Dreamweaver® 4 Weekend Crash Course™

Dreamweaver® 4
Weekend Crash Course™

Wendy Peck

Hungry Minds™

Hungry Minds, Inc.
New York, NY • Cleveland, OH • Indianapolis, IN

Dreamweaver® 4 Weekend Crash Course™

Published by
Hungry Minds, Inc.
909 Third Avenue
New York, NY 10022
www.hungryminds.com

Library of Congress Control Number: 200101671

ISBN: 0-7645-3575-7

Printed in the United States of America

10 9 8 7 6 5 4 3 2 1

1B/SR/QT/QR/IN

Distributed in the United States
by Hungry Minds, Inc.

Distributed by CDG Books Canada Inc. for Canada; by Transworld Publishers Limited in the United Kingdom; by IDG Norge Books for Norway; by IDG Sweden Books for Sweden; by IDG Books Australia Publishing Corporation Pty. Ltd. for Australia and New Zealand; by TransQuest Publishers Pte Ltd. for Singapore, Malaysia, Thailand, Indonesia, and Hong Kong; by Gotop Information Inc. for Taiwan; by ICG Muse, Inc. for Japan; by Intersoft for South Africa; by Eyrolles for France; by International Thomson Publishing for Germany, Austria, and Switzerland; by Distribuidora Cuspide for Argentina; by LR International for Brazil; by Galileo Libros for Chile; by Ediciones ZETA S.C.R. Ltda. for Peru; by WS Computer Publishing Corporation, Inc., for the Philippines; by Contemporanea de Ediciones for Venezuela; by Express Computer Distributors for the Caribbean and West Indies; by Micronesia Media Distributor, Inc. for Micronesia; by Chips Computadoras S.A. de C.V. for Mexico; by Editorial Norma de Panama S.A. for Panama; by American Bookshops for Finland.

For general information on Hungry Minds' products and services please contact our Customer Care department within the U.S. at 800-762-2974, outside the U.S. at 317-572-3993 or fax 317-572-4002.

For sales inquiries and reseller information, including discounts, premium and bulk quantity sales, and foreign-language translations, please contact our Customer Care department at 800-434-3422, fax 317-572-4002 or write to Hungry Minds, Inc., Attn: Customer Care Department, 10475 Crosspoint Boulevard, Indianapolis, IN 46256.

For information on licensing foreign or domestic rights, please contact our Sub-Rights Customer Care department at 650-653-7098.

For information on using Hungry Minds' products and services in the classroom or for ordering examination copies, please contact our Educational Sales department at 800-434-2086 or fax 317-572-4005.

For press review copies, author interviews, or other publicity information, please contact our Public Relations department at 650-653-7000 or fax 650-653-7500.

For authorization to photocopy items for corporate, personal, or educational use, please contact Copyright Clearance Center, 222 Rosewood Drive, Danvers, MA 01923, or fax 978-750-4470.

Hungry Minds™ is a trademark of Hungry Minds, Inc.

This book is for
Shawnda, Danille and Brian
My kids, my strength, my partners

Credits

Acquisitions Editor
Michael Roney

Project Editor
Sharon Eames
Patsy Owens
Valerie Perry
Mildred Sanchez

Technical Editor
Shawn Rasmor

Copy Editor
Lane Barnholtz
Rich Adin
C.M. Jones

Project Coordinator
Dale White

Permissions Editor
Carmen Krikorian

Graphics and Production Specialists
Joe Bucki, Sean Decker,
John Greenough, Adam Mancilla,
Gabriele McCann, Laurie Stevens

Quality Control Technicians
David Faust, Linda Quigley,
Susan Moritz, Carl Pierce,
Charles Spencer

Media Development Specialist
Angie Denny

Media Development Coordinator
Marisa Pearman

Book Designer
Evan Deerfield

Proofreading and Indexing
York Production Services, Inc.

About the Author

Wendy Peck jumped the fence from fashion design to professional graphic design in 1989 and began teaching computer graphics at the college level and for corporate clients in 1992. In 1997, after being on the Web for four years, she again changed her focus, turning her attention to Web design. Today, she divides her time between writing articles on graphic design for WebReference.com (www.productiongraphics.com), and other publications, while reserving about half of her time for designing Web sites. Wendy lives with her rapidly shrinking family (kids in their late teens who are moving out one by one) in Northwestern Ontario. She works from her home office, or increasingly, from the road, because she is an obsessive traveler. The Midwestern and south central United States is her favorite haunt.

Preface

Welcome to *Dreamweaver 4 Weekend Crash Course*. We make the promise that you can learn Dreamweaver in just one weekend. It may seem impossible to master a program as rich and powerful as Dreamweaver in such a short time, but you can. I have been using Dreamweaver for years and have discovered that most of Dreamweaver's power falls into selected key areas. Once you understand the big picture, the details fall right into place.

With that in mind, I have designed this book with two levels. In the first section of the book, you will create a simple Web site, allowing you to learn the foundation techniques in a simple context. Only when you are comfortable with the essential methods for creating reliable HTML code with Dreamweaver and have learned to avoid many of the pitfalls of Web design will you move forth and design a complex Web site. Then you can draw on your new knowledge from the early sessions and add many of Dreamweaver's most advanced features to help you build a major site.

This is not a book on HTML, JavaScript, or CGI but I have not ignored the fact that Web pages are built with HTML and other code. You will learn how to work with the design view, allowing you to see the code Dreamweaver creates as you build your pages. At the same time, you will learn how to make sure that the code you produce will display on most browsers. However software, or even code alone, does not build effective Web sites. You will learn to organize a site plan, ensuring that your visitors can easily navigate your site, and learn how to place external scripts. Finally, I will provide field-tested methods for creating great pages in an efficient manner. I earn my living using Dreamweaver, so I know time counts.

Dreamweaver has been a key tool for enterprising graphic artists and programmers to build careers and businesses creating Web sites. Many employers now list Dreamweaver knowledge as a required skill, and this number is increasing every day. Some people use Dreamweaver to maintain their own business sites; others use it to build Web sites as a rewarding hobby. Whatever your goal, you are just one weekend away from mastering one of the most popular Web creation tools on the planet. Find an undisturbed space, put a "do not disturb" note on your door, and get ready to emerge Sunday evening with a valuable new skill.

Who Should Read This Book

This book is for beginner to intermediate Dreamweaver users. It is also perfect for those who understand the correct mouse moves to create a Web page in Dreamweaver, but do not feel that they understand the "why" behind much of what they do. In this book, you are never asked to blindly click — you always know why you are doing what you are doing. If you fall into any of the following categories, this book will help you reach your goals.

- Beginners who want to learn Web design
- Intermediate Web developers who want to fully understand Dreamweaver and enhance their site building skills.
- Individuals who are working in the field, but wish to (or must) add Dreamweaver skills to their list of qualifications.
- Back-end developers who wish to (or must) add more page design skills to their list of qualifications.
- Print designers who want to add Web design to their list of qualifications.

How to Use This Book

This book is a trip right through the center of the most important and well-used features in Dreamweaver. It has been designed to be a complete course, providing all the information you require to boost your Dreamweaver skills to a very high level. You will get the most from this book if you complete every exercise. Some techniques may be very familiar to you, but there are so many tidbits of information, including the essential answer to why you would use a particular method, that the time spent completing any exercise will not be wasted. If you have experience with a technique, you will move very quickly through the steps. Each lesson builds on the exercises completed in the previous chapters, so skipping exercises may leave you without the prepared pages you require to complete a later exercise.

Finally, probably the most important reason for completing each exercise is for later reference. The topics in the book are clearly marked and will be easy to locate a few months from now. Reviewing a technique in the book later on will be much more effective when you can also open the document, study the code, and compare the exercise you did then to the project you are currently completing.

Overview

The concept of this book is simple. You will design a simple Web site with four pages to start the process. All graphics are provided on the accompanying CD-ROM, so you can work quickly through building the pages. In the second part of the book, you will build a Web site using liquid table design, templates, Library items, and three different types of menus. The site is enhanced with a Flash movie and impressive details like a Print Page button and the new Flash buttons included in Dreamweaver. In other words, by Sunday evening, you will have created a site containing features that are found in the largest sites on the Web.

Friday Evening

In the first four sessions, I will introduce the material I will cover, the Dreamweaver interface, and how Dreamweaver sites work. You will create a document that includes text and graphics by the end of this part.

Saturday Morning

By the end of this part, you will have pages on the Web. You will work through the basics of page layout, tables, and moving your site to the Web during these sessions.

Saturday Afternoon

In this part you start to add interaction to your site. Links, image rollovers, and placing scripts are all part of these sessions of the book. Before this part ends, you will also do some work with Dreamweaver's templates and Library items to start automating your work.

Saturday Evening

You definitely move past beginner as you start your second site at the beginning of this part. You will concentrate on planning the site, creating the templates you will use, and move on to preparing templates and Library items to use when you compile the second site on Sunday.

Sunday Morning

This part moves you right into the topics that can separate a true Web developer from a "wannabe." You will be creating complex menus and JavaScript rollovers, controlling text with CSS (Cascading Style Sheets), and using automated site maintenance tools by the end of these sessions.

Sunday Afternoon

Don't think you will be winding down slowly to the end of the book, because you certainly do not want to miss the fun features included on in these sessions. Learn to work with layers and move objects around your pages with Dreamweaver's timelines. To complete the techniques, you will create a page with frames. The final step is to look at how you can apply your new knowledge in an efficient way as we focus on productivity to end the book.

Appendixes

This section includes what is on the CD-ROM, the answers to your Part Reviews, and information on using Dreamweaver with other software programs.

Layout and Features

The time symbols in the margin show you where you are in your lesson. You may wish to allow a few extra minutes for each session, rather than rushing past something you do not understand. I have also included "extra assignments" if you need or want more practice. Although I have carefully planned out the time so that the work can be completed as promised, you should work at a pace that is best for you.

Also scattered throughout the sessions are hints, tips, and relevant information about addendum topics and concerns. You'll find these items illustrated with margin symbols shown below. This is a cross-platform book. Instructions for Windows users appear in the text and instructions for Mac users, when different, appear in brackets.

This symbol means that the accompanying information is important for broadening your awareness of Dreamweaver features, procedures, or perhaps Web development in general.

This symbol adds information to the material you are studying, provides an alternate method, or a time-saving suggestion.

This symbol is your warning of common errors that you might make while working with a technique.

This symbol indicates where you can find more information on the current subject elsewhere in the book.

You will require many graphics to complete the exercises in this book. This symbol advises you to copy certain files from the CD-ROM to your computer. Occasionally, this symbol refers you to more information on a subject contained in the Resources directory on the CD-ROM.

The symbol ⇨ indicates a menu path. For instance, if you see File ⇨ Save, it means select the File menu, and then select Save.

Ready, Set . . .

One little weekend — such a small amount of time to invest for so much knowledge. **Go** get it . . . .

Acknowledgments

Until I wrote a book, I questioned the number of people who received special thanks from the author. Now I know how much restraint authors use with their lists. A book is a monumental project that involves so many; reaching the point where you can write a book involves even more.

My first steps were so capably handled by Michael Roney, my acquisitions editor. You made it easy, and from the first day, seemed to know I could do this. Sharon Eames, my project editor, answered first-book nerves and insecurities. You really know when to help and when to let go. Shawn Rasmor carried the huge job of technical editor. Your changes were wise and right on the mark. This is a much better book for your attention. Patsy Owens, project editor and calm-down expert. You came in late, meeting frayed nerves and confusion with calm and understanding. You are a marvel. Mildred Sanchez, project editor, proved once and for all that editors are exceptionally organized people, with soft spots for author concerns, no matter when they enter the project. Lane Barnholtz, copy editor — how can you take my writing and make it sound just like me . . . but better? Amazing.

Andy King, Managing Editor at WebReference.com, took a chance on me and gave me my first big break in the writing world. More than a year has passed, and I still love working with you.

My Mom, Isabel MacLean, vigilantly policed both our written and spoken grammar and taught us to work. Thanks Mom. My Dad, Jack MacLean, though he did not live to know that I would write a book, taught me to dream. My sister Debbie believed in me years before I did and insisted that I stretch to find where I should go.

Val. You are my best friend and the greatest fan a person could ever have. Your belief that I can leap tall buildings in a single bound makes me think I should try.

Elsie and Marion, you are a rich source of wisdom and sanity. You stood firm in your support, even when things were way out of control. Rob, your belief never once wavered, even when mine did.

Although many contributed, my kids, Shawnda, Danille, and Brian are the reason I can do what I do. "You can do this Mom." So many times the three of you kept me going with these words as my career changed direction completely. "Go for it Mom," you said while doing without so I could build a new business. "We're fine," you offered as I spent day after day, week after week glued to the chair in my office. No Mom could ask for better kids. I am fiercely proud of you.

Contents at a Glance

Contents

SATURDAY

Dreamweaver® 4 Weekend Crash Course™

☑ **Friday**

☐ Saturday

☐ Sunday

PART

I

Friday
Evening

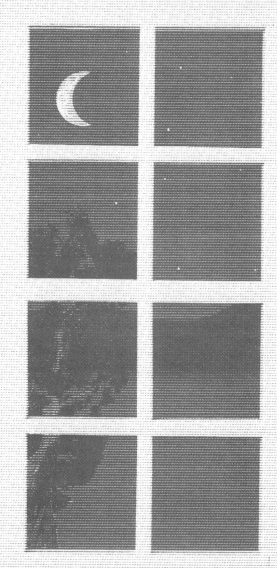

1

Introducing Dreamweaver

Session Checklist

✔ What will be covered

✔ Understanding HTML

✔ HTML versus WYSIWYG

✔ Understanding the limits of HTML

✔ What's new in Dreamweaver 4

✔ What is a host?

**30 Min.
To Go**

Before you start creating your first page, it is important to know where you are going and what you can and cannot expect from this course. Web development — more than most subjects — has no tidy beginning and end. One of the things that professional developers constantly struggle with is where to concentrate their learning efforts, because it is impossible for one person to absorb all there is to learn about the field of Web development.

I am a working Web designer. I have carefully identified the Dreamweaver features that I use constantly when creating client sites in order to determine what this course will cover. Some of the specialized and obscure features of this versatile program will not be featured, but you will learn what is necessary to create a full-featured site, containing unlimited pages with impressive visitor interaction, and even with a few bells and whistles. Most importantly, you will learn how to use Dreamweaver to create sites offering full browser and platform consistency.

Creating a page with Dreamweaver is a very small challenge, because the program automatically produces excellent HTML code. The real challenge is creating a page that will display consistently on the Web. That is the focus for this course.

Although Dreamweaver does create code automatically, do not allow yourself to be helpless when it comes to code. Your success will be directly related to the amount you learn about how the code you produce in Dreamweaver does its job. I will help direct you to the most important areas to study.

What Will Be Covered

First, this book is very much a hands-on exercise. I am not going to bombard you with page upon page of theory. You would most likely skip over those parts anyway, because you bought a software book to learn the software, right? The theory is included here, of course. How can you learn a program without understanding what concepts are being put to use? However, I will mix hands-on exercises and theory so that you learn the concepts as you apply the commands in Dreamweaver. It's the best way to teach in the classroom, and I am taking the role of the teacher in your home or office for the time that you spend on these exercises.

Creating sites

You will create two sites through the course. The first site is very simple, designed to teach you basic Dreamweaver functions such as how to place an image or create a table. I have deliberately kept this first site exceptionally simple to allow you to focus on the basic operations.

The second site is the opposite. Armed with the knowledge to create basic layout and to insert graphic elements, you will create a full-featured site that will rival mid-range commercial sites on the Web. You will create links, add forms, and create frames, plus add movies and sound. You will also use Dreamweaver to create JavaScript code, Cascading Style Sheets (CSS) and Dynamic HTML (DHTML).

Creating cross-browser code

I will cover many HTML issues in depth. HTML is a pretty simple concept. However, each browser interprets the code in a different way, and to make things worse, browsers are inconsistent across PC and Mac platforms. This is the main reason Web developers pull out their hair. Please pay special attention to the tips and notes that apply to cross-browser and platform issues. I acknowledged earlier that you are really here to learn the software, but knowing where to find a feature in Dreamweaver's menu is not going to help you if your page goes upside down in Internet Explorer on a Mac.

Lest you think I am exaggerating on this point. My own site — www.wpeck.com — was perfect on all PC browsers, and it also passed with flying colors on a Mac with Netscape. I was quite proud, until it was seen by a tester on a Mac with a recent version of Internet Explorer. The first column, which was only 200 pixels wide, pushed the second column to the bottom of the first column. Result? Only a bulleted list of features was seen on the first screen. The text content, the purpose for the site, was four screens below. Solution? One tag needed to be added. I cannot stress this enough: pay attention to the code!

DHTML and JavaScript create browser compatibility issues, as well. Whenever I talk about adding any code to Dreamweaver, I will always look at compatibility.

Using automated features

Dreamweaver offers the capability to work with templates and library items, which gives you the power to add elements to your site, and later, to change the entire site by adjusting one file. You will use both templates and library items on your second site. The Web is an ever-changing medium, and to keep interest in your site, visitors demand change. With a little forward planning, you can keep your content and style fresh with minimal effort.

You will learn how to manage your sites, automatically update changed pages, and check your site for problems. A small site can be managed manually, but you will be amazed at how confusing and time-consuming it can be to maintain a site of even 10 to 20 pages. Dreamweaver offers many tools to make this job fast and accurate, and I will cover that area in depth.

Optimizing your site

Download speed is crucial. The most carefully designed page will be missed by many visitors if you do not ensure that they see results quickly when they visit your site. Web surfers are not patient people. You will spend time learning to properly optimize code and graphics so that you do not sacrifice a fast-loading site for fancy layout or pretty pictures.

I will not cover dynamic content, which means creating pages from databases. Dreamweaver 4 was not designed for this purpose. I will also not cover graphic production. I assume that you have a source for images or that you can create your own images.

All images required for the exercises in this book can be found on the accompanying CD-ROM.

Dreamweaver UltraDev is a combination of Dreamweaver and a software program formerly known as Drumbeat. Dreamweaver UltraDev helps to automate the interface between a database and pages on the Web. The Dreamweaver portion of UltraDev is exactly the same as Dreamweaver 4. Once you have completed the exercises in this book, you will simply have to learn the interface issues. If you are interested in this area of Web development, visit www.macromedia.com and read through the information on Dreamweaver UltraDev.

Understanding HTML

When people talk about a program like Dreamweaver, they often say that you can design a whole site and never see a scrap of code. Software development companies add to the illusion with marketing statements that promise you will be able to create exciting Web sites without knowing HTML.

I will not call this a lie, because it is not. You can create Web sites without even knowing how to view your code in Dreamweaver. However, if you want to create sites that are stable and reasonably consistent for every viewer, you will have to understand exactly how HTML works.

I was able to go further without viewing code when I first started with Dreamweaver. My first projects were not complicated from a layout or functional standpoint. However, as I started to push to new levels and the issue of liquidity emerged, I found I was often working in the code window. Had I not started with a solid understanding of how HTML worked, and the syntax and operation for each tag, I would have been held back from reaching my goals. Do not think of learning HTML as a problem; rather, think of it as an opportunity for more freedom in your design work.

See Session 8 for a full discussion on liquidity in Web design.

**20 Min.
To Go**

What is HTML?

Design people like me tend to call HTML (Hypertext Markup Language) *programming*. Programmers will come up fighting and say it is not a programming language, but a markup language. My argument that HTML has funny little symbols and that you must type perfectly or it will not work, so it must be programming, holds no credibility. The programmers are right. HTML is a basic set of codes that tells a browser how to display text and images.

HTML is quite logical and, if you speak English, often self-explanatory. Each set of instructions is called a *tag*. Tags are placed around content to tell the browser how to display text and images on the page. Opening tags look like this `<tag>`, and ending tags look like this `</tag>`. As an example, the tag for boldface type is `<b>`. To make the word "Title" appear in boldface type, the tag would be: `<b>Title</b>`, and the word would appear on the page as **Title**. If you wanted "Title" to be both bold and italic, the code would be `<b><i>Title</i><b>`, with the final appearance as ***Title***. See, quite logical. A little memorization and you will be well on your way to understanding code.

You are not studying HTML in this course, so I will not delve into codes here, but I do urge you to learn this language. You should have at least one comprehensive HTML book in your library. I recommend the *HTML 4.01 Weekend Crash Course* by Greg Perry. Not only is this a great reference book for basic code, but it also offers hands-on instruction.

Hand Coding versus WYSIWYG

The battle rages on as it only can in the computer world. Many Web developers truly believe that the only respectable way to create HTML code is to work in a text editor and to type your code by hand. Another group of developers has an equally strong conviction that you cannot create a nicely designed page unless you can view the final appearance as you work. This work is done in a WYSIWYG (What You See Is What You Get) editor such as Dreamweaver.

However, because of the strong coding tools in Dreamweaver, this debate is losing momentum. Dreamweaver is primarily a WYSIWYG editor, but, particularly with the new additions in Version 4, it is also a powerful hand-code editor.

Remember a while back I mentioned that each of you will use Dreamweaver in a different way. This is one of the areas where people naturally find their own working style. I am a visual designer, a transplant from the print production world. I tend to design pages visually, and I spend more and more time with the coding window open as the site develops. I know other designers who use the visual editor only for specific jobs, such as creating tables and JavaScript rollovers. Still, other designers would not dream of using automated JavaScript, yet they rarely open the HTML window. The combinations are endless, and there is no right way.

In this course, you will be working primarily in the Document window, which is the visual portion of the program. Figure 1-1 shows my normal working screen with Design View and the Properties Inspector active. You should check your HTML code as you go along. For specific tasks only, you will type your code directly into the Code Inspector window. This should give you enough experience with how each function works to carry on and find the combination that is perfect for you.

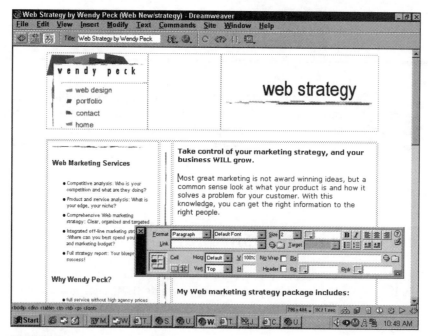

Figure 1-1
The screen arrangement that I use most often is shown here. I rarely close the Properties Inspector, but only open a code view or other panels or inspectors as required.

The important thing is to become comfortable with both visual and code work in Dreamweaver. If you restrict yourself to one or the other, you will not realize the full potential of the program.

Understanding the Limits of HTML

HTML was never meant to provide pretty layouts. It was designed to present information in a legible page. Of course, give humans a tool and before long, we will naturally be pushing the limits. And we have aggressively pushed the bounds for HTML.

However far innovation, creative use, and changing standards have taken HTML, it is still a limited graphics-layout tool. Add to this that the same HTML page might be displayed on a monitor with low resolution and 256 colors, or on a super-sharp, ultra-high resolution screen with millions of colors, it is a wonder that any pages look good on the Web.

But wait: there is one more problem. Browser software does not offer any true standards. As designers have pushed the bounds of HTML, new tags have been added. New concepts such as Cascading Style Sheets (CSS) have been developed to control text and positioning. JavaScript has exploded in response to increasing demand for pages with interactivity and motion. Browser software has kept up with change, but each software developer has chosen different ways to respond to advances. In fact, browser-specific tags now in use have been added by software developers and adopted by Web developers. Unfortunately, these special tags are only recognized by the browser that introduced them. Web design can be a minefield.

Dreamweaver smoothes many of the bumps for you when dealing with HTML and related languages. Much of what I have described in the preceding paragraph is invisible in Dreamweaver, because the program automatically chooses the tried and tested route to deliver most design and layout requirements. For plain pages with text, tables, and a few images, you do not even have to think about the non-standardized browser issues. However, start to stretch those bounds, even by a little, and you will have to put some remedial action into place.

How do you know? Trial and error and test, test, test. Dreamweaver does include excellent preview capabilities that reveal the most glaring differences between major browsers. As you design, you must make sure to at least check your page with Internet Explorer and Netscape Navigator. Developing this habit early on will eliminate much of the problem. You will soon recognize how your design style works in these browsers.

Dreamweaver 4 has added new tools for troubleshooting problems in various browsers. Learn and utilize every feature available to you. Throughout this course, I highlight common problem areas in browser compatibility, and I present methods to create consistent results. Keep your eyes open for these tips and notes.

Although designers would not naturally choose to work within the limits of HTML, an element of pride often results from taking a weak layout language and creating beautiful, functional pages.

If you are moving into the Web development world from a print background, begin this minute to forget everything you have ever known about creating a page. Keep your design principles in place; good design is still good design. But your success in this field depends on letting go of the control you have in print. Imagine opening your print portfolio and finding that all of your samples have changed color, font, or even layout. Designing for the Web is much like that.

What's New in Dreamweaver 4

When you already have one of the most complete and intuitive Web creation programs, what can you add to a new version? There are not many new capabilities to add, because there is little that any Dreamweaver version cannot do. The major improvements in Version 4 enable designers to do their work faster and more accurately, and to break new ground in testing.

The new code handling capability is the most impressive change for me. Before now, your code was displayed in a window called the HTML Source Inspector. Now a full-featured HTML editor is on board, and you can view your work in code view or design view, or in split screen view. Figure 1-2 shows the split screen. A simple click in the toolbar presents your desired view. The new HTML editing tools list is also impressive and fully customizable. I will cover how to use this feature as you get into the course.

A new toolbar at the top of the screen adds instant access to several important features such as code view (see Figure 1-2), browser preview, and design notes. The toolbar also offers limited File Transfer Protocol (FTP) capabilities from within your document.

The new JavaScript Debugger helps locate those often-elusive errors in your code. You can debug code for any of your preview browsers, giving you the opportunity to flush out problems right inside your document.

On the design front, the new Layout button offers click-and-drag table creation. You can create one table, or you can visually create a series of nested tables. Once you move from Layout view to Standard view, the new tables can be edited like any other table. Note the two views shown in Figure 1-3.

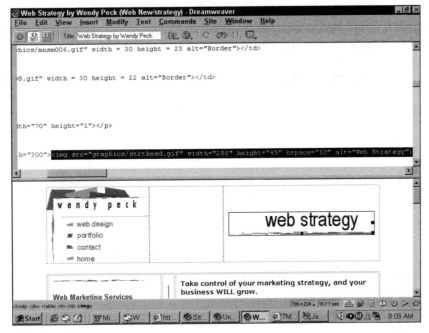

Figure 1-2
A full-featured code editor is integrated into Dreamweaver 4. The split-screen view is shown.

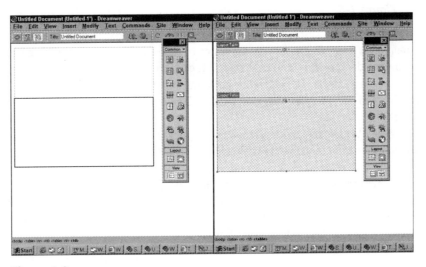

Figure 1-3
Layout view (right) provides click-and-drag table creation. The same table is shown in Standard view on the left.

An interesting new feature enables you to create Flash menu buttons from within Dreamweaver. One screen defines preset buttons, with fully editable text and rollovers automatically included.

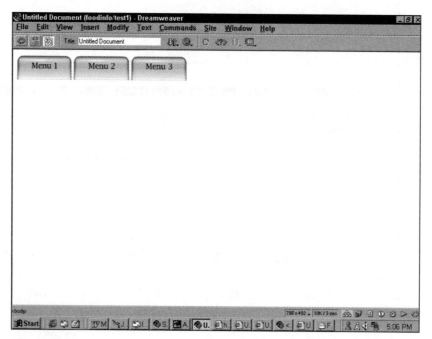

Figure 1-4
Preset Flash buttons can be added with a few mouse clicks.

Templates and CSS are now much easier to use. Finally, you can add a new CSS file to your document in a logical way. Integration with Macromedia's Fireworks continues to increase. You can work back and forth between Fireworks and Dreamweaver on the same slices, not losing link or rollover information — a great time-saver.

As Web sites become more and more complicated, the time spent organizing data and managing documents with several people working on a project becomes important. Dreamweaver 4 has added several tools to help.

The new Assets Manager is one of my favorite features. You can now have all the assets — images, colors, external URLs, scripts, Flash, Shockwave, QuickTime, and Templates — in one window with a visual display. When you work on a site with many pages, this feature saves hours.

For group work, you can now type your design notes on the document screen or e-mail the person who has a file checked out. The new site reporting features are wonderful, enabling you to request a preset report or to define your own report for troubleshooting on your site.

In general, though much of Dreamweaver remains familiar, a few of the new enhancements will become "can't live without" features within a few sessions. The Assets Manager and Code View window have become so much a part of my working habits, I don't think I could give them up. Oh, and I really like the Site Reporting, and ...

**10 Min.
To Go**

What Is a Host?

Finally, as the end to this session, I want to introduce an area you will need to be familiar with as you create your first pages. Most of this book will cover work on your local computer, because you really do not work directly on the Web. Web designers create files and then upload the files to the Web, where they can be seen by anyone with an Internet connection.

Moving the files is a simple concept. You transfer files using FTP much like you move a file from your hard drive to a floppy disk or other portable media. Dreamweaver 4 has a built-in FTP function, so you need nothing else to move your files.

However, where do you put the files? What is a host? A *host* is simply where you put your files. A host is a company (it's location does not matter) that has set up a place to store your files and to make them available to the entire Internet. Most companies charge for this service — consider it rent for your site. Some free hosts exist, though you usually must tolerate ads on your pages, because the host must be earning revenue in some way to keep the service going.

The range of services that each host offers varies dramatically. For this course, you need a full service host, because you will be wandering into some advanced areas. I have included a list of free, low-cost, and full-service hosts on the CD-ROM included with this book, and I have made sure that any hosts listed offer the services required for this course.

A list of free, low-cost, and full-service hosts can be found in the file hosts.html in the Resources folder.

If you prefer to find your own host, or already have one, you need to ensure that it offers full FTP and Common Gateway Interface (CGI) capability (preferably with direct access to a cgi-binfolder).

It's okay if you do not understand that last statement. By the end of the course, you will fully understand what FTP and CGI mean, but to get there, you need to have a host. If you are trying to find your own host, just include exactly what I have typed in the preceding paragraph in an e-mail to your prospective hosting company. The hosting company should be able to tell you if it has the required capability.

You will need to have a host in place by the start of Session 5, Saturday Morning.

Domain names

Before you leave the topic of hosts, I do want to cover one last detail. Many people confuse hosting with domain names, and I want to clear up any confusion.

You do not need to have a domain name to complete this course. All free servers provide you with an address that you can share with others so that they can access your files.

Here is my site as an example. My domain name is wpeck.com. It could also be wendypeck.com (which I also own), wpeck.net, wpeck.org, or wpeck.ca. These are all domain names.

I registered my domain name with networksolutions.com because, at the time, it was the only place to register a domain name. Currently, hundreds of domain registrars offer this service, most offering a one-year registration for under $20.

See a list of domain name registrars in the Resources directory. The file is named registrars.html.

This is completely separate from your hosting company, though. Many beginners get quite turned around by this subject. To make things a little complicated, you must provide information about your host when you register your domain. The registrar for your domain name must know where the files that go with the domain name will be stored. You must provide both a primary and a secondary Domain Name System (DNS) address for your host. DNS is the system that translates

Internet Protocol (IP) addresses (which are numerical addresses) into easy-to-remember domain names.

Go back to my earlier example. My domain name is wpeck.com, and I registered it at Network Solutions. My host is forsite.com. To register my name, I provided the following DNS information from forsite.com to Network Solutions:

Primary DNS
Name: NS.FORSITE.NET
Number: 204.180.41.2
Secondary DNS
Name: NS1.FORSITE.NET
Number: 204.180.42.2

I then contacted forsite.com, and I asked that an account be set up for me to host wpeck.com. Once all the work filtered through the system, anyone seeking wpeck.com was then pointed to forsite.com, and forsite.com directs wpeck.com traffic to my folder.

After you work through the system once, it all becomes clear.

If you are registering a domain name, be as sure as you can possibly be that you will not want to change hosts. Much work is involved in moving a host — often confusing and usually frustrating work. If you are forced to move your domain name to a new host, though, I advise an overlap of at least one month. Let your original host carry on for 30 days past the time that you plan to activate your new host. It can take several days for all the kinks to be worked out of the system. If you have your files on both hosts during the transition time, you will not face downtime for your site.

Done!

REVIEW

In this session, you learned what will be covered in this course, and you had an introduction to some of the basic ideas in Web design. It is important that you remember the following points:

- You will get the most from this course if you work through each exercise.
- You will create two sites as you work through this course.
- You should make a commitment to learn at least the basics of HTML.

- New features in Dreamweaver 4 speed up your work and make it easier to work with others on the same project.
- You need a host to complete this course.
- A domain name is a separate issue from your host (although you need a host in order to create a site that can be reached through your domain name).
- You do not need to register a domain name to complete this course.

Quiz Yourself

1. What is the main reason for learning HTML code, even though Dreamweaver produces it for you? (See the "Understanding HTML" section.)

2. HTML stands for what? (See the "Understanding HTML" section.)

3. Designing pages that display consistently for every visitor is a challenge. What two factors most influence how the pages you create will display? (See "Understanding the Limits of HTML.")

4. What are the three views available in Dreamweaver 4? (See the "What's New in Dreamweaver 4" section.)

5. What is a host? (See the "What Is a Host?" section.)

6. What is a domain name? (See the "What Is a Host?" section.)

Session Checklist

✔ Understanding the site window versus the document window

✔ Understanding the document window

✔ Working with panels in Dreamweaver

✔ Focusing on the Properties Inspector

✔ Using the menus

✔ Viewing your document

**30 Min.
To Go**

A lthough I could spend this entire book discussing HTML and Web design theory (and some have), let's roll up our sleeves and get started. This topic is never ending and constantly changing. The best way to learn basic Web development is to leap in and get your hands dirty. Once you have created a few of your own pages, much of the information that confuses you today will become clear.

You must start by finding your way around in Dreamweaver. There are a few differences from most other programs you have worked with It is not a simple page creation program. Dreamweaver's sole purpose is to create Web pages. Web pages are not useful unless . . . well, unless they are on the Web.

That statement is not as dumb as it may sound. Dreamweaver can be a little confusing in the beginning; half of its power comes from its ability to manage your site. To exercise the control it needs to keep the files on your site connected to one another, Dreamweaver creates its own organizational area for the files you have stored on your hard drive.

You will be creating documents in Dreamweaver, but you will be creating Web sites as well. Dreamweaver offers two separate areas that are very closely tied and interrelated, but which are also very separate. One area is called the Site window, where site information is stored and where the FTP capability that will transfer files to the Web resides. You can only have one site window open at a time. The second area is called the Document window. Individual documents will be opened or created from the Site window, and you can open as many documents as you desire at the same time.

Just hold onto the idea that there are two separate — but connected — areas and you are well prepared to move on.

Recognizing Site and Document Windows

Dreamweaver works with two windows: A site window, which displays and transfers files for a site, and the document window, where actual pages are created and edited. You are going to learn how to work with each window in the next two sessions, but I want to pause and give you a chance to become familiar with each window first.

Site window

When you define a site, as you will do in the Session 3, Dreamweaver scans the folder you specify and creates its own management window with the files it finds (See Figure 2-1). The files from your root directory are shown on the right side of the screen with the heading Local Folder, referring to the files on your computer. You can move, rename, and delete files from this screen, and the changes will be made on your hard drive. If you make the changes to files when you are not working in the Dreamweaver screen, the Dreamweaver site window will reflect those changes, as well. This window is simply an extra listing of what is on your hard drive in the specified folder.

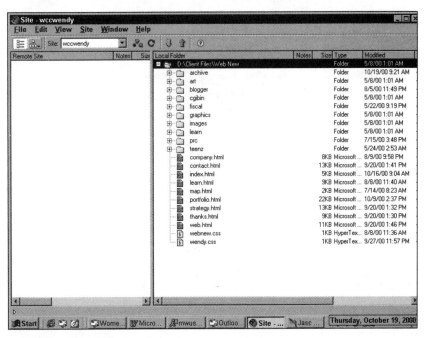

Figure 2-1
The Dreamweaver 4 Site window with only local files shown in the right pane.

The reason Dreamweaver creates its own system to list your files becomes evident as soon as you connect to the site. You will learn how to do this in the next session, but I want you to understand the concept now. Note in Figure 2-2 that there are now two listings. The files shown in the right pane are the same as those shown in Figure 2-1, but there is now a listing in the left pane, as well.

Note that the Connection button is now depressed — the little icon is joined and the light is displayed. This indicates that you are connected to the site. The files listed in the left pane are those that are stored in your directory on your host's computer.

The site window is the control center for everything you will do in Dreamweaver. Experienced Dreamweaver users would never dream of moving or deleting an important Web site file in any other way but through the site window. Your hard drive is not smart enough to know when one file might be important to another. Dreamweaver is. If you change the location or name of any file within a Dreamweaver site, the program checks all links before the change is made and allows you to change your mind or update the files. It's like having a warning buzzer that prevents you from making a mistake with your files.

Connection icon

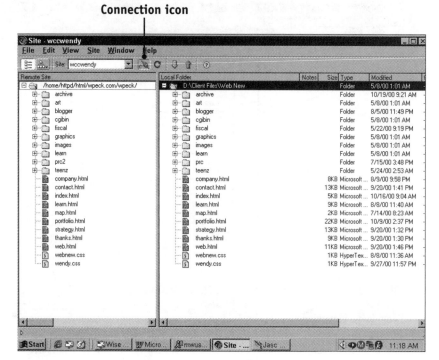

Figure 2-2
When Dreamweaver is connected to a site, both the local files (right) and the host files (left) are displayed.

Document window

The Document window has a very different look from the Site window. In fact, it resembles a word processing or desktop publishing window and is usually quite comfortable to use, even for new users. As you can see in Figure 2-3, it is easy to imagine what your page will look like while you work. (If you are a Dreamweaver user who has upgraded from a previous version, note the new toolbar at the top of the screen.)

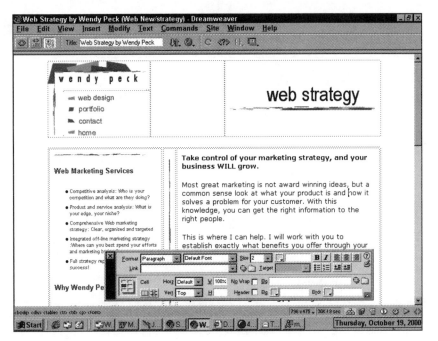

Figure 2-3
The Document window with the new toolbar

All changes to your document will take place in this window, and several documents can be open at one time. Dreamweaver creates a new window for each document that you open. It is not unusual to be working on many documents in a site. The page title for the page will be listed on the button in the taskbar for that window. In the sample shown in Figure 2-4, there are three documents open, plus the Site window. Note the page titles on the buttons.

You are going to move on now to the features in the document window, but I wanted to make sure that you understood the difference between the Site window and the Document window. It is the interaction between these two windows that makes Dreamweaver so powerful and, at the same time, so easy to use.

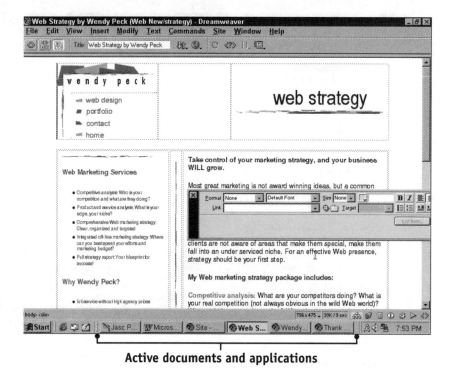

Active documents and applications

Figure 2-4
The Site window is shown here, as well as three Document windows. The "Web Strategy" document is active, although only a portion of the name is visible.

Understanding the Document Window

Now that the two types of window are clear in your mind, take a closer look at the Document window. This is where you will spend most of your time as you design your site.

You should start with a tour around the desktop. The screen shown in Figure 2-5 is what you will see when you create a new document in Dreamweaver. I have closed the Property Inspector, which opens by default; you will be working with this window later in this session. I also have clicked with the right mouse button (Ctrl-Click for Mac) to open the context menu so you can see all the menu options.

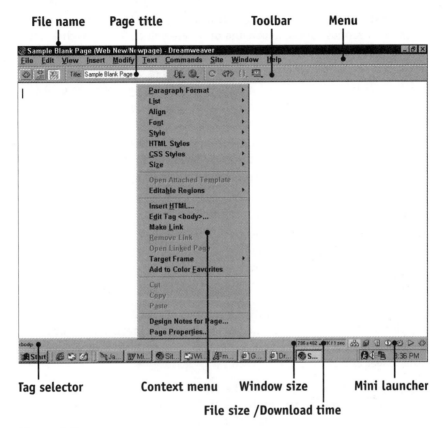

Figure 2-5
The Dreamweaver 4 desktop with a context menu open

- **Menu.** Most functions in Dreamweaver can be accessed through the menus. I urge beginners to use the menus. Find out why in "Using the Menus," later in this session.

- **Toolbar.** The toolbar is a new feature in Dreamweaver 4, and offers instant access to common actions as well as the code views.

- **Page Title.** This is the title that will appear when a visitor to your Web page bookmarks your site. Search engines also look for page titles for relevant words in the search terms. This is a very important feature, which previously was buried in the Page Properties menu.

- **File Name.** Displays the path and name for your file.

- **Context Menu.** A right-click (PC) or Ctrl-Click (Mac) of the mouse button presents various menus, depending on where you click. If you click a table, the Table menu appears. Context menus really save time.

- **Window Size.** Dreamweaver offers simulations of various browser resolutions. Click Window Size and choose the resolution you wish to duplicate to see how your page will look at smaller resolutions. This feature is valuable for liquid designs which you will create in Session 8.

- **File Size/Download Time.** This section displays the total size in kilobytes (K) of your page, and the approximate download time required. There are no excuses for slow-loading pages because you always have the size information available as you create your page.

- **Launcher Bar.** One-click access to the Site, Assets, HTML Styles, CSS Styles, Behaviors, History, and Code Inspector.

- **Tag Selector.** Lists the appropriate tags for the selected object. Clicking a tag in the Tag Selector automatically takes you to the location of that tag in code view.

You will be looking at each of these features in greater depth as you move through the course. This is just the bare-bones of the Dreamweaver tools. You are going to move next to the rich array of palettes, or small tool windows, that Dreamweaver offers.

**20 Min.
To Go**

Although you might be tempted to skip over the tool instructions, I urge you to resist. I am the world's most impatient person when I am learning software, preferring to get in and "get dirty" rather than taking the time to slowly study what is available to me. With Dreamweaver, however, that is a mistake. To help keep your workspace clean, many of the powerful tools are hidden — tools that can shave hours from your work, and help you to produce better pages at the same time.

Working with Panels in Dreamweaver

The Dreamweaver developers must have known from the beginning that every user of Dreamweaver software would have different needs. The system of panels (some are called Inspectors) for storing many of the tools is perfect. If you are working on interactivity, you can work with the Behavior panel open. While you set up frames for your site, you can have the Frames panel open. When you move on to edit your text, close all your panels and work with a wide-open screen. This can be easily accomplished by selecting Window ⇨ Hide Panels, or by pressing the F4 key on your keyboard. Restore the panels you had open by selecting Window ⇨ Show Panels, or by pressing the F4 key again. Figure 2-6 shows three panels open at once.

I will cover the functions and contents of individual panels as you proceed through building your pages, but there are some general methods that will help you get the most from the panels in Dreamweaver. You have some powerful customizing tools to work with, and you should always be on the watch for ways to streamline your panels.

I do not recommend that you customize your tools just yet. Let your work patterns develop a little and then make your changes. Be sure to teturn all tools to their default positions in this section.

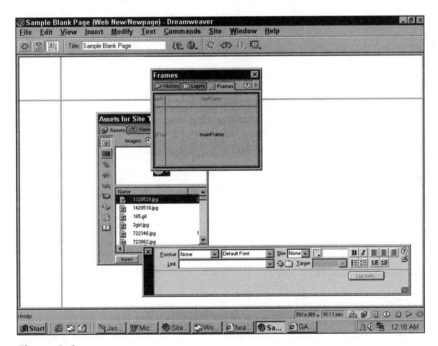

Figure 2-6
The Frames, Assets, and Properties Inspector panels are open on this screen. I usually work with the Properties Inspector open all the time, which is shown in the lower-right corner of the screen. I then open and close other panels as required for each stage of the page production.

Manipulating panels

Obviously, to put a panel to work, you must open it. There are many ways to open most panels. To open any panel, take any one of the following steps:

1. Select Window from the main menu and a drop-down list will appear.

2. Select the panel you wish to open. For this example, choose Behaviors.

    OR

1. Click the symbol for the panel you wish to launch from the Launcher bar in the lower-right corner of your screen. For this example choose Behaviors.

> **You will learn how to add or remove panels from the Launcher/Launcher bar in Session 30.**

To close a panel, simply click the *X* at the top right of the panel window.

You can move the panel by clicking in the title bar at the top of the panel window and then dragging it to a new location.

You also might want to resize a panel using the following steps:

1. Move your mouse over any border on the panel until the cursor changes to a double-pointed arrow.

2. Click and drag the border to the size you need, and then release the mouse button.

3. Repeat these steps for the next border until you are satisfied with the size.

Customizing panels

Many Dreamweaver panels are combined into one window. For example, the Behaviors panel is combined with CSS Styles and HTML styles in one window. The arrangement of your panels can be changed. You might find that you use two panels frequently, but if they are located on different panel windows, you have two panel windows open, even though you are not using all of the panels in each window. Or, you might only use one panel and would prefer that the window was smaller. Fortunately, you can mix and match panels as you desire.

To move a panel to a new window, take the following steps:

1. Open the Behaviors Inspector as previously described.

2. Open the Assets window.

3. Click the Behaviors tab in the Behaviors window. Drag the Behaviors tab to the Assets window and then release the mouse button. The Behaviors tab now shares a window with the Assets and Reference window (see Figure 2-7).

4. Click the Behaviors tab in the new location and drag it back to its original position. It should now be sharing a window with the CSS Styles and HTML Styles window.

You also can drag a panel off the current panel window and drop it anywhere on the screen. It will then form its own window.

No matter where a panel is moved to, if that panel is active (that is, the tab is to the front), the window title will reflect the active panel.

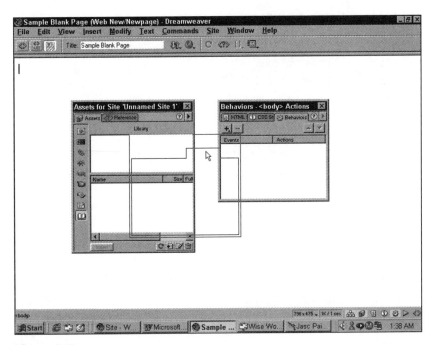

Figure 2-7
Moving the Behaviors Inspector to a new window

Focusing on the Properties Inspector

If I had to choose just one panel in Dreamweaver, the decision would be instant. It would have to be the Properties Inspector, as shown in Figure 2-8. In fact, most users find that it is impossible to work without this tool. The Properties Inspector displays information about the selected object, and also provides easy access to editing for the object.

What does this little gem control? Text, and everything about text. You can specify any of the following items:

- fonts
- font attributes
- font color
- alignment
- ordered and unordered lists
- HTML styles like H1, H2 and Paragraph
- links

It also controls most table functions, such as:

- table columns
- number of columns and rows
- merge and split cells
- add or remove borders
- apply a background color to tables, rows, columns, and individual cells

The Properties panel provides controls for images, such as:

- creating links
- image source
- image size
- adding or removing borders
- alignment
- adding Alt tags
- naming images for JavaScript
- adding vertical or horizontal space
- creating image maps

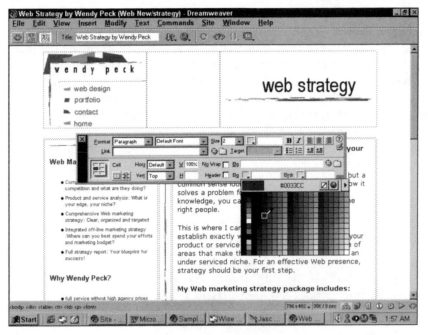

Figure 2-8
The little power panel — the Property Inspector

It's not hard to see why you will find it hard to work without this tool. I like the shape of the panel, because it rarely seems to get in my way. I usually work with the Property Inspector expanded, but occasionally will return to the default setting with some properties hidden. You can toggle the two views by clicking the arrow in the lower-right corner of the panel.

Using the Menus

There is nothing especially surprising or difficult about the Dreamweaver menu system. However, I did want to make sure that I touched on the subject of using menus. I have already mentioned this, and no doubt will again, but I am a firm believer that you should use menus when you are learning a program.

Too often, people rush to memorize keyboard shortcuts by the dozen. They feel that if they know them all, they know the program. I have spent a lot of time teaching people to use a wide range of software, so I speak from classroom experience when I say that is not an efficient way to learn a program. When you learn a shortcut, what you have accomplished exactly is, well, you have learned a shortcut. Period. That's it. You have no concept of where that function fits within the whole scheme. You are not steadily mapping out the entire program.

However, when you learn keyboard shortcuts by using the program's menus, you end up in the same place as you would using shortcuts, but you also know the program intimately. Every menu item that has a keyboard shortcut will list that shortcut to the right of the menu listing. You can learn those shortcuts as you work.

Take a look at Figure 2-9. Notice how the Insert ⇨ Table entry shows Ctrl+Alt+T as the shortcut. Yes, it takes a little longer to open the menu than to type a few keys, but look at what else you are learning without even concentrating. While you are in your early stages of learning Dreamwewaver and you area creating a few tables, you also are learning where you can find the tools to change your head tags or create frames.

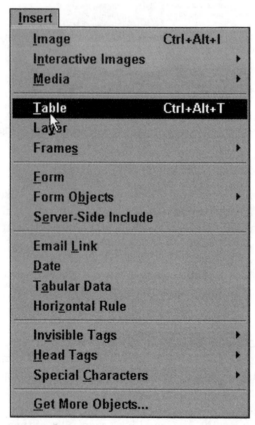

Figure 2-9
Adding a table. Note that the shortcut is listed to the right of the menu item.

Most of us have a great deal to remember. I prefer not to have information that I never use floating around in my head (there are days when it feels like not one more thing will fit in). When you access a menu for an option, make sure you let your eyes drift to the right. See that shortcut over and over.

Eventually, you will decide that you are accessing that menu item too often, and you will switch to the shortcut. You will not have to memorize it, because you have seen it many times. And don't forget, you have unconsciously noted everything that the menu contains.

You may rarely use the item above or below the menu item you use so often, and you will unconsciously skip the shortcuts on those items. I still do not know the frames shortcuts because I rarely use them. For the occasional page that I create with frames, the menu options will do just fine.

I will occasionally list a keyboard shortcut for your convenience. In fact, I just listed the shortcut to toggle your Properties Inspector on and off. Some shortcuts save so much time, or are used so often, that it only makes sense to use them from the start.

10 Min. To Go

Viewing Your Document

When you create a document in Dreamweaver, it is only an approximation of how it will look. To truly see how your page is progressing, you must know how your page will look on the Web. As you will see in the next Session, however, uploading your page — while not complicated — would be time-consuming if you had to upload the page to check it each time you make a change.

Luckily, Dreamweaver offers a quick, easy, and surprisingly reliable preview method right on your computer. Your document does not have to be saved before you preview it. All features, such as JavaScript or media, will function properly as long as your browser has that capability enabled or it has the necessary plug-in installed.

Defining your browser list

You have to tell Dreamweaver which browser you would like to test. The first browser you install will be set as the default browser. You can define up to 20 browsers to use for the preview, as long as those browsers are installed on your computer. As a bare minimum, you should have Internet Explorer and Netscape installed on your computer and defined as preview browsers in Dreamweaver.

Both Netscape and Internet Explorer are included on the CD-ROM included with this book. If you do not have both installed, please do so, because they are both required for this course.

To define a browser in Dreamweaver, take the following steps:

1. Select File ➪ Preview from the Browser ➪ Edit Browser list.
2. Ensure that Preview in Browser is selected in the left portion of the window.
3. Click the + (plus sign) to open the Add Browser window.
4. Type in a name that you will recognize for the browser in the Name section.
5. Click Browse to indicate where the browser is stored on your computer, and then select the browser file.
6. Choose Primary or Secondary browser. You can preview your documents in your primary browser by pressing the F12 key. Pressing the Ctrl+F12 keys (PC) or the Command+F12 keys (Mac) will activate a preview in your secondary browser. You must use the menu to preview with any other browsers.
7. Repeat these steps to add another browser, if desired.
8. Click OK. Your browser is now ready for a preview.

Previewing your document in a browser

Figure 2-10 is a preview of a document in Internet Explorer. To preview your document, take the following steps:

1. Choose File ➪ Preview from Browser ➪ choose the desired browser from the list. A new window will pop up in front of your document with your browser displaying your file.
2. Close the browser window to return to Dreamweaver.

Dreamweaver creates a temporary file to display your document in a browser. If you do not close the browser window when you return to Dreamweaver, and you then request another preview, it will load the same preview into the original window.

You're almost at the action point. In Session 3, you will be defining a site, and then you will start making pages.

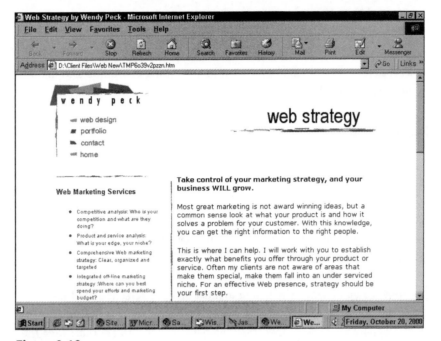

Figure 2-10

A Document previewed in Internet Explorer

Done!

REVIEW

In this session, you learned how to find your way around the Dreamweaver Document window and the panels, as well as how set up a browser to preview your document. Just to recap:

- There are two distinct window types in Dreamweaver: The Site window and the Document window.
- Dreamweaver creates and maintains its own listing of files on your hard drive when you define a site.
- When a site is connected through Dreamweaver FTP, both local files and files stored on the server are displayed.
- The Site window controls all automated features for maintaining your site.
- You create pages in the Document window.

- Dreamweaver panels allow you to choose which tools are on your screen.
- The Properties Inspector offers controls for almost all of the elements in your document.
- Pages created in Dreamweaver must be previewed in a browser to know exactly how it will appear on the Web.

QUIZ YOURSELF

1. How many document windows can you have open at one time? (See the "Document window" section.)
2. Where will a page title be displayed when a page is on the Web? (See the "Understanding the Document Window" section.)
3. What is a Dreamweaver panel? (See the "Working with Panels in Dreamweaver" section.)
4. How do you change the size of a panel on your screen? (See the "Manipulating Panels" section.)
5. How do you move a panel from one panel window to another? (See the "the "Manipulating Panels" section.)
6. Name four actions that can be done through the Properties Inspector? (See the "Focusing on the Properties Inspector" section.)
7. What is the total number of browsers you can have available to preview your document? (See the "Viewing Your Document " section.)

Session Checklist

✔ Understanding the Site window

✔ Touring the Site window desktop

✔ Defining a new site

✔ Creating a root folder

✔ Defining a Dreamweaver site from existing files

✔ Understanding folder structure and links

✔ Changing a filename

✔ Viewing dependent files with a Site Map

**30 Min.
To Go**

Now that you have learned some general Dreamweaver principles, you will move on to some hands-on work. In this session, you will take a closer look at the Site window, and then you will move on to defining a root folder. Finally, you will define a site using existing files, and you will create a site map.

Understanding the Site window

The Site window is not complicated. In fact, it resembles most of the file management–type listings you will see. There is a lot of power hiding in this simple window, though, and you will find that as you build more and more pages, or multiple sites, that this is where Dreamweaver has so much to offer.

Touring the Site window desktop

What better place to start than with a guided tour of what the Site window offers? The Site window includes a few strange names that are worthy of a short introduction — and it always helps to know the terminology used in a new program.

You have already taken a look at the file listing in the Site window. Zoom in on your view in a little as you prepare to create your first site. Figure 3-1 shows a Site window that is not connected to the host. Note that there are no listings in the left pane. I prepared this view to make it easier to read the labels on the screen.

Many people, myself included, are more comfortable with local files displayed in the left pane of the Site window. However, Dreamweaver ships with local files in the right pane by default, so all illustrations in these sessions represent the default. You can easily change the display so that local files display on the left and remote files display on the right. From the Site or Document window, choose File ⇨ Preferences ⇨ Site, and then choose Left for the Always Show: Local Files value.

- **Menu.** As in most programs, nearly every command available in Dreamweaver can be accomplished through the menu system. From this menu, you can activate any site maintenance operations, such as moving files to and from the server, or checking local or remote listings for a file. You can also open a listed file, create a new file, or preview any file in the browser.

With each new version, Dreamweaver's Site and Document operations become more integrated. This is for user convenience, though, not to blend the important separation between document creation and site management. Make sure you always keep the two functions separate in your mind.

- **Files/Map View.** The default — and most common — view is the Site Files view, as shown in Figure 3-1. Dreamweaver also offers a Site Map view, which offers a graphic representation of the files shown in the Files view. The Map view can be very helpful for monitoring the structure of the site. As you can see in Figure 3-2, it is easy to trace which files are related to one another.

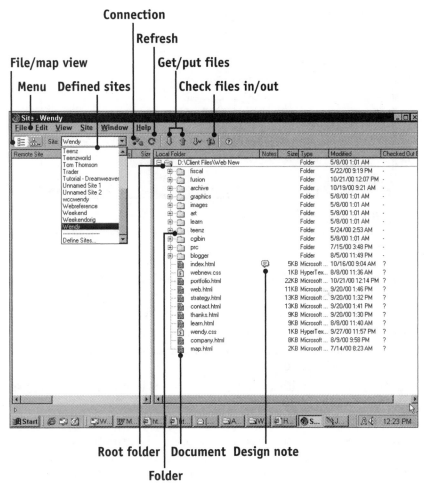

Figure 3-1
The Site window with File view. Dreamweaver is not connected to the server, so only the local files are shown.

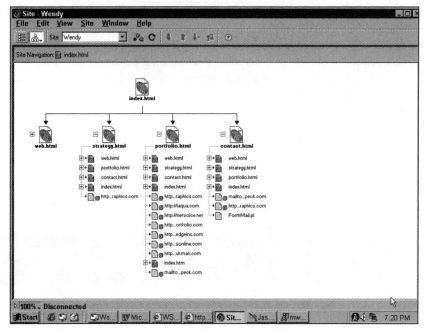

Figure 3-2
The Site Map view in the Site window. This is the same site shown in Figure 3-1.

- **Defined Sites.** When you have several defined sites (which you will do in the "Defining a Site" section, later in this session), they all appear in this drop-down window to provide you with fast access to any site.

- **Connected/Disconnected.** This screen shows a disconnected view. When connected to your server, the two sides of the plug will be joined and a green light will appear.

- **Refresh.** When you need to refresh the view of your local or remote files, one click will do it.

- **Get/Put Files.** Dreamweaver terms for retrieving files from, and sending files to, the server. The terms are from the local perspective. If you "Get" files, you are retrieving them from the server to your local folders. When you "Put" files, you are sending them from your local folder to the server.

- **Check Files In/Out.** When more than one person works on a site, it is very easy for one person to overwrite updates of another person. Checking files in and out prevents errors like this. I will cover this subject much more closely in Session 18.

- **Folder/Document.** Folders are on your hard drive, they have just been recorded by Dreamweaver in order to maintain your site. Documents are also stored on your hard drive, and will usually be created in the Dreamweaver document window. However, HTML pages created in any manner will appear in the Dreamweaver Site window when they are stored in the root folder.

- **Root Folder.** The root folder is the path to where your site is stored on your hard drive; it is specified when you define your site.

- **Design Notes.** Dreamweaver provides the opportunity to create notes that do not show when visitors see your page on the Web, but which can be read by people working on the site. In this case, I was the only person working on this site, and my notes on the index page simply track what changes I have made and why. This is a handy feature, even when you work alone. For a team, design notes are amazing communication tools. You can keep design notes on your local file, or you can choose to upload them to the server for others on your team to read.

This ends your basic tour of the Site window. It is simple and quite logical. Next, you'll take a quick look at some of the most important menu items, and then you'll define a root folder for your first exercise.

Learning the Site window menus

I am not going to hop on my soapbox about using menus again. However, I cannot resist a gentle reminder that you will gain a better understanding of this program if you use menus to start.

It is boring to step through each individual menu item, and I will be hitting all important menu commands in the upcoming sessions. Therefore, I won't take you on a full tour at this time. However, because the Site window menus include both document and site commands, I wanted to spend a little time unraveling the structure before you leave the Dreamweaver exploration stage.

The File menu for the Site window can be a confusing place; it offers an almost equal mix of site and document commands. For example, you can rename a folder, which is very much a site command. You can also create a new document, which causes the Document window to open. In fact, most of the commands in the File menu are document open, view, or check commands.

The Site window is like "command central" for working with Dreamweaver. When I am working on a site, although I can open a file through the Document window, I have a tendency to click back to the Site window. Quickly double-clicking a file listing opens the selected file (a shortcut for File ⇨ Open), and I find it invaluable to see the entire site structure repeatedly as I work.

The rest of the menus, however, contain only site-related commands. For example, the Edit menu concentrates on finding files through various methods, and the View menu lets you tell Dreamweaver how and what you would like to see in your site listings.

Files are moved — and most of the site management is done — in the Site menu. This is the powerhouse menu for the Site window, containing the features you must get to know intimately.

**20 Min.
To Go**

Finally, the Window menu controls the overall appearance of the Site window.

Defining a Site

You've arrived. Time to start creating that site I have been promising. However, hold on to those ideas for a few more minutes. You're not quite ready to start making pages yet. To create a successful Web project, you must work through an organizational phase.

Although it is natural instinct for many to just jump in and organize later — especially for us creative souls (yes, that can be taken as a confession that I am a jump-in-blindly type personality) — you just cannot do that in Dreamweaver. In fact, that is an exceptionally bad idea for Web design in general. Pages in a Web site are always connected through links, and they often include menus that must be created in a separate program. Failing to plan properly will always result in more work, or worse: fragmented navigation.

The payoff for a little organization, however, is creative freedom. Do your homework, set up properly, and let Dreamweaver automatically look after all the irritating little details that can bog down your creative process. You will be paid back in hours for the minutes you spend now.

Creating a root folder

The first step is to create a folder for your site. The folder can be located anywhere on your hard drive. For the sessions in this book, create folders in the root folder on your hard drive. This is only to provide consistency between what your screen shows you and the illustrations that I will be including in the book.

In my design work, I store all my sites in a directory called Client Files on a separate hard drive. In some cases, I have more than one site defined within one client folder. The location is not important, because you will tell Dreamweaver which folder will be your root folder.

Using your normal folder creation method, create a folder named "Weekend."

Defining a new site

Now that you have created your folder, you can tell Dreamweaver where the folder is located, and then create your site. You are building a site from scratch in this example. The next section covers finding an existing site with Dreamweaver.

To define a site with your Weekend folder as the root folder:

1. Open the Dreamweaver Site window.

2. Select Site ⇨ Define Sites. The Define Sites window opens.

3. Select New. The Site Definition window opens.

4. Make sure that Local Info is highlighted for the category type. Type **Weekend** into the Site Name area.

5. Click the folder at the end of the Local Root Folder option. Locate and select the Weekend folder that you created. The Local Root Folder will now read C:\Weekend\.

6. Make sure that the Enable Cache option is selected.

7. Click OK. An alert will appear telling you that Dreamweaver is about to scan the files in your folder and create a site cache.

8. Click OK, and then click Done on the next screen. Your site has been created (see Figure 3-3).

Dreamweaver's Site window now lists Weekend in the Site drop-down list box. The Weekend folder is listed in Local Files as the root folder. This is your working site for the next few sessions. You will return to it later. Now, it's time to build a Dreamweaver site from an existing set of files.

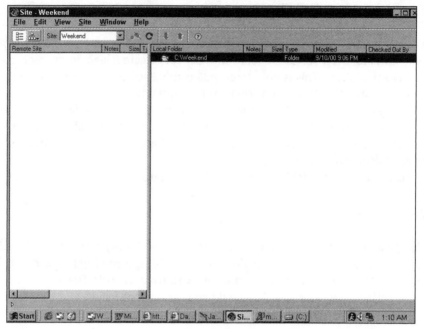

Figure 3-3
Your Site window should look like the window shown here once you have defined your site.

Defining a Dreamweaver site from existing files

You may have been building Web sites long before you decided to use Dreamweaver. No matter how you created existing Web sites, you can build a Dreamweaver site from your existing files, and put the power of site management and document editing to work for you now. In fact, the method used is identical to the steps you took in the "Defining a New Site" section, earlier in this chapter, but the results are different because Dreamweaver will find your existing files.

Locate the Session3 folder on the CD-ROM and copy the folder Weekend2 to your hard drive.

Copy the Session3 folder to your hard drive. It does not matter where you place this folder, as long as you can find it. Follow the instructions from the previous exercise to define a new site called Weekend 2. Your Weekend 2 site should contain two documents called index.html and secondpage.html. There should also be a folder labeled "art," containing a file named weekend.gif. Your screen should closely resemble Figure 3-4.

If you would like to create a new site from your existing files, follow the instructions to define a new site, but specify the location for your root folder. The root folder normally contains the start page (index.html) for your site.

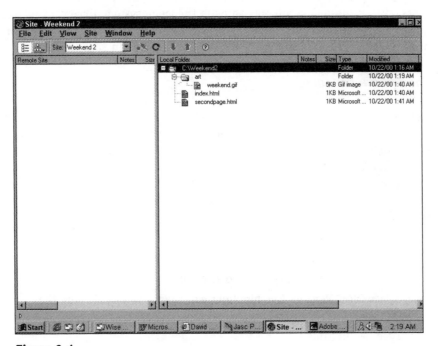

Figure 3-4
The Site window with the Weekend 2 site active. Note how Dreamweaver lists all files in the directory. The "art" directory is expanded here. Simply click any + (plus sign) to expand the folder view. Click the – (minus sign) to collapse the folder view.

**10 Min.
To Go**

Understanding Folder Structure and Links

As your final preparation to start creating documents, you should study the way in which Dreamweaver works with folders and links documents. You will start to see how much of the responsibility for keeping track of changes falls to Dreamweaver, rather than on your shoulders. You are working with a site that has only two pages and one graphic file. As you work through making changes, remember that the action and result would be the same if you were making changes that affected 50 pages or 500 pages.

HTML supports only one page per document. You direct visitors to your site by linking one page to another. In almost all Web sites, each page links to many other pages, even if those links are only through the menu system. Once you add one link to a page, it is no longer independent. Make any change to the location or name of the linked page and you will have a broken link in your site.

Changing a filename

Suppose you realize that you have made errors in your filenames, but you have pages linked to those pages with the incorrect names. Changing a filename is easy anywhere, but change just one character and your linked pages will no longer be able to find that file.

As one who has created and maintained sites without any automatic control, Dreamweaver's ability to quietly keep track of every single link is still magic to me. Enough talk! Here it is in action.

To change a filename:

1. Open the site window and activate the Weekend 2 site.
2. Click the file secondpage.html to select it.
3. Select File ⇨ Rename. The highlight will change to include only the filename.
4. Type **page2.html**.
5. Click away from the listing, or press the Enter key to accept the filename. The Update Files window opens, as shown in Figure 3-5. This window lists any files that are linked to the file you are changing, and asks if you want to update the files. Choose Update. Any reference to secondpage. html will be changed to page2.html in the listed documents.

Figure 3-5
Choosing Update will automatically change the link references in all of the listed files.

Viewing dependent files with a Site Map

Take a look again at Figure 3-4, shown earlier in this chapter. You now know that index.html and secondpage.html are linked, because Dreamweaver had to update index.html when you renamed secondpage.html. But there is nothing that indicates that link. You can easily see links in documents, but there is no indicator in the Site window.

You can see all dependent files, as well as the entire structure of a site, by changing the view. In Figure 3-6, you can see index.html linking to both the image, weekend.gif, and the file page2.html (remember that you changed the filename in the last exercise).

To create a Map view of your site:

1. Make sure the Weekend 2 site is active. Select Window ⇨ Site Map, or click the Site Map icon near the upper-left of the screen.
2. Select View ⇨ Dependent Files.
3. To give the listings more room for a small site, you can enlarge the columns. Select View ⇨ Layout and the Site Definition window will open. Make sure that the Site Map Layout is active, and then change the Column Width to 200. Click OK.

Your screen should closely resemble the screen shown Figure 3-6. The + (plus sign) indicates that there are more levels of linked files. In this case, however, the links will go on forever because the two files are linked to each other. You can collapse levels using the – (minus sign) key on the keyboard.

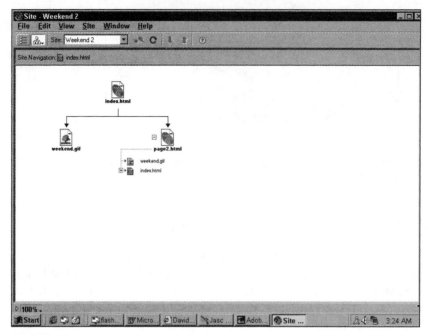

Figure 3-6
Site Map for the Weekend site. Note how the index.html page is linked to both an image and another page. The second page is also linked to an image, as well as back to the index.html page.

Note that the image file, weekend.gif, has no lower levels. However, it is linked to both index.html and page2.html (look for the image file in the page2.html list of dependent files). It does not take a lot of imagination to see how the Site Map view can help you organize your site. The Site Map can be saved as a graphic file, and you can print it as well.

To restore the file view, click the Site Files icon, or select Window ➪ Site Files.

You should now have a very good understanding of how Dreamweaver goes about managing your site for you. The solid foundation that you have built here will pay off over the next couple of days as you delve deep into Dreamweaver's capabilities.

Done!

In the next session, you will move back to the Document window and build your first page.

REVIEW

You have just learned how to find your way through the Dreamweaver Site window and understand how files are linked. You will want to make sure that you remember the following items:

- You can change where the local and remote files are displayed in the Site window by selecting Edit ⇨ Preferences.
- All file management tasks are handled in the Site window.
- You can create notes for any file using the Design Notes feature.
- The Site window controls the entire site.
- Any site must have a root folder, and the root folder can be located anywhere on your hard drive.
- You can set up a Dreamweaver site from your existing files.
- Always make changes to site files from within Dreamweaver, not through your hard drive.
- A Site Map provides an instant overview of your site.

QUIZ YOURSELF

1. When would you use Check Files In/Out? (See the "Touring the Site Window Desktop" section.)
2. What happens when you Get a file? What happens when you Put a file? (See the "Touring the Site Window Desktop" section.)
3. What is a root folder? (See the "Touring the Site Window Desktop" section.)
4. What do you need before you define a new site? (See the "Defining a New Site" section.)
5. Why must you make all changes to files in the Dreamweaver Site window? (See the "Understanding Folder Structure and Links" section.)
6. How can you create a site map that displays dependent files? (See the "Viewing Dependent Files with a Site Map" section.)

Creating a Document

Session Checklist

✔ Creating and opening a new document

✔ Viewing HTML

✔ Entering and editing text

✔ Placing an image

✔ Saving a document

***30 Min.
To Go***

N ow that you have successfully defined a site, it is time to add pages and begin to build your Web site. In this session, you will create a blank document and add basic elements, like images and text to the page. You will also continue to work within Dreamweaver's Site window, which is vital to preparing a good foundation for your site.

As I have mentioned in previous sessions, I usually refer only to menu commands in my instructions. Although almost every command can be accomplished with a keyboard shortcut, I believe that you will save time in the long run when you start out using the menus. When you seek a menu item, you are exposed to every other command within that menu. Although the other menu items may not register at the time, repeated access imprints the structure of the program, as well as neighboring commands, into your mind. In addition, shortcuts are listed with the menu commands, and you will quickly remember the shortcuts to the features you use all the time. Why carry 50 shortcuts in your memory when you only use 15 commands most of the time?

Creating HTML Documents

Each page on a Web site is an individual document (because HTML does not offer multiple-page capability.) There is no limit to the length of a single HTML page, although experienced designers rarely create pages that will fill more than two or three screens in the published document. Later in this course, you will learn to create links that will connect your pages — much like pages in a book.

Publishing to the Web bears little resemblance to printing a page from your printer or sending a file to a professional print shop. Many experienced computer users have difficulty with the transition from print to Web pages. To avoid confusion and frustration, I strongly recommend that you think of working with Dreamweaver as an entirely new concept, rather than trying to translate your former knowledge to Web publishing.

 If you have HTML coding experience, I recommend that you resist the natural tendency to do most of your work within the HTML editor. Dreamweaver will save you time once you have mastered the basic techniques. You can always check and tweak the code once it has been produced, but to write standard code by hand is defeating the purpose of the program, and it will also delay your learning progress.

Creating a blank document

In the last session, you defined a site called Weekend. If this is the only site you have defined, Dreamweaver will open with Weekend as the default site. If you have defined other sites, select the Weekend site from the drop-down list at the top of the screen.

Follow these steps to open a new document in the Dreamweaver Site window:

1. Select File ⇨ New File from the Main Menu. An entry will appear with the label untitled.htm. The filename label will be highlighted. In the label, type **session4.html**. You have created a blank document in the Weekend site. Please make sure that your Site window is exactly the same as the window shown in Figure 4-1. This will be important later.

2. Double-click session4.html in your Site window. Your document will open.

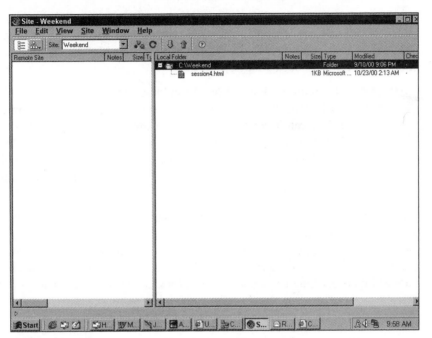

Figure 4-1
A blank document is created in the Dreamweaver Site window. This file is in the root directory for the site.

You can create a new document by using the File ⇨ New command from the main menu in an open document as well, but it is best to manage your files from the Site window as you learn the program. The entire structure for your Web site is clearly laid out in this window, and it is essential that you fully understand how each file relates to others as you create Web documents. The number of files and folders grows very quickly as you build a Web site. If you do not fully understand how your Site is structured, you will be confused as the site grows, and you will find the automated features for site management difficult to use.

Entering text and checking HTML

Using an HTML editor like Dreamweaver will normally create some confusion in the beginning. Technically, you can complete an entire Web site without seeing any HTML code. However, this concept should be considered more as a marketing statement by the software manufacturers than the description of a realistic workflow.

To create a Web page that will display properly in any browser and on any platform, there will be times when you will need to work with HTML code. I will refer to HTML code throughout this course, highlighting the most common adjustments and providing troubleshooting hints.

If you do not know HTML, I would advise that you gain at least a basic understanding of the language. You can learn it separately, or you can make sure that you are constantly observing the code that Dreamweaver produces while you create your documents. You should also have at least one comprehensive HTML book in your library. I recommend the *HTML 4.01 Weekend Crash Course* by Greg Perry.

Start right away to work back and forth between the visual display of your page and the HTML code window. When you created your document in the last step, it opened in a new window with a cursor in the upper-left corner. Although this looks like a blank page, Dreamweaver has already entered HTML code for you. Before you type anything on the page, take a look at the code that is already in place.

To view HTML code and then add text, follow these steps:

1. Locate the Code and Design View icons at the upper-left portion of your screen, as shown in Figure 4-2. The third icon, which is the Show Design View icon, should be depressed.

Show Design View icon

Figure 4-2
The Design view icon is active, meaning that no code view is showing.

2. Click the Show Code and Design Views, which is the middle Design View icon. Your window will split and the top portion of the screen will display the HTML code for your document. It should resemble the screen shown in Figure 4-3.

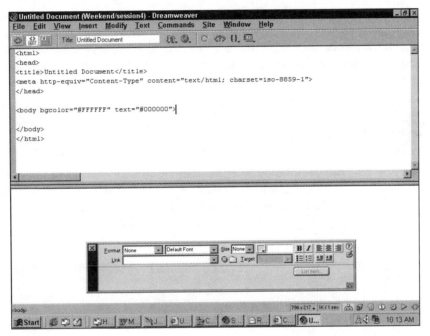

Figure 4-3
*HTML code for a "blank" page in Dreamweaver. Note that the cursor is not
at the upper portion of the HTML screen, but at the end of the* <body
bgcolor="#FFFFFF"> *tag. All code above this point creates the document
(Head) and sets the background color to white instead of the default gray.*

3. Return to Design View. Start your document with a simple text entry.

4. Type **If this is so easy, why does everyone make such a fuss about
   HTML?** Take another look at the HTML code. Note how the text you typed
   now appears with the code.

5. Return to Design View. Place your cursor at the end of the sentence you
   typed and press Enter to move the cursor to the next line.

6. View the HTML code again. Whoa! Where did all that code come from?
   HTML does not read the Enter key action like a word processor. You must
   have a <p> tag to indicate that there is a paragraph. Dreamweaver automatically sets that up. And the ? That is simply the code for a nonbreaking space, meaning a space that does not start a new line. HTML
   demands that content be placed in a tag. Dreamweaver uses this code as
   a placeholder until more content is added.

7. Type **OK, so maybe it is a little more complicated than it looked at
   first**.

Check your code and you will see that the placeholder code is now gone. There is a lot going on behind the screen in Dreamweaver. Keep checking as you move through the rest of the session. Not only will you gain understanding of the way HTML works, but you will also gain an appreciation for the work that Dreamweaver saves.

You also have the option to view your HTML in a separate window, which some people prefer. Although I recently recommended that you use menu commands to start, I am going to give you two shortcuts to open the HTML window. You will use this feature too often to hold the shortcut back. You can open and close the HTML window with the F10 key, or by clicking the HTML Source icon, which is located in the lower-right corner of document screen, as shown in Figure 4-4.

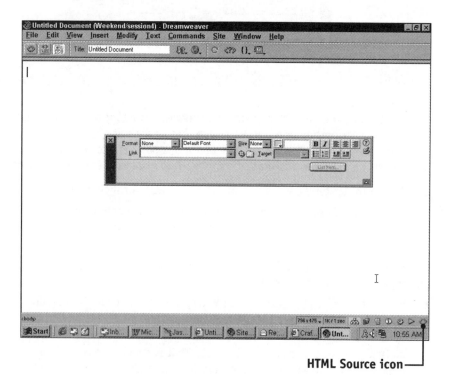

HTML Source icon ⌐

Figure 4-4
HTML Source icon

I cannot overstress the importance of making a commitment to become HTML-wise. You can learn a lot about how HTML code works by following the code as you create your document. Dreamweaver has an excellent reputation for creating "clean" code, which generally means that it does not produce a lot of extra code to accomplish a specific task. As you work through the exercises, even if I do not specifically direct it, peek at the code that is produced as you add an image, create a link, or complete any other action. Before you know it, you will have the skill to enter your own code and overcome the few little areas where Dreamweaver does not offer every option.

20 Min. To Go

To learn how to edit HTML in Dreamweaver, see Session 11.

Part I—Friday Evening
Session 4

Editing Text

HTML fonts are one of the main reasons I suggested that you leave any print experience behind. Because a page you create for the Web will be read on the reader's computer, you have very little control over the final appearance of text. Your page will use their fonts to display the text, which means that the font you use must be installed on all the computers that might display the page, severely limiting choice.

You will learn about CSS (Cascading Style Sheets) in Session 22. CSS handles text much more efficiently and provides tighter control.

Choosing your fonts

Dreamweaver has, again, done much of the work for you in choosing fonts that will work on your page. A printed page depends on fonts within the computer, which is delivering the file to the printer. Web pages read the fonts from the visitor's computer. This means that you must use fonts that are likely to be installed on any computer, because you have no way to determine which fonts will be present on that viewer's computer. Dreamweaver only provides the accepted list of fonts that are typically available on any computer.

Follow these steps to choose a font in Dreamweaver:

1. Open the Properties palette by choosing Window ➪ Properties.

   The second drop-down window from the left contains preset font choices. You can create your own set of choices, but the existing sets cover most practical Web options. Note that there are several fonts listed with each choice. When a browser loads a page, it will check the user's system for the first font in the list, and then check for the second, and so on, until it finds a font that it can display. The final entry in each of Dreamweaver's preset styles offers either san-serif or serif as a choice. If the browser cannot find one of the named fonts, it will use the computer's default serif or san-serif font to display the page.

2. Highlight the first sentence you typed.

3. Choose Verdana, Arial, Helvetica, and sans-serif from the drop-down menu options. The font changes.

Changing font color and attributes

The Properties palette is also used to change font color and attributes for your text. Follow these steps to change color or attributes:

1. Highlight a word in the first sentence.

2. In the Properties palette, click the Bold icon to change the text to bold.

3. Click the Text Color well, and then choose a color from the fly-out color palette, as shown in Figure 4-5.

4. Check the code again to see the HTML code behind the text's appearance onscreen.

Changing font size

HTML offers only relative text sizing — not text sizing by point size, which is common in the computer world. This simply means that each text size is set in relation to the other text in the document. Standards for relative font sizing vary across browsers and platforms. The implications and final results of using this method to set text size is complicated and confusing (and well worth hours of study). However, it is outside the scope this course. The concept is easy to grasp, though, and Dreamweaver makes setting the chosen relative size easy.

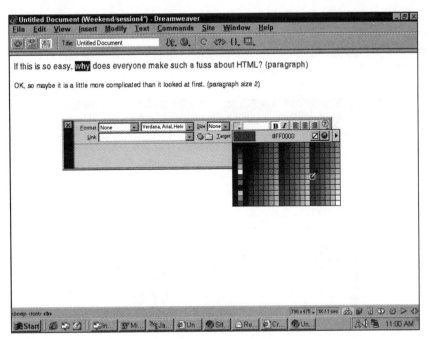

Figure 4-5
The Properties palette is used to change text attributes. The color fly-out features only Web safe color choices. Note that the text is highlighted—a necessary step for any text editing.

Follow these steps to set a relative size font:

1. Highlight the second sentence and choose the value "2" from the dropdown Size option in the Properties palette. Because the default font setting is "3," the text becomes smaller.

2. Check your code again in the HTML window to see the code that Dreamweaver has entered while you worked in the document.

Applying an HTML style

You can also assign an HTML style to your text. H1 is the largest headline style, and H6 the smallest. The styles are designed to be used in a hierarchical way, with H1 forming main headlines, H2 forming a second level heading, H3 forming a third level heading, and so on. Although the styles continue up to H6, H4 through H6 are rarely used. The Paragraph style is meant to be the normal body text. See Figure 4-6 for samples of the HTML styles.

HTML styles automatically add a break, so no line break is needed. They can only be applied to full paragraphs. You do not need to highlight all the text you wish to change. Simply place your cursor anywhere in the paragraph and then choose a style.

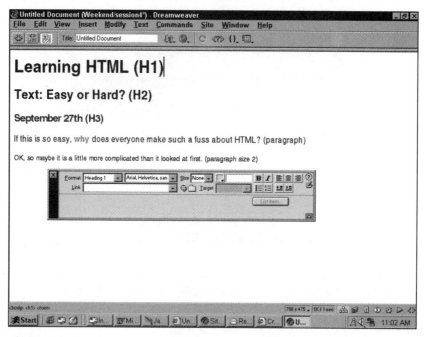

Figure 4-6
A selection of the most commonly used HTML styles. The font has been changed to Arial, Helvetica, sans-serif *for the headlines and* Verdana, Arial, Helvetica, sans-serif *for the paragraph text. Note how the Properties palette reflects the settings of the paragraph containing the cursor.*

**10 Min.
To Go**

Inserting an Image

You've learned to insert text into your page, but the Web has gone far beyond simple words. You want images — and lots of them. Fortunately, Dreamweaver makes it very easy to insert images. However, you must return to the Site window to organize where you store the images.

Creating a new folder

Images are best kept in a separate folder from the HTML documents. With graphic menu bars and rollover images, it is not unusual to create sites that contain several hundred images. Without organization at the start of the project, many hours are wasted locating files. Dreamweaver also needs to know where the images are stored, and it is much better to establish the location for all files first, before you place them in your document.

Follow these steps to create a new folder:

1. Activate your Site window. You will now create a folder for your images.

2. Highlight the main folder at the very top of the Local Folder window. New folders are placed as a child of the active folder. Because you want your graphics folder to be on the first level, you must start from the original folder.

3. Select File ⇨ New Folder from the main menu. Dreamweaver places a new folder under the starting folder with the default name "Untitled" active. Type the word **art**.

File size is always a concern with HTML documents, because size determines the download speed for the final page. I will cover optimizing your graphic images later, but you can also keep your file sizes smaller by choosing small names for common directories. For example, using the word "art" instead of the more common "graphics" saves five bytes for every image. Five bytes may not be worth mentioning, but what if you have hundreds of images, many which appear on every page of a 30-page site? For a large site, the savings are significant.

On the CD-ROM that accompanies this book, you can find lots of graphics to use as you design your Web pages. The images can be found in the Weekend\Art folder on the CD-ROM.

Inserting an image

Start adding the artistic elements to your page. Take the following steps to insert an image:

1. Activate your document. Like text, an image will be placed at the cursor location.

2. Click at the end of the last sentence in your document and press Enter to advance the cursor to the next line.

3. Select Insert ⇨ Image from the main menu. Locate the image 4insert.gif in the Weekend\Art folder on the CD-ROM that accompanies this book. Highlight the file to select it. Note that the image size and file size information is listed below the preview on the right side of the window. See the Select Image Source window in Figure 4-7.

4. Click OK to accept the choice and return to the document.

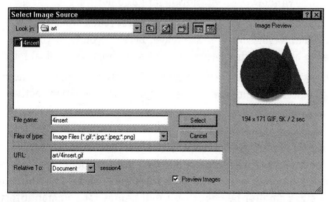

Figure 4-7
The Select Image Source window. Dreamweaver only lists image files that can be viewed on the Web. PNG format files can be viewed by some browsers, but they are not in common use yet. GIF and JPG files are the only formats commonly used today for the Web.

Click the image in your document and you will see selection handles around the border of the image. Note that the Property palette reports the image size, as well as the path leading to the image.

You can click and drag an image to a new location, or delete it with the Delete key. You can also resize an image by clicking and dragging the selection handles, but that is absolutely not recommended.

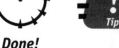

Done!

Although you can resize an image in Dreamweaver, it is the worst possible way to accomplish a size change. Browsers take longer to load resized images, and the quality is usually very poor. Dreamweaver is not well-equipped to resize an image without affecting the quality of the image. Images should be resized in a image editing program like Fireworks, Photoshop, or Paint Shop

Pro. You can resize the image in Dreamweaver to determine the desired size, but you always should return to an image-editing program to resize the image.

REVIEW

In this session, you learned how to create a document in Dreamweaver. Here are some important points to remember:

- It is best in the beginning to use Dreamweaver's site window to create new documents.
- Dreamweaver places text or images at the cursor's current position.
- A basic understanding of HTML code is important, even when using Dreamweaver. Make it a habit to always check your code in the HTML Source window.
- You have very little control over text when publishing pages to the Web. Dreamweaver offers only the fonts that are commonly found on most computer.
- Text must be highlighted to change font attributes. However, an HTML style is applied to an entire paragraph, so highlighting the entire paragraph is not required.
- Create a separate folder to contain the images for your site. Organization is the key to effectively using Dreamweaver.
- Do not resize images in Dreamweaver.

QUIZ YOURSELF

1. How many pages can an HTML document contain? (See the "Creating HTML Documents" section.)
2. Where should you create a new document if you are a beginner? (See the "Creating a blank document" section.)
3. Why does Dreamweaver offer such a small selection of fonts to use? (See the "Editing Text" section.)
4. HTML offers only "relative font size." What does this mean? (See the "Changing font size" section.)
5. How do you move an existing image in a Dreamweaver document? (See the "Inserting an Image" section.)

PART

I

Friday Evening

1. Dreamweaver is a WYSIWYG editor, which means you can produce Web pages without understanding HTML code. Why is it important to learn HTML code?

2. HTML code is not necessarily displayed in the same way in different browsers. Why?

3. Why can you not have total control of text in a Web page?

4. The Assets Manager is a new addition to Dreamweaver 4. Name three tasks that can be done through the Assets Manager.

5. What is the primary purpose for the Site window in Dreamweaver?

6. Why is it a good idea for beginners to use the menu system as they learn Dreamweaver?

7. What is a context menu?

8. What is a Dreamweaver panel?

9. What must you do before you can preview a document in a browser?

10. Before previewing a page in your browser, is it necessary to save the document?

11. What is the difference between *getting* and *putting* files in Dreamweaver?

12. What are Design Notes in Dreamweaver?

13. When you define a site, what is the purpose of the Root Folder?

14. How many pages can an HTML document hold?

15. What is a Dreamweaver site map?

16. What is the shortcut to open the HTML Inspector in Dreamweaver?

17. Why does Dreamweaver offer such a small selection of font choices in the Properties Inspector?

18. Where do you adjust font size and color directly on a page in Dreamweaver?

19. Why should you create a new folder for the graphics and images on your site?

20. What graphic-file types can be used for display on the Web?

☑ Friday

☑ **Saturday**

☐ Sunday

PART

II

Saturday Morning

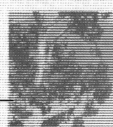

Introducing FTP

Session Checklist

✔ What is FTP?

✔ Using Dreamweaver FTP

✔ Setting Up FTP for your site

✔ Creating a folder on your remote site

✔ Transferring files to your remote site

✔ Transferring an entire site to remote server

✔ Editing files and folders on your remote site

**30 Min.
To Go**

So far, you have defined a site and created a document. There is just one remaining piece to pull it all together: getting your files onto the Web. I explained how hosting works in Session 1, and I am assuming that you have a host in place to receive your files. If you do not, please pause and complete this step.

You will find a list of low- and no-cost hosts on the CD-ROM, in the file hosts.html in the Resources folder.

What is FTP?

FTP is an acronym for File Transfer Protocol. FTP is the vehicle that Web designers use to publish their work. Instead of sending a file to a printer, Web designers send it to their servers using FTP. As a concept, it is really that simple. FTP is simply the tool that is used to transfer files from a hard drive to a server, and it makes the work accessible from a Web address.

Dreamweaver offers built-in FTP capability. When you have your FTP settings correctly specified, transferring files is no different than copying files from your hard drive to a disk. Invisibly, though, Dreamweaver keeps track of all your files and links, as you learned in the last session.

You are not required to use Dreamweaver to place your files on a server. FTP has been around for a long time, and there are many excellent programs available, which can be used to transfer files from your computer to a server. However, when you use a separate program, you lose many of the automated site management tools that make Dreamweaver so powerful. For any of the work you will complete during this course, I strongly recommend that you use Dreamweaver's FTP, even if you are very comfortable with another FTP program.

Dreamweaver FTP

Dreamweaver's Site window *is* the FTP screen. When you transfer a file from a local folder to the server, you are using FTP. Dreamweaver checks the file to see if there are any dependent files, and then asks you if you would like to transfer those files along with the file or files you have specified. Dreamweaver also checks to make sure that you have saved the file you are transferring, and gives you the opportunity to save the latest version if you have omitted that step. Other FTP programs can get your file to the server, but they cannot offer the extra safety features.

The following will apply to you only if your host has full FTP capability. Many free hosts allow pages to be added only through the page building tools offered on the site. In these cases, you will have to prepare your pages in Dreamweaver and copy your code to the appropriate template. If you are serious about Web design, I would advise that you make the commitment to a site that will allow full FTP access. Many of the low-cost hosts charge under $10 per month. Check hosts.html in the Resources folder on the CD-ROM for a listing of these services.

Gathering information for FTP setup

The first time you set up FTP, it may seem difficult. However, as long as you fill in accurate information, it will work, and the second time you use it is always easier. The secret is to collect the correct information. I will discuss each piece of information you will need to help ensure that you start with the right values.

Let's take a quick look at where you will enter the information so that you know where you are going. Figure 5-1 shows the Remote Info screen on the Site Definition window for the Weekend site you set up in the Session 3. I will take you there to enter your information in a few minutes. For now, I just want to move through each section to help you gather the correct information.

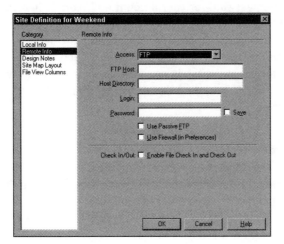

Figure 5-1
The Site Definition window for the Weekend site, with the Remote Info section active and FTP chosen for Access.

- **FTP Host.** This is the address for your host. It may be a simple address like foresite.net, or it may be DNS (Domain Name System) numbers such as 209.43.2.115. If you are uncertain, check the host's Web site, or ask your host for the correct entry. Unless this entry is correct, you will be unable to connect to your host.

- **Host Directory.** This directory is different for each host, and it states the path required to find your files on the remote server. Often, there is a long path to specify where your files will be stored. Check your host's Web site for this information, or ask your host for the correct path. Without the correct path specified, you may be able to connect to the host, and you may be able to place your files, but nobody will be able to find them from the Web.

- **Login.** This is the user name you chose (or were assigned) when you signed up with your host. Unless this is correct — and it is usually case-sensitive — you will not be able to connect to your host.

- **Password.** When you signed up with the host, you chose — or were assigned — a password; passwords are nearly always case-sensitive. Without the correct password, you will not be able to connect to your host. You can have Dreamweaver save your password so you do not have to type it in every time by checking the Save option next to your password.

**20 Min.
To Go**

Dreamweaver hides the actual characters of your password and will not allow this entry to be copied. For safety, you should write down the password for your account and store it in a very safe place. For client work, I write all FTP information on the inside of the file folder I create for each client, including address, directory, user name, and password. I keep the same information for my own sites in my daily planner, which I always have with me. Use the method that works for you, but do record the information.

Setting up FTP for your site

Now that you have all the correct information at hand, you can activate the FTP function for your Weekend site. You must provide FTP information for each site you define.

Take the following steps to define your FTP settings:

1. Open Dreamweaver's Site window.
2. Select Site ⇨ Define Sites and the Define Sites window will open.
3. Select the Weekend site from the list and choose Edit. The Site Definition window opens.
4. Select Remote Info from the Category.
5. Select FTP from the Access drop-down list box. Several blank fields now appear.
6. Type the address for your FTP Host as previously described.
7. Type the correct path for your Host Directory as previously described.

If you are planning to place your files in a remote folder that is not the root folder for your server, you must create the folder on the server before you specify it as the Host Directory for your site. For example, I have the Weekend site in a folder called weekend on my wpeck.com **site. Before I was able to specify the whole path, including the weekend folder, I had to connect to the root directory and create the weekend folder in my remote root directory. I then changed the Host Directory for the Weekend site to the weekend folder in my root site.**

8. Type your user name (log-in) and password as previously described.

9. Click Save to save your password for future sessions.

10. Leave all other options unchecked and click OK. Click Done in the Define Sites window to complete the process.

If your Internet connection is behind a firewall, see your technical advisor for instructions on setting up your FTP.

If the information you gathered is correct, and if you entered it all perfectly, you should be ready to connect to your server.

11. Select Site ⇨ Connect, or click the Connect button beside the site listing drop-down list box. An alert window will open informing you that Dreamweaver is attempting to connect to your server address.

If all the information you entered was correct, you will quickly see a listing in the left column that reflects the path you entered as your Host Directory. In Figure 5-2, you will see that there is a long path to the directory. In fact, the final directory, weekend, does not have room to display correctly.

Congratulations! You are now ready to start publishing to the Web. Be sure to test that all systems are go while you become more familiar with files and folders in Dreamweaver.

On the other hand, you may not be celebrating right now. If your FTP connection did not work, step through the process again, right from the start. If that does not solve the problem, get in touch with the technical support people for your hosting company. Make sure you include all the entries you made while attempting to make the connection. Use the titles that you find listed near the beginning of this section, and type in the settings that you used in your unsuccessful attempt. Most likely, the support staff will instantly spot your error and quickly get you up and running.

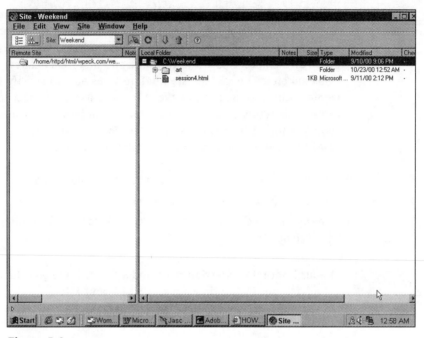

Figure 5-2
The Weekend site is connected to the server when you see the root folder for the remote site.

Tip

Dreamweaver creates a log of FTP activity during a session. If you select Window ⇨ Site FTP log, you will see everything that happened during your FTP session. Read through to see if you can identify the problem. It may not make sense to you, but it could help your technical support representative solve your problem for you. Simply select the text in the file and paste into an e-mail to transfer the report. This will let your technical support person know exactly where you are having trouble.

Creating a folder on your remote site

In Session 4, you created a document with the highly creative name of session4.html. You also created a folder called art, into which you placed 4insert.gif, an image from the CD-ROM. Now you want to transfer these files to the Web.

It is vital that you keep the same structure for your remote files as you have for your local files. To that end, I am actually going to make you work a little harder for this exercise than is required. I will not make you do that forever — just for this one little exercise. But I will not keep you in the dark.

Although Dreamweaver can do the work for you, it's important for you to know how to create a folder on a remote site yourself. You might occasionally want to make a few manual changes. Rarely, the automatic transfer and folder creation does not work right.

Take the following steps to create a folder on the remote site:

1. Make sure that the Weekend site is active and connected to the remote server.

2. Highlight the folder where you would like to place the new folder, in this case, the root directory on the remote site.

3. Select File ⇨ New Folder, or right-click (PC) or Command-Click (Mac) the root folder and choose New Folder from the pop-up menu. A new folder will appear with its name, Untitled, highlighted. Type **art** to name the folder.

The remote and local folder structures are now identical.

**10 Min.
To Go**

Remember from earlier exercises and discussions that Dreamweaver keeps track of all files and folders, which files are linked to other files, and so on. Well, that makes for easy file transfer of files. To transfer everything you have in the Weekend directory, simply tell Dreamweaver to transfer the session4.html file to the remote server. It will ask if you want to include all the dependent files. When you say yes, all files are then transferred. Because the image that is required in that document is in the art folder, Dreamweaver creates a duplicate folder so that it can maintain the same structure as you have for your local site.

Transferring files to your remote site

Now that the file structures are identical, it's time to transfer your files.

I have made a lot of noise recently about using menus and not shortcuts to learn the program faster. Now, I am going to change that advice for transferring files, because drag-and-drop is really the best way to transfer files. As your site builds, you will often find that you are transferring one file to a second- or third-level directory. When you drag and drop files, you can easily place them exactly where you want them to go.

Take the following steps to transfer a file:

1. Make sure your Weekend site is open and that you are connected to the remote server.

2. Highlight session4.html in the local folder window (on the right side). Click and drag the file to the remote site, and place your cursor over the root folder. Then release the mouse button.

3. An alert window will appear asking if you would like to include the dependent files. Select Yes. Watch the lower-left portion of your screen to see transfer details, such as which file is currently transferring to the remote site.

With all folders expanded in both the remote and local sites, your screen should closely resemble the screen shown in Figure 5-3. Note that while you only specified that the file session4.html should be transferred, the file 4insert.gif was also transferred, because the session4.html requires this image to display properly.

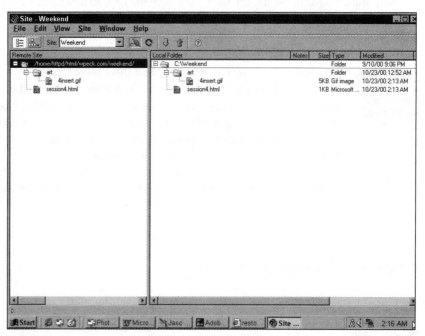

Figure 5-3
Both the remote and local sites are identical.

You should be able to see this page on the Web now. Open your favorite browser and type in the correct URL for your site in your address bar; for example, www.youraddress.com. You will also need to tell the browser which file to view, because you have not yet created an index.html page. (Index.html is the common name for the start page on any Web site, and all other pages link from there.) In this case, though, you are going to tell the browser to go to your address and find the specific file. To carry on the example, the full address is www.yourname.com/session4.html.You may have set up a weekend folder as part of another site, as I have done on my own site.

Transferring an entire site to the remote server

As I mentioned earlier, you can create a Dreamweaver site from files you created before you started using Dreamweaver by simply defining a site as you did in Session 3. Now you need to get that site onto the Web, but you don't want to do it one file at a time.

In Session 3, you created a second site called Weekend 2. Now you are going to create a new folder in the Weekend remote site to place the Weekend 2 site. Although this may seem a little confusing to start, it is another idea I want to present to you while you have examples with only a few files that are not critically important. In effect, you are going to create a site within a site.

Take the following steps to prepare to transport the Weekend 2 site to the remote host:

1. With the Weekend site active, and following the instructions in the previous section, "Creating a folder on your remote site," create a folder in the Weekend remote site called weekend2. Make sure that the Weekend site root folder is selected when you create the new directory.

2. Activate the Weekend 2 site. Following the directions for creating FTP settings, create FTP settings for the Weekend 2 site. Use the same values as you did for the Weekend site, but add /Weekend2/ to the Host Directory path. This sets the path to the Weekend root folder and points to the weekend2 folder.

3. Connect the Weekend 2 site to the server. Note how the root folder for the site is the path to the Weekend site with the addition of weekend2 (hold your mouse pointer over the root folder to see the full path, as shown in Figure 5-4. Although the Weekend 2 site is located in a folder on the Weekend site, as far as Dreamweaver is concerned, the Weekend 2 remote site starts with the weekend2 folder.

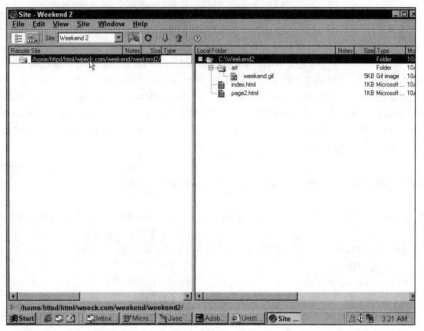

Figure 5-4
Although you know that the weekend2 folder is part of the Weekend site, Dreamweaver ignores anything in a site listing that is above the root folder.

You are now ready to move the Weekend 2 site to the server. You will do this with one action. Although you only have a few files and one folder in this site, the exact same operation would transfer a site with many folders and hundreds of files.

Take the following steps to move the Weekend 2 site:

1. Make sure that the Weekend 2 site is active and connected to the server.

2. Highlight the root folder on the local site (which will be C:\weekend2 if you have created the folders exactly as I have).

3. Click and drag the root folder on the local site to the root folder of the remote site.

4. An alert window will pop up asking if you wish to put (transfer to the server) the entire site. Click OK. The entire site will be transferred to the remote server.

5. Click the Refresh button beside the site listing in the upper part of the screen. This will rearrange the files and folders to display exactly as the local site is delayed. The order of appearance makes no difference. I simply want to avoid confusion at this point.

Because you are transferring the entire site, you will not be asked whether you wish to have the dependent links transferred with the files. All files in that site will be transferred, which naturally includes all dependent files.

The remote site and local site are now identical.

To see the connection between the Weekend and the Weekend 2 site, activate the Weekend site again. As you can see in Figure 5-5 (all folders have been expanded), Weekend 2 is a folder in the Weekend site. Because Weekend 2 is a level below the Weekend site on the remote server, it will show in the Weekend remote site. It is not, however, part of the Weekend local site, because Weekend 2 has a completely different root folder.

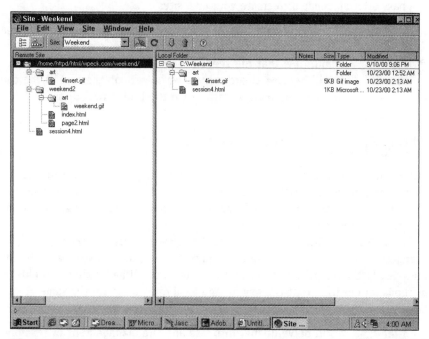

Figure 5-5
The Weekend site shows the weekend2 folder. Yet when the Weekend 2 site is active, there is no indication of the Weekend site, because the Weekend root site is one level higher than the Weekend 2 site.

Part II—Saturday Morning
Session 5

Finally, activate the Weekend 2 site again and you will see that there is no indication of the Weekend site, except in the path to the Weekend 2 root folder.

 The path to view your Weekend 2 site on the Web will be http://yoursite.com/weekend2/. **Because you do have an index.html page on this site, you do not need to specify a filename.**

I hope that you have managed to follow this discussion. I know it is confusing, but it is vitally important for you to understand the relation between root and local sites, as well as root folders on the local and remote sites. It is not unusual to have small sites within larger sites, and it is the best way to see how the local and remote sites relate to one another. Once you have fully mastered the concepts, you will have a lot of freedom to create your own sites.

 If you only have a tentative grasp of the last exercise, make a point to come back a little later in the course and follow through again. Now that the seeds have been planted, you will find that it will become clearer as you work through the rest of the course and become more familiar with the folder structures.

Editing files and folders on your remote site

There is no difference in how you work with files on the remote or the local site. As long as you are connected to the Web, you can delete, move, or rename a file on the remote server exactly as you do on the local site. Simply choose a file from the remote directory and edit as desired.

Be careful here: Always consider that Dreamweaver must be aware of any changes. Most often, changes are best completed on the local site, with the files uploaded to the remote site to update the site. You will be looking at sophisticated methods for ensuring that the remote and local directories are the same in later Sessions.

 I will delve deeper into site and file management in Sessions 10, 12, and 26.

In the next session, you will be building pages with more definition. You will start on new pages that will form your first small site.

Done!

REVIEW

- File Transfer Protocol is used to transfer files from your hard drive to the Web.
- You should always use Dreamweaver's FTP to move your files.
- Every host has different settings for FTP.
- You can edit files and folders on the remote server, but it is best in most cases to make changes on your local copy and upload them to the remote server.
- You can drag and drop local files to your remote server.
- Dreamweaver will transfer an entire site to the Web.

QUIZ YOURSELF

1. Why should you always use Dreamweaver to transfer files for your site? (See the "Dreamweaver FTP" section.)

2. If your FTP connection to a host is not working, what information should you send to the technical support division of your hosting company? (See the "Setting up FTP for your site" section.)

3. How can you make sure that your password is saved for future FTP sessions? (See the "Gathering information for FTP setup" section.)

4. Where can you find the FTP Site log, and how can it help technical support assist you? (See the "Setting up FTP for your site" section.)

5. The remote and root folders can be different. How can this be, and why might it be a good idea? (See the "Transferring an entire site to the remote server" section.)

Defining a Dreamweaver Site

Session Checklist

✔ Why use tables?

✔ Creating a paper mock-up

✔ Creating and editing a table in Dreamweaver

✔ Aligning a table

✔ Inserting an image

✔ Inserting text

✔ Aligning elements in a table

**30 Min.
To Go**

In this session, you will start to build a working site. All of the images and text you require will be provided for you so that you can concentrate on learning the techniques. This is the first of two sites you will create. The first site will include all of the basic techniques you require for every site you will build. The second site, starting with Session 17, will provide the opportunity to work with Dreamweaver's advanced features.

You will start this project by learning about tables. Although they were never meant to provide page layouts in the original HTML specifications, designers looking for more page layout control quickly put tables to use. The Web has never been the same.

Why Use Tables?

Used properly, tables are the best tools to control your layout. Using them properly usually means planning your layout and tables carefully before you start to build your page. I cannot stress this point enough. Some people plot their table structure out on paper before they start designing. I find that I start with a test page, planning my tables and layout in Dreamweaver, but not moving to production until I have very carefully tested the layout. I rarely use my test page, preferring instead to use it as a testing ground, and then I recreate the table structure on a clean document.

Whether you test tables on paper or on the computer, make sure that you make this stage a regular part of your creation process. It is very difficult to change your table structure on a page with all the content in place. Successful tables and clean code work hand in hand. It is much faster to work cleanly than to clean up the mess later.

There are some purists who still say that you should not use tables for layout. You will hear this from a small and dwindling number of people, though. The only alternative to tables, other than having no layout control, is working in layers (covered in Session 27). Working with layers is easy for the designer, but, unfortunately, this technology is not yet fully supported, even by modern browsers. Your choices, when creating pages for the general Web population, are tables or nothing. Even if you ignore the graphics aspects of using tables for layout, it is hard to present information in an easy-to-read format without having a columnar structure.

However, I have some sympathy for the purist stand. Tables are often badly used — more so when a program like Dreamweaver is used as the creation tool. Tables are so easy to build in Dreamweaver, it is quite common to get carried away by the impulse to control every single inch of the screen. Placing one table inside another table — known as nesting — can be a very effective way to create your layout. However, moderation is the key.

Never nest many tables to create your layout. Tables must be used intelligently. If you find you are creating tables within tables within tables, you are heading for trouble. Not only will your page load very slowly, but many browsers do not handle multiple table layers well. A little creative thinking will usually present a much better option than nesting many tables.

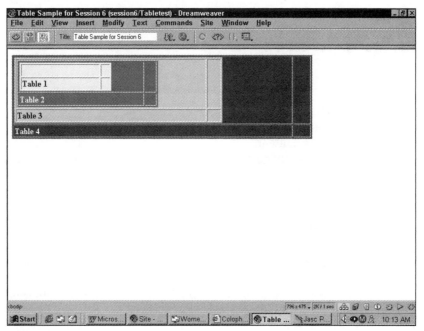

Figure 6-1
Four layers of nested tables — exactly how tables should NOT be used for Web design. Although it is an easy way to control layout, the increased load time and unpredictable results in some browsers make the cost too high.

Keep my warnings in mind as you move on to creating tables. I don't want to cripple you with fear, but if I am going to overemphasize just one point, this is a good place to pick. Clean, working tables will make your design life a pleasure. Tables with too many layers, or over-manipulated code, leaving behind spaces and assorted disorder, will lead to self-destructive behavior that can leave you bald.

Creating a Table in Dreamweaver

I know die-hard hand-coders who use Dreamweaver for one task only — creating tables. To create a two-row, two-column, empty table, you need the following code:

```
<table width="75%" border="1" cellpadding="10">
  <tr>
    <td> </td>
    <td> </td>
  </tr>
```

```
<tr>
  <td> </td>
  <td> </td>
</tr>
</table>
```

Now imagine that you require four columns and four rows, and you can see why you might be reluctant to do the typing, not to mention the confusion factor once the cells are filled with content.

Dreamweaver provides the tools to create and edit tables easily. Make sure you understand the basics of this section before you move on to the next session, which stretches your table beyond the basics.

Building your table

To simulate the production method I recommend, you will start with a test page. I will guide you step-by-step through the table creation, of course. As the final step in creating your table, you will create a new page with a fresh table into which you will place images and text.

Creating a paper mock-up

As I mentioned earlier, many designers prefer to plot their direction on paper before they open Dreamweaver. Figure 6-2 is a sample of a hand-drawn table layout. By the end of this session, you will have created a table with this structure. Notice how I have drawn the cells of the table and then worked the content over several cells. You must have a general idea of how tables work before you can create a drawing like this. You will cover all techniques required to create this table in this session.

Drawings and test tables can be a little like the chicken and egg question. Which really comes first? If you are new to tables, you may have better luck experimenting with a few test tables in Dreamweaver before you attempt to draw a mock-up diagram. But why bother if you have already figured it out in the test file? A drawing will help you to see the structure of your tables, and can help keep you on track as you insert your content. This is especially true if you are using nested tables.

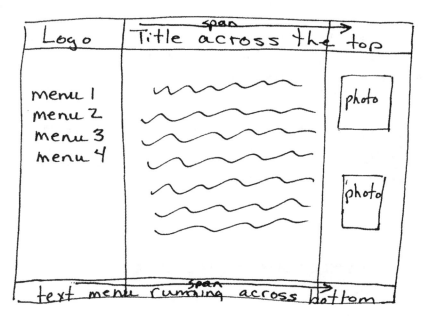

Figure 6-2
A hand-drawn table layout provides a quick way to design your table.

Creating a table

Now that you know where you are going, start building your table. You will work from a blank document in your Weekend site.

1. Open Dreamweaver and make sure that the Weekend site is active.

2. Create a new document (see Session 4). Name the new document tabletest.html and open it.

3. Working in Show Design View, select Insert ⇨ Table. The Insert Table window will open.

   Take a look at the mock-up drawing shown earlier in Figure 6-2. You can see that you will need three columns and three rows for this table. Type **3** for the Row value and type **3** for the Column value. Do not leave the Insert Table window yet.

4. Set the Cell Padding (margin between content and cell border) to 10 and the Cell Spacing (distance between cells) to 0.

5. Set the width to 500, and then choose Pixels from the drop-down menu. This means that your table will be 500 pixels wide. You will use percentages for widths when you build your second site.

6. Make sure the border is set to 1. This will place a 1-pixel border around the table and between each cell. For no borders, the setting should be 0.

Although you do not want a border on your finished table, it is a good idea for beginners to lay out their tables with the borders turned on. It is much easier to see where the table cells are located with the border visible. The border can be turned on and off at any time.

7. Click OK, and your table will appear on the page as shown in Figure 6-3.

Figure 6-3
Empty table with borders turned on for easy editing.

Aligning a table

Usually, the first task you will want to do with a table is align it on the page. If the table is to be aligned to the left of the page, do nothing; left alignment is the default table alignment. Soon you will look at aligning content within the cells. This exercise is to align the entire table to the right, center, or left of the page (content is not affected by this command).

Take the following steps to align a table on the page:

1. First, you must select the table. Place your cursor somewhere in the table, and then select Modify ➪ Table ➪ Select Table.

2. With the table selected, choose Center from the Align drop-down menu in
the Properties Inspector. Your table will now be located in the center of
your document.

**You can also select a table by holding your mouse pointer just
above the top or bottom border of the table until the move symbol (two double-pointed arrows, as shown in Figure 6-4) appears.
Click to select the table. When selected, the table border will be
darker and the sizing handles will appear.**

When the table is selected, the properties for the table are listed in the
Properties Inspector, as shown in Figure 6-4.

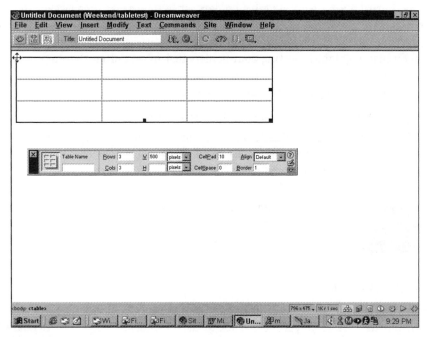

Figure 6-4
*Selection handles indicate that the table is selected. Note the Move cursor
that indicates when a table can be selected. The Properties Inspector lists
properties for the selected table.*

**20 Min.
To Go**

This is a perfect time to take a peek at the HTML code that you have produced. Open the HTML window (F10), or click either the Show Code View button or the Show Code and Design View buttons. Trace through the main table properties `<table>` and through the series of table rows `<tr>` and cells `<td>` to understand the structure of your table.

Editing a table

Even with the best preplanning, you will often need to adjust a parameter or two for your table. With the Properties Inspector, adjusting a table is a breeze. Your table must be selected to make changes, but any properties, including the number of rows or columns can be adjusted. you are going to remove the border from this table. I usually work with my table borders set to 0, because Dreamweaver does show an outline for the table cells, but this is a good adjustment to keep in mind. Once your table is filled with content, borders and structure may become hidden in tightly placed graphics. Setting your borders to 1 px will often show a problem that is invisible when the border is set to 0.

Take the following steps to edit table borders:

1. Select your table as you did in the previous example.

2. Change the Border value to 0 in the Properties Inspector. As shown in Figure 6-5, note that Dreamweaver marks the table and cell position with dotted lines when the border value is set to 0.

For accurate proofing, you can make even the dotted table borders disappear. Select View ⇨ Visual Aids ⇨ Table Borders to toggle table borders on and off.

Merging table cells

Your table is starting to look a little like the diagram shown in Figure 6-1, but you have a little work to do yet. Refer back to the diagram and note that there are two areas with "span" notations. The top row has only two columns, and the bottom row of the table has one column. You must join the column cells to create this layout.

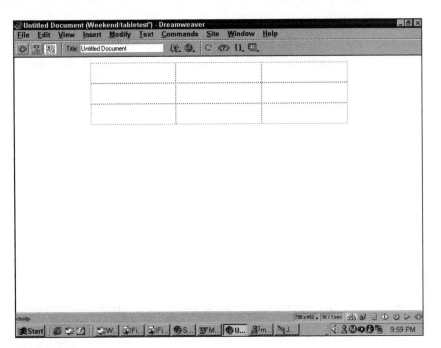

Figure 6-5
The same table as the one shown in Figure 6-4, but with the borders set to 0.

The HTML code required to merge columns is <td colspan="x">, where x is the number of columns you need to join. You can use the same technique to join rows using the code <td rowspan="x">>, where x represents the number of rows you want to combine. Although this is not an HTML course — and Dreamweaver produces this code automatically for you — you need to be familiar with this set of codes to troubleshoot any tables you create.

Take the following steps to merge columns for your layout:

1. Click inside the top-center cell and drag across the center and right column of the top row. Both cells will be selected, as indicated by darker borders.

2. Click the Merge icon near the lower portion of the Properties Inspector in the Cell section. (Notice the position of the cursor in Figure 6-6.) The selected cells will be merged.

3. To merge the bottom row, click in the lower-left cell and drag across all three columns to select them.

4. Click the Merge icon as to merge the cells. Figure 6-6 shows the completed merge from Steps 1 and 2, with the lowest row of cells selected and ready to be merged.

I recommend that you go back to the beginning, create a new document, and work through this entire exercise again. Even better, try to do it without following the text step-by-step. It is very important that you have the methods described here well-seated in your memory. Work through the exact same steps, but name the file you create in the first step index.html.

**10 Min.
To Go**

If you are already familiar with Dreamweaver tables, or you feel quite confident that you know how to create a table and merge cells, simply save the file you created as index.html.

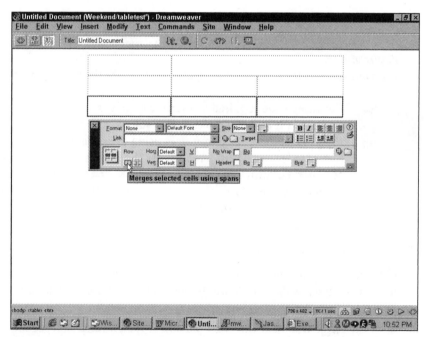

Figure 6-6
Your table now closely resembles the diagram. Don't worry about the difference in the row heights; The content will force the height as it is inserted into the cells.

Inserting Content into Tables

Now that the table is constructed, you can start to add your content. You have already inserted one image, but now you want to place an image into a table cell. There is a lot more to consider when inserting images into tables. I am just going to have you start from scratch. First, you must copy the content files from the CD-ROM that accompanies this book.

Files for this exercise are in the Session 6 folder on the CD-ROM. Copy the following graphics files into the c:\Weekend\art folder (or into the art folder in the root directory for your Weekend site): logo.gif, menu6a.gif, menu6b.gif, menu6c.gif, menu6d.gif, photo6a.jpg, and photo6b.jpg.

Copy worddoc6.doc and textdoc6.txt to c:\Weekend (or into the root folder for your Weekend site). Check your Site window, with Weekend active, to ensure that they are in the right location (see Figure 6-7).

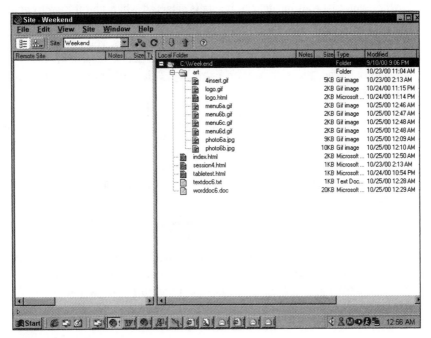

Figure 6-7
Your Weekend Site window files should be the same as this list if all files have been saved to the correct location.

Inserting images

Place the logo in the upper-left cell of your table to start.

1. Place your cursor in the upper-left cell of the table. Your image will be inserted at the cursor's location.

2. Select Insert ⇨ Image. The Select Image Source window will open. Select logo.gif from the art folder. A preview of the logo will appear in the right side of the window. Click OK.

Don't worry that your cells seem to be moving at this point. You will get your content into the appropriate places and work on the layout in a few minutes.

3. Insert your cursor into the left column of the second row. Repeat Step 2 to insert the file menu6a.gif.

   When you place an image, the image is selected when you return to your document. You are going to place four images for the menu directly beneath another in the same cell. To accomplish this, you must get your cursor back and place a line break to place the next image. With the image selected, press your right-arrow key. This will move the selection from the image to the "line."

4. With your Shift key held down, click Enter. This inserts a break (<br>) tag, which moves the cursor to the next line without the extra space that a paragraph tag (<p>) inserts.

5. Insert the image file menu6b.gif. This is a good time to look at your HTML code to see how your table looks with content, as well as the <br> tag.

6. Repeat Steps 4 and 5 to insert the menu6c.gif and menu6d.gif image files.

7. Repeat the Steps 3-6 to insert both photo6a.gif and photo6b.gif into the middle row of the right column. Refer to the hand-drawn diagram in Figure 6-2, shown earlier, if you need a guide to place the photos.

Inserting text

Now that you have the images in the table, you are going to add the text. Don't worry if everything looks out of balance. It is important to get the content into place before worrying about fine-tuning the layout. Now enter your text manually and paste text in from a file.

Take the following steps to create the headline:

1. Place your cursor into the second column of the top row. Type **A tour through our country.**

2. Highlight the text you just typed. In the Properties Inspector, change the font to Arial, Helvetica, sans-serif. Change the font size to 4. Click the "B" icon to add the bold attribute to the text.

Take the following steps to insert the body text:

3. Open the file worddoc6.doc (Microsoft Word) or textdoc6.txt (plain text). Select all the text and select Edit ⇨ Copy to copy it.

4. Insert your cursor into the middle cell of the second row and choose Edit ⇨ Paste.

Now that the images and text are all in the table, it's time to fine-tune the layout. You can specify widths for columns to hold the content in place.

Specifying column width

Although the columns and rows are correctly set up, you must instruct the browser as to how wide to display each column. Different browsers will display information — especially tables — in many forms. You can add some control with specified widths.

I will be delving much deeper into controlling column layout in Session 7, which moves into Liquid Design.

This sample is a very simple fixed-width table. You must keep a few basic table principles in mind. First, no matter what width you specify for a column, it will never be smaller than the largest graphic it contains. You could specify that every cell in a column should be 75 pixels wide, but if you have a graphic in any cell that is 100 pixels wide, all cells in that column will expand to 100 pixels. The column can be larger than the largest image, but it cannot be smaller.

Never use Dreamweaver's click-and-drag sizing for columns and rows. It is tempting to drag a cell border and place it where you want it; it works very well in Dreamweaver. But browsers do not always — or even often — follow. You will rarely require row heights when designing a table, but when you are making a row larger or smaller by dragging, a height is automatically entered. This adds unnecessary code, which increases a visitor's download time. It can also cause a great deal of frustration.

You are much further ahead in plotting your tables out as you have done here, and in specifying your table parameters numerically. It is the little things like this that enable you to make your pages compatible with all browsers.

Place your widths in the second row. You cannot specify the width of a merged cell, and row two has no combined cells. Placing a width command in one cell controls the width for the entire column.

Take the following steps to correct the layout of your table:

1. Click inside the left column of the second row. Make sure that you can see the cursor and that you do not have an image selected. Your image is 137 pixels wide, so you want your column to be 137 pixels. Enter 137 as the W value, near the center of the lower section of the Properties Inspector

2. Click inside the right column of the second row. Specify 100 for the width of the column.

   The left column and the right columns in this table require the space for the images. Because the table width is fixed at 500, a little math will give you the correct size for the center column. Subtract the two column widths from the total table size to determine the width for the center column (500 – 137 – 100=263).

3. Click inside the center column of the second row and specify 263 pixels for the width of the column.

Your table should now closely resemble the sample shown in Figure 6-8.

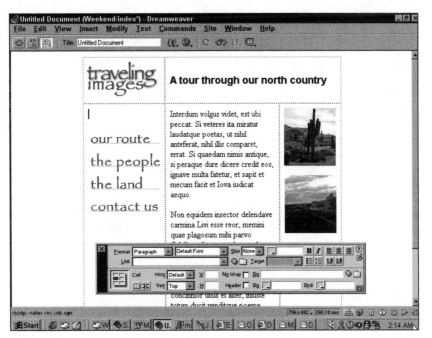

Figure 6-8
The corrected layout after specifying column width

Aligning content in tables

You can align each table cell independently, both horizontally and vertically. Left alignment is the default setting.

Never specify left justification when it is not needed. HTML naturally defaults to left alignment, and specifying left does nothing but add code, which adds to download time.

Take the following steps to change the alignment for a cell:

1. Place your cursor in the upper-right cell containing the headline.

2. Select Center from the Horz (Horizontal) drop-down menu in the Cell area of the Properties Inspector (see Figure 6-9).

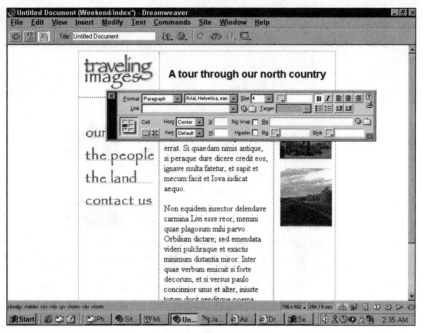

Figure 6-9
Setting the horizontal alignment (Horz) for the cell changes the headline text alignment to center.

Done!

The rest of the cells in your table are fine with the default alignment.

You also can select an entire column or row and specify justification. Simply move your mouse pointer over the upper border of the column or over the left border of a row until the cursor changes to a solid arrow (see Figure 6-10). Click and the entire row or column will be selected.

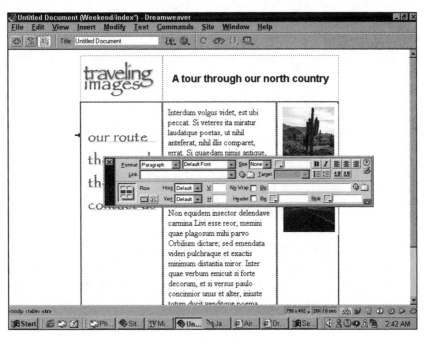

Figure 6-10
When the cursor changes to a solid arrow, you can click and select the whole row or column.

REVIEW

- Tables are used for most cross-browser-compatible Web page designs.
- Properly designed tables can help you control layout.
- Nesting tables can increase download time and cause problems for some browsers.
- Most table editing is accomplished with the Properties Inspector.
- Merging tables cells can help you create a more exciting page layout.
- It is important to watch your code as you are building tables; much of the troubleshooting work you do will involve tables.
- Text can be added by typing directly into Dreamweaver, or by cutting and pasting from a word processing program or a text editor.
- Setting column widths can help to control your layout, but column heights rarely need to be adjusted and should be avoided.

Quiz Yourself

1. What is the main purpose for tables in Web design today? (See the "Why Use Tables?" section.)

2. Why should you not "nest" tables? (See the "Why Use Tables?" section.)

3. Why should you view a table with a border of 1 pixel when your design does not call for borders? (See the "Creating a Table in Dreamweaver" section.)

4. Where can you find all information about a selected table? (See the "Building your table" section.)

5. How do you enter a nonparagraph line break
? (See the "Inserting images" section.)

6. Why should you never use Dreamweaver's click and drag function to move column or row borders? (See the "Specifying column width" section.)

7. What is the default justification for any element in Dreamweaver? (See the "Aligning content in tables" section.)

Using Tables for Liquid Design

Session Checklist

✔ Understanding monitor resolution

✔ What does resolution mean for design?

✔ Designing for varied resolutions

✔ Understanding liquidity

✔ Creating liquid design in Dreamweaver

✔ Creating a table using percentage values

✔ Inserting a clear GIF placeholder

**30 Min.
To Go**

When you are designing your page, the hardest thing you will face is not where to place your graphics or text, or even what colors you should use. The hardest part of designing for the Web is that you have no idea what monitor, what platform (Mac or PC), and what browser will be used to display your page.

This chapter is devoted entirely to overcoming the differences in monitor resolution that will display your pages. You will build a page that will grow and shrink as the monitor resolution changes, preventing horizontal scrolling at low resolutions, and yet filling the screen for high-resolution monitors. The term *liquid design* is a popular way to describe this design principle. More than almost any other design technique, adding liquidity to your design gives your work a profes-sional look and feel. Any designer can make a page that looks good at one resolu-tion on one platform and in one browser. The skill comes in being able to say, "Bring them all on — my page is ready."

Understanding Monitor Resolution

Resolution is, quite simply, the number of pixels that your monitor uses to fill your screen. It is expressed in a pixel value, with the width first. If your monitor is set to 800 × 600 pixels, your monitor is using 800 pixels across and 600 pixels down to show everything onscreen. If you are viewing a document that is 850 pix-els wide, you must scroll to the right to see all the information. Likewise, if the monitor has more than 600 pixels of information to display, a scroll bar will be provided to allow you to see the information on the lower edge of the document.

Computer users of some experience can change the resolution settings for their monitors, but most do not. The vast majority of monitors are never changed from the factory-set resolution, which means that as a designer, you are building pages that will be seen on monitors ranging from 600 pixels wide to over 1500 pixels wide, and that value is increasing as each new generation of monitor is introduced.

Although monitor size and resolution have some degree of asso-ciation, you must not make the mistaken assumption that the two are directly related. There is no reason why a 15-inch moni-tor cannot be set to either 640 or 800 pixels wide. Likewise, a 17-inch monitor is most likely set to 800 or 1024 pixels wide, but it also can be set to 640 pixels and — if your eyes are very good — even into the 1200+ pixel range. In fact, your monitor resolution is at least as closely related to your video card capa-bility as it is to your monitor size.

What does resolution mean for design?

In Web design, try to any keep scrolling to a minimum. Web designers turn them-selves inside out to prevent horizontal scrolling, because scrolling in two direc-tions is frustrating and confusing for visitors.

I have included an optional exercise for you. If you are entirely comfortable with how content and monitor resolution work together, this exercise will waste your time. If, however, you have only a minute grasp of this concept, you should take a few minutes and see a graphic creating a scroll.

Locate the session7 folder on the CD-ROM. Copy the file linetest.html to your Weekend site root folder. Copy the files redline400.gif and redline1200.gif to the art folder of your Weekend site root folder.

Take the following steps to see a horizontal scroll caused by a graphic:

1. Copy the files to your Weekend folder as described in the preceding CD-ROM note.

2. Open the linetest.html document. Note how you must scroll a long way to the right to see the end of the red line. This line is 1200 pixels wide.

If your monitor is set for a very high resolution, you will not see a scroll. Reset your monitor resolution to a width less than 1200 to see the effect described here.

3. Let's replace the 1200-pixel line with a line that will fit. Double-click the red line to open the Image Source window. Select redline400.gif and click OK. The scroll disappears. Even if you use a smaller view for your window, the line will still fit without a scroll as long as the window size is greater than the length of the line (plus a few pixels for the window borders).

4. Note how the text wraps to the window, no matter what the size. This session will address keeping text in place later in the session. For now, it is only important that you understand that graphics can create a horizontal scroll, and that you should work hard to prevent this from happening in your design work.

5. You can delete the files used for this exercise because you will not need them again.

Now that you have seen the result of content forcing a scroll, you should see a little more clearly why monitor resolution is so important to us as Web designers. When you are designing for print, you can do nothing unless you know the size of the paper for your project. But in Web design, you simply do not know the size of your paper.

Designing for varied resolutions

You must choose a main resolution for your design work. I have always worked with the lowest common resolution for my design work. When I first started with design, that meant 640 × 400 pixels. As the older monitors and video cards dropped out of service, and the number of people using 800 × 600 pixel resolutions increased to over 50%, I switched. Even though monitor widths such as 1024 pixels are now quite common, I still do my work with my monitor set to 800 pixels wide.

I almost always design for scroll-free display at an 800-pixel width. If I can create a scroll-free display for 640-pixel width monitors without affecting the design, I will work hard to create that effect. However, the number of low-resolution browsers in use is reducing every day, and it is very difficult to create pages that display without a scroll at low resolution and still fill a 1024-pixel-wide screen. Many designers — myself included — are prepared to sacrifice perfect viewing for the lowest resolution visitors have available in order to offer easier navigation and access to information for the vast majority of users.

**20 Min.
To Go**

There is a compromise, even when you choose to allow a scroll at 640 pixel widths. It is a good idea to place the most important information in the left and center portions of the screen. Place the least critical information in the area that can only be accessed by scrolling when seen on a low-resolution monitor.

Understanding Liquidity

Once you understand the resolution "problem" and have enough information to make your personal or professional choice as to which resolutions you will use as your targets, you are only a short distance along the road to creating liquid design. The major work comes when you try to create liquid pages or, as one of my students paraphrased, "stretchy" pages. However, I have never lost my delight at how Dreamweaver makes such short work of complicated tables — the backbone of liquid design.

The terms *liquid, ice,* and *jelly* have become a popular way to explain the different types of pages commonly in use on the Web. Liquid implies that the content will stretch and shrink as the window resizes. Ice pages contain content at a fixed size; the pages look exactly the same no matter what the monitor resolution or window size may be. Ice pages are anchored to the upper-left corner of the screen. Jelly pages, like Ice pages, have content with a fixed width. However, Jelly pages are centered on the page so that the extra space around the content in a higher resolution monitor will be divided equally on either side of the content.

Liquidity works through variable width tables, using the principle that text line length will naturally expand and shrink as its container becomes larger or smaller.

In the last session, you placed a table. You made that table 500 pixels wide. Whether you view that table with a 640-pixel-wide monitor or at the highest resolution, cutting-edge monitor, that table will still only cover 500 pixels. However, you have a powerful tool in another HTML table command — <table width="x%">, where x is the percentage of the screen you wish your table to fill.

Compare the sets of tables in Figures 7-1 and 7-2. In Figure 7-1, two tables are shown. The upper table has a table width of 95%, while the lower table has a fixed width of 760 pixels. On an 800-pixel-wide display, the two tables are nearly identical.

However, skipping down to Figure 7-2, you will see quite a difference between the previous figure. This view is in a reduced window. See how the upper table is still displaying all the content with a slight margin on either side of the table — 95% of the screen is still filled. The right portion of the lower table is not even visible though, because the table is fixed and the window is now smaller than that fixed size.

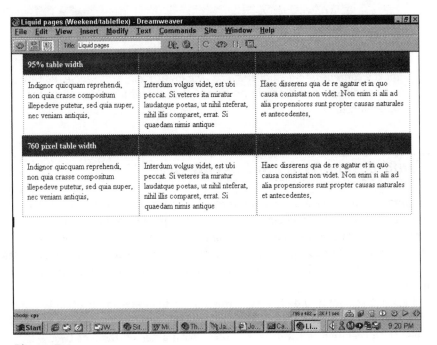

Figure 7-1
The upper table is set to 95% width, with the lower table set to 760 pixels.
On an 800-pixel-wide display, the tables are nearly identical. Figure 7-2
shows where they differ.

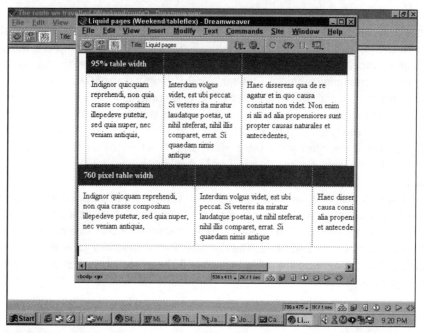

Figure 7-2
When the window size is reduced, the upper table set to 95% simply shuffles all the content into a smaller space. The lower fixed width table, however, cannot adjust, and the right portion of the content is hidden. Note the scroll bars have appeared.

Liquid Design Basics in Dreamweaver

Although it does take a little more work in the planning stages, the rewards for using liquid design include better use of screen space (often called real estate) at higher resolutions, and a more professional appearance for your pages. Designers may hate to see horizontal scroll bars on their work, but it can be equally disturbing to see your carefully balanced page tucked up in one tiny little corner of a huge screen.

I am not so sure how dedicated I would be to liquid design if I had to hand-code my designs, however. Liquid design depends heavily on carefully planned tables with specified cell widths, and often with a nested table or two. Dreamweaver makes short work of tables, no matter how complicated they are. If you do your planning right, Dreamweaver gives you the tools to quickly deliver dynamic, liquid design. Let's learn how to do it.

Creating a table using percentage values

Start with a table having borders and no content. You will create this table in exactly the same way as you created the fixed width table in Session 6, but you will specify different values.

1. Activate the Weekend site and create a new document. Name this document route.html.

2. Select Insert Table. The Insert Table window will open. Create a 3-column, 3-row table with a Cell Padding value of 10 and a Cell Spacing value of 0. Specify the width as 95% and the border as 1.

3. Before going any further, stop and reduce the size of your Dreamweaver window. Increase it again. Note how the table becomes smaller as the window gets smaller. This is the basic principle behind liquidity.

4. Just to make sure you have the difference down solidly, edit your table to have a width that is approximately 100 pixels less than your own monitor resolution. Select the table and change the width in your Properties Inspector to be 800 pixels – 100 pixels = 700 pixels.

You will have to change the % to pixels value in the drop-down box beside the Width entry field.

5. Reduce your window size and you will see that the table stays the same size but creates a horizontal scroll: *non*liquid design.

6. Return the table width to 95%.

Adjusting cell size with percentage values

That's pretty cool, but what if you don't want equally sized columns? No problem . . . well, maybe a few problems, but nothing that can't be solved. You have to find the problems first, though.

Take the following steps o specify the size of your columns:

1. Insert your cursor into the left cell in the second row of the column (you will edit the first row later in this session). In the Properties Inspector, specify the cell width (W) as 20% (make sure you type the % sign; without the % sign, the 20 means 20 pixels).

2. Insert your cursor into the center cell in the second row of the column. In the Properties Inspector, specify the cell width (W) as 50%.

3. Insert your cursor into the right cell in the second row of the column. In the Properties Inspector, specify the cell width (W) as 30%.

How's your math? Add the cell percentage widths of 20 degrees + 50 degrees + 30 degrees and you get 100%. But wait! Isn't your table 95% wide? Yes, it is, but the two numbers are NOT related. The table is taking up 95% of the available window. The cell widths must add up to 100% of the table width (for this example).

10 Min. To Go

With a table set up as this one is, the table width will range from approximately 570 pixels wide for a 640-pixel-wide resolution — 95% of approximately 600 — don't forget there are a few pixels needed for window borders, scroll bars, and so on — to over 1000 pixels for a 1200-pixel-wide resolution. The cell widths will adjust according to the size of the table. For example, the left column, which is set for 20% of the table width, will range from approximately 114 pixels to over 200 pixels wide for the same resolutions previously described.

But what if you need more control than that for your design? Read on.

Combining percentage and fixed column widths

First, let me offer a caution. You can exhibit a reasonable amount of control over how your page displays, even with liquid design. However, when you are using percentage widths, you will have to accept that, rather than designing exactly how your page will look, you are designing for a range of appearance. A page designed to be perfect at 800 pixels wide will look a little squished at 640 pixels. It is also likely to be a little more spread out than you would like at 1200 pixels wide. You are working to provide a great page to the majority of browsers, and an acceptable page that is easy to use for all who fall outside of your defined range.

What you can do is control at least part of the page so that menu columns and graphics display as they should. This is most often accomplished by combining fixed and percentage column widths in one table. The most reliable setup is to have the left columns fixed, and to have the columns at the right expanding and contracting.

First, let's edit the table that you created earlier to reflect the widths required to create the next page in your site, which is very similar in layout, except that it will be a liquid design. You are going to make the left column an exact size so that the text will always be in the same position in relation to the menu items. After you have set the left column, I will discuss what you need to do with the photo column.

You may wish to open the file index.html in the Weekend site, because you will be following closely to this layout as you build the next page.

Creating a fixed width column

To begin, you will make the left column a fixed width. Insert the first menu item before you adjust the width, as you will take the width value from the graphic.

Before starting the next exercise, locate the session7 folder on the CD-ROM. Copy the files photo7a.jpg, photo7b.jpg, and space.gif to the art folder of your Weekend site.

1. Open the Weekend site and the document route.html (it may still be open).

2. Turn off your borders by selecting the table and specifying Border 0 in the Properties Inspector.

3. Insert your cursor inside the left cell of the top column. You are going to add the logo file to this cell. Select Insert ⇨ Image. The Insert Image window will open. Locate the file logo.gif in the art folder. Select the file, and then click OK to return to the document. You will not see much change in the table.

4. Make sure that the graphic you just placed is selected (selection handles and a border will appear around the image). You need to know what width to set your left column, and you will use the graphic width to tell you. You want this column to be consistent no matter what resolution the viewer is using.

    Look at the W and H values in the Properties Inspector. These list the width and height of the selected graphic. Your width is 137. Make a note of this value.

5. Press your right-arrow key once to deselect the graphic. The cursor will move to the right of the graphic but remain in the same cell. You need to position your cursor here in order to specify the width of the cell. Replace the 20% value listed in the W field with 137 (make sure the % sign is removed). This sets your cell width to 137 pixels.

You will not see any change if you are working with an 800-pixel-wide display, because the 20% width at this resolution is very close to the 137 pixels you just set. But trust me: this setting is important.

6. You also want to place the photos into the right column. Insert your cursor into the right column of the middle row. Then, insert photo7a.jpg and photo7b.jpg with a <br> tag between them.

See Session 6 for detailed instructions on inserting two photos into a column.

Plain numbers always refer to pixels in Dreamweaver. For table widths you choose % or pixel from the drop-down menu. For all other entries, you will have to specify the % sign if you want a percentage value.

What do you have now? You have a graphic inserted that will prevent that column from ever shrinking smaller than the image, or 137 pixels. In addition, you have told Dreamweaver to make that cell 137 pixels wide, which means that it will not be larger than it is now.

There are exceptions that I will cover in the next session, but for your purposes here, this is a true statement.

Controlling percentage and fixed width column layouts

You have a decision to make at this point. The left column is fixed. But what are you going to do with the other two columns? There are two choices for a liquid design. You can set the columns so that both columns flex with the number of available pixels. The result would be that your text would have longer and shorter lines, depending on the page size. In addition, the column containing your images would expand and contract. Because the images are a fixed size, the only thing that can happen is that the white space will increase or decrease. With larger images, this might be a good choice, but you are risking having very small images floating far away from the text, which would likely look disjointed.

Isn't it too bad that you can't set the outer column to be fixed, and just let the text expand and contract to fill the window? The good news is that you can do that. The bad news is (YOU knew that was coming, didn't you?) that you do have to watch how far you ask your text to stretch. Good communication calls for short paragraphs, especially on the Web. When you are asking your text to do all the stretching to make a page liquid, you risk having one-line paragraphs at high resolutions, which look hideous and are very hard to read.

The answer? Add a little extra space to the photo column. That will give you very short lines of text on a 640-pixel-wide screen. Remember, though, that you are more concerned about your mid-range resolutions. Your photos are 100 pixels wide. If you set the right column to 150 pixels, you can help the text a little. But you must do more than just set the width of a column to add white space.

Using a transparent GIF to control layout

Most browsers will not observe your 150-pixel cell measurement. They do not respect white space and will push your text right over to the photos anyway. You have to convince the browser that you really want that space, and you will use a neat little trick to do that. You will insert a 1px × 1px image that has been created as a transparent graphic, meaning that it is completely invisible.

Follow these steps to then place this graphic at the end of the cell:

1. Position your cursor to the right of the second image and press Enter to move the cursor to follow the images. Press Enter one more time to allow some separation between the photos and the transparent GIF you will place. This image is invisible, so you want it away from your content for easier editing. Insert the image space.gif from the art folder in your Weekend site. Do not proceed until you have read the next step; you need the image to remain selected.

2. Check your Properties Inspector and you will see the size listed as 1px × 1px. Change the width (W) value to 150. This will force the graphic to 150 pixel and will hold the column at that width.

3. Use your right-arrow key to deselect the graphic and position the cursor in the cell. Specify 150 for the cell width (W) value.

4. With your cursor still in the cell, set the cell alignment to Center in the Horz drop-down menu in the Properties Inspector.

Centering the photos in this column allows you to play with a few more pixels toward a liquid design. You could align to the left and have the photos close to the text, but a wide white space would occur at the right because the 95% table width setting allows ever larger margins as the resolution is increased. Setting the alignment to the right would align your photos nicely along the edge, reducing that white space, but the photos would then appear too far from the text for solid unity. By using center alignment, you cheat both problems a little. Liquid design is a series of compromises. You do get very good at spotting the opportunities before too long.

Adjust a transparent GIF to the size you require using the image size command, but never resize a graphic in Dreamweaver. The capability is there, but that does not mean you should use it. If you decrease the size of a graphic, you are forcing a visitor to download a larger file than is required. If you increase the size of a graphic, the quality will be very poor. (You will lose quality if you make an image smaller in Dreamweaver, as well.) Graphic programs have better controls for retaining image quality as the size of the image is reduced. Often, I will resize an image in Dreamweaver just to determine the required size, but I *always* take the image back into a graphics program to properly resize it.

Using 100% width for a column

The final step in setting the parameters for your table is to specify what your center column width should be. So far, you have a 200-pixel column containing the 200-pixel logo graphic. You have a 150-pixel column held open by a 150-pixel GIF file, and which contains images that are 100-pixels wide. Your table is 95% of the screen width. What are you going to do with the center column?

If you specify that the text column have a fixed width, you no longer have a flexible table. But how can you tell what percentage of the table remains available? Good point; you have fixed widths in a flexible table. I was not bad in math, but that is way past what I can calculate.

Luckily, the solution has nothing to do with calculated numbers. In fact, you can use 100% as a message to the browser to "use whatever is left for this column." It seems a bit strange, but think about it for a minute. You have a left column that cannot be less than 200 pixels because the graphic will not collapse. You have the same setting for the right column because you inserted a 150-pixel graphic — the transparent GIF). The table is going to cover 95% of the screen no matter what, as long as graphics do not override that width. By telling the center column that it is to take up 100% of the space, you are telling it to cover what is left.

Remember that browsers do not always respect the widths you specify. You have the two outer columns set so that they can be no smaller than the specified width. The 100% command tells the browser that you do not want it to decide that the left or right column deserves more space.

Finishing this page

Follow Figure 7-3, shown earlier in the chapter, to finish the page. Refer back to Session 6 as you put the first page together if you need guidance to place the menu images. You must copy one more menu item, menu6.gif from the session7 folder on the CD-ROM, to the art folder in your Weekend site. Note that you use the new file, but you omit the file menu6a.gif. You are creating the page that matches that menu item; you do not want it to appear in your menu list, because that is very confusing.

Don't worry at this point if the page is not perfect. You will be making a few changes as you move through the techniques in later sessions, and you will do a final check before you can call this complete.

Done!

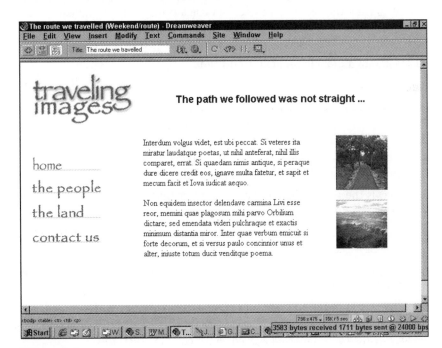

Figure 7-3
The final appearance for the route.html page at this point. You will make changes as you learn new techniques.

REVIEW

- You must be aware of monitor resolution at all times when you are designing for the Web.
- The most common monitor resolution widths today are 800 pixels and 1024 pixels.
- It is a good idea to place the least important information on a page at the right if you are designing a page that will have a scroll at 640-pixel-width display.
- Tables with percentage values are an efficient way to create liquid design because they collapse and expand with varied monitor resolutions.
- You can use a combination of fixed and percentage width columns in a column with a percentage width.
- Although you can control the appearance of a liquid page to some extent, you cannot completely control it.
- Browsers will ignore even fixed-width cell sizes if there is no graphic content to keep the cell at that size. You use a transparent, or invisible, GIF file to force cell widths when there is no content.
- Never resize a photo or image in Dreamweaver. It is better to take the image into a graphic program to resize it.

QUIZ YOURSELF

1. What does it mean when a monitor is 800px × 640px? (See the "Understanding Monitor Resolution" section.)

2. What is the result when a graphic is larger than the screen width? (See the "What does resolution mean for design?" section.)

3. What do the terms Liquid, Ice, and Jelly mean? (See the "Understanding Liquidity" section.)

4. When you set a Dreamweaver table to a width of 95%, what is it 95% of? (See the "Creating a table using percentage values" section.)

5. When the number 100, with no value such as pixel or %, is entered into the Properties Inspector of Dreamweaver, what size will be applied to that value? (See the "Creating a fixed width column" section.)

6. When a column is specified to be 200 pixels, and a graphic is inserted that measures 250 pixels, what will the resulting size of that column be? (See the "What does resolution mean for design?" section.)

7. Why should you never use Dreamweaver to reduce the size of a photo? (See the "Using a transparent GIF to control layout" section.)

8. Why does a transparent GIF image keep a column at the same size as the GIF file's width? (See the "Using a transparent Gif to control layout" section.)

8

Enhancing Tables with Background Color and Images

Session Checklist

✔ Adding a table background color

✔ Adding a table background image

✔ Adding a table row background image

✔ Adding a table cell background image

✔ Setting up a preview browser

✔ Previewing your page

✔ Troubleshooting table backgrounds

**30 Min.
To Go**

In the last two sessions, you put basic pages together. You learned how to make your content fill the screen and how to plan your pages so that as many visitors as possible would see attractive, meaningful pages. With that base, you can move on to adding design touches that will make your site more visually pleasing.

You will add backgrounds to — and learn how to make links that will — connect your pages to one other, as well as to other pages on the Web. You will soon see why I wanted you to be so careful with your folder structure and file placements in the first few sessions. Even those of you who may not keep perfectly organized desks must not let that habit creep into your Web design. Almost everything you do from this point forward will create a chain of documents and images that will only work so long as every file is in the perfect place.

Enhancing Tables

Tables are the basis for most layout on the Web. Table backgrounds are the perfect place in which to add color, because very little code is required to specify table or individual cell background color. You can fill a page with color without adding to the download time for your page.

In addition to adding color, you can also add images as table backgrounds. This is a little more complicated, because not all browsers will interpret table background images in the same way. I will discuss this in the "Inserting Table Background Images" section, and you will then learn some workarounds to common problems.

You can add background color to full tables, rows and columns, or individual cells. In addition, you can nest one table inside another. The range of possibilities is endless. One of the best ways to learn more about how to use tables creatively is to find sites on the Web that you like. You can view the source file for any Web page in your browser. Study how the designer has constructed tables and used backgrounds to create the look. With Internet Explorer, you can also save pages — and even entire Web sites — to your hard drive that you can later open in Dreamweaver. However, you must never use the code you save to produce your own pages without requesting and receiving permission from the creator, preferably in writing.

Never, for any reason or under any circumstances, use another designer's code, or even a portion of their code, for your own work, without permission. Studying how a page has been put together is a time-honored way to learn from excellent quality work. However — and I cannot stress this strongly enough — that code belongs to someone else and it is illegal, as well as highly unethical, to use any portion of code produced by another. Study it, learn from it, and perhaps even drop a note to thank the site owner for the inspiration, but always produce your own code.

Start with the easiest of all table background enhancements: adding a table background. You are going to create a special page for the table background exercises, because no single page should ever have as much added to it as you are going to learn. (You will not be working on your document in this session; although you will apply what you learn here in future sessions.) Make sure that you save the test pages. They will be a valuable resource for the future.

You should check your code with each step you take, especially when you are working with tables. It is important to understand where the color commands are placed in the code. When you start into complicated liquid layout, reading your table code becomes very important for troubleshooting.

Adding a table background color

Take the following steps to add a background to an entire table:

1. Open your Weekend site and create a new file named tablecolor.html. Open the new document.

2. Create a 3-column, 3-row table with the following parameters: CellPad 10, CellSpace 10, Width 95%, and Border 0.

3. If there are no dotted table borders showing when you return to the document, you will have to turn on your table borders. Select View ⇨ Visual Aids ⇨ Table Borders.

4. Select the entire table. Place your cursor anywhere in the table and select Modify ⇨ Table ⇨ Select Table from the main menu, or move your mouse pointer over the upper-left corner or lower border until you see the move cursor (a double-pointed arrows) and click to select. You can also place your cursor anywhere in the table and click the <table> tag located in the lower-left of your screen to select the entire table.

This is the last time I will provide detailed instructions on how to select a table. I will simply ask you to select the table. You may wish to mark this page.

5. In the Properties Inspector, click the color well for Bg Color. Select a light color from the color palette; I used a light yellow (see Figure 8-1). The color number will appear in the Bg Color field and your table will fill with that color.

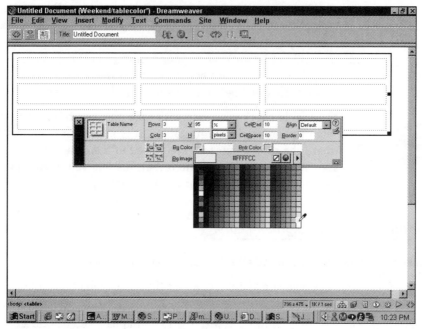

Figure 8-1
Choosing a background color for an entire table.

Adding a cell background color

Often, you may only want to add color to one cell, or to a few cells. The process is similar to adding the color to the entire table, but your selection method will be different.

1. Place your cursor in the left column of the top row. To change the color in one cell, you do not need to make a selection. As long as your cursor is in that cell, the color will be added.

2. Click the color well beside the lower Bg field near the lower portion of the Properties Inspector. Choose a dark color from the color palette and the cell will fill with that color. Note that the color number has been inserted in the Bg field (see Figure 8-2).

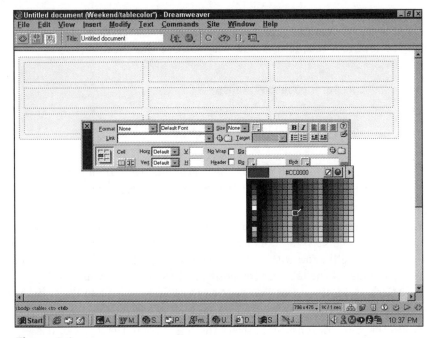

Figure 8-2
Choosing a background color for a single cell.

If you want to add color to more than one cell — but not to a full row or column — select only those cells.

3. With Ctrl (PC) or ⌘ (Mac) depressed, select the first and third cells in the bottom row. Choose your background color as you did in Step 2, but choosing a different color. The selected cells will fill with the chosen color.

Adding background color to a row or column

Although you can add color to rows or columns cell by cell, that is not efficient. In the case of table row backgrounds, it creates extra code.

Row background color

Now take a minute or two to see this in action, because it is a very simple way to illustrate how you can create unnecessary code.

1. Click inside the first cell of the second row. Apply a black background to this cell. Repeat this action one at a time for the remaining two cells in the row. Your code for that row will look like this code:

```
<tr>
  <td bgcolor="#000000"> </td>
  <td bgcolor="#000000"> </td>
  <td bgcolor="#000000"> </td>
</tr>
```

   Now select the row and remove the background color from the cells. Choose a background color for the row, and then compare the code with the preceding sample code.

2. Select the entire row by placing your cursor anywhere in the table and choosing the `<tr>` tag from the lower-left portion of your screen. You can also choose the row with your mouse. Move your mouse pointer over the left border of the table, at the position of the row that you wish to select. When the cursor changes to a thick arrow, click and the entire row will be selected.

3. In the Properties Inspector, select the full entry in the Bg field. Use Delete to remove the entry. The selected row now has no background color. Do *not* deselect the row.

4. Redo the background color, but apply it to the entire row. With the row selected, click the color well beside the Bg field. Choose black from the upper-left corner of the color palette. Again, deselect to confirm the change.

5. Check your code. It should be the same as the following codew. You do not have to be a code expert to realize that this is a lot less code. To be exact, the difference is 34 characters — and 34 bytes — nearly 30 percent less.

```
<tr bgcolor="#000000">
  <td> </td>
  <td> </td>
  <td> </td>
</tr>
```

Never think that a little extra code will do no harm. Although you are only saving a few bytes with this one example, sloppy work as you apply attributes can add significantly to the download time over many entries and many pages. It also makes the code much harder to troubleshoot when you encounter browser display problems.

Column background color

Although adding a background to a row and to a column is identical in method, the resulting code is different. The row background is controlled by the <tr> background command. However, HTML has no column background command, so backgrounds are applied on a cell-by-cell basis — it cannot be avoided. I wanted to make sure I stated that clearly so that you do not spend time trying to figure out why you have exactly the same code for this exercise that I was so adamant about preventing in the previous exercise.

Take the following steps to apply a background to a column:

1. Select a column by holding your mouse pointer over the top border, within the area of the column that you wish to select. When the cursor changes to a thick arrow, click to select the column. You can also select a column by clicking and dragging from the first cell to the last cell in the column.

2. Click the color well beside the Bg field and select a color. The cells in the column will fill with the chosen color.

Removing a background color

Take the following steps to remove a background color from a table, row, column, or cell:

1. Select the table, row, column, or cell from which you would like to remove the background color. Use the same selection methods that you used to add the color.

2. Highlight the color number in the Bg or Bg Color field of the Properties Inspector, and press Delete to delete.

Cell padding and spacing with background color

Cell padding and spacing can be confusing. Padding refers to the amount of margin within each cell, while spacing refers to the distance between cells. For separating text and images, the two commands do not differ much. However, as soon as you add color to backgrounds, they become fundamentally different.

I would like you to see this in action. The table you created earlier has a Cell Padding and Cell Spacing value of 10. You are going to add a bit of text to a few cells. You will then copy the table and change the values.

1. Type **Test padding and spacing** into one light-colored cell and into two cells that are side by side, preferably with the same colored background. You will have to change the color of your font to a light color if you have used dark colors for your backgrounds. Note how the text does not spread right to the edge of the cell. This is cell padding at work. The distance between the dotted table borders is the cell spacing.

Don't worry if the text forces the table out of balance; it does not matter for this exercise. However, If you would like the practice, set the column widths to 33%, 34%, and 33% to bring it back into line.

2. Select the entire table. Then, select Edit ⇨ Copy to copy the table.

3. Click at the right edge, behind the table, to place the cursor. Press Enter two times to move the cursor down.

4. Select Edit ⇨ Paste to paste a copy of the table.

5. Select the new table and change the CellSpace to 0. The cells are now right against one other with no spacing. See how the text still has a margin in the cell? This is because you did not change the CellPad value. Figure 8-3 shows the two versions.

Save the file that you have worked with for this exercise. It will make a good reference document for you in future exercises.

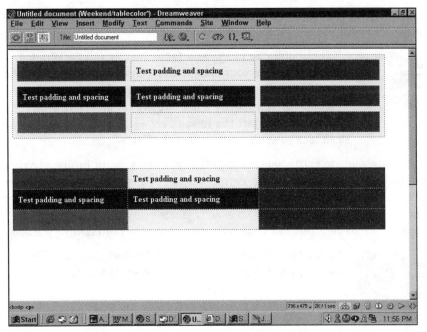

Figure 8-3
The upper table has cell spacing and padding set to 10. The lower table has the cell spacing set to 0 and the cell padding remains at 10.

Inserting Table Background Images

Color is fun to work with and adds very little to file size, but you can also add a lot to your pages by using images as backgrounds for your tables. Technically, any image can be used as a background, but there are some limitations. First, any time you talk about graphics, you must consider download time. Technically, you could add a different background image to every cell in a table. However, each image would slow your page load. You must always walk a balance between appearance and load time.

But why would you use an image as a background rather than just placing an image? There are many reasons. First, a table background will not affect table size. Remember when you placed an image and the image size forced your column and row size? A background will not do this. The cells will shrink and grow, showing more or less of the background as determined by other content.

If you want to place other content, such as another image or text over your image, you must use a background.

You can place an image as a table, row, or cell background. However, before your imagination runs too wild, I would like to caution you. Netscape has a peculiar quirk with table backgrounds. If you specify a background for an entire table, Netscape will start the image over again with every cell, which can lead to some pretty unusual effects.

You are going to create another page that you can save for future reference. It can be valuable to have a simple, correct version of a technique to refer to when you are having trouble with that technique later on. Once you have added content, it can be tough to trace down exactly where everything should be. Comparing correct code to your troubled code is the fastest way to trace down a problem.

Locate the session8 folder on the CD-ROM. Copy the file back8.gif to the art folder of your Weekend site.

Inserting a table background

Now create a table and add a background.

1. Open your Weekend site and create a new file named tableback.html. Open the new document.

2. Create a 3-column, 3-row table with the following parameters: CellPad 10, CellSpace 10, Width 95%, and Border 0.

3. If there are no dotted table borders showing when you return to the document, you will have to turn on your table borders. Select View ➪ Visual Aids ➪ Table Borders.

4. Select the entire table. In the Properties Inspector, click the Browse for file icon beside the Bg Image field. The Select Image Source window will open. Select the file back8.gif from the art folder.

Your table now has a background. You will return to this table in a few minutes for further discussion, because you will be previewing the table in both Internet Explorer and Netscape. However, you are moving on to placing a row background and cell background before previewing.

Inserting a table row background

When you do not want a background to cover your entire table, you can specify that the background image will appear only in a row. The background information is added to the `<tr>` tag. You are going to create another table to add the row, and then add the cell background.

1. Place your cursor to the right of the table you created in the pervious exercise. Press Enter two times to move the cursor down.

2. Create a 3-column, 3-row table with the following parameters: CellPad 10, CellSpace 10, Width 95% and Border 0.

3. Select the top row. In the Properties Inspector, click the "Background URL of cell" folder beside the upperBg field. The Select Image Source window will open. Select the file back8.gif from the art folder. Your background will appear in all three cells, but there will be white spaces between the cells.

4. Change the cell spacing to 0 to abut the cells together.

5. Type **This is the top row** in the first cell of this row (the reason for this entry will become clear in a few minutes).

Inserting a table cell background

Finally, you will add a background to a cell. The background information will be added to the `<td>` tag.

1. In the same table, select the first cell of the second row. In the Properties Inspector, click the folder beside the top Bg field. The Select Image Source window will open. Select the file back8.gif from the art folder.

2. Repeat Step 1 for the second and third cell in the third row.

3. Type **Cell background** in each of the three cells with cell backgrounds. Your table should now resemble the sample shown in Figure 8-4.

Leave the table backgrounds for a few minutes, and set up your preview browsers. Once you can preview the tables, I'll discuss what you can and cannot do with table background images.

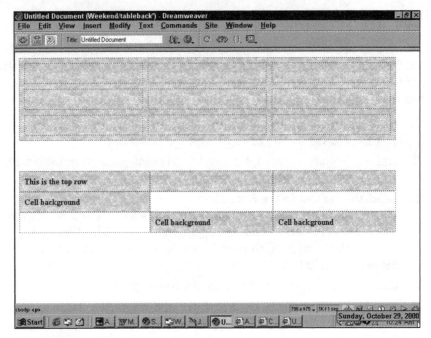

Figure 8-4
Final appearance for background image test tables

Previewing a Dreamweaver Document

Although Dreamweaver provides an accurate view of a finished page, browsers
interpret code in different ways. As you work, you should preview your page often,
at least in the two most popular browsers: Internet Explorer and Netscape. In addition to letting you know that the browsers are interpreting the code to match the
layout you created, a preview will also activate functions that do not display in
Dreamweaver, such as JavaScript.

**You must have Internet Explorer and Netscape installed on your
computer for this course. If you do not have a recent version of
both programs installed, please install them from the CD-ROM
included with this book.**

Before you preview your document, however, you must tell Dreamweaver where the browsers are located on your hard drive. You can install up to 20 browsers for previewing in Dreamweaver, and you can set two of those programs to preview your page with a keyboard shortcut. These are known as your primary and secondary browsers. Primary browsers will deliver a preview with F12. Secondary browser previews are launched with Ctrl+F12 (PC) or Command+F12 (Mac).

Adding a preview browser

Take the following steps to specify a preview browser (the browser must be correctly installed on your computer before adding to the browser list in Dreamweaver):

1. Select File ➪ Preview in Browser ➪ Edit Browser List. The Preferences window will open. Make sure that Preview in Browser is highlighted in the Category listing.

2. Click the Browser's + (plus) button. The Add Browser window opens. Type a name that you will easily identify in the Name field.

3. Click the browse button beside the Application field. The Select Browser window will open. Navigate to the folder where your browser is installed (usually in Program Files on your main hard drive). Choose the application file for that browser. Figure 8-5 shows all of the windows open as you choose your browser.

4. Specify whether you would like this browser to be the primary or secondary browser in the Defaults section of the window. Click OK to return to the Preferences window.

5. Repeat these steps for any browsers you wish to add. Click OK to return to your document.

If you cannot find where your browser is installed, use the search feature on your computer to locate the browser by name. The correct file will be an Application-type file, and it will display the browser logo in the file listing. You can also check the file's properties to confirm that a file is an application. Make note of the path to the file and return to the Select Browser window to specify that browser.

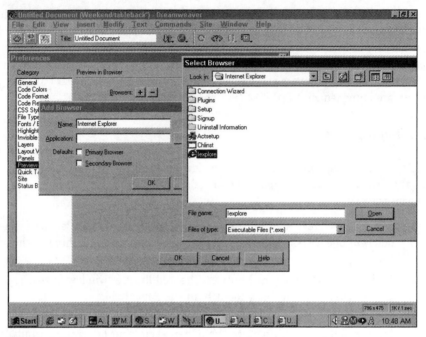

Figure 8-5
Choosing a preview browser in Dreamweaver.

Previewing your Dreamweaver document

Once you have your preview browsers set up in Dreamweaver, you are ready to see how the browsers are interpreting your pages. You are about to be introduced to one of the toughest elements of Web design. The code you have produced is correct — well, technically correct. However, each browser has its own quirks.

It is a great idea to start a notebook or an electronic note file to keep track of all the browser oddities you discover. Today, you may remember that Internet Explorer will not display a code. A month from now, you may forget completely, or you may fail to remember how you worked around the problem. You will save hours in the future if you take the time to make a few simple notes now.

Take the following steps to preview your page in a browser:

1. Activate or open the file you used for the previous exercise (tableback.html).

2. Select File ⇨ Preview in Browser ⇨ Internet Explorer (or whatever you called your Internet Explorer entry). A new window will open with your file displayed in Internet Explorer.

3. Repeat for Netscape. Do not close the preview windows.

Don't panic when you see the preview of this page. Hold on for just another minute or so and what you are seeing will be discussed.

You are now ready to preview any page you create in Dreamweaver. If you would like to add other browsers — for example, Opera — the steps you take are exactly the same. For the major Web population, however, previewing in the two major browsers as you work will suffice.

I will discuss how you can have your pages tested with a wider variety of browsers and on different platforms in Session 25.

Table Backgrounds and Browsers

If you have not already done so, preview the document that you created in the background images session in both Internet Explorer and Netscape. Leave both windows open and compare. Considering that these two previews came from the same document in Dreamweaver, the differences are rather astounding. Figure 8-6 shows the result, but you will be better able to see the subtle differences on your own monitor at full size.

Assessing the browser interpretation of table backgrounds

Internet Explorer is doing a great job of displaying a unified background in the table and in the cells in the second example. But where is the table row background? Welcome to Web design.

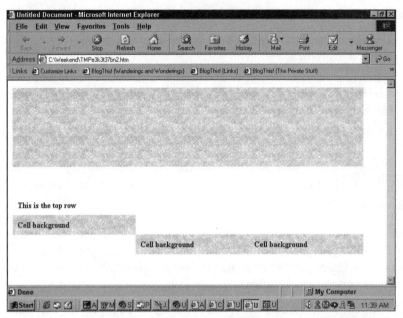

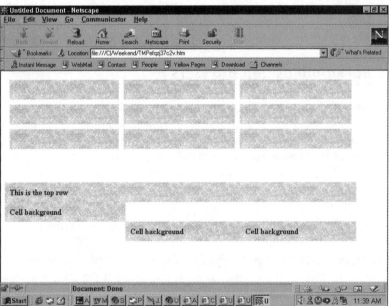

Figure 8-6
One page and two displays. Notice how the Netscape version places spaces between the table cells, and that Internet Explorer does not display the row background.

Just to protect myself, since I have been around this industry for a while, I am going to add a disclaimer. You *may* be seeing a table row background with your platform and Internet Explorer combination. However, many combinations will not display it — in fact, I have not found one that does. My disclaimer also tells a lot about this industry, because it is almost impossible to make an absolute statement about *every* browser on both platforms.

Now look at the Netscape preview. Netscape is not kind to table backgrounds, as you can see in the upper table. You can remove the gaps by specifying 0 cell spacing, but the pattern will start over with every cell. It is almost impossible to get a seamless table background in Netscape by using a background for the entire table.

But isn't that a table row background working perfectly? Yes, it is. Well . . . almost. Look closely at the row and you will be able to see a break in the pattern at each cell. The <tr> tag is recognized, but the background image starts over with each cell.

Working around browser interpretations of backgrounds

Comparing what Internet Explorer and Netscape can do to your table backgrounds, it becomes clear fairly quickly that this is an area that takes great thought and planning. Often, the fix you would apply to correct a problem in Netscape creates a new and different problem in Internet Explorer.

First, if there is another way to accomplish the effect you desire, I would recommend you use it. However, there is too much power in backgrounds — especially <td> backgrounds — when creating liquid design to dismiss them as too complicated or buggy.

One way around the problem with backgrounds is to use nested tables. You will explore that process in Session 19.

You can create a JavaScript "sniffer," or code that will determine what browser and platform your visitor is using (creating a "sniffer" will be covered later in the course). The code then calls for the appropriate page, which has been custom designed for that browser and platform. This is not a popular method, however, because you must create as many sites as the combinations of browsers and platforms you wish to serve.

Never design your page for just one browser and then place a notice on your site that the visitor should use only that browser. It does not take much extra studying to learn how to create code that can be used by all browsers. If you are — or you plan to become — a professional designer, you *must* learn to create cross-browser-compatible code. That is your job!

I have included this set of examples so that you can study what the effects are and make decisions based on what you have seen here. I never create a background for any table tag that has a horizontal repeat, and usually only use the `<td>` tag to add a background image for liquid design (your second Web site for this course will incorporate this method).

Each design situation is different. You may come up with a very creative solution to use a background in your table that will work for only one situation — the one you are working on. However, having the samples you created here to refer back to later as you are trying to work around some of the problems will be truly valuable.

Finally, once in a while, it is not a table background you require, but a page background. The next session discusses this.

Done!

REVIEW

- You can add background color to full tables, table rows, or table cells.

- To add a background color to a table column, you apply a background to all table cells in that column.

- You can select an entire row or column in a Dreamweaver table by clicking in the left or upper border for that row or column.

- You can remove a background color by deleting the entry in the Properties Inspector.

- Table background images can be applied to full tables, table rows, or table cells.

- Netscape and Internet Explorer interpret table backgrounds in very different ways.

- You can add up to 20 browsers to the Dreamweaver preview list. Two of those browsers can be assigned as Primary and Secondary browsers and can be launched with keyboard shortcuts.

- When using table backgrounds of any type, you must plan and test carefully.

Quiz Yourself

1. Why is important to not copy another designers code directly? (See the "Enhancing Tables" section.)

2. What are the three different types of background codes that can be added to a table? (See the "Enhancing Tables" section.)

3. There is no code for adding a background to an entire column. How do you add background color to a column? (See the "Adding background color to a row or column" section.)

4. What is the difference between cell padding and cell spacing? (See the "Cell padding and spacing with background color" section.)

5. How does Netscape interpret a table's background? (See the "Inserting Table Background Images" section.)

6. What is the benefit in specifying a Primary and Secondary browser in Dreamweaver? (See the "Previewing a Dreamweaver Document" section.)

Adding Backgrounds, Meta Tags, and Links

Session Checklist

✔ Adding background color to a page

✔ Adding background image to a page

✔ Setting page margins

✔ Adding meta tags

✔ Adding links to images

✔ Adding alt tags to images

✔ Adding links to text

✔ Creating a text menu

**30 Min.
To Go**

Over the last few sessions, you have been working with tables. In the overview of the Dreamweaver program, that might be seen as backwards, since you are just now moving on to setting basic attributes for pages. However, since tables control almost all layout, I prefer to have that knowledge as the first step.

Now you will focus on the overall appearance of your page. You will learn to add page titles, keywords and page descriptions, and background color, and as well as how to set your margins. Finally, you will learn how to create links without text and images. By the time you finish this lesson, you will have all the tools needed to finish your first site.

Creating a Page from a Previous Page

When you are building a site, you want your pages to be consistent. When you build your second site (starting in Session 16), you will be working with templates, which guarantees consistency. However, you do not know how to do that yet, so you will work from the Route page as your "template." To start this session, create a new page from the last page you created. Open your route.html page and save it as a new document for your site.

Locate the Session9 folder on the CD-ROM and copy the files photo9a.jpg, photo9b.jpg, and back9.jpg to the art folder in your Weekend root folder.

Take these steps to USE another page as a template:

1. From your Weekend site, open the file route.html. Immediately save it to a new file by selecting File ➪ Save As. The Save As window opens. Confirm that you are in the Weekend root folder, and then save the file as people.html.

2. The menu for this page is incorrect. There is a link to the people.hmtl page — the very page we are creating. To correct the menu for this page, delete the graphic menu item "the people," which is the file menu6b.gif. With your cursor in the same location, insert the file menu6a.gif, which is the menu item to link to route.html. Your menu will now offer links to all pages in the site except the current page, as it should.

It is very annoying to visitors to be offered a menu choice for the current page. It is not hard to make sure that you have only those menu items on the page that will lead your visitors to a different page.

3. Replace the photos at the right. Double-click the top photo and the Select Image Source window will open. Choose photo9a.jpg. The original photo will be replaced with the new photo. Repeat this step for the second photo, replacing with the image photo9b.jpg. At this stage, you could also delete the original photos, and then insert new photos later.

When you are using an existing page as the beginning of a new page, never make any changes until you have saved the file to a new filename. It is too easy to get caught up in the changes and, without thinking, just save the changes. You then have to recreate the original page. Make that an absolute rule. Open the file and immediately choose Save As, and specify a new filename.

5. Highlight the headline text and type **Without the people, what can you learn about a new place.** Return the text alignment to the default (left) by clicking the Align Center icon in the upper-right corner of the Properties Inspector. The Align Center icon will return to the nonselected state. (When no Alignment icons are depressed, the default value is used.)

6. The text can remain, or you can highlight the existing text and type or paste in new text. Check once again to make sure that this is the people.html page (the filename is listed in the title bar on your screen), and then save the file.

　　Now you can move on to making some changes to your new page using the Page Properties settings.

You can use this method to save several pages. However, if you are creating a larger site, you should do your initial design and then create a template. You can make changes to a single file, and then have those changes applied to any document that uses that template as a base. You will look at templates very closely in Session 16, and you will use them to build your next site.

Setting Page Properties

Anything that affects the entire page is created through the Page Properties window. This includes page settings for text colors, margins, and background. There is also a very handy feature for those who design the page look in a graphics program before creating the HTML code in Dreamweaver. Called the Tracing Image, Dreamweaver will display a graphic representation of a page you have created in a graphics program. You can adjust the transparency of the image until it is barely visible, and then build your HTML page on top of it, using the image as a guide.

　　We will walk through a step-by-step example for each of these page property features, but let's start by adding a background color to the page.

Adding background color

The background color that you choose for your pages can set the whole tone for your site. You are going to add a color to this page to illustrate the method, and then you will use a background image for another background.

For most Web sites, you will choose one effect and carry it throughout the site. This site is being created just for learning purposes.

Take these steps to add a background color:

1. With the people.html page open, select Modify ⇨ Page Properties. The Page Properties window will open.

2. Locate the Background color well and click to open the color palette. Choose a light color if you want to keep black text, or choose a dark color and change your text to a light color. You can click Apply to see the changes before you accept the new color and return to the document. When you have a color you are happy with, click OK. Yikes! What about that white menu? Don't worry — you will fix that in just a few minutes.

I am hoping that you have noticed another problem. If you have gaps between your menu items, as shown in Figure 9-1, , they can be repaired almost immediately. Consider yourself lucky that you hit this topic. The fix is simple, but finding this one can be an all-day procedure if you do not know how to look for it.

Also, notice the HTML code in Figure 9-1. See the two little spaces between the image and the <br> tag? That's the culprit. Remove those spaces and your menu will tighten right up. HTML is supposed to ignore spaces, but it does not always do so. Make note of this tip somewhere, because it will occur again. In fact, if you ever have gaps on your pages that do not make sense, look to your HTML code to see if you have spaces lurking inside.

3. Change the background color to white for the cells containing the logo, the menu items, and the headline. (See the last session if you need to brush up on how to do this.)

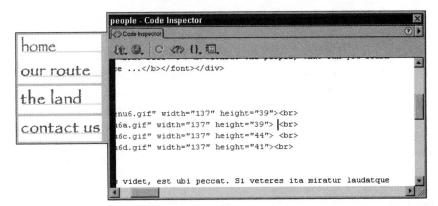

Figure 9-1
Spaces between graphics are usually caused by a space between an image and the <br> tag. You can avoid the spaces by hand-coding the <br> tags between images, but I find it faster to troubleshoot the problem as it occurs.

Adding a background image

You can also use an image for a background. Many first-time Web designers leap to the idea of including an image that fills the background. Although it can look great, it can also ruin your site if you are not careful.

First, you must make the image at least 1500 pixels wide to be sure that it will not repeat. If the image also has a vertical repeat, the image must also be considerably longer than you expect the vertical scroll to be on your page, or again it will repeat. Think of an image of a person, perhaps with the opacity reduced in the graphic program for a faded effect. The image looks great, but if that person appears again at the right or lower edge of the screen — that's not so great. Making a graphic, which is that wide and deep, either takes a special image or it needs the world's best file-size optimizer — or both.

What is realistic, however, is to use a background image that is designed to repeat in only one direction. The file you will work with for this exercise is a graduated full background, which changes from white to gray. The image is only 20 pixels high, although it is 1500 pixels wide. The file size is small — just over 800 bytes.

Small, textured tile patterns are also perfect, because they are designed to seamlessly repeat over any background distance. The background you used for your table in the last session is a perfect example of a tiling background image.

Having warned you of the pitfalls with background images, let's get one in place:

1. Open the Route page again and create a new file called land.html using the same steps as you used in your earlier exercise.

2. Select Modify ⇨ Page Properties to open the Page Properties window.

3. Click the folder beside the Background Image field and select the file back9.jpg from the art folder. Click Apply if you want to preview the effect, or click OK to accept the change and return to your document.

You will now have a background that gradually darkens across the page. If you are using 640 pixel-wide resolution, the shading will reach light gray only as it approaches the right edge of your screen. People viewing the image using an 800 pixel-wide resolution will see a medium light gray at the right edge. Those using higher resolutions will see a darker gray. Even though this image is 1500 pixels wide, it does not cause a scroll.

Adding a page title

20 Min. To Go

Your page title is important. This is the information that will display in the title bar of the visitor's browser as they view your page. It will also be the text that appears in the bookmark listing when someone bookmarks your page. Try to make your page title meaningful. Include enough information to identify the main site on each page, because your visitors might not bookmark just the first page. Make each page title different, as well, because it might only be the content on the bookmarked page that has attracted your visitor's attention.

To create a page title, do *one* of the following:

1. Type your title in the Title field in the Dreamweaver toolbar.

2. Select Modify ⇨ Page Properties and type your page title in the Title field near the top of the Page Properties field.

Setting page margins

Setting margins for your page adjusts where your content will appear on the screen. Although you can use margin settings to increase space to the left and upper portions of your screen, the most common use for this command it to reduce the margin to 0 so that your content will fill the screen.

This is another important command for creating liquid pages (see Session 7 for an introduction to liquid pages). To illustrate how this works, you will add a table to the top of the Land page in the Weekend site. You will learn how to make it tuck right up under the upper edge of the window and stretch fully from left to right on the screen.

Take the following steps to create a border line:

1. Open the land.html file from the Weekend site. Insert your cursor at the beginning of the table. You might need to select the table and use your ← key to place your cursor. Insert a paragraph break by pressing the Enter key.

2. Create a one-row, one-column table with cell spacing and padding both set to 0. Set the width to 100% and the border to 0.

3. Place your cursor inside the table and specify a cell background color (you could also use a table background to achieve the same results).

Now you have a table forming a very thick line. There are two more adjustments to make to this line. You want the line to be right in the upper-left corner and to stretch right across. You also want the line to be thinner. Let's start with the placement.

Set the margin width to 0 in the Page Properties window. Internet Explorer and Netscape have different codes for margins. For both browsers to recognize margin settings, you need to have two sets of commands. Luckily, each browser ignores the other browser's commands for this setting, and Dreamweaver makes it easy for you to enter the code.

Take these steps to set margins:

1. Select Modify ⇨ Page Properties to open the Page Properties window.

2. Locate the margin settings near the center of the window. Specify 0 for Left Margin, Top Margin, Margin Width, and Margin Height. Click OK to return to your document.

Your line now stretches from edge to edge on your screen. However, it is too thick, and it is not as easy as you may think to trim it down. The problem is that Dreamweaver has placed a nonbreaking space in the table, because a table cell must contain data to be displayed in a browser. The code that is creating the colored table cell is as follows:

```
<td bgcolor="#990000"> </td>
```

If you remove the nonbreaking space, your table will collapse and disappear completely. This is another place where a the transparent GIF can help you. (See Session 7 to review how to place a clear GIF placeholder.) You will replace the nonbreaking space with an invisible graphic and specify the height you want to make your line. You could simply specify the height of your table cell, but Netscape would still ignore it. You will also set the length of the line to 500, because

Netscape seems to prefer longer lines to display empty cells. (To be honest, I do not have a reason for you, nor do I remember how I started using longer lines. I just know it always works.)

Although those were a lot of words to describe getting ready to place an invisible graphic, they were all necessary. Now we'll place the transparent image:

1. Place your cursor inside the table. Select Insert ⇨ Image and choose space.gif from the art folder in your Weekend site. Click OK to return to your document. The space graphic will be selected; do not deselect it. It can be very difficult to select a tiny, invisible graphic, so you will need to increase the size of the image before you deselect it.

2. With the graphic still selected, specify 500 for the image width and 8 for the image height.

3. Check your code. Note that the nonbreaking space has disappeared. As soon as you insert any content, Dreamweaver removes the nonbreaking space.

4. Remove the extra space between the table and the line so that the table rests right up next to the line. With your cursor at the right edge of the first table, press Shift+Enter to add a <br> tag.

Therein lies the secret to creating lines that run from edge to edge. Adding the zero margin settings and the 100% table width, as well as inserting the transparent image to hold the table open, are the standard features for this technique. You can also easily create a double line by using a table with two rows. Simply specify a different color and insert a clear graphic in the second row, as well. The two rows can be different heights. The beauty of this technique is that no matter what resolution your visitor is using, this line will always stretch from margin to margin.

Netscape allows room for a side scroll bar, even if there is insufficient content to require the scroll bar. If you are working with an edge-to-edge design and a gap appears at the right side of your screen, chances are, that you do not have enough content to call for a scroll bar. You can fix this by adding several paragraph spaces (pressing the Enter key) to trick Netscape into thinking it needs a scroll bar.

Adding Head Properties

Head content includes any information that falls between the <head> and </head> tags at the beginning of any HTML page. This is where you place meta tags, or information about the document. Some meta tags have been defined in Dreamweaver and can be entered separately, including keywords for search engines and page descriptions. The head also contains many specialized codes, such as JavaScript. For this exercise we will add a page description, keywords and an author Meta tag.

You will be learning how to add JavaScript in Session 13.

So that you can easily edit your page's head content, you can enable a small bar that displays an icon for each head tag. Select View ➪ Head Content from the main menu. Keep this view open while you walk through the following exercises so that you will be able to see the new items added to the head content.

Adding a page description

The text you specify as a page description will appear in search engine listings. Take the following steps to add your page description:

1. Select Insert ➪ Head Tags ➪ Description, and then type **The story of a trip across this great country** (or feel free to create your own description). Click OK to accept the changes. Note that a new icon has been added to the head content display.

I have used dull words just as an example for this page. Of course, when you have a lively description that really paints a picture for your potential visitors, they are much more likely to visit.

Inserting keywords

Many talented people are making a living exclusively by helping businesses achieve high listings in the search engines. I am not so bold as to claim anything I could say on the subject in one paragraph would even scratch the surface. Add this to the list of subjects you must research to promote your site. It is a vital component of marketing your site, whether the site is personal or commercial.

To add keywords, select Insert ➪ Head Tags ➪ Keywords. Type in **trip, tour, family, place names** (add some state or province names here), or use your own keywords in the Insert Keywords window. Click OK to return to the document. Note that a new icon has been added to the head content display.

Adding other meta tags

You can enter any data you choose in a meta tag. Designers often use meta tags to add a creation date and author information. The tag consists of two separate entries. The name entry gives the tag a title, such as creation date, and the content entry contains the listing "March 23, 2001."

To add an author tag, select Insert ⇨ Head Content ⇨ Meta and the Insert Meta window will open. Make sure that Name is selected in the Attribute drop-down box and type **Author** in the Value field. Type your name in the Content area. Click OK to return to your document.

Editing head content

Once you have created a head tag, you can easily edit it. Make sure you have Dreamweaver set to display head content (View ⇨ Head Content). Click any tag in the head section and the Properties Inspector will display all the relevant information — which you can edit. Figure 9-2 shows the keywords tag.

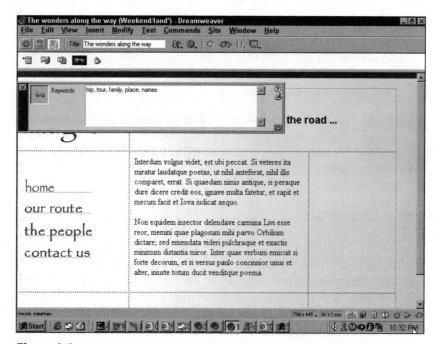

Figure 9-2
Click any head tag and you can edit content in the Properties Inspector window.

Creating Links

**10 Min.
To Go**

We are coming down to the end of the basic steps required to create an entire site. I promised you that you would have a site on the Web by noon today, and we are right on schedule. The one task left is to create links to allow visitors to visit all of your pages. You will create links to other pages, as well as to other sites on the Web. You will also create one special link to automatically open a visitor's e-mail program so they can send you a note.

Your site is still a little rough, and it will be when you upload it to the Web for the first time. But, you need room for improvement, because you have more techniques to learn. Knowing how to retrieve and edit a file, and to then get the file tucked safely back on your server, is extremely important. You will fine-tune the site and learn to perform the correct FTP transfers at the same time. For now, let's get those pages connected.

You will spend a lot of time on links, and different types of links, in Session 12.

Adding links to images

Images are often used for menu items. The menu you created for your first site was created from graphics. It takes a surprising amount of code to create a link, but Dreamweaver makes short work of this operation.

Take the following steps to create a link from an image:

1. Open index.html from the Weekend site.
2. Click the "our route" graphic menu item to select it.
3. In the Properties Inspector, click the folder next to the Link field. The Select File window will open. Choose route.html and click Select to return to the document. The graphic will not change appearance in any way, but when it is selected, you can see the link information in the Properties Inspector.
4. Make sure that the border value is set to 0.
5. Repeat Steps 1 through 4 with the next two menu items, choosing people. html and land.html, respectively, for the linked files. Ignore the Contact menu items for a few minutes.

That is all there is to creating a link with a graphic. You can now go through the rest of your pages and create links for all your menu items.

If you find an unexpected blue border on your image, setting the border value to 0 will remove it.

Adding Alt tags to images

Have you noticed the little information tags that pop out when you hold your mouse pointer over a graphic? That is the Alt tag in action (see Figure 9-3). People who browse with image display disabled off will see a note telling them about the image that is supposed to appear in that location. If the graphic is a link, the Alt tag usually provides some information about the link.

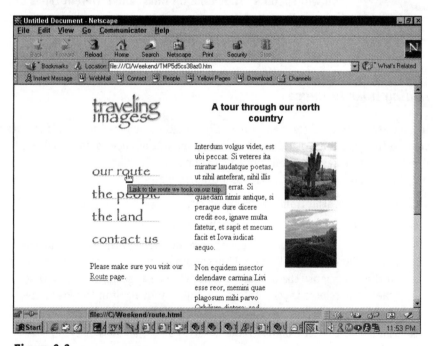

Figure 9-3
Alt tags display as the mouse pointer is held over a graphic. These tags help people who cannot display or see graphic displays.

Visually impaired people depend on voice translators to tell them what is on a Web page, and Alt tags are read to tell the visitor about that image. You can also use Alt tags to provide the visitor a little more information about the link. In short, Alt tags are a very good idea. They are required for your page to be validated by any industry-standard rating systems, such as the W3C (World Wide Web Consortium) or Bobby, which many government agencies insist upon for their sites.

W3C offers a code validation service with which you can test your pages for W3C validity (`http://www.w3.org/`). Bobby is a service provided by CAST (Center for Applied Special Technology) to test HTML pages for accessibility (`http://www.cast.org/bobby/`). It is an excellent idea, especially if you are a beginner, to visit both sites, study the issues around accessibility and valid code, and also to test your pages.

Dreamweaver makes it very easy to add Alt tags. Take the following steps to add Alt tags:

1. Open the index.html page from your Weekend site.
2. Select the "our route" graphic.
3. Type **Link to the route we took on our trip.** in the Alt field in the right side of the Properties Inspector.
4. Repeat Steps 2 and 3 for each graphic on the page. For the menu items, create a sentence similar to the one you created in Step 3. For the photos and logo, you can type just what it contains, or you can type something similar to **Picture of _____.**

There isn't a lot of work involved to make a big difference to those who cannot use graphics to help them gain access to the information on the Web. It also adds a professional touch to your pages.

Adding links to text

In much the same way that you added a link to your images, you can change any text into a link. The difference is that the text you want to link must be highlighted. There is no limit to the number of words you can use to create a single link. Just select all the text you want to include, as described in the following steps:

1. Open the index.html file from the Weekend site.
2. Insert your cursor beneath the menu in the left column. Press your Enter key to create a space between the menu item and the cursor, if necessary. Type **Please make sure you visit our Route page.**

3. Double-click, or click and drag, to select the word Route. In the Properties Inspector window, click the folder beside the Link field (on the left side of the window). Choose route.html from the Select File window. Click Select to return to the document.

   Your text will now appear blue with an underline (this is the default link appearance). You will learn how to adjust link colors in a later session. Figure 9-4 shows the link appearance with the linked file displaying in the Properties Inspector.

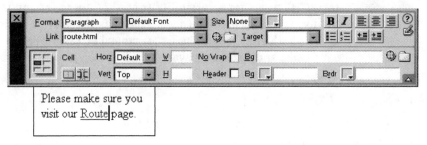

Figure 9-4
Text with an added link. Note how the linked filename appears in the Properties Inspector.

Special links

The links that you just created connect your visitors to other pages on your site. You can also create links that link to other sites, or that open your visitor's e-mail program so they can send you a note. These links can be added to images or to text, each using a different type of link code.

You will learn about linking to a specific place on the page with Named Anchor links in Session 12.

Linking to other pages

To add a link to another Web address, select your image or text, and type in a full Web address.

1. In the index.html document, insert your cursor below the text you added in the last exercise. Type **You can buy books at Amazon.com**.

2. Highlight Amazon.com. In the links field in the Properties Inspector, type http://www.amazon.com. Your text will change to indicate that it is a link. When your visitor clicks this link, they will be taken to the Amazon.com site. For links to other sites, it is important that you specify the full address for an external site, including the http:// portion of the address.

Linking to e-mail

If you want your visitors to be able to send you a note directly from your site, you can choose to add a **mailto** link.

1. In the index.html document, select the "contact us" graphic.
2. In the links field in the Properties Inspector **type mailto:(your email address)** with no brackets; for example, **mailto:wpeck@wpeck.com**. Your text will change to indicate that it is a link. When your visitor clicks the link, their e-mail program will be opened, and a new message will be started, ready for them to type their note.

Although I have used the menu items as a "mail to" link, this really is not the best method to use. The mailto command should be used for a direct "send us an e-mail" style link. The contact link should lead to another page. In the interest of quickly moving you through the material, I have elected not to have you build one more page. It would be great practice for you, however, to create a contact page, and then add a "mail to" link to that page if you have time.

Creating a text menu

Now that you know how to create a link from text, you can build a text menu. Although most main menus are created from graphics, it is a good idea to include a text menu at the bottom of each Web page. Visitors will not have to scroll back to the top for the menu, and those without graphics enabled can use the text option.

I prefer to create my text menus in a table. I also tend to nest the menu table in the main table, although some would disagree with this method. If you do not want to nest tables, you can place it below the main page table. However, you can use this exercise to learn how to nest a table, as well as create a text menu.

Take the following steps to create a text menu in a table:

1. Open the index.html document from the Weekend site.

2. Insert your cursor into the last row of the layout table. This row should have all of the cells merged to create one large cell from your work in Session 6. If the cells are not merged, select the cells and merge them.

3. Select Insert ⇨ Table, and then specify a table one row and four columns. Set the cell padding to 10, and set the cell spacing to 0. Set the width to 100%, and set the borders to 0. Click OK to return to your document. The original table row now contains our new table.

You might wonder why the new table is staying within the 500-pixel main table when the new table has a width of 100%. Shouldn't it be across the entire page? When a table is placed within another table — or into a table cell — the 100% refers to 100% of the cell or table it is contained within. If you want to see this in action, select the new table and copy it. Place your cursor below the main table and paste the new table. Now that it is outside the original table — even though it has the exact parameters — this table will stretch across the page (see Figure 9-5).

Make sure you delete the table that is outside the main table. You created that table simply to understand the 100% width constraint principle.

4. Type **the route** into the first table cell. Type **the people** into the second table cell. Type **the land** into the third cell. Type **contact us** into the final cell.

5. Select the four cells of the menu table by clicking and dragging. Set the cell alignment to center by choosing Center from the drop-down Horz menu in the Properties Inspector.

6. Create a link for the first menu item by selecting the text and linking to route.html. Repeat this step for the next two menu items, choosing the appropriate file for the link.

7. Select "contact us" in the menu. Create a "mailto" link as described earlier.

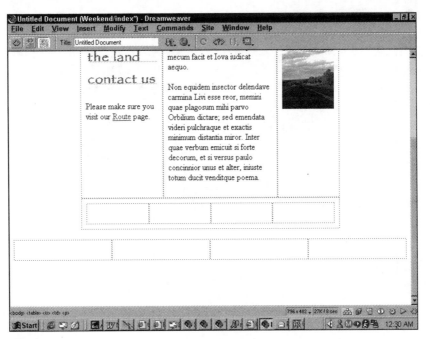

Figure 9-5
The table shown at the bottom of the page, and the table that is nested at
the bottom of the main page table, are exactly the same table. The width is
specified to be 100% in both, but the table inside the main table is con-
strained to 100% of the main table width. The lower table is stretching to
100% of the page.

Your text menu (shown in Figure 9-6) for this page is complete. You must create
the same menu for each page. You can copy this table and paste it into each
document. However, the text will need to be changed for each page, because you
do not want the active page to be listed. You also want to add a home menu. Each
page will have a four menu items. For example, route.html will have home, the
people, the land, and contact us as menu items.

This was a fast and furious lesson. It's time to leave document creation and
focus on FTP issues for the next session.

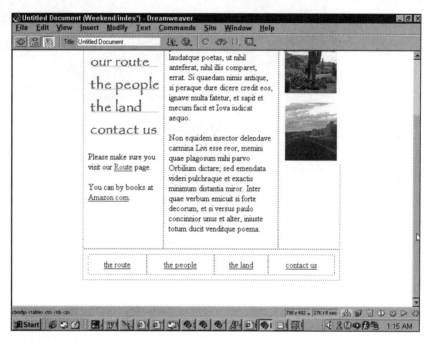

Done!

Figure 9-6
The completed menu for index.html

REVIEW

We have covered a lot of material in this session, although much of it was similar in nature. The important things to remember are:

- You can use one page to create another page for a small site, but be careful to immediately rename the file so that you do not overwrite your original file.

- When you add background color or images, it is very important to preview your work in both Netscape and Internet Explorer, because they treat the codes for this properties in very different ways.

- When you add page titles, descriptions, and keywords, you should choose your words with care, because these properties are used by the search engines.

- Setting page margins to 0 allows you to stretch your design content from margin to margin and right to the top of the page.

- You can create your own meta tags to present information in the head of the document. Head content can only be seen in the document code.
- Alt tags are very important for many Web users.
- Links are added in much the same way for both text and images in Dreamweaver.
- Text menus provide an extra level of navigation for your visitors, and they can be very useful for those who cannot view images.

QUIZ YOURSELF

1. Where do you change the page background color or image in Dreamweaver? (See the "Setting Page Properties" section.)

2. Why is a title important for your page? (See the "Adding a page title" section.)

3. What margin settings are necessary if you want to have your content cover the entire screen on your finished page? (See the "Setting page margins" section.)

4. Where does a page description appear with a finished page? (See the "Add a page description" section.)

5. Where do you specify link information for both text and images? (See the "Creating Links" section.)

6. Where do Alt tags appear on a final page, and what other purpose do they serve? (See the "Adding Alt tags to images" section.)

Using Dreamweaver Site Management

Session Checklist

✔ Moving files

✔ Using global replace

✔ Transferring multiple files

✔ Finding a file on the remote server

✔ Retrieving files from the server

✔ Synchronizing a site

✔ Updating files

**30 Min.
To Go**

Y ou have your rough site completed, and now it is time to transfer it to your server. When I am working creating a new site, I would not use this exact workflow. I usually create the first page drafts, and then place them on the server to make sure everything is working right. My next step is usually to take the remaining pages to a very finished state before transferring them to the server. Dreamweaver makes site management much easier, but I still prefer not to transfer my files back and forth more than necessary.

For this exercise, though, I want you to have working examples to learn Dreamweaver's site management tools, so you are placing files that you know need to be edited. You will transfer the files to the server, and you will then retrieve them to make your edits. Although I always try to minimize the number of trips back and forth, it is a rare page that does not make several journeys from remote to local and back again, despite my best efforts.

The information contained in this Session is very valuable to your future work and, perhaps more important, your sanity. A site that is out of control can make your work life truly miserable.

Now it's time to get those files to the server.

Preparing Your Site

Before we tap into the full power of Dreamweaver's site management tools, you are going to clean up your local folder. As you have worked through the previous sessions, you have created a few extra files that have no purpose for the site. As you learn to work with Dreamweaver sites, you will develop ways to keep working files — such as graphics files or word processing documents — in a location that makes sense for you.

I tend to make a client directory, and then assign a folder beneath the client directory as my site root folder. This is my way of keeping all files for one client in one folder, while not cluttering the root folder with working files. You will find methods that work for you to separate your working files from the files that you need on the server.

I am going to keep things simple and have you create a new folder that will hold all of your reference files and any working files you create. Not only will this clean up your site and provide a folder to exclude when you synchronize, but you will also see the Dreamweaver file tracking process in action.

You probably thought that I was just teaching you messy habits. When it comes to files, if I am leading you down a less-than-obsessively neat road, I have my reasons. Keeping your files neat and in logical order is the single most important thing any computer user can do to make their work time more productive. It is at least twice as vital for Web designers.

I often create a test folder within the root folder for a site. Occasionally, I want to experiment with a new technique, or do a "what if I did it this way" exercise while building a site. With the test files in the root folder, all related files can be used from the correct location, yet I have all my testing files in one place to exclude from the synchronization process.

Transferring files within a Dreamweaver site

You need only four documents for the Weekend site. You already created the following page files you need to have your site work: index.html, land.html, people.html and route.html. These are the pages you need to have your site work. However, you also created several reference files and imported text files. These you will move to a new folder.

1. Open the Weekend site window. We will first create our new directory. A new folder will be placed below whatever folder is selected when you create the folder. Click on your root folder listing to highlight, and choose File ⇨ New Folder **OR** Right-click (PC) or ⌘-Click (Mac) and choose New Folder from the drop-down menu. Name your folder **resources**.

2. Now that you have a folder, move your extra files into the folder. Click to highlight all files except the files you need for your site index.html, land.html, people.html, and route.html).

3. Click and drag, moving your mouse pointer over the resources folder. Release the mouse button and the Update files listing will appear.

    Dreamweaver has quickly searched through your site and checked for any links that will be affected by the move you are requesting. In this case, you should receive a list that reflects only the files you are moving, since these files are not linked to any other documents. However, each of these files must be updated, because their relation to any dependent files will change. Dreamweaver will automatically make the link changes if you choose to update the files.

4. Select Update. Dreamweaver will check the local and remote sites for these files and make changes. If you are not connected to your server, Dreamweaver will attempt to connect you.

If you had moved these files to a new folder outside of Dreamweaver, the Site window would reflect the changes, but the links within the files will not have been changed. You would discover that your graphics files and any other connected file would be broken when you opened the document again, and you would then have to manually change every link.

Using the Find and Replace command

It is not unusual to discover that you have made an error, or that you have changed your mind on a word you have used throughout every page. This is especially true if you have used one page to create other pages. Often, we find this just as we are getting ready to upload our site.

Dreamweaver has nearly unlimited find and replace capability. You can search and replace plain text, HTML source codes, and specific tags, or you can use the advanced text search to customize what you would like to find. You can perform your searches in the current document only, in the current site, in a specified folder, and — a wonderful addition to version 4 — in selected files (choose files in the Site window).

First, I would like you to go back and add the text menu to each of the pages we created over the last few sessions.

Take the following steps to add the menu:

1. Open the four documents that remain in your Weekend site root folder.

2. On the index.html document, select the table containing the text menu (see Figure 10-1). Make sure that you have the entire table selected, not just the cells. You will have one selection boundary, and the Properties Inspector will show the table values, such as rows and cells.

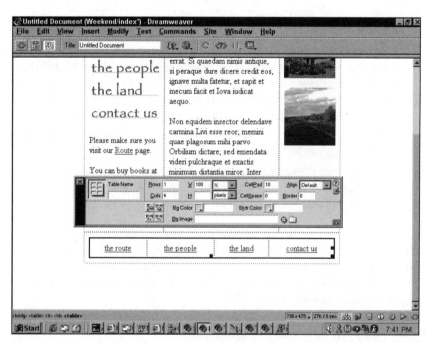

Figure 10-1
A fully selected table

3. Copy the table. Select Edit ➪ Copy, or press Ctrl-C (PC) or ⌘-C (Mac).

4. Activate the route.html file. In the bottom row of the table, select and merge the cells by clicking the merge cells icon in the Properties Inspector.

5. Insert your cursor into the merged cells and paste the menu table. Select Edit ➪ Paste, or press Ctrl-V (PC) or ⌘-V(Mac).

6. Delete the entry "the route" and type home in its place. Create a link to index.html.

7. Repeat Step 6 for the land.html and people.html files. You must delete the link for the page you are editing; that is, for the land.html file, you will delete the text "the land" and add the text "home." You will have to shuffle entries around so that the order remains the same as it is in the menu.

8. Close all files except index.html.

20 Min. To Go

   I took you the long way around, but you are ready to do a replace now. You are going to change the contact menu item to read "contact" instead of "contact us." Since you are going to replace the menu item in all the files in a folder, you can perform the replace from any page or from the Site window. If you were performing a replace on only one page, you would need to have that page open.

1. Select Edit ➪ Find and Replace. The Find and Replace window will open.

2. To replace text or code through the entire root folder, choose Folder from the drop-down Find In menu. Click the folder icon to specify the root folder for your Weekend site.

3. Choose Text from the Search For drop-down menu. Type **contact us** in the field beside the Search For menu.

4. Type contact in the Replace With field.

5. Click Replace All. An alert will pop up, warning you that you cannot undo changes in documents that are open. This is a warning to be heeded. When you are replacing text across an entire site or folder, make sure that you know exactly what you are doing. Click OK.

If I am doing a global search and replace, I will usually test my replace on one page before I do the global search and replace. It is easy to neglect to include a space or similar tiny error. However, if you are making changes that cannot be undone across 50 documents, you want to make sure that you have it right.

6. Dreamweaver will go to work and list all the changes it makes. A pop-up alert will appear to let you know what changes have been made. Click OK. Note that the changes that have been made are also listed in the Find and Replace window. Figure 10-2 displays the setup for the replace that was performed, along with the completion message.

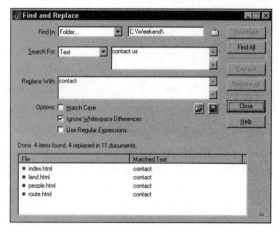

Figure 10-2
The search parameters and results for the global search

Search and replace can save so much time. Remember the spaces we had between our image code and the <br> tag? I will often run a source code search to replace "space
" with <br> for an accurate and almost instant way to guarantee that my code is correct. If you catch yourself doing the same thing over and over again, perhaps a search and replace exercise is the answer.

Even when you cannot use the replace feature, the find feature can be very handy. Specify the term you would like to find and where you would like to find it (folder, site, etc.). You can then use your F3 key to move from one instance to the next, making corrections as you go.

Transferring Files

When you think of transferring files, you must think of it as a continual process. Rare is the Web site that is placed on the server and left alone. Designers are always making small revisions, updating information, improving on our work, and so forth. After all, that is what the Web has opened for us: the ability to publish constantly.

You have created a small site for this portion of the course. Technically, you could put this site on the Web very easily because you only have a few files. In fact, clicking the file you want to transfer and dragging it to the server side of the Site window is the full technique for transferring a file in Dreamweaver.

However, I built this course on a small, simple site to start. Transferring the files to the server and learning about Dreamweaver's powerful site management tools is one of the main reasons I chose to structure the course this way. It is much easier to follow what is happening when you are only working with a few files.

 Although you are working with a small and simple site, please pay special attention to this section. This process is not difficult, but it can be confusing when you are working with a larger number of files. The time you spend making sure you fully understand the Dreamweaver site management tools will be repaid to you many times over.

Deleting a file on the remote server

In Session 5, you transferred files to the Web. You transferred a single file and an entire site. In this Session, you are going to transfer multiple files. To start, however, you are going to delete one file from your remote site. As part of Session 5, you placed the file session4.html on the remote server. However, this is a resource file and there is no reason for it to be on our server.

Take the following steps to delete a file on the remote server:

1. Open the Weekend site window. Connect to the server.

2. Select the file session4.html.

3. Do one of the following: Select File ⇨ Delete, press your Delete Key, **or** right-click (PC) or Control-click (Mac) and select Delete.

You can delete a folder in the same way. Simply select the folder and proceed as above.

Transferring multiple files

You can move one or many files by selecting, and then clicking and dragging the selection to the remote side of the Site window. Select continuous files by selecting the first file, and then pressing your Shift key before selecting the last file you want to transfer. You can also select multiple files that are not in contiguous order by clicking each file while pressing the Ctrl (PC) or Command key (Mac).

Take the following steps to transfer multiple files to the server:

1. Open the Weekend site and connect to the server.

2. Select the four files that we created for the site.

3. Click and drag any of the selected files to transfer all of the selected files. Drag them to the remote side of the Site window, and then position your cursor over the listing at the top of the screen. This is your root folder, and you want to make sure that your files are in the root folder (see Figure 10-3).

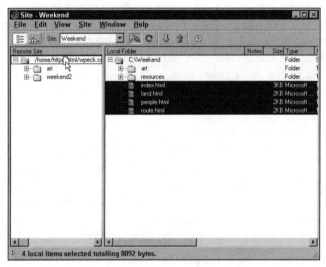

Figure 10-3
Files selected and dragged to the root folder on the remote site

4. An alert window will appear asking if you would like to include dependant files. Click Yes. Dreamweaver will check the files you are transferring and include any graphic or other dependent files, creating a folder for the extra files that are in a separate folder on the local site as it works. On the first transfer of any file, you should always say yes to this; Dreamweaver can effortlessly make sure that all the files you require will be placed in the correct folder on the remote server.

As the files are transferring, watch the status bar at the bottom of your screen. The left side tells you which file is transferring and the size of that file. The right side provides a progress bar so that you can track the transfer progress. You can also stop a transfer by clicking the red icon in the lower-right corner, or by pressing your Esc key.

5. Your site should be fully uploaded to the site. View the site on the Web using the address `http://www.youraddress.com/Weekend/`. You have an Index file, and that file will automatically appear when you request the Weekend folder.

The links are not all in place yet; you still have some work left to do without edits. Your lower text menu should enable you to navigate your site.

Finding a file on the local or remote server

You have a small site with a very simple structure. You can see every file on the remote server simply by expanding folders. However, most sites are much more complicated, and it is not unusual for even a personal site to grow to more than 20 pages, with several folders containing images — or sub-pages. Dreamweaver offers a really simple, terrific search feature to find the matching file, or to find multiple matching files on your local or remote server. To show the power of this feature, make sure that all the folders are collapsed on your remote server.

1. Open the Weekend site and connect to the remote server.

2. Expand the art folder on your local site and select menu6.gif. Press your Ctrl (PC) or ⌘ (Mac) key and select the file index.html.

3. Select Edit ⇨ Locate in Remote Site from the main menu. Dreamweaver will select the index.html file and open the art folder on the remote site to select menu6.gif.

4. Now try it in reverse. Select a file or several files in the remote site and select Edit ⇨ Locate in Local Site.

This may seem like a silly thing to rave about. Although I do not use it often, this feature saves time and many mouse clicks when I do.

Retrieving files from the server

Copying files from the server to the local folder is the same procedure as copying files from the local drive to the server, only in reverse.

1. Open the Weekend site and connect to the server.
2. Select the land.html file on the remote server.
3. Click and drag the file to the root folder of the local site. You will be asked if you would like to copy the dependent files. You can click NO this time, because all the files you require for that page are already on the local site.

 Be careful downloading files from your remote site to your local site however. If you have made changes to your local copy and you attempt to download that file from the remote site, another alert will appear confirming that you want to overwrite the local copy of that file. Pay attention when this alert appears. If you say yes, any changes you have made to the local copy will be overwritten.

Synchronizing a Site

The nearest comparison that I can draw for what happens when you synchronize a site comes from my childhood. Somewhere, we had picked up the idea that all covert operations started with everyone synchronizing their watches. Without that, how could we ever pull off a successful mission (try as I might, I cannot remember what the missions were) if our watches were off by even a minute.

Synchronizing your Dreamweaver site is exactly the same principle. You are taking a snapshot of the remote and local sides of the site. Where differences exist, those differences are corrected. If you are working alone, the changes are almost always made on the remote side because you do your work on the local site. However, if you are working as part of a team, you may well be Getting (transferring from remote to the local) as often as you Putting (transferring from the local to remote) files.

 See Sessions 3 and 5 for basic information about transferring files with Dreamweaver.

No matter which direction the corrections are taking place, the important thing is that you are exactly matching the two sides of your site. When you are working on a site, it can be tough to keep track of which files you have updated. You may have made one tiny change to a graphic file, plus adjusted one word in many documents. When you are synchronizing your site, even the tiny graphic file edit will not be left behind.

You have some decisions to make. You have things on your local site that you do not want to upload to the remote site. Remember, you also have the Weekend 2 folder on your remote site that you do not want on your local site.

You have several choices available to you when you synchronize your site. You can choose to synchronize the entire site or just selected files on the site. You also can choose whether you will have files transferred from the local site to the remote, the opposite, or both.

A question may be running through your head. Why did I bother to show you all those methods for uploading and downloading files if all you have to do is synchronize your site and it will all be looked after? Good question. The answer is that you are often working on one or two files, and you want to test the results on the server. You do not need to go through the synchronization step for simple working steps like that. If you are working back and forth with single files, it is usually faster just to upload them and synchronize the site when you are finished to make sure you have not left any files behind. Synchronizing is not difficult, but nothing is faster than a click-and-drag from the local to the remote site.

Enough talk. Let's synchronize your site.

1. Open the Weekend site and connect to the server.

2. Select Site ⇨ Synchronize. The Synchronize Files window will open.

3. Choose Selected Local Files Only from the Synchronize drop-down menu.

4. Select Put newer files to remote from the Direction drop-down menu (see Figure 10-4).

5. Select Preview. The Synchronize window will open.

    The preview window you see enables you to go through the files that Dreamweaver has found and decide whether those files will be updated. For the files that you are working with here, I would have simply chosen the four documents and the art folder rather than the whole site, because we have files that we do not want to include. However, I wanted you to work through the process of eliminating files.

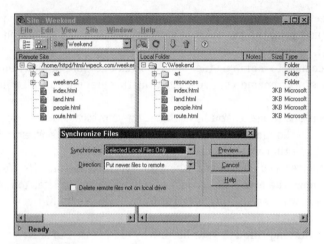

Figure 10-4
Synchronizing only selected folders

6. Uncheck all the files that are in the resource directory. Only files that remain checked will be placed on the server. See Figure 10-5 to see the documents that form our site with checks, as well as the files without checks. Click OK.

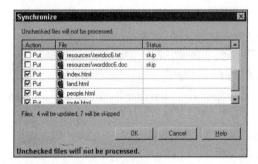

Figure 10-5
Ready to synchronize. The files that will not be transferred to the remote site are unchecked.

Dreamweaver goes to work placing all the files that you have edited. You will make a few changes in your documents now, and then you will synchronize again. This should be a regular pattern for you if you wish to take full advantage of the power of Dreamweaver's site management tools.

Editing and Updating Files

Time to put a lot of what you have learned into practice, and on your own, too. This is where I give you a list and tell you to do it. If you are following along with the timing of this course, you will not be able to get this done all at once. It is a lot faster when I am guiding your every keystroke. All we really need for the next part of this course is to make changes to a few of your files. You can then go back when you have time to finish all of the details.

Here is your "to-do" list. All references can be found in Session 9.

- Add the gray background image (see "Adding a background image") to the other pages, or remove it from land.html page so that all of your pages match.

- Make sure that all of your pages have a working text menu (see "Creating a text menu").

- Add links to your graphic menu items on all pages (see "Adding links to images" and "Special links").

- Set margins to 0 and add a line at the top of the page, or remove the line from the top of the Land page (see "Setting page margins").

- Add Alt tags to your images (see "Adding Alt tags to images").

- Add titles to all pages (see "Adding a page title").

- Add meta tags like keywords and description.

- Check your pages for errors in alignment.

Once you have made one change to at least three pages, you are ready to update your site. You will simply repeat the synchronization exercise discussed earlier in this session. Make sure you remember to deselect the files in the resources directory.

I have covered all of the basic functions you need to build a site. From here, we head for some exciting techniques. I promised that you would have a site on the Web by now, and you do. Give yourself a big pat on the back. Your reward will come soon. You have worked hard to get through the basics, and now you can have a little fun.

Done!

REVIEW

We tapped into the powerful features that Dreamweaver offers for site management with this session. If you have come to Dreamweaver with the experience of having manually created sites, you probably have a mile-wide grin right now. Unless you have maintained a site with just your memory, you may not fully appreciate what you have just learned. However, there are a few key points that you should remember:

- It is crucial that you keep your site folders very tidy. Without great housekeeping habits, it will be nearly impossible to use the automated features for Dreamweaver site management.

- When you move files within a Dreamweaver site, the links are automatically checked and you are given an option to update the files.

- If you perform a search and replace action that included files which are not active (open), any changes cannot be undone. It is best to test the replace feature with a single page before performing a global search or replace.

- Clicking and dragging will transfer any selected files either to or from the remote site. Select continuous files using the Shift key; select non-contiguous files using the Ctrl (PC) or Command (Mac) key.

- Synchronizing a site is simply making sure your remote and local sites are exactly the same. You can exclude any files from the synchronizing process.

QUIZ YOURSELF

1. When you click and drag to transfer a file in the Dreamweaver site window, what does Dreamweaver do for you? (See the "Transferring files within a Dreamweaver site" section.)

2. Dreamweaver has a command that will replace a phrase or piece of code throughout the entire site. What should you do before you tell Dreamweaver to Replace All? (See the "Using the Find and Replace command" section.)

3. How do you delete a file on the remote server? (See the "Deleting a file on the remote server" section.)

4. What is synchronizing a site in Dreamweaver? (See the "Synchronizing a site" section.)

5. Once you have synchronized your site, when should you use it again? (See the "Editing and updating files " section.)

PART

II

Saturday Morning

1. What capability does using Dreamweaver's FTP feature offer that using other FTP programs does not?

2. List the four pieces of information about your remote host you need to set up the FTP for a Dreamweaver site.

3. What single action transfers an entire site to the remote server?

4. Why should you avoid nesting multiple tables, especially to many levels?

5. Why is it a good idea to plan your tables well before you start building them?

6. Why would you work with your table borders turned on when you do not wish to have table borders in the final version?

7. What is the difference between setting table width to a fixed size or a percentage?

8. If a column contains only text, and you want it always to display at 200-pixels wide, what can you do to ensure that the table is always at least 200-pixels wide?

9. When you place a table inside a cell of another table and set a percentage width for the new table, what determines the width of the new table?

10. Does Dreamweaver allow you to specify both fixed and percentage values for columns in the same table?

11. When you wish to add a background color to only one cell in a table, how do you accomplish this in Dreamweaver? What HTML tag is affected.

12. How do you delete a table's background color in Dreamweaver?

13. How does Netscape Navigator display a multicell table that has a background image added.

14. Internet Explorer does not display a background image when the background is specified as part of which tag?

15. How do you add a background color or image to a page in Dreamweaver?

16. In the Page Properties window, you can set page margins to zero. Why must you add four commands to change two margins?

17. Where do you add a link to an image in Dreamweaver?

18. Suppose you want to change the page margins on all 25 pages of your site. How do you do this in Dreamweaver?

19. How can you transfer multiple files from the local site to the remote site or the visa versa?

20. Why do you choose to synchronize a site?

PART

III

Saturday
Afternoon

Session Checklist

✔ Editing HTML

✔ Customizing Dreamweaver HTML

✔ Placing a script in Dreamweaver

✔ Editing your script

✔ Previewing imported scripts

**30 Min.
To Go**

Way back in Session 1, I read you the riot act about learning the code that runs your Web site. This is where you will learn how to work with your code, and why it is important to understand what goes on behind the Dreamweaver screen.

This session covers checking, editing, and adding code in several different ways. Dreamweaver offers customizing features for the HTML code, and we will take a look at that feature.

Once you know how to work with the HTML screens, you will move on to placing code from a different source. There are thousands of free, or reasonably priced, cripts available, which you can add to your sites. These scripts are often very high quality, and can offer exciting features for your sites. You will learn how to place a script, which will also teach you how to copy scripts between your own documents.

Editing HTML

Whether you are troubleshooting or typing nearly all the code you require for a page, the methods are the same. Let's work through a sample of each oepration so that you are familiar with all of Dreamweaver's HTML editing capabilities. Version 4 has added HTML editing power, so even if you are familiar with earlier versions, you will find new information here.

Working with HTML in Dreamweaver

First, you are going to look at some basic codes and get used to working with the code windows. You have three choices for viewing code within Dreamweaver. You will type or edit code using each method so that you can discover which way is the most comfortable for you. When I first started using Dreamweaver 4, I tended to use the pop-up code window. That was natural, since no other choice was available in Dreamweaver 3.

However, I have noticed that I am using the code view in the main window much more. My choice is not based on logical calculations for the best method; it is developing naturally. If I am using the mouse, I have a tendency to click the top bar for code view. When I am using the keyboard, the F10 key is natural from my long experience of having used that shortcut in earlier versions. It makes no difference.

All Dreamweaver HTML viewing methods can be interchanged and achieve the same result. You do not have to be consistent with how you view code. You can go from the window display to split screen view to full screen code view and back again, as your working style demands.

Editing HTML in the Code Inspector window

The original HTML display method in Dreamweaver is a separate window known as the Code Inspector.

Create a new document and type some code by hand in the Code Inspector.

1. Create a new document and save it in the Resources folder in your Weekend site as handcode.html.

2. Open the Code Inspector using one of the following methods. You can click the <> icon in the lower-right edge of your screen, press the F10 key, or select Window ⇨ Code Inspector from the main window. Click and drag the window borders if you would like to have more room to work.

3. Dreamweaver has already placed the minimum amount of code required to create a document with a white background, rather than the default gray, and that code will be visible in the Code Inspector. Check the code below to confirm that you are starting with the same code.

```
<html>
<head>
<title>Untitled Document</title>
<meta http-equiv="Content-Type" content="text/html;
charset=iso-8859-1">
</head>

<body bgcolor="#FFFFFF" text="#000000">

</body>
</html>
```

4. Enable your line numbering so I can point you to specific lines in your code. Locate the icons at the top of the Code Inspector window. Click the View Options icon, which is the last icon on the right. Select Line Numbers and a list of numbers will appear down the left side of the window, as shown in see Figure 11-1.

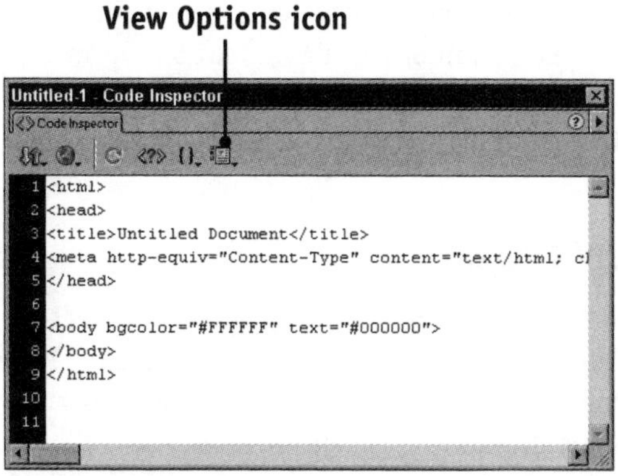

View Options icon

Figure 11-1
The Code Inspector window with the Line Numbers option activated. Line numbers are enabled using the View Options icon.

5. Now you can change your background and text color by typing code. In the Code Inspector, delete the line containing the background color and text color (line 7). It is not necessary to delete the entire line in real working circumstances. We could just replace the color number, but I want you to have a whole line of code to type in.

6. Type in the following code:

```
<body bgcolor="#330099" text="#FFFFFF">
```

7. Place your cursor on the next line (line 8). Type in the following code:

```
<p>Now my background is blue and my text is white.</p>
```

 Although all of the above line — except the <p> and </p> tags — is actual page content, it can still be typed into the code window. In fact, there is nothing that Dreamweaver can do that cannot be done in the Code Inspector or other code view windows. Remember that an entire Web site can be built using nothing but a text editor.

8. Click outside the Code Inspector window, or close the Code Inspector to see the results.

9. Place your cursor at the end of the text line on the screen and press Enter to move the cursor down. Type **All of my text will now be white.** The new line that you typed should have the same attributes as the line you typed in Step 7.

10. Open the Code Inspector window and locate both lines of text. They should be the same, with the exception of the actual text shown in Figure 11-2. Note how the cursor is in the same place in the main document and in the code window.

Editing HTML code with a split screen

Split code view and design view are new features in Dreamweaver 4 — features that I learned to love very quickly. Unless I am working on a very long script, I find that the half-screen view gives me a good overview of the code I am working with, and yet I can still see what is happening on the design screen.

We will enable split-screen view and add an image using only HTML code. We are going to continue working with the document from the previous exercise.

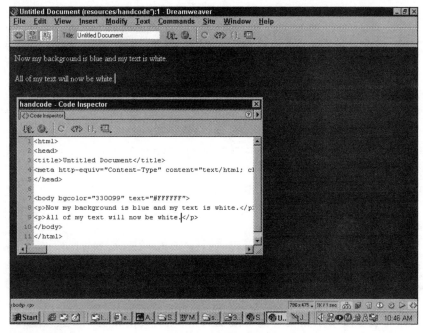

Figure 11-2
The finished code and screen appearance for this exercise.

In the Session 11 directory on the CD-ROM, locate the file image11.gif, and then copy it to the Art folder in the root folder for the Weekend site.

1. If it is not already open, open handcode.html from the resources directory of the Weekend site. Close the Code Inspector window if it is still open.

2. Enable split-screen view by clicking the Show Code and Design Views icon (see Figure 11-3) in the toolbar in the upper-left corner of the Dreamweaver screen.

**Show Code and
Design Views icon**

Figure 11-3
Show Code and Design Views icon

You can specify whether the code window or the design window will display at the top of your screen. Click the View Options window on the far right of the toolbar at the top of your screen, and then click Design View on Top to toggle the arrangement of the screen view.

3. Using the design view screen, place your cursor at the end of the last row of text and press Enter to move the cursor down one line.

4. Type the following code between the <p> and </p> tags.

```
<img src="../art/image11.gif" width="200" height="150">
```

The full line of code looks like this:

```
<p><img src="../art/image11.gif" width="200" height="150"></p>
```

The code you typed first states that this is in a paragraph, and then indicates that it is an image, displaying the path to the image. The image size follows. Finally, the end paragraph tag ends the paragraph.

While you are working in the split screen, select your image in the design screen. Note how the selection is repeated in the code section of the screen. Select the text in the code screen and note that it is selected in the design screen, as well. This should help you to really grasp the idea that the two windows are different presentations of the same information.

20 Min. To Go

Editing HTML code using the full window

Finally, when you have a heavy coding task ahead, you might want to work with your code using the full screen . I will repeat my warning here for those of you who come from a hand-coding background. Dreamweaver has very powerful hand-coding features; with a full-screen code window at your disposal, you may be tempted to ignore the design view and many of the other tools as you produce your pages. But you lose so much of Dreamweaver's power when you work only in code. If this is a potential problem for you, try limiting yourself to a split screen with the code and design views. You then have the best of both worlds at your fingertips.

You are going to add a very simple table to your working document, taking advantage of the larger code area to see the code for the full table.

1. Open the document handcode.html if it is not already open.

2. Enable the full code view by clicking the Show Code View icon (see Figure 11-4) in the toolbar in the upper-left portion of the Dreamweaver screen.

Show Code View icon

Figure 11-4
Show Code View icon

3. Place your cursor at the end of the last row of text, and then press Enter to move the cursor down one line.

 When you are working in any HTML view in Dreamweaver, pressing the Enter key has no effect on your document. It simply moves the code down one line. Technically, HTML ignores white space (throughout this book, I do list exceptions to that rule).

4. Type the following code, pressing the Enter key to start new lines, and pressing the Tab key to align it in an easy-to-read format.

```
<table width="75%" border="0" cellspacing="0" cellpadding="10">
    <tr>
        <td>Text for Row 1 Column 1</td>
        <td>Text for Row 1 Column 2</td>
    </tr>
    <tr>
        <td>Text for Row 2 Column 1</td>
        <td>Text for Row 2 Column 2</td>
    </tr>
</table>
```

Try to trace the construction of this table. I have included text that will identify exactly where you are in the table. The <tr> tag creates a row, and the <td> tag creates a cell.

5. Click the Show Design View icon to proof your code. It should resemble Figure 11-5.

Show Design View icon

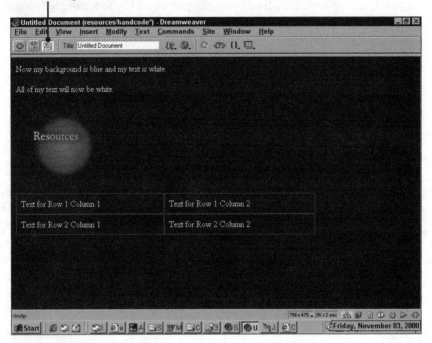

Figure 11-5
Dreamweaver display with Design view active

Those are your three choices for editing HTML code within Dreamweaver. You can also set up an external program to launch from within Dreamweaver in which you can edit your HTML code.

Customizing Dreamweaver HTML

HTML has many correct forms, so it is natural that many people have preferences for code style. Some prefer tags and/or attributes to be in uppercase (capital letters). Dreamweaver's default is lowercase. Hand coders have developed their own system for creating tables or frames that is easy for them to understand and edit. Dreamweaver offers the option to specify the way code is written.

Even if you do not have a preference for the way code is written, adjusting the color-coding for tags can help to quickly identify common trouble areas. I have my `<td>` tags set to display in a hot pink color, because that is one tag that is very fussy about where spaces in the code may be placed — especially for liquid design. I also have my <br> tags set to a gold color so I can spot them in an instant. The tags that you choose to highlight might also be different. If you put some thought into how you want your code to display, you will find that your code work in Dreamweaver will speed up dramatically.

The changes you will make in this section apply only to the way the code appears in the code window; they have no effect on the actual display of your page.

Changing a Code Color

You can easily change default tag colors so that they display in a different color for easy identification:

1. Select Edit ⇨ Preferences and choose Code Colors from the Category listing in the left side of the Preferences window.

2. The color codes in the upper section apply to general colors for the HTML screens. For example, the Background for the code colors is #FFFFFF, or white. This means that your code will appear on a white background. Other values include black for text — which is your text content — and a dark blue for tags. I find the default codes in this section are to my liking, but if you would prefer a change — perhaps you would like to see a greater difference between the text and the code color — simply click the color well next to the attribute you wish to change and choose a new color. You will have to return to one of the code windows to see the changes take effect.

3. Tag color is changed in the Tag Specific section. Scroll down the list to find the <br> tag. Click BR to select it. If you have made no changes to this tag, the Default option will be chosen.

4. Click the radio button next to the color well to indicate that you want a custom color applied to this tag. Choose a new color from the color palette. (I have mine set to #FF9900.) You will have to return to a code window in Dreamweaver to see the result.

5. If you would like to return to the default color for a code, simply repeat the process for choosing a new color, but click the default color radio button. The default color will be returned.

Although specifying color for your code will help, you can overdo it. Color tags show up easily because they are the color in a sea of black. If you have a rainbow of code — with each tag displaying in a different color — you will be no further ahead. Pick the tags you work with the most and assign a color that will stand out.

Customizing HTML code styles

If you would like to change the way that Dreamweaver writes specific code, you can do so from the same menu.

1. Select Edit ➪ Preferences. Choose Code Format from the Category listing in the left side of the Preferences window.

2. You will change the preferences temporarily so that your tags will be created in uppercase. Choose <UPPERCASE> from the Case for Tags drop-down menu, and then click OK.

3. If you are not in Design View, change to it now. Insert a table to see the new code style.

4. Change to code view and you will see that your tags are now written in uppercase letters.

5. Unless you really like this setting, repeat the process, but this time, choose lowercase in the Case for Tags menu. (We will be using the default for the course.)

You have many more options to customize Dreamweaver. We will be looking much more closely at customizing settings in Session 30.

Now that you are a little more comfortable working with HTML code, we are going to move on to placing a premade script into your page.

Placing Scripts into Dreamweaver

**10 Min.
To Go**

There are countless scripts available on the Web to enhance your pages. You will also find that you use scripts, which you have written yourself over and over. These scripts must be placed in Dreamweaver's HTML code view so that you can control the placement of the code. The process is not sophisticated — no more than cutting and pasting code into your code window in most cases — but you must be precise. It is very important to understand the structure of an HTML document to achieve success in placing complicated scripts.

For this exercise, we will use a simple date script from JavaScriptSource.com. You can find the original code at `http://javascript.internet.com`, as well as in the datescript.html document in the Resources folder on the CD-ROM.

Never use another person's code without observing the copyright laws. If you did not write it, you need permission to use it! There is no gray area with this subject. Many scripts are freely offered on the Web, but they usually have conditions. One common condition is that the author's notice must remain in the script. Others restrict the use of their code without payment to non-commercial sites. Still others are for sale as shareware (which means that you are free to download and test, but are expected to send payment to the creator of the script if you use it for your final pages). Be aware and observe these important laws. Next year, you may be writing code, and those same laws will be protecting your work.

Understanding document structure and scripts

I have strongly suggested that you learn HTML coding. Placing scripts is one very good reason for knowing your HTML. Scripts often require that elements be placed in very specific places in your document. If you cannot read the HTML code, you will be depending on luck — not a good idea with anything for Web design.

The two areas that you must know are the Head and Body of an HTML document, as well as the <body> tag (see Figure 11-6). Many scripts have at least two parts: one which must be placed in the Head area of your document (or between the <head> and </head> tags); and the other sections which must be placed inside the <body> tag. Still others must be placed alongside — or inside — other tags (within the body area, between the <body> and </body> tags). Well-written instructions for placing scripts will include very clear instructions about where each section of code must be placed.

Document body

Body tag

Document head

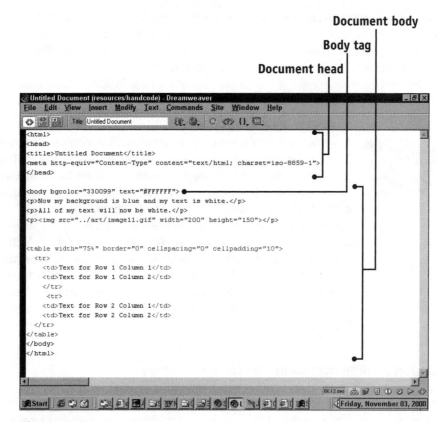

Figure 11-6
Common areas for placing scripts into HTML documents.

Although you can place scripts without knowing any JavaScript or CGI, it is a better idea to at least gain a working knowledge of how these languages work. You will usually want to change a few parameters; without reasonable knowledge of what makes the script work, you will be helpless if there is a problem. In addition, you will have a much easier time with the Dreamweaver Behaviors if you understand JavaScript. Even with automatic features, you will achieve better results when you know why the code is working the way it is.

Placing a script

The script we are using is placed only where we want the date to appear. Take the following steps to place the date script:

1. Open the handcode.html document from the Weekend site if it is not already open.

2. Open the file datescript.html from the Resources directory on the CD-ROM. You do not have to save this document to your hard drive; we are simply cutting and pasting the contents into our document. You also can visit `http://javascript.internet.com/clocks/properdate.html` to copy directly from JavaScriptSource.com. While you are there, you can browse though the many scripts that are also available.

3. Highlight the script code, beginning with `<SCRIPT LANGUAGE="JavaScript">` and ending with `</script>`. Copy the code.

4. In handcode.html, make sure you are in code view, and then place the cursor where you would like the date to appear. I have placed it below the table on the bottom of the page. Make sure that you leave a line or two between the table and the script in your HTML code. It will not affect the placement in the document; it just makes editing much easier. Most scripts add a lot of code to your page. Without good spacing, it is very tough to edit your code later.

You may prefer to place your cursor at the correct location while you are in Design View. When you switch to Code View to paste your script, the cursor position will be maintained.

5. Paste the script into your document. Switch to Design or Design and Code View and you will see a marker where the script has been placed, as shown in Figure 11-7. If you do not see a marker, you may have turned off viewing for items that do not display in Dreamweaver. Check View ⇨ Visual Aids. Invisible Elements must be selected to see the placement of the JavaScript.

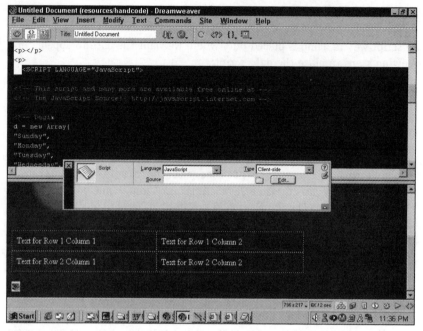

Figure 11-7
Code and design window shown, with the date script highlighted in the code window, and represented by an icon in Design View. Note that the Properties Inspector is showing that the icon represents JavaScript.

6. Click the icon for the JavaScript to select it. The Properties Inspector will indicate that you have a JavaScript script at this position. You can edit your script using the Edit button.

    To see your script in action, you must preview your page in a browser.

7. Choose File ⇨ Preview in Browser, and then choose the browser you wish to test. It is a good idea to test any new script in at least Internet Explore and Netscape Navigator.

You can find a list of script sources in the document scripts.html in the Resources folder of the CD-ROM.

It takes a lot more to explain what we have done here than it does to actually accomplish the task. We have worked on a test document, so the pressure of working around the code you have created for your site did not exist. You will edit this script in Session 13, and you will also use it in Session 15 when you create a library item. You will then place it in your pages. Make sure you save the file.

Done!

While this information is fresh in your mind, why not try to place a different script? There are many available. I do recommend that you test a new script on a new page, however. Place the script and test it in a browser before repeating the placement in your document. That may seem like a lot of work, but when you are working with a two- or three-part script, it is easy to make one tiny error that will affect either the script or your HTML. Once you have the script in your test document, it is a very quick cut-and-paste to move it into place in your working document.

REVIEW

We devoted our time this session to working with code windows. You should be starting to feel more comfortable with the available options. Keep the following in mind as we move on:

- Dreamweaver code viewing options are completely interchangeable and require no consistency. Viewing the code windows is simply another way to see the same information presented in layout form in a design view. (See "Working with HTML in Dreamweaver.")

- You can have the line numbers displayed in Dreamweaver HTML views. (See "Editing HTML in the Code Inspector Window.")

- You can type code directly into any HTML viewing window in Dreamweaver. (See "Editing HTML with a Split Screen.")

- Changing HTML code colors can help make your code easier to work with, yet it does not affect the document display. (See "Changing a Code Color.")

- You can change how Dreamweaver creates code by changing the settings for Preferences. (See "Customizing HTML Code Styles.")

- When placing a script into Dreamweaver, you should work in code view and be careful with the placement of your code. Creating a test document is recommended when you are using a new script. (See "Placing a Script Into Dreamweaver.")

QUIZ YOURSELF

1. What are the three different methods for viewing your HTML code in Dreamweaver? (See the "Working with HTML in Dreamweaver" section.)

2. What effect does pressing the Enter key have when you are working with your code? (See the "Editing HTML CODE with the full code window" section.)

3. How do you change the code color in Dreamweaver? Why would you change code color? (See the "Changing a Code Color" section.)

4. If you want your tags to appear in uppercase characters, where can you specify that option in Dreamweaver? (See the "Customizing HTML Code Styles" section.)

5. What is the most common way to insert a third-party script into your document? (See the "Placing a Script" section.)

6. How can you edit a script without using a code view? (See the "Placing a Script" section.)

Producing and Checking Links

Session Checklist

✔ Understanding Relative and absolute links

✔ Named Anchor links

✔ Previewing your links

✔ Checking links in Dreamweaver

✔ Changing links site-wide

**30 Min.
To Go**

Without links (short for hyperlinks), the Web is just print material on a monitor. It is the interconnected nature of the Web that makes it an entirely new way to communicate or conduct business. For this reason, it is also what must be in good order for a site to work. This session covers the different types of links we have to use, and how to keep links in working order.

Dreamweaver is a powerful ally for working with links. In Session 6, you learned how easy it is to use the Properties Inspector to add links to your documents. In Session 10, you transferred a file and watched as Dreamweaver updated the links that were contained in that file. In this session, you are going to look behind the actions to discover what links are and how they work.

Understanding Relative and Absolute Links

There are two basic types of links. Absolute links are independent of any folder structure on your site. Relative links are written in relation to the root folder on your site.

A link is simply an address to a different location. Let's compare them to street addresses. If you're in a coffee shop on Main Street and someone asks you to tell them where they can find a shoe store, your answer might be, "Tippy Toes, right next door." Chances are that they will find the store. Now imagine that you are at home and the same question is asked. You will have to add that the store is on Main Street, at the very least. Imagine that you are in the next town. Now you have to add the name of the town where Tippy Toes is located, as well as the fact that it is on Main Street, before the store can be found. All of these examples are relative. They consider the location of the person looking for the store, and they include enough information to reach the store from that location.

Suppose you wanted to remove all doubt about where the store is located, no matter what the location is of the inquiring person. The answer will be the same for all of the above examples. Tippy Toes is on earth, in the Northern Hemisphere, in North America, in the United States, in Kansas, in Sedgwick County, at 555 Main Street. You would get some strange looks if you gave this answer while you were in the coffee shop next door to Tippy Toes, but it is technically correct. This address would be an absolute address. No matter where on earth you are, this description of the location of Tippy Toes will be correct.

Absolute or relative links are usually not right or wrong. In fact, in many cases, they are completely interchangeable. Often, however, one or the other is most appropriate for a particular application. Let's look more closely at both types.

Relative links

I try to use relative links whenever I can. I like the flexibility they offer when working with Dreamweaver. Absolute links are . . . absolute. Once you create them, they will stay the same, and they will not be updated by Dreamweaver if you decide to move your files to a different directory. For this reason alone, I recommend that you use relative links unless there is a compelling reason to use absolute links.

 See the next section on absolute links to know when they should be used.

If you are linking between two documents in your root folder, the relative link is as simple as can be. In Dreamweaver, you simply click the folder with the Link section of the Properties Inspector and choose the file. When we created the links for our index.html page, the link to the Route page was a simple statement in the Properties Inspector; it appeared in HTML code as `<a href="route.html">Text for the link</a>`. If the file that you are linking to is in another folder in the root folder, the path includes the folder. In the following code, `<a href="resources/handcode.html">Text for the link</a>`, note the addition of the resources folder to the path. See Figure 12-1 for the Dreamweaver representation of the same link.

Figure 12-1
Link showing a relative path to a lower-level folder

 The path will be marked by ../ (two dots and a single forward slash). if the linked page is above the folder in which the HTML page is saved. See Figure 12-2 for both the code and the Properties Inspector representation of a file that is two levels above the document holding the link.

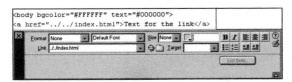

Figure 12-2
Both the Properties Inspector and the code version of a path to a file two levels above the document containing the link.

Relative links are generally used unless there is a reason to use an absolute link. Links that are contained within a site — just like links to the other pages on the same site — are almost always best as relative links. If you do change your directory structure, Dreamweaver will adjust your links for you, saving you a great deal of work and providing perfect accuracy. However, there are cases where absolute links must be used.

Absolute links

Absolute links are a must for any link to another site. For example, if you are linking to Amazon.com, you must use the absolute link http://www.amazon.com.
(See Figure 12-3 for the code and Properties Inspector view of a link to an external
site.) Anything less than the full address will not take your visitor to the site.
Large organizations often insist on absolute links for their Web pages, as well.

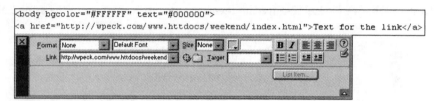

Figure 12-3
*Both the Properties Inspector and the code view display the entire path to
the link.*

It makes no difference in HTML whether we point to our Route page from our
home page as http://yoursitename.com/route.html (absolute) or we point to
our Route page by specifying route.html (relative). The two examples of link codes
below both lead to the same place for a visitor.

The links lead to exactly the same location:

```
Relative Link:
<a href="route.html">Text for the link</a>
Absolute Link:
<a href="http://wpeck.com/www/htdocs/weekend/route.html">Text for
the link</a>
```

**For quick and accurate absolute links, copy the address of the
site you want to link to from the browser address bar, and then
paste the link into the links section of the Properties Inspector
(or directly into your code). More broken links occur from typos
than from any other type of error.**

**20 Min.
To Go**

Named Anchor Links

You do not always want to link outside of the document that you are creating. For pages with long text passages, it is a good idea to give your readers links to individual topics within the page. In other cases, you might want to direct your visitor to a special place on a page to match the link. This is done using a Named Anchor link.

These links are a little different in that you are creating the link and naming it yourself. The name for the link does not appear on the finished screen, and it will only make sense to the page creator. The general concept is to place a note in your code with a name, and then create a link that points to that note by name.

Your site pages are not long enough to show the effect of the named anchor, so I have included a page with text from an article I wrote. You will add several named anchors to this page.

Copy the file namedanchors.html from the Session12 folder on the CD-ROM to the Resources folder in your Weekend site.

1. Open the file namedanchors.html from the Resources folder of your Weekend site. This page is fully formatted, but we want to add links from the menu on the left to the lower sections of the pages.

2. The first step is to create the anchors that we will link to. In Design view, insert your cursor at the beginning of the page headline. Select Insert ⇨ Invisible Tags ⇨ Named Anchor.

3. In the Insert Named Anchor window type **top**. Click OK. An icon will appear beside your headline. (If you do not see an icon, select View ⇨ Visual Aids ⇨ Invisible Elements.) This icon represents your anchor. Click the icon and see the listing in the Properties Inspector, identifying this object as an anchor and displaying the name. You can use the Properties Inspector to edit the name. Figure 12-4 shows the results.

Use lowercase letters for filenames and links whenever possible. For Web use, filenames and folders are often case-sensitive. If you get into the habit of using lowercase letters all the time, you are less likely to create a case error in a link. Lowercase titles also are less work. Why use the Shift key over and over again when it is not necessary?

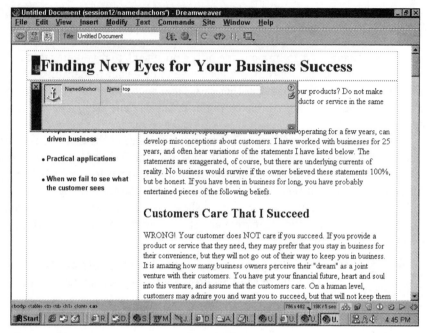

Figure 12-4
The Named Anchor icon is at the beginning of the headline. Note that the
Properties Inspector offers the opportunity to edit the anchor name.

4. Repeat Step 3 to add the following anchors:

   Insert an anchor named **custcare** beside "Customers Care that . . . .".
   Insert an anchor named **customerdriven** beside "Prepare to Be a
   Customer . . . ."
   Insert an anchor named **pracapp** beside "Practical Applications."
   Insert an anchor named **failtosee** beside "When We Fail to See . . . ."

5. Now you will create links to the menu items. Ignore the anchor in the
   headline for a few minutes. In the menu area at the top the screen (in
   the left column), select all the text in the first menu entry ("Common
   errors . . . ."). In the Properties Inspector, locate the Links field. Type
   #custcare. Note that the menu item is now underlined, indicating there
   is a link. When we preview this document, clicking this link will display
   the location in the page of the matching named anchor at the top of our
   screen.

6. Repeat Step 5 for the remaining menu items, matching the menu item to the appropriate anchor.

   We are going to add another handy feature for our readers, and then we will insert links to allow them to move back to the top of the page and the menu without scrolling.

7. Scroll to the second headline ("Prepare to Be . . . ."). We will place a link to the top of the page at the end of the text, just above this headline. Insert your cursor at the end of the last paragraph in the first section and type **Back to Top**. Add a link to the named anchor "top" by adding a link as #top. Right-justify your text.

8. Repeat Step 7 at the end of each section. Dreamweaver will copy the link information along with the text. Of course, this will only work when every link is exactly the same.

9. Preview the document in your browser. Click the links to navigate up and down on the page.

There is a copy of the completed exercise in the Session12 folder on the CD-ROM. The file is named nameanchorcomplete.html.

You can link to a specific place on another page in the same way. Simply create the link to the page you are pointing to, and then add the anchor code at the end of the link. For example, if the page you just created was in the root folder of My Business Site, the link http://wpeck.com/namedanchor.html#customerdriven would lead directly to the section. "Prepare to Be a Customer Driven Business."

**10 Min.
To Go**

Previewing Your Links

By now, you may have noticed that Dreamweaver offers no live action for your links. You must preview the links in your browser to test them and make sure they are taking your visitors where you want them to go.

You do not need to be connected to the Web to preview links between local files. However, to test a link from your site to another site, your Web connection must be active.

Open your Weekend site again and preview how your links are working.

1. Open index.html from the Weekend site.

2. Select File ⇨ Preview in Browser and choose your browser (or press F12 for a preview in your Primary browser).

3. Click all links on all pages. Keep a notebook handy to note which links are not working (you may not have finished creating all the links).

4. Edit any links that are not working and preview again. Repeat until all links are working.

Testing and Editing Links

Dreamweaver can save a lot of editing time for you by identifying links that are broken, or by identifying files with orphan links (no links leading to the files). You can check a single document, selected files, or the entire site. You can also change a link through your entire site.

Dreamweaver does not check your external links to ensure that the sites you are connecting to are still active. There is software available that will do external link-checking. See the file utility.html in the Resources folder on the CD-ROM for links to external link-testing software.

Testing links

There is no excuse for having broken links with Dreamweaver. You have many methods available to you for testing links. To use the following method to test links, you must test your links before uploading, because this operation is performed only on your local files.

Checking links in a single document

This is the fastest way to make sure that all of your links are working before you upload your pages:

1. If it is not already open, open index.html from your Weekend site.

2. Select File ⇨ Check Links. The Link Checker window will open. If there are any broken links, they will show in the white section of this window.

3. Select External Links from the drop-down menu in the Link Checker window. Any external links for this page will appear in the white area. You should have at least two external links: one to Amazon.com. and one to the mail recipient. There will be three external links if you created two mail links.

4. The Orphaned Files option only works when you are checking all links in a site (see below).

Checking links in selected documents

When you want to check links only in selected documents, use the following method:

1. Open your Weekend site if it is not already open.

2. Select the files that you would like to check.

3. Select File ➾ Check Links. Any broken links for the files you selected will show in the window.

4. Select External Links from the drop-down menu in the Link Checker window. Any external links for the selected files will appear in the white area.

Checking links on an entire site

Finally, you can check all the files on a site for broken links:

1. Open your Weekend site if it is not already open.

2. Choose Site ➾ Check Links Sitewide.

3. View broken links and external links as discussed above. With a site-wide check, you can also identify any orphaned files. Orphaned files have not been linked TO from any other page. We have several orphaned pages on our site, since the files in our Resource section are not referred to by any other page.

Changing links across your site

Suppose you link to an external page as a resource from your page, and that link changes, or that you find a better source. If you only require that the actual link be changed, you can make the adjustment across your site with one simple action. We are going to change your Amazon.com link so that it goes directly to the books section on that site.

1. If it is not already, open your Weekend site.
2. Select Site ⇨ Change Link Sitewide. The Change Link Sitewide window will open.
3. In the Change All Links To field, type **http://www.amazon.com**.
4. In the Into Links To field, type **http://www.amazon.com/books/**.
5. Click OK, and a list of the files that contain the link you wish to change will display. Click Update and all the links to Amazon.com on your site will be edited. (We only have one link to Amazon.com on this site.)

You can also select a file that you wish to alter links to, as well. Browse for or enter the name for the file you wish to replace, and browse for or enter the file you wish to replace the file with from the Change Link Sitewide window.

It is always important to pay special attention when you are working with links. Although they are so simple to work with, they do control your entire site. Never treat a link casually; one typo or other error can make your site impossible to navigate.

We will now move on to creating JavaScript rollovers, where links form only a small part of a much more complex operation.

Done!

REVIEW

We have looked at several different aspects of links. While everything in this session is vitally important to the success of your site, there are a few areas that deserve special attention.

- Relative links refer to a location based on the path from the current page to the linked page. They will be updated when changes are made within a Dreamweaver site. Relative links are also more flexible.
- Absolute links are the complete address to a location.
- Named anchor links are used to create a link to a specific place on a page. They can be used with relative or absolute links.

- Links cannot be tested from within the Dreamweaver working environment. You must preview in a browser to see the links in action. To test links outside the current site, you must be connected to the Web.
- You can check for broken links within a Dreamweaver local site.
- You can change a link to another across your entire site.

QUIZ YOURSELF

1. What is the difference between absolute and relative links. (See the "Understanding Relative and Absolute Links" section.)
2. What is the benefit to relative links? (See the "Relative Links" section.)
3. When must you use absolute links? (See the "Absolute Links" section.)
4. What is a Named Anchor? (See the "Named Anchor Links" section.)
5. Which types of links can you test without being connected to the Web? (See the "Previewing Your Links" section.)
6. How can you easily change a link throughout your entire site. (See the "Changing Links Across Your Site" section.)

Generating JavaScript Rollovers

Session Checklist

✔ Introducing JavaScript

✔ Editing JavaScript

✔ Creating a simple JavaScript rollover

✔ Identifying JavaScript actions

✔ Creating a complex rollover

**30 Min.
To Go**

L et me begin by saying that this session is not really about JavaScript, or at least, not about learning how to write JavaScript. Countless great books have been written about JavaScript composition, requiring more than a book or two. In this session, JavaScript is either placed from another source, or created automatically with Dreamweaver tools. I would like to suggest again, though, that the more knowledgeable you are about JavaScript, the more you can achieve when using Dreamweaver's tools.

Introducing JavaScript

Dreamweaver has powerful JavaScript creation tools called *behaviors*. Some JavaScript code is created invisibly, as in rollovers. If you chose not to view the code, you would not even know that JavaScript was written into your page. You can become a little more involved in the JavaScript creation process by using the Behaviors function, a feature that writes the code, but with your direction. Both features are examined in this session.

What is JavaScript?

JavaScript is a Web-based scripting language that has only been around for a little over five years. It has nothing to do with the programming language, Java. Developed to overcome the limitations of HTML, JavaScript has added much of the interactivity on the Web today.

Cross-browser support for JavaScript is very good, and it is a relatively simple language to learn. JavaScript is used on almost every site today, if only for image rollovers, which you will create in this session. JavaScript is used to check for browsers, platforms, resolutions, and so on. It is also used to create the popular drop-down menus, validate information entered in forms, and provide password protection. As a flexible language, JavaScript's uses are endless, and developers continue to invent new ways to use it every day.

For many designers, the tools in Dreamweaver, and free or purchased scripts, satisfy all their JavaScript requirements. Even though you can use JavaScript without knowing the first thing about it, I recommend that you gain at least a working knowledge.

You do not have to write your own scripts. I try to avoid writing my own, partly because I do not consider myself a JavaScript expert, and I am also a careless typist. However, I do read JavaScript very well, and can usually spot a problem fairly quickly. I also know enough to edit scripts, and have written my own scripts when nothing else would do — I do not like to compromise ideas. I recommend achieving at least this level of competence with JavaScript.

In the meantime, you can learn how to work with JavaScript in Dreamweaver.

Editing JavaScript in Dreamweaver

You placed a JavaScript script in Session 11 by simply working in the HTML code. However, you can also edit your placed script from within Dreamweaver, either through the code view of the main document, or by using the Properties Inspector. Go back to our placed script and use the Properties Inspector to remove the words "Last update" from the JavaScript display in your document as well as the `<center>` tag.

To edit a script:

1. Open the document `handcode.html` from the Resources folder in your Weekend site.

2. Select the script icon in your design view. The Properties Inspector indicates that JavaScript is selected.

3. Click the Edit button in the Properties Inspector. The Script Properties window opens.

4. Scroll to the end of the script and locate the following code:

   ```
   document.write("<center>Last update: ");
   ```

   Highlight and delete ("`<center>Last update: `").

5. Locate the following code:

   ```
   document.write("</center>");
   ```

   Highlight and delete ("`</center>`").

6. Close the Script Properties window.

Now, follow these steps to move the script to the top of the page:

1. In design view, insert your cursor in front of the first text entry. Hit Enter twice to make room for the date script.

2. While still in design view, click the JavaScript icon to select it. Confirm that the JavaScript is selected in the Properties Inspector.

3. Click and drag the icon to the top of the page.

4. Preview your page in your browser. See Figure 13-1 for the correct results.

You have placed a JavaScript script, edited it, and moved the script to a different location in your document. Now you are ready to create JavaScript rollovers.

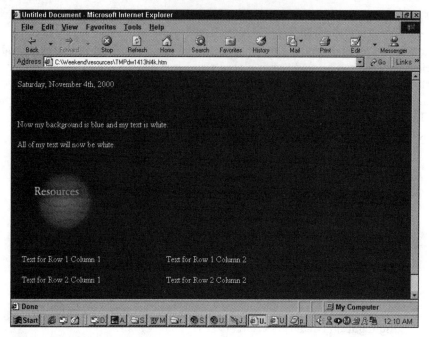

Figure 13-1
Final results for the date code script placement

Creating a Simple JavaScript Rollover

**20 Min.
To Go**

In a simple rollover, one image is replaced with another when the mouse is held over the original image. This has become a universal symbol on the Web for an image that is also a link, with most menus using at least a simple rollover.

Rollovers are easy to create. They add an element of movement to your page, and help your visitors to understand the navigation on your site. You will create a simple rollover, which means that the image changes to another in the same place.

Creating a rollover

To create a rollover, Dreamweaver generates three sections of code, placing JavaScript into the document head, into the <body> tag, and also into the document body where the rollover is to be placed. Check your code before you place the rollover so you can view the change.

Copy the files menu6over.gif, menu6aover.gif, menu6bover.gif, menu6cover.gif, and menu6dover.gif from the Session13 folder on the CD-ROM to the Art folder of your Weekend site.

1. Open the `index.html` file from your Weekend folder. (You are going to replace the image menu items with JavaScript rollovers.)

2. Select the first graphic in the menu. Delete it.

3. Keep your cursor in the same location as it was when you deleted the file in Step 2. Select Insert ⇨ Interactive Images ⇨ Rollover Image and the Insert Rollover Image window opens.

4. Type **route** for the Image Name value.

5. Click the Browse button next to the Original Image field. Select the file menu6a.gif from the Art folder. The image that you specify in this field is seen before the mouse is passed over it.

6. Click the Browse button next to the Rollover Image field. Select the file `menu6aover.gif` from the Art folder.

Never use images of different sizes for rollover images. The original and the rollover image must be the same size. Also, be careful that the elements in your original and rollover graphics line up when preparing rollovers. A 1-pixel difference when positioning the two images can cause an effect that is quite disturbing.

7. Verify that the Preload Rollover Image option is checked. This prompts the browser to load the rollover image into the browser cache when the page is viewed. When the mouse is passed over the rollover image, a pre-loaded image displays instantly.

8. Add the link for this menu item. Click the Browse button next to the When Clicked Go To URL field. Select route.html.

9. Click OK to return to the document.

   The menu item continues to resemble a simple graphic link, even when you roll your mouse over the item. Dreamweaver does not display live JavaScript. To see the results, preview your document in a browser.

10. Preview the document in your primary browser. Move your mouse over the top menu item and the image should change. Preview the document again in your secondary browser to ensure that your rollover is working in both.

11. Repeat Steps 2 to 10 for the other menu items on the page, changing the details for each menu item. The graphics you used to create the menu originally are used again as the original image. The rollover images have the same name as the original with the addition of the word "over." For example, if menu6b.gif is the original then menu6bover.gif is the rollover image.

That's all there is to creating a simple rollover. It is almost as quick and easy as creating a simple graphic menu link, but it does add a lot to your page.

Understanding JavaScript code placement

As mentioned previously, Dreamweaver places code into three sections in the HTML code, beginning with the first section in the document's head area . A small excerpt from the head code is included below. Note that the first few lines are in HTML code. The JavaScript starts with <script language="JavaScript">.

```
<html>
<head>
<title>Untitled Document</title>
<meta http-equiv="Content-Type" content="text/html; charset=
iso-8859-1">
<script language="JavaScript">
<!--
function MM_swapImgRestore() { //v3.0
  var i,x,a=document.MM_sr;
for(i=0;a&&i<a.length&&(x=a[i])&&x.oSrc;i++) x.src=x.oSrc;
}
```

The second section containing JavaScript is the <body> tag. An example of that code is included below. This time, the JavaScript instructions are within an HTML tag, and it is instructing the browser to preload the listed images.

```
<body bgcolor="#FFFFFF" text="#000000"
onLoad="MM_preloadImages('art/menu6aover.gif','art/menu6bover.gif'
,'art/menu6cover.gif','art/menu6dover.gif')">
<table width="500" border="0" cellspacing="0" cellpadding="10"
align="center">
```

Finally, Dreamweaver places code to instruct the browser where to display the JavaScript, and what actions to take. These commands are included in the link tag for each set of images.

```
<p><a href="route.html" onMouseOut="MM_swapImgRestore()"
onMouseOver="MM_swapImage('route','','art/menu6aover.gif',1)"><img
name="route" border="0" src="art/menu6a.gif" width="137"
height="39"></a><br>
```

**10 Min.
To Go**

Creating a Complex JavaScript Rollover

This rollover is becoming increasingly popular, and with good reason. When you roll your mouse over one image, another image in a different location appears. When used properly, a lot of visual information is presented in a small space.

Using the Behaviors palette accomplishes this task. Instructing Dreamweaver to write the code, step by step, is more involved than placing code from another source, or using the menu to create a simple rollover.

This process can be very confusing, but once you get the concept, it is easy. I have designed a very simple menu for simple explanation and construction. The menu items have names to help you track what is happening and grasp the concept. You can view the finished menu in the Session13 folder on the CD-ROM in the file rollover.html. Figure 13-2 shows the original and the rollover for each of the three menu items.

Figure 13-2
The original menu is shown at the top left. Note how the menu item changes color and an image appears when the mouse is passed over it.

Now, you are going to create a document in the Resources folder to build the menu. You will use this menu type for the second site you build. It is best that you work on this menu with nothing else on the page as you learn. Building another for the new site helps reinforce the method.

Locate the Session13/Rollover files folder on the CD-ROM. Copy all files in that folder to the Art directory of your Weekend site.

Preparing to create a complex rollover

This exercise is divided into two parts. First, you prepare the initial menu by placing images, and naming the images you place. This is very important. Once you have prepared the entire menu, you will add the behaviors that run your rollovers.

To prepare your menu for a complex rollover:

1. Create a new document and save it to the Resources folder of the Weekend site as rollover.html.

2. Create a table with three rows and two columns and the following parameters: Cellpadding 10, Cellspacing 0, 350px wide, and Border 0. Merge the three cells in the right column to form one cell. Place your menu titles in the cells in the left column, with your rollover image in the right column.

3. Place the image topmen13.gif in the top row of the left column.

4. Name your images so JavaScript understands which images to change. Click the image you just placed to select it. In the Properties Inspector, type **top** in the Name field (this is not labeled in the Property Inspector window) at the top left of the window. See Figure 13-3.

5. Create a "dummy" or, more precisely, a "null" link, because the behavior must be attached to a link. Type **#** into the Link field in the Properties Inspector.

If you are creating a rollover that links to another page, as you would expect for this menu, you can create the correct link now, or return at a later time to enter the correct link. Because you are just doing an exercise here, you need not worry about creating the links. When you create the menu for the next site you build, you can create complex rollovers with working links.

Name

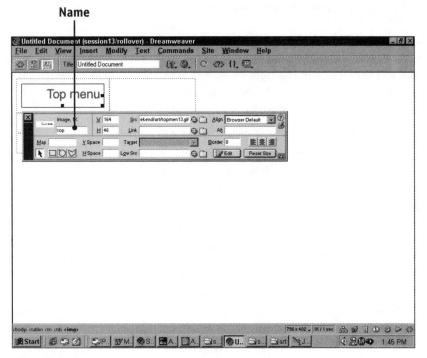

Figure 13-3
Images are named in the Properties Inspector in preparation for attaching Behaviors.

6. Repeat Steps 3, 4, and 5 to place the second and third images. Each is placed in a separate cell in the left column. The second menu image is midmen13.gif and should be named **middle**. The bottom menu image is named botmen13.gif and should be named **bottom**.

7. You also need to place an image in the right column. When menu items are not activated by the mouse, this image is displayed. In this case, place a blank image to hold the place for the rollovers. Place the image menu13blank.gif in the right column and type **blank** in the Name field.

Although the images in this exercise are very close to one another, an image can be placed anywhere on your page. However, ensure that images affected by the mouse action are noticed. If you place them too far from where the visitor is focused, the effect may be lost.

Attaching behaviors to the images

You are now ready to add the JavaScript to this image and create a double rollover. Each of the menu items on the left has two separate rollovers added to them. The image you just placed in the right column is used only to receive the images called with the menu images when the mouse rolls over it.

To add behaviors to our images:

1. Open the Behaviors palette, if it is not already open.

2. Select the top menu image. Now add behaviors to change the menu item image and also place an image where the blank image currently resides. Both actions are included in one behavior.

3. Click the + (add) in the Behaviors palette to add a behavior. Select Swap Image from the menu that appears. The Swap Image window opens.

4. Add a behavior to change your menu item to a different image when the mouse is held over the image. In the Images section of the Swap Image window, the entry image "top" should be highlighted. Remember that "top" was the name of the first menu item. Click the Set Source To "browse" button. Select the file topmen13-over.gif from the listing in the Select Image Source window. Click Select to close this window and accept the file. *Do not click OK in the Swap Image window yet.* You have only completed half of the rollover so far.

5. Complete this behavior by replacing the blank image with the image that should display with the top menu item. In the Images listing of the Swap Image window, select "blank."

 Don't worry — the changes you made to "top" are still there, even though you cannot see them. To confirm, simply click that image name again in the list to view the Set Source To field that contains the instructions you just completed.

6. With "blank" selected, browse for the image menu13_1swap.jpg. Highlight the file and click Select to return to the Swap Image window. Now click OK, because you have done what you needed with that image.

7. Preview your rollover in your browser. When the mouse passes over the top menu item, the words turn to gold, and an image appears to the right. If you are getting that result, you have created the behavior correctly and can move to the next menu items.

8. Repeat Steps 2 through 7 to complete the menu. The middle menu item requires midmen13-over.gif for the swap with "middle," and menu13_swap2.jpg for the swap with "blank." The bottom menu item requires botmen13-over.gif to swap with "bottom," and menu13_swap3.jpg to swap with "blank."

 It is time to check your code again. Your simple document is exploding with code. See if you can trace which section of the code is performing which part of the action. It is all there for you to view, and if you follow it bit by bit, much of it makes sense.

Done!

If you are still a little uncertain about how to do this exercise, I recommend you start again from scratch. This technique may seem confusing until you have a "Eureka! I get it" moment. Once you understand how this menu works, you are well set to create your own, and to apply other behaviors.

REVIEW

You now have the skills to add action to your pages. Because the techniques included in this session are used often, it is important to remember a few vital points:

●   JavaScript provides a great deal of the interactivity on the Web today, through features such as rollovers. It also works behind the scenes collecting and verifying data.

●   You can write or edit JavaScript in any code window in Dreamweaver.

●   Always use images of exactly the same size for rollover states. It is also important that elements on the rollover states are placed in exactly the same place on the image.

●   JavaScript is placed in the head, the <body> tag, and in the body of your document.

●   Complex rollovers can change images that are in different locations from where the mouse initiates the action.

●   Naming images is critical for any JavaScript. It is to your benefit to give each image a name that easily identifies it.

●   Behaviors are attached to links for rollovers.

QUIZ YOURSELF

1. Why is it important to gain a working knowledge of JavaScript? (See the "What is JavaScript" section.)

2. What are the three locations where Dreamweaver places JavaScript code when creating a rollover? (See the "Creating a Simple JavaScript Rollover" section.)

3. What must you do to test a rollover in Dreamweaver? (See the "Creating a Simple JavaScript Rollover" section.)

4. What is a complex rollover? (See the "Creating a Complex JavaScript Rollover" section.)

5. What do you need on your page to prepare for a complex rollover? (See the "Preparing to create a complex rollover" section.)

6. Behaviors are Dreamweaver's way to create JavaScript code. What behavior do you use for complex rollovers? (See the "Attaching behaviors to the images" section.)

Session Checklist

✔ Understanding how forms work

✔ Working with CGI

✔ Building forms in Dreamweaver

✔ Setting form parameters

✔ Activating a CGI Form

**30 Min.
To Go**

We will be building a form in this session. We will look, in a very brief way, at making that form run with CGI. However, you will have to do some work on your own to get this form running. There are too many variables, such as how different hosts handle CGI scripts, as well as variations in the CGI scripts that run forms. I am aiming at introducing you to the concept of how CGI runs forms in the hopes of pointing you in the right direction to learn more.

If you have had to fill in your name and e-mail address on the Web, chances are that you have used a form. If you have had to fill in your address and select choices on a survey form, you have almost certainly used a form powered by CGI.

Forms are used to collect information on the Web. The results are generally returned by e-mail for most small Web sites, and they can often be sent directly to a database for more complex information processing, or for high traffic sites. The form we will create will be a simple contact form, with the results to be returned by e-mail.

You also create easy surveys or polls for your site, which are run by free and low-cost scripts readily available on the Web. If you are ambitious, you can also add message boards and chat rooms to your site in the same way. There is no shortage of applications run by CGI scripts, but the concept can be confusing when you first start. Although we will be referring only to a form for this exercise, the concept is much the same for many other types of CGI applications.

Understanding How Forms Work

Dreamweaver offers very simple and powerful tools to create a form. If you want a text field on your form, a few keystrokes will create it in Dreamweaver. Do you need a radio button, a checkbox, or a button to submit information that is labeled with other than the word Submit? Dreamweaver delivers, and without much more work than placing a simple image in your document.

Do you feel a "but . . . " coming on here? Well, there is one, and it is a big one. Creating the form objects is only half the battle. In fact, for hair-pulling potential, you are not even close to halfway finished when you have designed a perfect form.

The form we create in Dreamweaver is much like the shell of a car. No matter how pretty it is, and no matter how perfect it is, that car is going nowhere with just a frame and body. CGI is like the engine for that car. Without the body and frame, the engine sits like a lump, no matter how powerful or advanced it is. In fact, until extra pieces are added to a car — small, seemingly inconsequential pieces — neither the frame nor the engine can do what it was designed to do.

Working with CGI

Luckily, when you place a CGI script, you will need to do very little to the CGI part. Unlike JavaScript, your form script is not placed into your code. You simply refer your form to an external CGI script.

A form powered by CGI on the Web has been created by HTML elements that enable the form to display on the page. A set of CGI instructions is waiting to take the information that is put into the form and send it to the correct place. Between the two elements are instructions that do not show on the screen as part of the form, but are also not part of the CGI script. These instructions are entered into the HTML code to connect the form and the CGI script.

Perhaps this sounds a bit complicated. It is. But don't be discouraged. As long as you work carefully, there is no reason why placing a simple CGI form is beyond even a beginner's basic ability.

Building Forms in Dreamweaver

There are two parts to building a form in Dreamweaver. The first essential action is to create a form. The second is adding form objects, such as text fields and check-boxes, to your form. All form objects must be inside a form.

I am using FormMail, a free script from Matt's Script Archive (`http://www.worldwidemart.com/scripts/`) as a sample script for this exercise. This is a very simple — yet incredibly versatile — script designed by Matt Wright and offered at no cost. If you use this script, please make sure that you leave the credit in the code. It is all Matt asks in return for using this powerful tool.

Creating the basic form

You should be feeling fairly comfortable with tables by now, so you are going to create your form inside a table. Although it slightly complicates the construction, it is hard to create an attractive form without having a table to help you with the layout.

Let's create a form and add some form objects to it.

1. Create a new document in the root folder of the Weekend site and name it contact.html.

2. For simplicity's sake, add your form before you add anything else to the page. Select Insert ➪ Form. A red border will appear; this border represents the form. You can also confirm that a form has been created by checking the Properties Inspector. If you cannot see red borders, select View ➪ Visual Aids ➪ Invisible Elements.

**20 Min.
To Go**

Connecting the form to a CGI script

A form cannot run on its own. You must provide the route for the form to find the required information (CGI Script) to operate.

1. Tell the form which CGI script will be used to power the form. Click the folder next to the Action field and select the CGI script you want to use. If you are using Matt's FormMail script, locate and select FormMail.pl in the cgi-bin folder.

CGI scripts are always stored in a special folder. The name of this folder is usually cgi-bin, although you will occasionally find the name is cgibin. Your server is the one that sets this folder's name. Whatever name is required for your server is the one you should create on your local site.

Placing a table in a form

A table is used to create an orderly form.

1. Place your cursor inside the form borders. Create a table with two columns and five rows. Specify CellPadding 10, Cell Spacing 0, width 350 pixels, and Border 0. Your page should resemble the one shown in Figure 14-1.

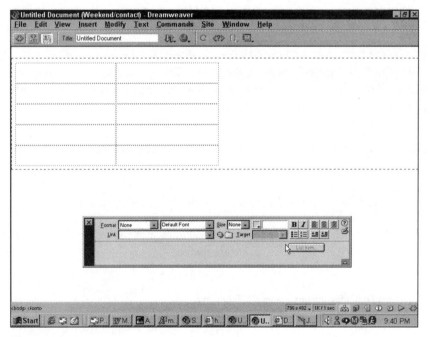

Figure 14-1
Table placed inside a form

2. Place the text that will identify what information is required for each form object first. This is simple text in a table. You will create the form objects in the next exercise. Type **Name** into the first row in the left column. Type **Email** into the second row in the left column. Type **Travel for** into the third, type **Interests** in the fourth, and finally, type **Comments** into the fifth row.

3. Set the left column width to 75 pixels. Merge the two cells in the bottom row. Your form should now resemble the form shown in Figure 14-2.

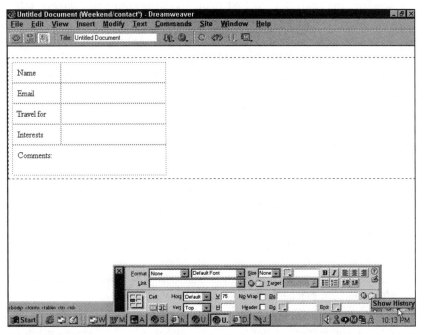

Figure 14-2
Text titles entered into the table within a form

Adding form objects

You are ready to start adding form objects now. We will start with the text field, which is used anytime you want to have a response typed in by the visitor.

Adding a single-line text field

This form object is used for any text entry.

1. Place your cursor into the first row of the right column. Select Insert ⇨ Form Objects ⇨ Text Field. A text box will appear.

2. With the text box still selected, type **name** in the field beneath the title TextField in the Properties Inspector. This identifies the form object for later use.

3. With the text box still selected, specify 30 for the Char Width value. This specifies the width for the text field, and is measured in characters. If you would like to restrict the number of characters allowed for this field, type the value in the Max Char field. Leave the default value of Single Line for Type and the Init Val fields blank.

4. Repeat Steps 8 and 9 to specify the Email text field, using **email** for the TextField name.

Adding a radio button

Radio buttons are used when only one choice will be allowed.

1. In the right column in the Platform row, type **Business**. Select Insert ⇨ Form Objects ⇨ Radio Buttons. Type **Personal**. Insert another radio button.

   Since radio buttons work together, the RadioButton name (as entered in the Properties Inspector) for all buttons in a series must be the same. In this case, we will name the series "travelfor." The entries in the Checked Value field will eventually be the result that is returned in our results if that selection has been checked.

2. Select the Business radio button. Type **travelfor** in the name field to the right of the Properties Manager. Type **business** in the Checked value field. Select Checked as the Initial State.

3. Select the Personal radio button. Type **travelfor** in the name field to the right of the Properties Manager. Type **personal** in the Checked value field. Leave the Initial State as Unchecked.

**10 Min.
To Go**

Adding a checkbox

Checkboxes are used when you want to allow your visitor to select multiple choices.

1. In the right column in the Interests row, select Insert ⇨ Form Objects ⇨ Checkbox. Type **Domestic travel by car**. Holding your Shift key down, press Enter to move the cursor to the next line. Insert another checkbox and type **Domestic air travel**. Press Shift+Enter to insert a break. Insert another checkbox and type **International travel**.

2. Like the radio buttons, we want the CheckBox name to be the same for each checkbox. Type **interests** for the CheckBox value in all three checkboxes.

3. Type the following names into the Checked Value fields: **domcar** for the first, **domair** for the second, and **international** for the third. Leave the initial state as Unchecked for all.

Adding a multiple-line text box

We started with a text box that only required one line. When you would like to offer more room for comments, you can create a multiple-line text box.

1. In the bottom row, place your cursor at the end of the word Comments. Press Shift+Enter to insert a break.

2. Select Insert ⇨ Form Objects ⇨ Text Field. A text box will appear.

3. Type **comments** in the TextField name field, and set the Char Width to 40.

4. Choose Multi line as the Type. Specify 10 in the Num Lines Field. This value specifies the vertical height of the text area that will display.

5. Choose Virtual from the Wrap drop-down box. This setting will allow scrolling if the text entered exceeds the size of the text box.

6. You can specify text that will appear in your form to help guide your visitors. Type **Please leave a comment.** in the Init Value field.

Inserting a form button

You have your form elements in place for your visitors to enter information, but you must provide a way to send the form results to yourself. This is handled with a form button.

To add a button:

1. Place your cursor at the end of the last text box at the bottom of the form. Press Enter to move the cursor down. Select Insert ⇨ Form Objects ⇨ Button. A button will appear.

2. Repeat Step 1 to place a second button. Now we will rename the buttons.

3. Select the first button. Type **Submit Form** in the Label field. The button will change to reflect the new text. All other values will remain the same.

4. Finally, you would like to provide an easy way for your visitors to clear the entries they have made and start over. Select the second button. Type **Reset** for the Button Name. Click Reset Form in the Action field. The label will change to reset.

Always preview forms often in both Internet Explorer and Netscape, since the results in the two browsers rarely match.

You have now constructed a form. See Figure 14-3 to check your results. Now let's move on to creating hidden fields, which are used to organize the results that are returned to you.

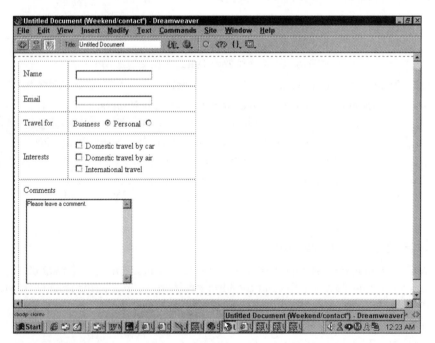

Figure 14-3
The completed form in Dreamweaver

Setting Form Parameters

You connected the form to a CGI script when you started your form. However, when you consider that you edit almost nothing in the actual CGI form script, you will soon realize that something is missing. How is the CGI script going to know what to send for results? It won't unless you provide that information.

Each CGI script will have a set of parameters that it needs to have satisfied for the script to work. In addition, there will be optional fields that you can specify to obtain the information you require. The CGI script will contain every field that is offered as an option (more than you could ever need for one form), but you supply information with your form that tells the script which values to send. This information is specified in hidden fields.

To determine which values you require, and which can be included as an option, look for a help section where you find the script. The help section for Matt's FormMail script, for example, is excellent and provides all the information you need to determine which hidden fields you will deliver the results you require (`http://www.worldwidemart.com/scripts/readme/formmail.shtml`).

Creating hidden form fields

A hidden field is a special HTML tag that enables you to add information to your form that cannot be seen on your pages, but which provides specialized information that can be read by the CGI script. They are quite simple to add once you know the values you require.

Take the following steps to add a hidden field:

1. In the contact.html document, place your cursor at the beginning of the table. Make sure the cursor is inside the form. Select Insert ⇨ Form Object ⇨ Hidden Field. An icon will appear at the top of your form. You will create a hidden field for each piece of information you must pass on to the script.

2. Make sure the hidden field icon is selected. In the Properties Inspector, type **recipient** in the HiddenField name field. This is the one required field for the FormMail script. Type your e-mail address into the Value field.

Although only the recipient file is required for the FormMail script to work, the result of a form with only this field would be a blank e-mail. You still must specify which information you require.

3. Create four more hidden fields following the steps in Step 1. You should now have five hidden field icons.

4. Select the second hidden field icon. Type **Subject** for the name, and type **Travel Interests** for the value. This field will place Travel Interests in the subject line of the e-mail you receive from this form.

5. Select the next hidden field icon. Type **print_config** for the name. This field is the most important field for the quality of our information. When you list your form object names here, the CGI script knows to return the results from these fields. Type **name, email, travelfor, interests, comments** for the Value. These names match the form objects that we created.

6. Select the next icon. Type **redirect** for the name. This field will enable you to direct your visitors to a specific page once they have submitted their form. I usually create a special page for this feature; For this exercise, just return to your front page. Type **../index.html** for the Value.

7. Select the final icon. Type **required** for the name. This field asks that the form not be accepted unless the specified fields have been completed. Type **name, email** for the Value.

You form is complete. This is as far as I can take you in this process, but I urge you to obtain a CGI script and follow the instructions to place the form on the Web. You will probably find it much easier to do your first form using FormMail.pl as the CGI script, because the form that you just built is ready to upload for that script. If you use another script, however, you will have to adjust the name fields to match the names in the CGI script.

Although I cannot give step-by-step directions for placing this form, I will give you some hints and a little more information to smooth your way.

Activating a CGI Form

There are a few things I found very confusing when I was trying to get my first CGI-driven form to work. I have touched on some of the confusion points in the early part of this session, such as the relationship between the form and the CGI script. Once I realized that the CGI was a fully external script, and that my form simply tapped into that external script, things became much more clear. I am so comfortable with the few CGI scripts I use now that it is hard to imagine it seemed hard. Perhaps if I can run through the things that confused me, and how I came to understand them, you will avoid some of the head-scratching time I put in.

Editing the CGI script

The FormMail script requires only one adjustment. You must specify the name of the domain that will be using the FormMail.pl file; in my case, wpeck.com. The entry is near the beginning and is noted with a comment in the script. The entry for my site is @referers = 'wpeck.com';

Although you need an adjusted script for each domain, you can run countless forms once the script is running successfully on that domain by simply specifying this script as the Action for a new form.

To edit FormMail.pl, use a plain text editor such as Notepad. The file will not show in the files listing for a text program. If you specify All Files, or type ***.*** for the filename and press Enter, you can then select the file.

You will need a separate FTP program such wsFTP (PC) or Fetch (Mac). A CGI script must be transferred to the server using an ASCII format, and you must set a parameter known as permissions. Permissions are stated as numbers (755 or 775, for example) and are simply codes. The codes represent different levels of security in the form as to who is allowed to read or write to the file. If you are not writing CGI, this is not something you must understand fully, but you do need to know how to set permissions. Scripts will usually offer information about this subject, and your hosting company should also be able to help. Note, though, that this only applies to the actual script and not to the form. The form document is transferred just like any other file.

That's really it. Give it a try. Although it seems confusing, there is a lot of help available on the Web, and the rewards are well worth it. There are exciting new CGI scripts coming into use every day, and you will find many very useful.

Done!

We have a very plain contact page for the Weekend site. Why not try out your new skills and create a contact page that matches the other pages. You can use the menu items from another page, or you can save one of the others as a template. Your form can then be copied to another page.

REVIEW

- CGI forms have two distinct parts: The form and the CGI script. Dreamweaver helps tie the two parts together, and also has powerful forms creation capability.
- The CGI script is connected to the form through the Action field in the Properties Inspector.
- All form elements must be placed within a form or they will not work.
- Forms are usually placed in tables for better layout. The table must be completely contained within the form.
- All objects in a Checkbox or Radio button group should have identical names.
- Hidden fields are used to communicate with the CGI script to achieve the end results we require.
- CGI scripts require permissions to be set, which is done using a separate FTP program.

QUIZ YOURSELF

1. Forms are made up of two parts. What are they? (See the "Understanding How Forms Work" section.)
2. What is the most common way to control the layout of a form? (See the "Building Forms in Dreamweaver" section.)
3. What is a cgi-bin folder? (See the "Connecting the Form to a CGI Script" section.)
4. What is the difference between a radio button and a checkbox in a form? (See the "Adding Form Objects" section.)
5. What is a hidden field? (See the "Setting Form Parameters" section.)
6. Where do you edit a CGI form? (See the "Editing the CGI Script" section.)
7. Why do you need a separate FTP program to transfer the CGI script to the remote server? (See the "Editing the CGI Script" section.)

Creating Library Items

Session Checklist

✔ Introducing the Assets Manager

✔ Understanding Library items

✔ Creating a new Library item

✔ Inserting a Library item

✔ Creating a Library item from existing items

✔ Editing a Library item

✔ Updating Library items globally

✔ Breaking the Library item links

✔ Deleting or editing a Library item file

**30 Min.
To Go**

S ome of you are going to say that I have held back information from you when you read the rest of this session. Much that we have done could have been done much more easily if I had introduced the Asset panel to you in the beginning. From a purely practical standpoint, you are right. However, you would also be totally in the dark about how the menu system works, and the structure of this program.

The truth is that I have kept many time-savers hidden. Over the next few sessions, as we start to build a second site, I will bring the various panels to you, suggesting where you can use them to save time. I do stand by my belief that you truly learn a program not just by actions, but through the menu system. When you know a program, you can use the time-savers with great knowledge and still know where to find those inevitable features that are not included in a drag-and-drop format.

Now I can bring the Assets panel to the forefront. When used with the Properties Inspector, you can accomplish a good percentage of the actions you require as you build a site.

Introducing the Assets Panel

The Assets panel is new with Dreamweaver 4. When I took my first tour through the program, I first read the listings of new features, and immediately came to attention when the Assets panel was described. I opened the panel for an existing site and began to click through the various types of information contained in that little window. Quite frankly, I was stunned as the implications to these listings started to settle in. This feature does change the way you work with Dreamweaver.

We will take a very short look at the basics of the Assets panel in this session. Library items — the focus for this session — are now stored within the Assets panel. However, I will leave most of our examination and hands-on exercises for the Assets panel to a later session.

 The Assets panel deserves a large amount of time devoted to explaining the features and how to use them in document creation. We do not have the time right now; I must discuss Library items and Templates to prepare for our next site. However, I have devoted an entire session to this feature. See Session 21.

Assets panel basics

The Assets panel gathers the assets for your site into one convenient location. Assets include images, links, external scripts, colors, media — almost any type of information that you place in a Dreamweaver document will be stored in the Assets panel. The assets are gathered from the site cache so that it will automatically track new or deleted files.

Once an asset is in the Assets panel, you have drag-and-drop convenience to add that element to another document in the site. You can also copy an asset to another site. To summarize, you can place almost any type of file from within the Assets panel — one very powerful feature.

Working with the Assets panel

Before moving on to library items and how they work in the Assets panel, I would like you to see how the Assets panel works with an image. You are going to create a throw-away document. (It is not necessary to save this file, since you are using it as a scratch pad just to become slightly familiar with the Assets panel.)

1. Open the Weekend site. Create a blank document. You can do this through the menu without saving the document. Select File ⇨ New if you are in a document screen, or select File ⇨ New Window from the Site window. There is no difference between a document created this way or through the New File method in the Site window.

2. To open the Assets panel, select Window ⇨ Assets. The Assets panel will open, and it may be showing assets in the windows.

3. Make sure that the Site option is checked near the top of the panel. Click the Image icon at the top of the left toolbar. You should now see a listing of all the images we have used in the Weekend site. Click any listing in the lower window to see a preview in the upper window. (See Figure 6-1.)

4. Scroll through the list of images to locate menu6.gif. Click and drag either the lower listing or the preview image for this file to the document window. The image appears at the location of your cursor.

You can place more than simply images using the Assets panel. You can also change the color of text.

1. Type **Testing type color** below the image you placed.

2. Click the Color icon, located just below the Image icon in the left toolbar. Highlight your text. Drag one of the colors listed in the Assets panel over the highlighted text. When you release the mouse button, the text will change to the color you dragged onto it.

Figure 15-1
An image is dragged from the Assets panel to the document. Releasing the mouse button places the image at the cursor point.

Since only the colors you already have in use in the site will be listed, you can guarantee color consistency from one page to the next. The list of click-and-drag operation carries right down the list of assets you have in a document.

I will cover the Assets panel in great depth in Session 21. In the meantime, we have enough to move on to Library items and Templates, the next session.

Understanding Library Items

The Assets discussion has helped introduce the idea of Library items very nicely. Library items are used in a similar way to Assets once they are constructed. You can drag and drop a Library item into your document just as you did in the above exercise.

Library items, however, are much more powerful than most Assets (Library items are assets). First, anything can be a library item — from a snippet of text to a full table. There is no limit to what you can create as a library item. Library items can contain scripts, images, links — anything that you can place on an HTML page.

The secret behind a Library item is that the code you specify is simply stored away in another file in the root directory for your site. When you place the Library item in your document, the document checks the stored file and displays the information — a wonderful time savings for placement alone.

You can only place elements for the body of a document with a Library item.

Editing Library items

20 Min. To Go

Suppose you find a better way to present the information that is stored in a Library item. You can edit the Library item and apply the changes to every document in which you have used the item. As an example, suppose you have your copyright information stored as a library item, and that it has been placed in over 100 documents. You would like to change the date of the copyright to the new year. To do that, you would open the Library item, change the date, and then save the changes. Update across your site, and the next time any of the pages that contain that library item are displayed, the new information will be available.

If you are familiar with SSI (Server Side Includes), you are probably noticing strong similarities. The concepts are exactly the same. The practical use is very similar. The difference is really only in how the two file types are displayed. SSI is more flexible when it comes to editing, because Library items are Dreamweaver-only commands. However, with Library items, there is no need to change filenames (like SSI's .shtml extensions), and Library items will display on the local server or the remote with equal ease.

Using Library items

Library items are also very easy to use. Although it takes a little time to get used to the idea, you are more likely to be confused by thinking they are more difficult than they are. Work through the exercises in this session and trust that they are just as easy as they seem. You will be thinking up new uses for library items very quickly, and you will then wonder how you worked without them.

Working with Library Items

You can build a Library item from scratch, or you can create one from existing information. You will build one of each type. The best way to learn about Library items is to start working with them. The more I talk, the more difficult they will sound, so let's build one.

Creating a Library item from scratch

Although Library items are created within what looks like an HTML page, make sure that you understand that you are creating *pieces* of a page. When we arrive at the edit screen, you will notice that the background for the page is gray. That is the default HTML background. Because you are editing information that will be placed in an existing page, we cannot add code that will fight with the other code on the page, such as the <body> tag. In fact, Library items must be placed only within the body of the document.

Take the following steps to create a Library item from scratch:

1. Open the index.html page of your Weekend site.

2. If your Assets panel is not open, select Window ⇨ Assets or Window ⇨ Library to open. Both routes will open the Assets panel.

3. Click the Library icon in the left toolbox of the Assets panel (last icon). This will open the Library section of the Assets panel, which should be blank.

4. Click the triangle at the upper-right side of the Assets panel to open the Assets Options menu. Select New Library Item. A new listing will appear in the Assets panel window with the name Untitled. Type **copyright** to name your Library item. Your Assets panel should resemble the one shown in Figure 15-2.

5. Click the Edit icon at the lower edge of the Assets panel (see Figure 15-2, shown earlier). A blank HTML page opens. Note that the window Title bar features the following listing: <<Library Item>> (copyright.lbi). This tells you that you are not editing a document, and it states the name (copyright) for this Library item.

6. Type **Copyright 2001 Your Name** (where "your name" is ... you get it). Highlight the text.

Edit

Figure 15-2
A Blank Library item has been named in the Library section of the Assets panel. Note the Edit icon.

7. Practice with the Assets panel to change the text color. Click the Color icon in the Assets panel (the second icon in the toolbox at the left). Click and drag color #993333 over your text and release the mouse button. This color should be in your list if you added the line at the top of the page during an earlier session. If it is not there, choose any dark color. Your text will change color.

8. Apply Center justification (Align Center icon at the upper-right of the Properties Inspector) to center the copyright notice on the page.

9. Select File ⇨ Save. Close the <<Library Item>> window to return to your document. The text you typed in the Library edit screen will now appear at the top of the Assets panel when the Library item is active.

You have now created a Library item that can easily be placed in any document in your Weekend site. Check the Site window and you will see that a new directory has been added. The Library folder, which was automatically created as soon as you added a Library item, contains the file copyright.lbi. Dreamweaver created this file when you created the Library item in this exercise.

Adding a Library item to a document

Now that you have a Library item to work with, you can place it in your document.

1. Your index.html document should still be open. Place your cursor to the right of the layout table and press Shift+Enter to bring the cursor below the table.

2. Make sure the Assets panel is open, and that Library is active in the Assets panel. Click and drag the Copyright Library item to the area below the table in your document. The line of text in our Library item appears in our document, with a yellow background. The background lets us know that it is a library item.

If you would like to view your page without the Library item background, select View ⇨ Visual Aids ⇨ Invisible Items to turn off the Invisible Items display. You can repeat these steps to view the Invisible Items again.

3. Click the text to select, and then check your Properties Inspector. Although the text is selected, the Properties Inspector lists this as a Library Item (see Figure 15-3).

Figure 15-3
Although it appears that text is selected, the Properties Inspector shows no text options, since this is a Library item.

4. Repeat Steps 1 and 2 in every document of the Weekend site to place your copyright notice on every page.

Now that your Library item is placed, you can make changes with one easy step. You will do that in a few minutes. However, I want to pause for a bit and talk about creating a Library item from existing information.

Creating a Library item from existing information

It is probably more common to create a piece of information within a document and then decide that you want that to become a Library item. You might also know you are creating a section of the page that will become a Library item later, but you want to design it within the context of the page. Any item can be used to create a Library item.

Take the following steps to create a Library item from existing information:

1. If it is not already open, open index.html from the Weekend site. You should have two statements under the menu: one is a reference to the Route page, and the other is a reference to Amazon.com.

   If you do not have these statements, type the following below the menu in the left column. (These links were added in Session 9.)

   a. **Please make sure you visit our Route page.** (Highlight the word Route and create a link to route.html.)

   b. **You can buy books at Amazon.com.** (Highlight Amazon.com and create a link to http://www.amazon.com/books/.)

2. Select the text in both statements. Open your Assets panel if it is not open, and click the Library icon to activate the Library function.

3. Click the side menu icon and select New Library Item. Note that the text you have selected appears in the upper window of the Assets panel and a new listing appears in the lower window. Type **notes** to replace the Untitled label.

4. Return to the document and click away from the text to deselect it. Your text now has a yellow background, indicating that it is a Library item. (If you cannot see the yellow, check to make sure that you have the Invisible Elements viewing enabled.)

   Although you created this information within your document, it is now the same as the Library item we created from scratch.

5. Add this Library item to every document, except Contact, in your Weekend site, just as you did with the copyright notice in the last exercise. (See Steps 1 and 2 of "Adding a Library item to a document," earlier in this chapter.)

**10 Min.
To Go**

Editing a Library item

Now that you have a Library item defined — whether you created it from scratch or from existing information — you can make changes in the same way.

To reduce confusion, save and close all documents in Dreamweaver with the exception of index.html. You are going to make changes from here, so it will be apparent to you that even without the document open, Library items can be updated.

Take the following steps to edit a Library item:

1. With index.html active, select Window ⇨ Assets to display the Assets panel. Click the Library icon to activate the Libraries area of the panel.

2. Double-click the Copyright item in the Library items listing to open it.

You can also open your Library items by opening the drop-down options menu and selecting Edit, by clicking the Edit icon at the lower edge of the Assets panel, or by right-clicking (PC) or Command-clicking the listing and choosing Edit. However, double-clicking is usually the fastest.

3. We are going to change the word copyright to a copyright symbol. Select and delete the word "copyright." With your cursor at the beginning of the sentence, select Insert ⇨ Special Characters ⇨ Copyright. A copyright symbol ((c)) will appear.

4. Select File ⇨ Save. An alert window will appear asking if you would like to update the library items in the list of files in the window. Click Update and the Copyright Library Item entries will be updated in all of your documents.

As soon as you click Update, the Update Pages window will appear, and you will see log entries added as Dreamweaver updates that library item in other files. Once the changes are completed, the window remains so you can see a list of the changes that have been made. Read through the listings to make sure that the files that contain the library item are listed.

5. Select Close to close the Update Pages window.

6. Open the other files in your site to confirm that the change has been made.

7. Repeat the above steps to change the color of the text for the Notes Library Item.

8. Close the <<Library>> window.

Although Dreamweaver prompts you to update your Library items with every edit, there are times when you will require a global update. You have that option, as well.

Updating Library items globally

If you choose not to update Library items after an edit or, if for any other reason, you want to update your Library items as a separate action, take the following steps:

1. From any document or the Site window, open the Assets panel and activate the Library items asset.

2. Click the triangle at the upper-right side of the Assets panel and choose Update Site. This will give you the option to update all Library items in the site, or to seek and update specific Library items. You also have the choice to update the entire site. If you want to update only the documents using one Library item throughout your site, choose Files That Use from the left drop-down menu and the Library item you want to update from the right drop-down menu.

That is how easy it is to have one-stop editing power over elements throughout your entire site. A little planning in the beginning can save you hours over the creation of an entire site. You will also gain consistency, because it is hard to remember exactly how you have worded a phrase, or which color you used for a specific note. Library items will be the same across every page, no matter how many changes you may make.

What if you would like to change the text contained in a Library item for just one page. Don't worry; you also have that option.

Breaking a Library item link

Suppose you would like a slightly different version of the Library item on one of your pages. You can break the link and then edit it, without affecting that Library item on any other page. Once the link is broken, however, changes you make to the Library item file will not be reflected where you broke the link.

Take the following steps to break a link:

1. Open the land.html file from your Weekend Site. We are going to break the link to the Notes Library item and edit the text.

2. Click in any of the text of the Library item to select. Click the Detach from Original button in the upper-right corner of the Properties Palette. The link is now broken.

3. Now note the Properties Palette. All the original settings for selected text are shown.

4. Position your cursor after "books" in the second paragraph of the former Library item text. Type **that feature our route**. Your paragraph should now say, "You can buy books that feature our route at Amazon.com."

You do not have to use Library items only for items that will be updated regularly. You can also use it for items that change slightly on every page, such as a text menu. Apply the Library item containing all menu items and then break the link. Remove the text item that represents the current page. Although you cannot do a global update (because the links are broken), you can quickly add a consistent menu to each page.

You now have the means to automatically insert repeating elements throughout your site. You can also share library items with other sites.

Sharing Library items between sites

If you would like to copy a Library item to a different site, Dreamweaver provides the way. Your copyright notice Library item could easily be used on a different site.
Take the following steps to copy a Library item to another site:

1. Open your Assets panel within the Weekend site (any document or the Site window). Activate the Library items asset.

2. Select the Copyright item from the list. Click the triangle at the upper-right side of the Assets panel and select Copy to Site. Choose Weekend2 from the menu that appears.

3. Your copyright notice will now be available in the Weekend2 site Asset panel.

Deleting or editing a Library item file

You can remove a Library item from any document by selecting and deleting it from within the document. However, if you wish to delete the main Library item from your Assets panel, it is a bit more involved. When you delete the Library item from the Assets panel, the library item is removed, but the content from that item remains in the documents. You must delete each entry to remove them. You can also use the content from a deleted Library item to recreate the item.

1. Open any document in the Weekend site.

2. In the Assets panel, click the Copyright Library item. Click the right menu, or right-click (PC) or Command-click (Mac) and choose Delete. Click Yes to deleting the file when you are prompted. The Library item is deleted, but the text remains on the pages.

3. On any document, select the Copyright Library item. Click Recreate in the Properties Inspector. The copyright listing returns to the Asset panel.

4. To edit the name of the Library item in the list, click the listing with two clicks (not a double-click, but two distinct clicks). Change the "c" to a "C" in copyright. Accept when you are prompted to update your files.

Keep your eye open for ways to use Library items for your work. It is often worthwhile to change an element to a Library item even after it has already appeared on many pages. It does not take much to delete the current entry and apply a Library item. The benefit is in future edits, of course.

Next, we will look at templates. They follow the same concepts as Library items, but they deal with entire pages.

Done!

REVIEW

We have just covered the topic of Library items and how much time they can save. To review and confirm what you have learned, there are a few key points that should be highlighted.

- The Assets panel can be used for many functions, such as adding images, changing colors, and using repetitive links.

- Library items can contain only content for the body of the site (that is, between the <body> and </body> tags).

- Library items are similar to SSI, although they will run on local as well as remote sites.

- Library items can be built from scratch or created from existing elements.

- Library items can contain images, text, tables, script information — almost any element that can be included in an HTML document.

- Library items can be edited, and the changes will occur wherever the Library item has been placed.
- You can break the connection to a Library item, but that element will not be updated if you edit the original Library item.
- You can share library items with other Dreamweaver sites.

QUIZ YOURSELF

1. What does the Asset panel contain? (See the "Assets Panel Basics" section.)

2. What is a Library item? (See the "Working with Library Items" section.)

3. What are the two methods that can be used to create a library item? (See the "Working with Library Items" section.)

4. When you edit a Library item and then edit the original file, what will happen to other instances of the Library items in your site? (See the "Updating Library Items Globally" section.)

5. When you break a link to a library item, what is the result? (See the "Breaking a Library Item Link" section.)

6. How do you copy a Library item to another site? (See the "Sharing Library Items Between Sites" section.)

Building Templates

Session Checklist

✔ Understanding Dreamweaver templates to get the most out of them

✔ Creating a new template from an existing document

✔ Creating a document from a template

✔ Editing a template

✔ Apply a template to an existing page

✔ Breaking a template link to a page

✔ Creating a template from scratch

✔ Renaming or deleting a template

**30 Min.
To Go**

In their simplest form, *templates* are patterns for your pages. You can create a template from scratch or — more realistically — you can turn an existing page into a template. The latter is more practical because it is a rare site that is fully planned before any page creation is done. To create a template from scratch, you must know exactly where you are going with your site design.

Dreamweaver templates are wonderful things; unfortunately, they are grossly underused. I believe this is the case because understanding how to create or edit a template is not the hard part, yet is the piece that is most often described. What you really need are clues about where to use templates. I am going to guide you through this process, and show you how to use templates to streamline your work and add consistency to it.

First, you will start by taking a look at what a template is. You also will learn what you can and cannot — and what you should and should not — attempt to accomplish with a template. Understanding templates will help to quell any confusion you may have when you start to work with them.

Understanding Templates

Remember when you created Library items in the last session and you were able to make global changes? Templates work under the same concept, but they control entire pages rather than just page elements. Of course, because they encompass a wider range of elements, there is also more to think about, and a great deal of planning ahead to be done.

You must fully understand what templates can do before you can make the best decisions for using them. The easiest time to decide where templates could be used — especially when you have never used them — is when your site is finished. However, because you build pages on templates, it is a bit late by that time. Try to sort through some of the potential uses and situations before you start to create your first template.

Planning ahead

If there is only one key to efficient use of templates, it is planning ahead. In the next session, you will be doing the planning for a new Web site, and you will see how much planning is required just to set up a site. However, I feel no remorse over making you work through this because the time you invest will be repaid many times over.

I have developed my working methods through experience — much of it bitter. Rushing into a site without adequate planning is just asking to have life become very complicated at a later stage. Skipping the planning stage usually results in undoing much of the original work. That hurts more than doing it right in the first place.

Templates can help simply because they force you to know several things, such as the appearance of your site and what will remain the same on each page. This usually forces you to have your navigation well-established. On the flip side, templates can also help you make changes that would be too time-consuming in the later stages of your site development. How do you find the balance between knowing exactly where you are going so you can set up a template and planning your templates so you can change as much as possible later? Start with knowing what a template can and cannot do.

What can a template do?

The simple explanation is that you can use a template to set up an entire page. Template zealots would have you believe that you can do a complete site redesign simply by changing your template. I'll admit that, technically, this is true. Reality, however, is a little different.

Unless you have a site that truly does not change from one page to the next except for the text that is on each page, the statement is not really true. A site that features 500 stories, each on its own page — and having a consistent menu — would fit into this description very well. The template you would use for a site like this could be very structured.

Most sites require a little more flexibility, which is not what templates are about. Templates are about locked areas. There are two different types of areas on a page created from a template: some areas can be edited at will, while others cannot be changed at all. Therein lies the problem. You want your pages to be consistent, but they often require small changes, such as removing the active page menu item to prevent confusion.

There is another big restriction with template pages: You cannot freely place items into the document head on a page created with a template. The document head area of a template page is automatically set as a non-editable area, with the exception of the page title. Although Dreamweaver will automatically place JavaScript script calls into the document head, CSS files must be manually attached to the template.

Do I seem to be talking you out of using templates? It may seem that way, but I am actually a huge fan of templates, and I strongly recommend that you use them whenever you can. In fact, the more you use templates and library items, the better your sites will be. You just have to know when, where, and how to use them. Next, take a look at some ideas, and then you will be ready to get the how-to rolling.

Strategies for using templates

How can you use the power of templates and still maintain your flexibility? Here are several ways.

- Use editable areas
- Break the link to the template
- Include everything with the template

Using editable areas

The first way that you can keep your flexibility is to be creative with editable and non-editable portions of your page. Menus beg to be included in a template because they usually appear on every page. However, they often change. as did the page in the Weekend site that we created in the early parts of this book. Removing the active page menu item reduces confusion. How can that be part of a template? Make the menu an editable portion of the page with all possible menu items included. On your page, simply delete the menu item you do not want. This strategy can be applied to any element that varies in a minor way from page to page.

Breaking the link to the template

You can break the link to the template on any page. Of course, you will not be able to automatically update that page, but you will still have the general page format as a base. On almost every template-based site, there will be at least one page where the template is too restrictive. Breaking the link to the template restores your full editing ability.

You can also plan your site to intentionally use broken links. If you create every page with a template and then break the link on every page, you will still have consistency. You lose all automatic updating capability, of course, but you have a quick and consistent start to every page.

Include everything with the template

This strategy comes right back to the planning stage. If you are going to require CSS (Cascading Style Sheets), make sure that the CSS references are included as you create your template. If you are going to effectively use templates for complicated sites, you cannot skip the planning stage. In fact, you are probably wise to build a few pages in the normal fashion before creating your templates. Changes happen through a project, but never more than in the first few pages that you put together. Once you have a clear direction, create your templates and quickly move ahead from that point. The time you spend creating the trial pages and well-planned templates will be recovered very quickly on a large site.

Session 22 covers the details involved in controlling text and CSS.

I can hear your fingers tapping on the desk. Time to move on. I agree. Next, you will do some work with templates so that all of the information I have dumped upon you can find a place to rest.

Creating a Template from an Existing Document

Start by creating a template based on the index.html page from the Weekend site, which we created in the first half of this book.

1. Open index.html. You are going to make some changes to this page and then create a new index page, so be sure to save it with a different filename. Save it as index1.html.

2. To prepare for the template, you want to add the Home menu item. That will place all possible menu items on the page. Insert a rollover image using menu6.gif and menu6over.gif from the Art folder.

3. Select File ➪ Save as a Template. The Save as a Template window will open. Type **weektemp** in the Save As field.

4. Open your Assets window and click the Templates icon, which is located just above the Library icon in the left toolbar. You should see the Weektemp listing in the lower portion of the screen shown in Figure 16-1. A preview of the template appears in the upper window.

Figure 16-1
The template listing for Weektemp. Note how the top window provides a preview.

You have just created your first template. However, it is not much use at this point because Dreamweaver creates a new template with the page title as the only editable region. Unless you are planning to create multiple pages that are exactly the same, you have to make some changes.

Take the following steps to create editable regions:

1. Highlight the headline text. Select Modify ⇨ Templates ⇨ New Editable Region. The New Editable Region window will open. Type **headline** to name this region.

2. Click your mouse pointer anywhere in your document to deselect, and then look at the headline region. The text is now surrounded by a box that has the label "headline." When we create a document from this template, the text that is shown here will appear, but it will be fully editable.

3. To help organize your template, add text that will state what is to be presented in this region. Highlight the text again and type **Insert headline here** (see Figure 16-2).

4. You will also need to be able to enter different text in the content region. For this example, delete all the text before you create the editable region. Highlight all text in the center column. Press Delete. With your cursor still in that cell, select Modify ⇨ Templates ⇨ New Editable Region. The New Editable Region window will open. Type **content** to name this region.

5. This time, Dreamweaver provides the text from the name you assign. You can edit this entry to make it more descriptive. Select the text within the curly brackets { } and type **Type the content for the page here**.

6. You can create an editable region for your photos, as well. You can choose to leave the photos in as placeholders or, as you are going to do in this example, you can delete them and enter enough information that a new image can be used. Select and delete the top photo at the right. For this one, right-click (PC) or Command-click the image. Select New Editable Region from the pop-up menu. Type **photo1** into the New Editable Region window.

7. Add specific information to make your template easier to use. Highlight the text within the curly brackets and type **photo size must be 100 px wide**. This will tell you (even months from now) the size of photo that is required for this section.

Insert headline

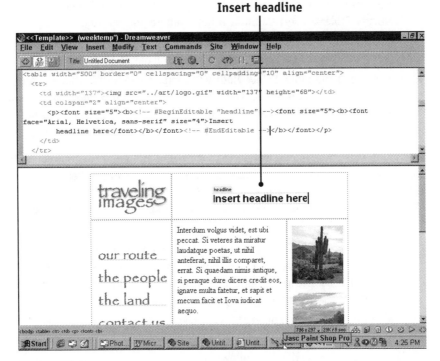

Figure 16-2
The headline region is now an editable region, as shown by the light blue border and label.

> If you wish to see the page without the template code, select
> View ⇨ Visual Aids ⇨ Invisible Elements and the template code
> will disappear. Repeat these steps when you want to redisplay
> the template codes.

**20 Min.
To Go**

The template page is starting to make sense. You have your menus in non-editable Regions, however, and you know that you will to want to edit these. For them to be most useful, you must make sure that all menu items are included on your template page. At the beginning of the last exercise, you added a Home rollover image to the graphic menu. The menu is now ready to be turned into an editable Region.

The text menu at the bottom of the page must be edited, however, for a useful template. You want to have all menu items present in your template, because deleting content is much easier than adding content — and it is much better for consistency. Start with the table and add the "home" link.

1. Insert your cursor in the cell containing the word "route." Select Modify ⇨ Table ⇨ Insert Column. A new column will be added.

2. Type **home** in the new column. Create a link to index.html. Your menu is ready for the template now, but you have to make it an editable region.

3. Select the entire table. Select Modify ⇨ Templates ⇨ New Editable Region. Type the name **text menu** in the New Editable Region window. When you create a page from this menu, you will simply delete one column from the table.

Although you are probably wondering where you are going to stop, you still have a few things to add to your template. Your graphic menu is very important, but the rollovers create an extra challenge. Let's move on.

Take the following steps to create an editable Region from a graphic menu with rollovers.

1. Select the menu graphics. Check your code to ensure that you have selected all the required code for those elements. It is likely that some code will *not* be selected from the Design view. For this example, your code will start with the following:

   ```
   <a href="#" onMouseOut="MM_swapImgRestore()"
   onMouseOver="MM_swapImage . . .
   ```

   Your code will end with the following:

   ```
   . . . src="../art/menu6d.gif" width="137" height="41">
   ```

   Make sure that all of the code is selected in Code view and return to Design view to finish. See Figure 16-3 to see the Region that can be left behind in a selection from the Design view.

2. Create an editable region from this selection. Type **menu** as the editable region title.

The non-editable sections of a page created with a template are shown in the code view with a yellow background behind the code. When you are editing your template, you will not see this because there are no non-editable regions in a template document.

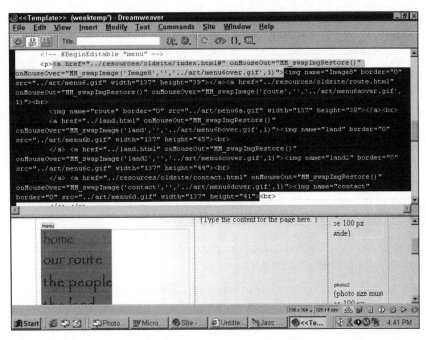

Figure 16-3
When this menu was selected from Design view, the code for the rollover was left behind. See the region highlighted by the light shading for the region that was not selected.

The library items that you have in your template should remain as non-editable regions. You can make changes to library items, and those changes will be passed from the library item to the template. The template will then update the content in any non-editable region so that the changes will appear in any documents based on that template.

You have now completed the content portion of your template. Take a few minutes to review what you have done, and ensure that you understand what is happening in your template document. You will soon be creating a document based on this template, but you first want to add a background and set the default text for the page. Head content is not editable in a template-based page, so any changes must be made in the template.

Add a background to your template:

1. In your Weektest template, select Modify ⇨ Page Properties. Select the file back9.jpg from the Art directory. Select Apply to see the effect, but remain in the Page Properties window.

2. Check to make sure that your Background value is white and that the Text value is black. Make the following changes for link text: Links — dark blue, Visited Links — dark purple, and Active Links — red.

That's it. You have created a template that can server as the base for an entire site. If you are wondering what you have saved (because almost all Regions are editable), read on. The savings will very quickly become obvious. You must remember the times that I said, "Repeat for the remaining pages," to truly understand the benefits.

Work with this template and you will see what I mean.

Creating a Document from a Template

Now that you have a well-planned template, it is time to put it into action. Use this template to create a new document:

1. To keep confusion to a minimum, close all documents in Dreamweaver, leaving just the Site window open and the Weekend site active.

2. Select New ⇨ From Template. The Select Template window will open. Select Weektemp. Click Select to close.

3. A new document has been created with our template features. You should save this right away. Eventually, you will overwrite our index.html document with this file; for safety, save it as indexnew.html.

4. You can quickly create this page by filling in the blanks. Highlight the text in the headline editable region and type **A tour through our North country**.

5. Select the text for photo1 and delete it. Insert the image photo6a.jpg from the Art folder. Repeat for the photo2 region, using photo6b.jpg.

6. To make the menu correct, delete the "home" graphic.

7. Correct the text menu by placing your cursor in the "home" column and selecting Modify ⇨ Table ⇨ Delete Column.

8. Add a title to your page by selecting the Untitled Document entry in the Page Title region of the toolbar and typing a meaningful name for your page.

9. Finally, select the text in the content editable region, and then either type text of your choosing or paste copied text from the original index.html document.

10. Repeat the above exercise with the route.html page, saving the new file as routenew.html. Don't worry that the table in the template is smaller. You will adjust that in your template in the next exercise.

Believe it or not, you have completed two pages. How's that for fast? You may have wondered where the timesavings were going to enter the picture, because most of your page had editable regions. However, you did not have any concerns about your page layout because that was all set.

Now let's see the true power of templates as you make changes to the template.

Editing a Template

I can see two problems with the sample page that I would like to correct. The first is to make the table flexible so that it will grow and shrink with monitor resolution. Second, there should be a caption region under the photographs. Return to the template to make these changes:

1. Open the Assets panel and activate the Template section. Double-click the Weektemp listing to open your template.

2. Place an editable region under each photo for the caption. Name them **caption1** and **caption2**. Highlight the name text and set it to Italic in the Properties Inspector.

3. Select the main table and change the width value from 500 pixels to 90%.

4. Select File ⇨ Save to save the template. The Update Template files window will open, listing the files that are attached to that template, and asking if you would like to update. Click Update.

5. Return to your documents, highlight the caption text, and then type a caption. Save your documents.

Now you have the knowledge to create a new page for each of the pages in the sample site based on the template. You have seen how quickly the pages can be compiled when you are using a template. Go ahead and do that for practice, but leave the contact page. You will handle that page in a slightly different way.

Applying a Template to an Existing Page

I'll be honest here and tell you that you need a fairly special page to use this function. Dreamweaver has to determine where all the content of a page will fit within the editable regions of a page. There is one page that will fit quite well, though. You have not added any design details to the contact page, so you can slide the template into the page easily. You will also break the template link with this page for reasons that will be evident as soon as you add the template.

Start by adding the template to the contact page:

1. Open contact.html.

2. Select Modify ⇨ Templates ⇨ Apply Template to Page. The Select Template window will open. Select Weektemp.

3. You are now presented with a window titled Select Editable Region for Orphaned Content. Dreamweaver is telling you that it found content on the page that you want to add the template to, and it does not know what to do with it. Select the Content listing. This will place all the content from this page into the content editable Region.

The resulting page is relatively complete. However, because this page has a special element and purpose, there are some Regions that are not perfect. You can fix that by breaking the link.

Breaking a Template Link to a Page

10 Min. To Go

When you added the template to the contact page in the previous exercise, the template added all of the design features for the site. This page will now fit nicely with the others. However, you do not need the photos on this page, and could probably do without the library items, as well. To make changes like this without affecting the other pages that are based on this template, break the link and edit your page at will.

To break a link:

1. Make sure the contact.html page is active. Select Modify ⇨ Templates ⇨ Detach from Template. That's all it takes. Your page has not changed, but it is no longer attached to the template.

2. Click the Library item below the menu and delete it.

Although you gain editing freedom with this page by detaching the template, you also lose the ability to edit it from the template because it is no longer linked. If you make changes to your template that you would like to have reflected on this page, you will have to manually enter the changes. It is best to take your pages as far as you can with the template intact before you break the link to avoid duplicated editing.

3. To remove the photos at the right, delete the entire column. With your cursor in the column, select Modify ⇨ Table ⇨ Delete Column.

4. Check to see if you have an extra copyright notice just below the form. If you added this library item to the Contact page in the last session, it would have come to this page with the rest of the content. Of course, the template also has a copyright notice. Delete the one below the form to correct it.

5. To finish this page, delete the "contact" menu item in both the graphic and text menus. Type **Contact Us** in the headline Region.

There is one final Region we should cover with templates. You can also build a template from scratch rather than from an existing page.

Creating a Template from Scratch

If you know exactly what you require, you may also build a template page from scratch. I prefer to work out the design of a page without the encumbrances of working in the template mode. Even when I know content is going into a template format, I build my template page as a regular Dreamweaver page and then create the editable regions. But that is a purely personal preference, and you should try both ways to see which suits your style.

To create a template from scratch:

1. Open the Assets panel from within the Weekend site. Click the Template icon on the left side of the panel.

2. Click the Assets panel side menu symbol, or right-click (PC) or ⌘-click (Mac) in the lower screen of the Assets panel and select New Template. A new listing will appear in the Template list. While the new listing is still selected, type **testtemplate**. The top window identifies this as a blank template.

3. To edit the template, double-click the listing, or click the Edit icon at the lower edge of the Assets panel. Your template document will open, and you can build your template as you would for any other HTML page. You must specify editable Regions as we did in the first template we created.

A template created from scratch can be applied and edited in exactly the same way as a template created from an existing page.

Renaming or Deleting a Template

The final housekeeping you must cover is what to do with a template when you want to change the name or dispose of it completely. Dreamweaver looks after most of the problems that could occur, but you must be careful whenever you are working with files that link to other documents.

Take the following steps to change the name of a template:

1. Open the Assets panel and activate the Templates region. Click twice on the template listing that you wish to change (two distinct clicks, not a double-click), or click the side menu of the Assets panel and choose Rename. The template name will be highlighted.

2. Type **testonly** as the new template name. Dreamweaver will ask if you want to update any files that are linked. Select Update.

Take the following step to delete a template:

1. Open the Assets panel and activate the Templates region. Click twice on the template listing that you wish to change (two distinct clicks, not a double-click), or click the side menu of the Assets panel and choose Delete. Dreamweaver will ask you to confirm that you want to delete this template. Select Yes.

Be cautious with this command because you will have to break the link to the template in any documents that are linked to a deleted template.

Never delete a template file from the Site window. If you want to remove a template, always use the above method. If you delete the file in the Site window, the listing will remain in the Assets panel and will continue to deliver errors. If that happens, create a new file in the Site window to match the template name, and then delete the old one from the Assets panel.

You have just been through a fairly deep tour of templates. You may still decide not to use them in your work, though I encourage you to at least try using a template to give you a consistent starting point for every new page. Even when you immediately break the link to the template, you will still save time and improve your consistency.

Your site should be very consistent now. Make a final check though the pages. If you are satisfied, overwrite the original documents from this site with the equivalent new files.

If you would prefer to keep the original files that you created, use the Site window to drag the original files into the Resources folder. Dreamweaver will keep track of the links for you. Then, simply rename the new files to the old filenames and your site will be complete and easily updated through templates.

Upload the new files to your site and pat yourself on the back. You have covered a lot of territory in a short time, and you have already reached a very high level of knowledge of Dreamweaver's basic features.

In the next session, you will start planning a new site. The new project will put all the skills you have learned to-date into action, while at the same time, you will learn about more of the more complex features Dreamweaver offers.

Done!

REVIEW

I hope that templates are making sense to you now. As long as you have a good grasp of the concept and remember a few important points, you should be well on your way to mastering templates.

- Planning ahead is crucial to success with templates.
- Templates can be created from an existing document.
- Editable regions are the only locations where content can be entered on a page created from a template.
- Selecting View ⇨ Visual Aids ⇨ Invisible Elements will toggle on and off the template codes on a page.
- It is better to set a template up with extra elements to be deleted, rather than adding them on every page. It is easier to delete than to add, especially for maintaining consistency.

- When working on a document from a template, unless the region you want to edit has been set up as an editable region, you must make any changes in the template file and then update. Changes will be applied to every document that was created from that template.

- A template can be added to an existing page, although all content on the existing page can be directed to an editable region of the template. You can specify which region will receive the content.

- A template link can be broken for a page at any time. However, when the document is not linked to the template, changes to the template will no longer automatically update the document.

QUIZ YOURSELF

1. What is the most important thing to do when designing templates? (See the "Planning ahead" section.)

2. What is an editable area in a Dreamweaver template? (See the "Strategies for using templates" section.)

3. Templates can be created with two methods. What are they? (See the "Creating a Template from an Existing Document " and "Creating a Template from Scratch" sections.)

4. Head items are not editable in a template with the exception of one. What can you edit on any template? (See the "Creating a Document from a Template" section.)

5. When you make changes to a template, what happens to any page that was created from that template? (See the "Editing a Template" section.)

6. When you edit your template, what happens to a page with a broken link between the template and the page? (See the "Breaking a Template Link to a Page" section.)

7. Why should you use the Assets panel to rename or delete a template. (See the "Renaming or Deleting a Template" section.)

PART

III

Saturday Afternoon

1. What is the best way to work with code in Dreamweaver?
2. When you are working in code view, what is the result in the document if you press your Enter key three times?
3. Why do you change the default code color in Dreamweaver?
4. What are the two areas of an HTML document where scripts usually have to be placed to work correctly?
5. What is one example of a common link on a Web site that must be an absolute link?
6. When you are working in Design View, how can you tell where a Named Anchor is placed?
7. If you discover that a link you have used in many places on your site has been changed, what is the easiest way to update all the links?
8. How can you edit JavaScript without leaving the design view?
9. What is a simple rollover in Dreamweaver?
10. What must you do to test a rollover in Dreamweaver?
11. When you use the Behaviors panel, what are you adding to the selected item?
12. Why do you use tables to layout a form?
13. How is a CGI script connected to a form?
14. What is the difference between a check box and a radio button form object?
15. What purpose does a hidden field serve in a form in Dreamweaver?

16. How can you identify every color you have used in your site without visiting every page?

17. Two methods exist for creating a Library Item. What are they?'

18. What happens when you have placed many instances of a Library Item, but decide to delete the Library item from the Assets panel?

19. When the content of a page that was created with a template is not located in an editable area, what must you do to make changes to that content?

20. When you wish to delete a template file from the Assets panel, why is it important to do this in the Assets panel?

PART

IV

Saturday
Evening

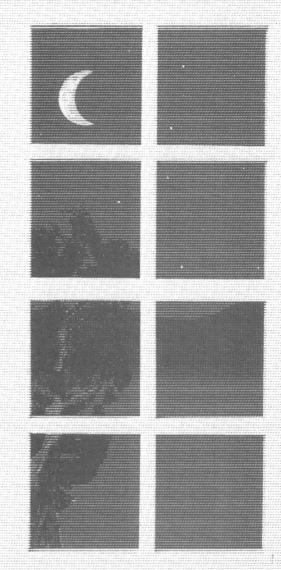

Planning Site Navigation

Session Checklist

✔ Planning site navigation

✔ Manipulating navigation tools in Dreamweaver

✔ Preparing a Navigation Bar

**30 Min.
To Go**

N othing is more important to a site than the navigation. If your visitors cannot find the information they require on your site, the best writing, graphics, or dynamic content in the world will not do the job.

Dreamweaver 4 offers powerful aids to construct navigation elements, and this session covers many of these features. You'll also discover how to create navigation codes automatically with Dreamweaver's tools and then how to create a library item or template to automate their placement on the page.

But first, you should plan how your navigation will work. This is not a navigation or usability book, but I cannot write about creating navigation without first briefly explaining how navigation should be structured.

Finally, in this session, you will get a peek at the Food Info site, the second site you will build for this course. In fact, you will build one small menu that you will use in that site.

Planning Navigation

Establishing a plan for site navigation is both my favorite and least favorite portion of Web design. It is exciting, and it often feels like completing a complicated puzzle. On the other hand, you are making decisions that will be difficult to change later because the graphics involved in creating navigation will be fully integrated into the overall appearance of the site.

To start the process, you must know why your visitors will be coming to your site. The look and features of the site are more dependent on *who* is coming to your site, but the navigation is best designed around *why* they have visited your site.

I will pause here and give a very short overview of the site you will build for your second project. You'll build the site for a fictitious business, called Facts on Food. It is an internet-only business, geared to providing information about food. Prime customers include students, teachers, chefs, writers, and serious hobby chefs. It is primarily an information and research site.

Establishing the why for a site visit

The crucial information you need to learn from this exercise is why visitors will come to the Facts on Food Web site. They will come to find background information about the food they are working with or writing about. This information includes cultural reference, history, common uses for foods, and some recipes. The site also has links to other information and recipe sites.

What's important about the Facts on Food Web site from the visitor's perspective? Fast access to the information is most important. Although a few may care to wander through the site for entertainment, the majority of visits would be with a goal at hand. Visitors will already know what they are looking for when they hit the front page. Keep this in mind when you design the site.

When you have a site that is geared for return visits, which is the only way a site like this can succeed, you must let your visitors get to information almost instantly. This is not the place for artsy, hidden menus. The other important consideration is that this will be a large site. You must provide obvious clues to let visitors know where they are at all times.

Listing navigation areas

You must first determine the logical order and grouping for information. The Facts on Food site will be divided into food areas, because a food area is the most likely starting point for a visit. For example, visitors will likely know whether they are looking for information on a meat or a spice before they arrive. This becomes the major navigation for the site, streamlining visitors into the correct category right away. However, visitors may want to know about both a meat and a dairy product. For this reason, make sure that visitors can get to another major area from any page.

Each food section of the site will have five divisions that will be offered from a secondary page within the major groups. Every page should also offer links with company information and a contact route, because it is impossible to tell where in the process this information may be needed. These topics will invite a visitor to contribute to the site, contact the site owners, or find out more about the company behind the site, which you will make available through another menu on every page. Table 17-1 lists these topics.

Table 17-1
Jump Menu Categories

Categories	Subcategories
* MEAT	History
* VEG PROTEIN	Cultural
* FRUIT/VEG	methods
* GRAINS	recipes
* DAIRY	resources
* SPICES	
CONTACT	
ABOUT US	
CONTRIBUTE	

* *Will have subcategories*

Finally, you want the returning visitor to be able to get anywhere on the site quickly. For this reason, you will provide a *jump* menu (a drop-down menu listing the entire site) and a search function. See Figure 17-1 for an early version of these areas.

Figure 17-1
Early proof for new Food Info site, reflecting the menu setup as described in Table 17-1. The jump menu, as highlighted here, will provide quick navigation for the entire site from any page in the site.

It sounds logical and quite simple once it is all laid out. However, it takes a lot of planning to create an intuitive and useful navigation system. Even for this imaginary site, I mapped out a couple of different structures before I settled on one to use in this session.

Creating a site map

Dreamweaver has a site map creation feature (see Session 3), but unfortunately, that only works once you have your site built. However, it is still a good idea to create a site map before you start on your site.

A *site map* simply lays out the physical structure of your site. You can use a graphics program to do this, or a spreadsheet, even a plain piece of paper with a pencil. The important thing is to create a visual map of the site layout, which can help enormously in spotting errors or missed connections.

I am more comfortable in a graphics program than with pen in hand, so I create my maps on the computer. See Figure 17-2 for a rough site map created in a vector illustration program. This map is the basis for this Session's exercises. I draw your attention to the word *rough* because I do not spend hours making a site map a beautiful piece.

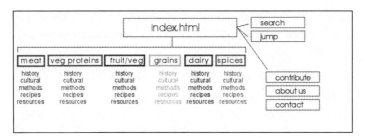

Figure 17-2
Site map created with a vector program, though a pencil and paper will work just as well

You will return to the navigation subject, once you have seen the various tools that Dreamweaver offers to create navigation areas. Most of you probably have at least the seed of an idea for a site. While you work along, watch for the perfect way to present the information you are looking to share with your visitors. You have many choices.

Manipulating Navigation Tools in Dreamweaver

You have already seen Dreamweaver's rollover navigation in Session 13, but much of the work you did on the rollover menus can be further controlled by creating a Navigation Bar. You will build one of the menus for the new site using this feature.

You can also create image maps quickly and easily. *Image maps,* which take a single graphic and make different parts of the image link to different places, were once very popular. Although mouseover navigation has replaced many image maps, the latter still have their place. You will learn about image maps in Session 26.

You will start with a jump menu. Dreamweaver makes creating these unglamorous, but most useful navigation aids, as easy as typing in your content. The method is easy to follow and will get you in shape to tackle the slightly more complicated navigation bars.

Creating jump menus in Dreamweaver

Jump menus do such a great job of offering tons of information in a very small space, that they remain indispensable for any serious information site.

They are also very easy to build. Dreamweaver has automated the process so well, that is it literally a fill in the blanks exercise. You will build one on a new page in our Resources directory of the Weekend site, using the information for the

**20 Min.
To Go**

new site as a practice run. Although you are only working with menus here, you are becoming more familiar with the JavaScript features in Dreamweaver.

To create a jump menu:

1. Create a new document and name it `jump.html` in the Resources directory of the Weekend site.

2. Select Insert ➪ Form Objects ➪ Jump Menu. The Insert Jump Menu window you see in Figure 17-3 will open. Through these steps, you will enter the items from the site map in this jump menu.

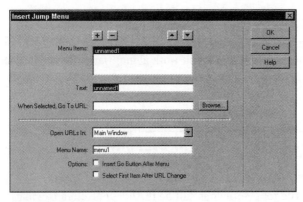

Figure 17-3
Initial Insert Jump Menu display

When the Insert Jump Menu window opens, the Menu Items area contains the item "unnamed1." Note how this same title also appears in the Text field. The Menu Items area reflects the text that is typed in the Text field. If you were to click OK right now, you would have a jump menu with one listing — unnamed1. However, you are going to rename this entry in step three and then add more entries in subsequent steps. As more menu items are added, the list in the Menu Items section will grow. To edit any entry, select it from the Menu Items list and change the text in the Text field. You are now ready to enter the menu items.

3. Make sure that the original text is highlighted, and type **Get around fast** in the Text field. Click in any other field and the new text will replace "unnamed1" in the Menu List.

 This entry is simply a message, not meant to be a link, so you will not add a URL link for this item.

4. Before you add other menu items, you need to set up the values for the menu as a whole. To name the menu, type **quick** in the Menu Name field near the bottom of the screen, replacing **menu1**.

5. You want the line "Get around fast" to appear in the closed jump menu at all times, so Click Select First Item After URL Change. This brings your menu display to the first item you enter every time the menu displays.

6. Now you will add the menu items. Since you will be listing all of your categories and their subcategories, you must consider how the areas can be defined. You will have a list of 39 items. If you type all entries in the same style, a user would never be able to distinguish the items at a glance.

 So, you will use uppercase letters for the main categories, and spaces and bullets to define the subcategories.

 Click the + to add an entry to your menu. "Unnamed1" appears again in both the Menu Items and Text fields.

7. Type **MEAT** in the Text field.

8. To state where the visitor will go by choosing this list item, enter **meat.html** in the When Selected, Go To URL field. Your listings should look exactly like the ones in Figure 17-4.

Meat.html **does not exist yet. However, from working out the details for the site, as explained above, I know what the main category page names will be. At this time, we will only add URLs for the main categories, not the subcategories. We can finish the menu when we have our pages in place and can ensure that the right filenames will be in the menu.**

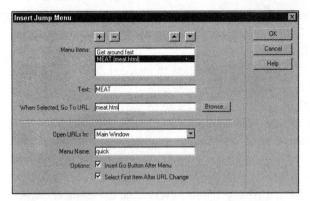

Figure 17-4
Insert Jump Menu window after the first two menu listings have been added.

The next steps create the entries for the Meat submenu items. You want them to be easily identified as sublistings so you will add an indent and a bullet. This is a little more work, but since this menu will appear on every page, it is well worth the investment to help visitors find their way quickly.

To include an indent, add an HTML space ( ). In fact, add two of them, because one space looks like an error, rather than an indent. To add a bullet, the HTML code is • .

1. Click the + again to add another listing. In the Text field, type ** ** two times. Type **•** to insert a bullet, and then type **history.** Your entry should read ** • history**, which will display as shown in Figure 17-5. You will add the URL in Step 3..

2. Repeat the previous step four times. In place of "history," type **cultural, methods, recipes, and resources**, respectively.

3. Referring to Step 6 in the previous list, continue to build your menu by typing the remaining main menu items: **VEG PROTEIN** (vegprot.html), **FRUIT/VEG** (fruitveg.html), **GRAINS** (grains.html), **DAIRY** (dairy.html), **SPICES** (spices.html). Also include their subcategories:

   - history
   - cultural
   - methods
   - recipes
   - resources

4. Finally, add the last three main menu items: **CONTACT** (contact.html), **ABOUT US** (about.html) and **CONTRIBUTE** (contrib.html).

5. When you have entered all your listings, click OK to return to your document.

6. Preview your document in both browsers. Figure 17-5 shows the expanded menu in Internet Explorer.

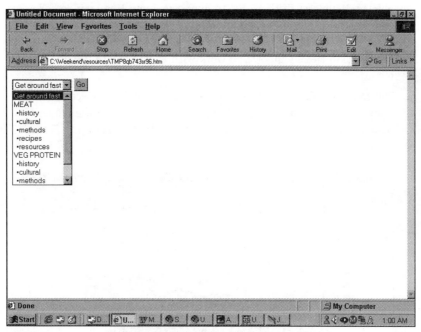

Figure 17-5
The jump menu previewed in a browser, where the HTML formatting of list items appears

The jump menu takes much more time to explain than it does to complete it. Once you have completed a few entries, "tedious" will probably be a more likely comment than "difficult." If you get bored, peek at your code; typing all of it is a lot more tedious.

Before you leave this section, you should learn to edit a jump menu.

Editing a jump menu

If you want to return to your jump menu to change a value or to add a value, follow these steps:

1. In design view, click the jump menu to select it.

2. Select Window ➪ Behaviors to open the Behaviors palette.

3. You will see the words "Jump Menu" at the right side of the Behaviors palette. Double-click this label to open the Jump Menu window. You can edit any entry by selecting and entering new text in the Text field. The Jump Menu window you open from the Behavior panel is identical to the Insert Jump Menu window you work with as you create the original jump menu.

4. You can also edit your entries through the Properties Inspector. Select the jump menu as above, but click the List Values button on the Properties Inspector. Clicking any entry selects it for editing, as shown in Figure 17-6.

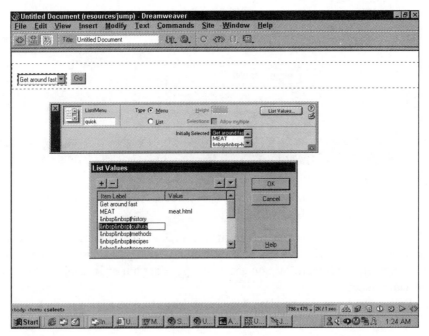

Figure 17-6
Editing jump menu items through the Properties Inspector

Creating a Navigation Bar

10 Min. To Go

Dreamweaver provides a streamlined method for creating graphic menus like the one you create for your first site in this course. You use the Interactive Images menu to place individual rollover images to create the graphic navigation. This section will show you how to use Dreamweaver's Navigation Bar feature, which will allow you to enter all of your rollovers in one spot.

You will also further streamline the menu process by creating a library item from the finished Navigation Bar. The menu you will create with this exercise is perfect for this route because it will not change for most pages on the site. Once again, you will create this menu in a document in the Resources directory of the Weekend site.

You can only place one Navigation Bar on each page in Dreamweaver, even though two or more menus are often on the page. Create a Navigation Bar for the menu that best matches the options offered.

Preparing the graphics for a Navigation Bar

I am not going to cover how to create the actual graphics because that is well outside the scope of this book. I used Photoshop 6 to prepare the graphics for this site and have included the Rollover window from Image Ready to illustrate the three states of the graphics shown in Figure 17-7: Normal, Over, and Down.

Figure 17-7
Rollover window from Adobe ImageReady showing three states of one menu item. You will use these graphics to build a Navigation Bar in Dreamweaver.

I use the rollover creation feature of Adobe Photoshop or Macromedia Fireworks to save my graphics, but I create my rollovers and navigation bars in Dreamweaver for more control and flexibility.

You will create a menu that contains three states. The Normal state is what you see when the menu is not in use. The Over state is what you see when the mouse is placed over the menu item. Finally, rather than removing the active link for this menu, you will use the Down state to create a third graphic that will indicate that the menu is active. In this case, choose the menu item background color to match the page color so that the active link will appear to be part of the page rather than part of the menu. You can use any graphic effect, but the Down state should give a clear indication to visitors that they are on the page represented by the menu item.

When you are building your own Navigation Bar, you will need all graphics prepared ahead of time. For this example, you can find the necessary graphics on the CD-ROM.

Preparing a Navigation Bar

There are several steps to preparing a Navigation Bar in Dreamweaver:

- Inserting the first menu item
- Inserting additional menu items
- Customizing Navigation Bars for each page

These steps are broken down in the following sections. Although the instructions appear to be very long, do not let this discourage you; they are all very logical, and you can complete them quickly.

Inserting the first menu item

With your graphics prepared, you can create a Navigation Bar that can be copied to many pages or placed in a Library item. To build the Navigation Bar, follow these steps:

1. Create a new folder in the Resources folder of the Weekend site. Type **navmen** as the name. You will be creating four pages that will cover all possible views for the Navigation Bar.

In the Session 17 folder on the CD-ROM, copy the Smmen folder to the Resources/Navmen folder on your Weekend site. This folder contains 9 files you will use to create your Navigation Bar.

2. Create a new document, and name it **main.html**.

Eventually, this menu will be placed on another site, so you will be doing no page formatting.

3. From the document you just created, main.html, select Insert ➪ Interactive Images ➪ Navigation Bar. The Insert Navigation Bar window opens.

   This window should look a little familiar from the Jump Menu window you used in the previous exercise. The unnamed1 listing appears in two fields. You will enter the information in the Element Name field, and that text will appear in the Nav Bar Elements listing. For this example, you have three menu items: contribute, about and contact. You have graphics to represent each, but you should use the same names that appear in the graphics to prevent confusion.

4. Type **contribute** in the Element Name field.

   As soon as you leave that field, the name will appear in the Nav Bar Elements list. The lower fields will always be related to the selected item in this list. You must now tell Dreamweaver which graphics to use with this listing.

5. First, specify the Up Image, which will be seen when there is no action on this item. Click the folder next to the Up Image field. Locate the file smmen1.gif in the art/smmen folder.

6. Next, specify the image that will be seen when the mouse passes over this menu item. Click the folder next to the Over Image field. Select smmen1over.gif.

7. Finally, place the image that will be seen when the page that matches the menu item is active. Click the folder next to the Down Image field. Select smmen1down.gif.

 Although you will not use it for this exercise, you have one more option. You can place an Over While Down state image that will display a different graphic when the mouse is passed over the link displaying the down position.

8. To specify the link for this set of images, enter **contribute.html** in the When Clicked, Go to URL field.

9. Activate Preload Images. This command will ask the visitor's browser to load the images into the cache so they will be available when needed.

10. Choose Insert Horizontally for this menu because the menu items are going to be side by side. If you were creating a menu like the one in the Weekend site, which was the first site we created, you would choose Insert Vertically. Uncheck the Use Tables option, as a table layout for this simple menu is unnecessary.

11. Your first menu listing is complete. But **do not** click OK yet. You'll pick up from here in the next exercise.

Inserting additional menu items

Including more menu items is mainly a repeat of inserting the first menu item, but you must first add a new listing.

1. Click the + button to create a new listing.

2. Repeat Steps 4–8 in the previous exercise for each new menu item. This exercise requires the following entries:

   Second menu item
   Name: about
   Files: `smmen2.gif`, `smmen2-over.gif`, `smmen2-down.gif`

   Third menu item
   Name: contact
   Files: `smmen3.gif`, `smmen3-over.gif`, `smmen3-down.gif`

3. When all three menu items have been completed and your window looks like Figure 17-8, click OK to complete.

4. Preview your menu in a browser. None of the links will work yet because you haven't added URLs.

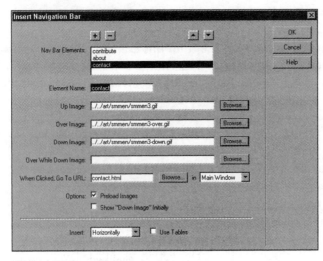

Figure 17-8
The final setup for creating your Navigation Bar

This forms the basis of the Navigation Bar feature's capabilities. Once the links are added, you can place this menu on any page, and the rollovers and links will work. However, the Navigation Bar will look the same on every page, giving the visitor no idea which page is active.

You may have noticed when you previewed the menu that the "down" images are not showing yet.

Because you want to let your visitors know that they are on a page in that menu, you have to do a little adjusting on each page. So, you will create three more pages, one for each of the menu items. On each page, you will set the menu to display the active menu item with a white background.

Customizing Navigation Bars for each page

To make the Navigation Bar display a down image, you must create a slightly different bar for each page. This sounds complicated, but it involves only one checkbox. Follow these steps to customize Navigation Bars for each page:

1. Create a new file in the Resources/Navmen folder, and enter **contribute.html** as the name.

2. Copy the Navigation Bar from `main.html` and paste it into `contribute.html`. Simply select the images in the Navigation Bar, and Dreamweaver will pick up the JavaScript to paste it into your new page.

3. With `contribute.html` active, select Modify ⇨ Navigation Bar. Highlight **contribute** in the Nav Bar Elements field of the Modify Navigation Bar window.

4. Click Show "Down Image" Initially. Click OK. The first menu item, contribute, will now be in brown type on a white background. This is the file `smmen1-down.gif` showing or your Down Image from that menu item.

5. Save this file.

6. Create a new file in the Resources/Navmen folder, and enter **about.html** as the name. Repeat Steps 2–4, substituting `about.html` for `contribute.html` in the steps. Save.

7. Create a new file in the Resources/Navmen folder and enter **contact.html** as the name. Repeat Steps 2-4, substituting `contact.html` for `contribute.html` in the steps. Save.

8. Preview your menu. You should be able to click back and forth among the pages you have created, and the active page menu item should always display with a white background.

So now you have created a text menu, a rollover menu with each image placed separately, a jump menu, and finally, a Navigation Bar. You have a built a strong toolbox of powerful methods to accomplish many different types of navigation. You will use these tools over and over as you design Web sites.

Done!

REVIEW

I am hoping you are now quite comfortable with Dreamweaver's automation. They certainly streamline the work flow and save many hours. You do need to keep a few very important things in mind though.

- The most important factor in creating a navigation system is "why" visitors have come to your site. You must know why they are there to build a navigation system that will serve their needs.

- Creating a site map to illustrate the site structure can save you many hours of work and make your site a more logical place to navigate.

- Jump menus offer navigation to your entire site in one small area. Dreamweaver makes creating a jump menu very fast and easy.

- To edit a jump menu, you must use Dreamweaver's Behaviors palette or edit through the Properties Inspector.

- When creating a Navigation Bar, you must have prepared all the graphics you wish to use. You can use graphics created in an automated slicing feature such as ImageReady or Fireworks to build your Navigation Bar.

- Enter all menu items in the Insert Navigation Bar window, at one time, to build your menu. You can edit the Navigation Bar at a later date by selecting Modify ⇨ Navigation Bar.

- Navigation Bars can be customized for each page.

QUIZ YOURSELF

1. Why is it important to create a site map before you start designing your site? (See "Planning Navigation.")

2. What is a Dreamweaver Jump Menu? (See "Creating jump menus in Dreamweaver.")

3. How can you quickly edit entries in a jump menu once it has been created? (See "Editing a jump menu.")

4. A navigation bar is a handy way to create a menu. There is an important restriction with a Dreamweaver Navigation Bar though. What is it? (See "Creating a Navigation Bar.")

5. What are the four states you can assign to entries on a navigation bar? See "Creating a Navigation Bar.")

6. What is the command to edit your navigation bar? (See "Customizing Navigation Bars for each page.")

Using Automated Site Management Tools

Session Checklist

✔ Checking files in and out

✔ Creating and using design notes

✔ Developing a new site

**30 Min.
To Go**

In this session, you define your second site. However, I will discuss a few new site-management tools before you do.

As Web design becomes much more specialized, it is not at all unusual for two or three people to be working on one project, even for relatively small sites. The graphics may be done by a graphic designer, the database work done by a programmer, and the interface between the Web and the database may be done by yet a third person. One-person firms often team up with other small firms with different skills. If your goal with learning Dreamweaver is professional, you will not go far into your career without working with others.

Fortunately, Dreamweaver provides two powerful tools for working with a group of people: the *check in and out system* and the *Design Notes* feature. In this session, you use Dreamweaver's site-management tools to define your second site, Food Info.

Using Check In and OutThe check in and out system notifies others that you are working on a file, and that it should be left alone. Dreamweaver also makes the files on the local site read-only unless that file has been checked out from the server. Changes are made and the file is uploaded to the server before another team member gets a green light to work on that file. Then the new person must also download the file, ensuring that the newest version is the one to be edited. It is a good system. However, it is not perfect for every site, and it does add a small level of complication. However, I encourage you strongly to learn it well, because the first day you work with another person, the check in and out system will become your most valuable ally.There are several to setting up the check in and out system. Like many of the techniques I have covered, these steps seem to take a lot of space to describe. After you have worked through the process once, though, you will find that it is simple, and mostly guided by common sense.

Preparing to check files in and out

Before you can use the check in and out system you must do some preparation in your site window. Please take a few minutes and make sure that your Weekend site, the one that you created in the first portion of this book, does not have extra files that should be deleted or stored elsewhere. Occasionally, it is a good idea to review your site with an eye toward keeping it meticulously clean. Any files that are not part of the site should be in the Resources folder of your Weekend site. If you have updated all of your original files, you can delete the second copies that you made, or move them into the Resources folder. You should have only five HTML files in your root directory: index.htm, contact.html, land.html, people.html, and route.html.

To enable your site for using the check in and out function, follow these steps:

1. Activate the Weekend site. Select Site ⇨ Define Sites from the main menu.
2. Make sure that Weekend is selected and click Edit. This will open the Site Definition for Weekend window.
3. Select Remote Info from the Category list at the left of the window.
4. Select Enable File Check In and Out near the bottom of the window. Several new fields will appear.
5. Type in your name and e-mail address in the Check Out Name and Email Address fields. Make sure that Check Out Files When Opening is checked. See Figure 18-1 for the correct settings.

If you will be using files from different computers, assign different names for yourself on each computer, such as Wendy (office)
and Wendy (portable). You will be able to tell which computer
holds the latest version if you neglect to check the file in.

6. Click OK and then Done to complete.

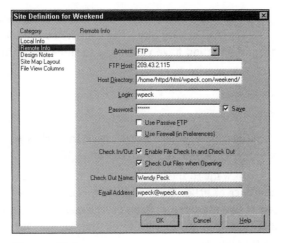

Figure 18-1
*Site definition settings for a site that has check in and out
capabilities enabled*

**20 Min.
To Go**

You are now ready to use the check in and out system with this site.
Dreamweaver uses your name and e-mail address to provide tracking and convenience for the people working on the site. When you check out a file, others can
tell who has the file based on information that is read from the entry you made.
They can also send an e-mail instantly to the address you specified in the site-
definition process.

Checking files in and out

Now that the site is enabled, you can start to use the check in and out system. If
you always work from one computer and never collaborate with another developer
on a site, you don't need to use this feature. Synchronizing your site will give you
the same results with less interference.

See Session 10 for a discussion of synchronization.

To use the check in and out feature, you should first upload the files that have been changed, either by dragging your files to the remote site from the local site, or by synchronizing your site (see Session 10).

Never check out a file when you do not know the status of your remote files. The act of checking out a file overwrites the local file. It is important that you have your most recent files on the remote site.

Start by checking out a file:

1. Connect to your server if you are not already connected.

2. Highlight index.html on the local site. Select Site ⇨ Check In *or* click on the Check Out File(s) icon in the toolbar as shown in Figure 18-2.

   You will be asked whether you want to include dependent files. If you will be working on the graphics or other dependent files, such as Library items, you should say Yes. If you are only working on the main document and have the dependent files are already in your local site, you can say No. This is obviously a faster choice.

Check Out File(s)

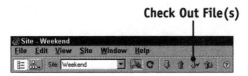

Figure 18-2
Check Out File(s) icon in the toolbar.

3. Your index.html file now has a green check mark in front of it on both the local and remote sites. If you hold your mouse over the entry, your name will be displayed in the status bar near the bottom of your screen. This is how others will know who is working on the file. You can open and edit your file normally. For this exercise, simply open your file and add a space or a line so that you have a change to save, and save your file.

When a file is checked out, someone else can still remove it. The check out process notifies others to leave the file until you return it, but nothing prevents another person from Getting or Putting a file (see Session 26). This is a tool for convenience of cooperative team members.

4. When you have completed your edits, Click the Check In icon, located right next to the Check Out File(s) icon. Again, you will be asked if you would like to include dependent files. Generally, the response should be the same as when you checked out the files.

Your file will be returned to the remote site and a lock icon appears beside that file on the local site as shown in Figure 18-3. This signifies that the file is now a read-only file. To save changes on the file, you have to check out the file again. This prevents you from making changes to the file that are not reflected in the remote site.

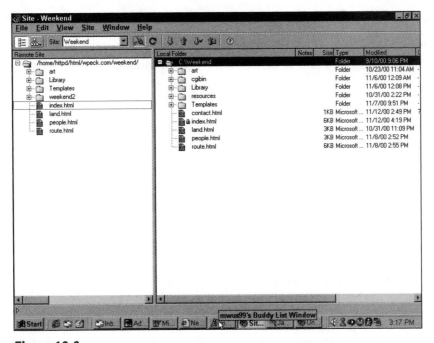

Figure 18-3
Note the lock icon beside the index.html file in the Local Site. This indicates that the file is now read-only.

Although you can turn off the read-only status by choosing File ⇨ Read Only, it is best to leave it intact. The automatic system provides confidence that you can upload your files. If you take a shortcut around any of the features, you risk forgetting one little detail. In fact, the confidence that comes from using the automatic system can bring your guard down and *cause* errors if you do not follow the proper procedures. If you use this feature, use it fully.

5. Double-click your index.html file again. Before the file opens, you will be asked if you wish to include dependent files. This is because Dreamweaver automatically checks out the file as soon as you open it. Say No and note that the index.html files on both the local and remote sites now indicate that the file is checked out.

That is all there is to protect files from being overwritten. However, if you always work alone from the same computer, synchronizing your site will give you the same results with less interference.

 This is the last time in the book that the check in and out feature will be implemented. If you wish to continue using this feature, you will find the instructions for the rest of the sessions will still be correct, with few exceptions.

Canceling file check in and out

To stop using the file check in and out system, you simply cancel it in the Site Definition window.

1. With the Weekend site active in your Site window, select Site ⇨ Define Sites.

2. Make sure that the Weekend site is selected in the Define Sites window, and click Edit.

3. Choose Remote Info from the Category list. Click on Enable File Check In and Out to deselect.

4. Click OK and then Done to save your changes.

**10 Min.
To Go**

That's it, you no longer have the file check in and out system working. You can repeat this process at any time to turn it back on.

Even if you do not need to check your files in and out, you may find that the ability to add design notes to your files is valuable. Dreamweaver provides the opportunity to write a note to yourself or to others. These notes will not appear on the published page, but can be accessed from within Dreamweaver.

Creating and Understanding Design Notes

The second powerful tool for teamwork is Dreamweaver's design note capability. However, this feature can be just as valuable when you are working on a site alone. Perhaps the best way to think of design notes is as Post-It notes for your documents. This is another feature that can seem mysterious and complicated until you have completed one. Any designer who is concerned with details should be using design notes regularly. When two people are working on the same file, design notes can be indispensable.

Dreamweaver 4 lets you enter design notes when you are in the document screen, which makes it quick to use. You can make notes about what is left to be done, and delete the references as you complete the task. Most Web pages are a series of many small tasks, and it is easy to forget a few little details. It is much faster to make four small changes and then upload them, than it is to make four changes, four times and upload four times. Design notes can help you organize your own work.

For group work, design notes are indispensable. The ability to draw a partner's attention to a problem or to request that a feature be added right on the actual page saves a great deal of e-mail, and improves communication dramatically.

Understanding Design Notes

First, Design Notes have nothing to do with your document. That is probably the most important thing to remember. They will not show up on your site, even if you choose to have them uploaded with the document. They lurk completely in the background unless you call for them from within Dreamweaver.

Dreamweaver has two levels of Design Notes. You can create a note for the entire document, which can include information about text, images, and so on. You can also create notes for individual images, which can significantly reduce communication breakdown. It is hard to make changes to the wrong image when a note is attached to that image.

Design Notes can save a great deal of time and confusion, and are extremely easy to use. Files with notes display an icon in the Site window. Notes are stored on your site in a folder named _notes in the same directory as the file with the Design Note.

The files for Design Notes will not show up in your Site window. They are accessible, however, through the file system on your computer.

Enabling Design Notes on your site

The first step in creating Design Notes is to enable your site. You only need to do this once, unless you wish to turn the capability off.

To enable your site for Design Notes, follow these steps:

1. With the Weekend site active in your Site window, select Site ⇨ Define Sites.
2. Make sure that the Weekend site is highlighted in the Define Sites window and click Edit.
3. Choose Design Notes from the Category list and the Design Note options will be presented.
4. Click on Maintain Design Notes to activate this site.
5. If you wish to share your notes with others who are working on your site, activate Upload Design Notes for Sharing. This setting will automatically upload any notes attached to a document when the document is uploaded.
6. Click OK and Done to save your changes.

If the Design Notes feature is not activated for a site, that option will be grayed out in the menu.

Your site is now ready to include Design Notes that you prepare. Dreamweaver only adds Design Notes to a document at your request.

Creating document Design Notes

Now that the site is ready to create design notes, you will first add one to a document:

1. Open index.html. Select File ⇨ Design Notes to activate the Design Notes window. The first window of the Design Notes window is where you will enter most information.
2. Select Revision 3 from the drop-down box.
3. Click on the calendar icon to add the date.
4. Type the following note or text of your own choice:
   Based on weektemp template
   To do:
   Change images ASAP
   Add counter

5. If you wish to have the Design Notes screen presented every time you open your document, activate Show When File Is Opened. This is not really necessary, though, because you can open it at any time. Click OK to return to your document.

Creating object-based Design Notes

The previous exercise created Design Notes that apply to the entire document. To create a Design Note for a single object — in this case, an image — the method is the same, but you start in a different way.

1. To create an image specific Design Note, right-click (PC) or Command+click (Mac) on an image. Select Design Notes from the pop-up menu.

2. In the top left of the Design Notes window, note that the image name and path is stated. This is the only indication that the Design Note is attached to an image rather than a file, as shown in Figure 18-4.

3. To enter Design Notes, follow Steps 2 through 5 of the previous exercise.

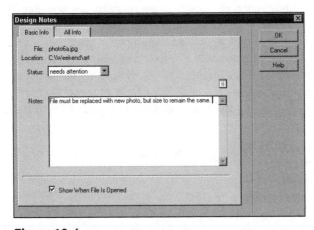

Figure 18-4
The filename and path is the only indication that this Design Note is attached to an image and not to the document.

Viewing and editing your Design Notes

The design notes only become valuable when you can access your past notes and add new information. To view and edit Design Notes, follow these steps:

1. To view and edit document Design Notes, select File ⇨ Design Notes. You can read the information or add new notes in the same way as you did when you created the Design Notes.

2. To view and edit image-based Design Notes, right-click (PC) or Command+click (Mac) on the image with a Design Note attached. Read the information or edit as you wish.

3. Click the All Info tab at the top of the window.

    This window has two roles. First, it tracks all notes that have been entered. You can also use this window to enter notes. To enter a new note from the All Info window, click the + and type **Author** in the Name field. Type your name in the Value field and the entry will show in the upper window.

4. To remove any entry in the All Info screen, highlight the entry and click – (minus sign). Your entry will be deleted.

Because this is such a simple concept, I will not use space to lead you step-by-step through more Design Notes. However, watch for opportunities to use a note. Perhaps there will be a technique that you would like to put in your own words, or a tip or caution from this book that you would like to add to your documents as you work. Design Notes do not take up much space and are completely out of your way unless you are using them. Using them is a good habit for beginner and expert alike.

You can now move on to creating the new site. You can choose to activate check in and out or Design Notes in the site.

Creating the Second Site

You are ready to leave Weekend behind and move on to the new and more complex site. The course was designed in this way so that the site design would not be held back by the basic techniques that you have concentrated on to this point.

From this point on, you are moving into the more advanced and more exciting elements of Web design. Before you leave the basics, though, remember that the techniques that you have covered are the techniques that you will use for most of your design work. With the exception of Cascading Style Sheets (CSS), which I use for every site, at the very least for text control, most of my professional work is done with the methods you have covered to this point.

CSS are discussed in Session 23.

By completing two sites, you will also complete the basics twice. It is a lot easier to remember a technique the second time it is used, because you already saw the results the first time it was used. My goal with this course is to give you a solid grounding in the techniques that you will use every time you create a site, and enough information on the more advanced topics to steer your future development.

With that said, just carry on and set up a new site.

The instructions for setting up this site are deliberately more vague than they were when you created the Weekend site, since you have already worked through the steps once. If you stumble, review Sessions 2, 3, and 5 for more detailed instructions.

The site that you create now will contain the Food Information site that you prepared menus for in Session 17. You must first create a new folder to serve as your root folder by following these steps:

1. Create a folder on your hard drive and name it **foodinfo**.
2. Open Dreamweaver and define a new site. Name it **Food Info**.
3. Specify the foodinfo folder that you created in Step 1 as the root folder for the Food Info site.
4. Set up your FTP information for the Food Info site. In most cases, this will be the same as your settings for the Weekend site.
5. Create a new folder for the Food Info site. Name it **art**.
6. Decide whether you wish to have Design Notes or check in and out capability for this site. If you wish to add either one, do so now. (I will not refer to either function).

Done!

That is as far as you must take this process for now. However, you will be working with the site in every session from now on, and will be adding folders in addition to the ones that Dreamweaver creates automatically. You will need this base for every site, though.

REVIEW

This session looked at two interesting site-management tools: check in an out and Design Notes. You should remember the following from this session:

- When you are working with other Web developers, Dreamweaver's powerful site-management tools can help prevent time-wasting file overwriting and miscommunication.

- You may be working alone, but on different computers. In this case, the check in and out feature can save you a great deal of confusion and time. Simply define your sites with different user names, and you will be able to tell at a glance which computer contains the most recent copy of any file.

- Files that are checked out from the remote site will have a green check mark in front of the filename.

- Files on the local site that have been checked back into the remote site will become read-only files until they are checked out from the remote site.

- It is vitally important not to work around any of the safety features in the check in and out system once you start to use it.

- You can add notes to any file or image in Dreamweaver using Design Notes.

- You can turn either Design Notes or the check in and out off and on at any time during the creation or maintenance of your site. The best idea, however, is to use it from the start.

- Creating a new site starts with the creation of the root folder. The root folder and FTP information are the only required pieces of information required to define a site. In fact, you do not need to define the FTP information, but you cannot upload to the Web without.

QUIZ YOURSELF

1. Where do you initially enable a site for using the check in and out feature? (See the "Preparing to check files in and out" section.)

2. How can you tell that a file is checked out of a Dreamweaver site? (See the "Checking files in and out" section.)

3. Where do you initially enable a site for design notes? (See the "Enabling Design Notes on your site" section)

4. You can create two types of design notes. What are they? (See the "Creating and Understanding Design Notes" section.)

5. How do you view design notes? (See "Viewing and Editing Your Design Notes.")

Creating a Template for the Working Site

Session Checklist

✔ Organizing with templates

✔ Building tables for your template

✔ Completing and troubleshooting your template

**30 Min.
To Go**

S ession 16 introduced you to templates. You created a template from the
Weekend site, but you had already been working with that site for a while.
Your template work was done with the site almost complete, so you did not
see all the benefits, or all the problems that can come from designing a site with
templates. This time you are inviting templates and Library items in from the
start. You will create your templates as soon as you have the basic structure for
the Food Info site, and you will build subsequent pages with your templates.

**You should return to Session 17 and mark Figure 17-2. This is
the site map for the Food Info site you are building, and it helps
to have it within easy reach as you work through the initial
stages of this site.**

You are about to build a fairly complex site. It will have two main menus, as
well as interior menus. You will create several templates because each level of the
site requires a slightly different look. By the end of this project, you will be comfortable with templates and have many ideas for working with them.

Creating Site Templates

Before you create your first template, you must know what the Food Info site is going to look like. You will use a few templates to build this entire site, so you must make sure that you have the basics in place. You can, and will, make changes, but as flexible as templates may be, you must have a basic plan. For this site, you will build the first page and then create your template.

I usually do initial design in a graphics program. I then move the graphics into Dreamweaver to create my HTML pages. However, the transition is not always smooth, and I have learned to make a test page before I carry on with my final HTML page, the one that will create my template. When you make many changes, snippets of code can be left behind. This page will be repeated many times and it is a good idea to work from a clean page.

Figure 19-1 shows what you will be building in this session. Don't worry if it looks a little complex right now. Later in this session, under the "Building Your Tables with Template" section, you'll find a breakdown of the table structure, and you will work through the exercises step-by-step.

When planning your template, it is wise to establish first what will not change for any page that you create with the template. In this case, you will be changing little of the top portion of the page. The logo will stay the same. The three decorative lines below the logo will remain the same. The drop-down menu and the search feature do not change. Nor does the basic setup of the lower portion of the page. Most of what you see in Figure 19-1 can be placed into locked areas on the template.

However, a few important areas will change. The message at the top right will be changed on all interior pages to reflect page names. You will also change the background color of that area to help visitors identify where they are in the site.

The menus will also change. The main menu, with the food categories will be put together with a navigation bar, so it must remain editable. Remember that you must change the down state on each page.

The small menu, containing contribute, about us, and contact menu items will stay the same for all but the three pages reflected by the menu items. You could leave this menu locked in the template, and then just break the template for those three pages. However, it's not always wise to detach a template because it is too easy to make changes and forget that the pages that have been detached. It's preferable to set this menu as a Library item, and break only the Library link to change the menu. With those decisions made, you can build your template.

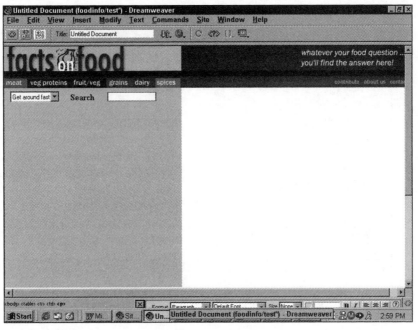

Figure 19-1
The competed basic entry page for the Food Info site

Build Tables for Your Template

You have a site map, but you must put together the page that will form your main page; The table breakdown in Figure 19-2 will help with this process. The top table is the page as it will be when complete. Because it is hard to see the table structure with all the backgrounds, there is another version of it without background colors and with table heights at default values. The lower sample displays the second table with a gray background and black borders for clarity.

Don't panic. I will step you through building the tables in the following instructions. However, I do want you to study the image to see if you can come to the instructions with a good understanding of what you will be doing rather than following them blindly. Creating tables that will work well for layout is the most important aspect of Web design.

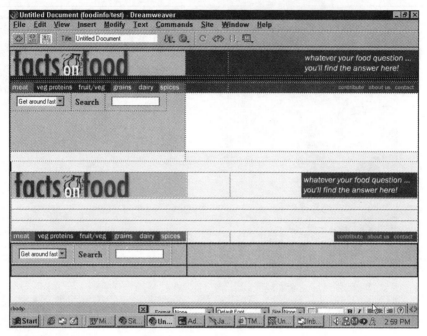

Figure 19-2
The table structure for the Food Info site

You start by creating a document for testing. You may stumble a little as you build these tables. After you have created the tables once, you can build them again — quickly and cleanly. It may seem like duplicating work, but I still do that in my design work. You will spend a lot less time whipping together a clean table than you will searching through code on 17 pages to clean up the snippet of code that caused problems, but did not show up until final testing.

Copy the following files from the Session 19 folder on the CD-ROM to the Art folder of your Food Info site: answer.gif, droptemp.gif, logo.gif, searchtemp.gif, and spacer.gif. Copy the following folders to the Art folder as well: smallmen and mainmen.

**20 Min.
To Go**

Creating the test page tables

You are now ready to create a template from scratch.

1. With the Food Info site active, create a new document and name it
   test.html.

2. In the Page Properties window, change your margins to 0. Remember that you will have to set all margin fields to 0 to make both Netscape Navigator and Internet Explorer understand the command.

3. Create a table with five rows and three columns. Cell spacing and padding should be set to 0. The width is 100% and the border is 0, but see note below.

You may wish to set your border to 1 as you build your table, because it makes it much easier to see what you are doing.

4. With your table selected, press your right arrow key to bring the cursor behind the table, but on the same line. Use Shift+Enter to move the cursor below the table. Do not worry if the cursor is too far down. You will be adjusting the code on this later in this session.

5. Insert another table with two rows and three columns. Cell spacing and padding should be set to 0. The width is 100%. Set the borders to 0 or to 1 if you would like to work with them turned on. Figure 19-3 shows what your page should look like.

6. Merge the three cells of the second row into one cell. Repeat for the third and fourth rows. These will be the decorative stripe cells.

7. Apply the background colors to the first table as follows. All colors extend across the entire row.

   Row 1: #990000 (Deep Red)

   Row 2: #000066 (Dark Blue)

   Row 3: #000000 (Black)

   Row 4: #990000 (Deep Red)

   Row 5: #663300 (Brown)

8. Apply cell background to the first cell in the first row of the second table. Use color #FFCC66 (Gold).

The first row of cells in the second table will hold all the content. The design has a gold background over 344 pixels at the left. The second row is simply to hold the control elements for this table. You will add those pieces later in this session.

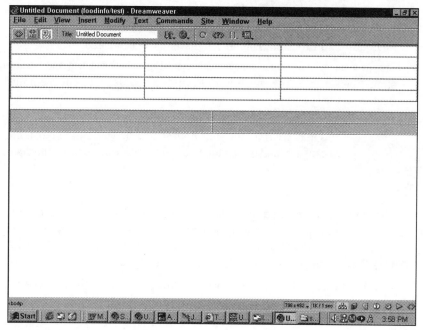

Figure 19-3
Two tables placed, with borders set to 1 for easier viewing. The background of the second table is set to gray to make it easy to separate them for this sample. Your tables should have no backgrounds.

That is the basic setup of the tables. Now you can place some graphics.

Adding content to your tables

Your basic tables are in place. The shape of the page will come from the graphic placement. Next, I briefly explain several new concepts that you will be using.

Table cells have a habit of not following a simple cell width statement. If the browsers would accept that cell width was absolute, your design would be much easier. However, when it comes to tables, you must assume that a browser will only use your table setup as a guide.

Some designers insist on controlling everything on the page, and still others say that because HTML is not an exact language, you should design with total flexibility. Some of us come down firmly — exactly in the middle. Many people, like me, have tried to find the best of both worlds and have spent a lot of time experimenting with techniques for liquid design.

The design that you will be working on is fully liquid, which means that it will display at low resolutions without a horizontal scroll (barely — many low-resolution monitors will see a tiny scroll), yet will stretch to fill the screen for high-resolution monitors. Yet, the left side of the page is static, providing some control over the appearance.

A valuable tool for accomplishing this is to use invisible placeholder graphics. All browsers respect a graphic and will not collapse a table cell that contains a graphic, even if the graphic is just a spacer. Browsers will collapse a cell containing text, though, so we often use a spacer to guarantee that important places on the page remain constant. You will use spacer graphics in this design.

You also use a combination of fixed widths and percentages for our table widths. In this case, the left columns are fixed, and you will allow the right column to expand and contract with browser resolution.

Keep this topic in mind as you put this table together and watch what each addition does to the table. Make sure that you have the files copied from the CD-ROM as noted earlier, and get ready to start adding content.

**10 Min.
To Go**

1. Place your cursor in the second cell of the first row. Place the image spacer.gif from the Art directory of your Food Info site. *Do not* click anywhere. While the graphic is selected, change the width to 50 in the Properties Inspector. This has no purpose right now other than to hold this cell open and visible if you are not using borders while you create your table. This width will be reduced when you complete the table.

   An invisible graphic that is 1 pixel × 1 pixel is hard to select for editing. You should always set the size before you deselect.

2. Place your cursor in the first cell of the first row and insert logo.gif. Set the cell width to 344 in the Properties Inspector. Make sure that your graphic is not selected, and that your cursor is in the cell containing logo.gif when you set the width.

3. Insert answer.gif in the last cell of the first row. Deselect the graphic, but make sure that your cursor is still in the same cell. In the Properties Inspector set the Cell Horz alignment to Right. The graphic will move to the right. Insert your cursor in the Cell W field and type **70%**.

Using a higher percentage for a flexible table cell value than the amount of space that remains unspecified in the table is really telling that cell to "take everything that no other cell is using." This is not a perfect solution because browsers, Netscape especially, are very democratic. Browsers will see that you have too much space in one column and give some to another cell, but this command does help to keep your fixed content fixed and the flexible content moving as it is supposed to. When this command works perfectly, the third column in this table ranges from approximately 250 pixels to more than 1000 pixels for the highest resolution monitors. Yet the color will always cover the area, and the graphic at the right will remain at the edge of the monitor.

4. You will enter your main menu graphics now. Place your cursor in the first cell of the last row in the first table. Insert the following graphics, one after the other with nothing between them. Use your right arrow key to deselect each graphic and to move your cursor into place to insert the next graphic. The graphics can be found in the Art/mainmen folder of your Food Info site. Place, in order: `mainmen1.gif`, `mainmen2.gif`, `mainmen3.gif`, `mainmen4.gif`, `mainmen5.gif`, and `mainmen6.gif`.

Although it is actually duplicating work, I prefer to place my menu graphics before I build any rollovers or navigation bars. I often make changes at this point, and I do not like removing and adding JavaScript functions any more than necessary. Plain images are simple to work with, and are just as effective for planning and constructing tables. When I create a rollover or navigation bar, I simply delete the original graphics.

5. Repeat the above for the menu containing contribute, about us, and contact items as well, inserting images in the third column of the last row in the first table. Use images from the Art/smmen folder and place the following images, in order: contribute.gif, about.gif, and contact.gif. Set the Cell Horz value to Right.

The first table is nearly complete, but we must set the size for the stripe rows. A nonbreaking space, which is automatically inserted by Dreamweaver when there is no content in a cell, is holding the rows open right now. Follow these instructions to insert an invisible graphic in each row to create our stripes:

1. Insert your cursor in the second row (blue). Insert spacer.gif. Before deselecting, set the width to 500 and the height to 5. Your row will instantly take on that height.

Technically, you should be able to leave the invisible spacer set to a 1-pixel width, set the height as we require, and still have the cell fill the screen. However, it is a better idea to set the width to 500 if the spacer is in an empty cell. Browsers do not always respect a tiny graphic, even though logic argues that they must. For a cell that is empty and providing only color, a 500-pixel width graphic will ensure that the cell will stretch across the page.

2. Repeat for the third (black) and fourth (red) rows, setting the spacer height to 5 for the black and 3 for the red row.

If your table rows do not redraw immediately, you can use Ctrl+Spacebar to force the table to redraw.

You have now completed the top table and your page should closely resemble Figure 19-4 if your table borders are set to 1 for the construction stage. To complete the page, you will set the cell widths for the bottom table and add a nested table for our jump menu and search areas.

Add settings for bottom table as follows:

1. For this table, you are using a control row below the content row. You will place spacer graphics in this row, and set the widths to keep the content area as simple as possible. Place your cursor in the first cell of the second row. Insert spacer.gif and set the graphic width to 344. This matches our top graphic and main menu width.

2. Set the same cell width to 344. Technically, you should be covered with these two actions — the graphic to hold the cell open to 344 and the width to hold the cell from expanding beyond 344. However, you must also make sure that the second cell in the row also knows that you really mean 344.

3. Place your cursor in the second cell of the control row. Type **100%** for the cell width.

   This tells the right column to fill any of the screen not held by a graphic. In most cases, this works. But you should put in a spacer graphic just in case a browser is in a generous mood and decides that you really do not mean to have that much in one column and shares some of the width with the left column. You can safely place a graphic that is 220 pixels wide without causing a scroll for low-resolution monitors (344 + 220 = 566 or just under the "safe" width of 570 pixels). This graphic does not really do anything because it is less than the full width of the screen. But experience has taught you that the browsers are much more likely to listen when they have a spacer graphic that is as large as possible.

4. Place your cursor in the right cell of the bottom row and insert spacer.gif. Specify a width of 220.

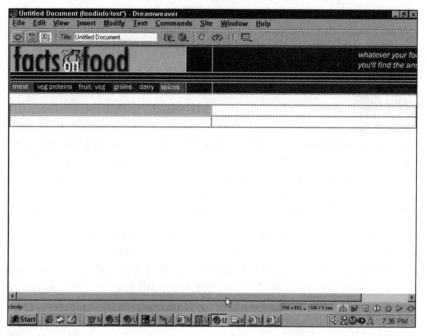

Figure 19-4
Test page with top table completed. Table borders are turned on for the construction stage in this sample.

You may think that I have spent too much time at my computer because I seem to think that browsers "make decisions." Well, I probably have spent too much time at my computer. But when you are trying to juggle all the HTML code, the JavaScript, graphics, different browsers, and different platforms, you do at times just say, "Fine! It makes no sense, but I will just do the fix." Placing a graphic to hold open a 100 percent table cell is exactly in that category.

Adding a nested table

Now you are going to add a jump menu and search area to the top of the main content area. To align these items, you will create a nested table, or a table within a table. This can be an effective way to overcome some of the limitations in HTML design.

Never use a nested table unless it is truly necessary. In addition to making your page difficult to edit, you are using a lot of code, and too many layers of nested tables can cause unpredictable results. I have seen examples of tables nested six deep, when the same effect could have been achieved with one or two tables had some planning been done at the beginning.

To add a nested table:

1. To make it easier to work, use your Enter key to add lines and open the first cell of the first table. (Should be the only gold cell.)

2. Place your cursor at the upper left of the same cell. Insert a table that is 1 row, 3 columns, with CellPad set to 8 and no cell spacing. Set the width to 300 pixels. Border is 0. Set the border to 1 if you want to work with borders until you finish your table. Your new table is positioned inside the original table. See Figure 19-5.

Now that you have the place, add the contents for the nested table, starting with placeholder graphics. The jump menu will be added in Session 20. The search function will not be activated as part of this book, but is an easy script to locate on the Web if you would like to do an extra exercise. (See Session 11 for general instructions on placing a script.)

1. Place your cursor in the middle cell of the new table and type **Search**. Apply bold to the text.

2. Place your cursor in the third column of the new table. Insert searchtemp.gif. Note how the columns adjust when the graphic is added. Don't worry about that just yet. We will correct the columns in the next section.

3. Finally, place the jump menu placeholder. Insert image droptemp.gif in the first column of the new table.

4. Set the cell containing the jump menu image to 70.

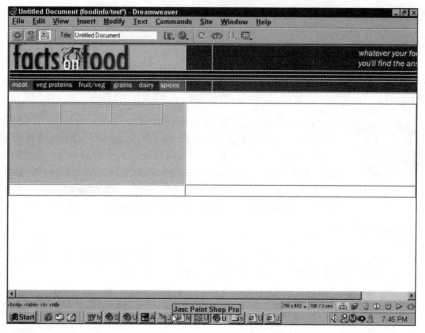

Figure 19-5
New table nested inside the original table. Borders are set to 1, but will be turned off when the construction is finished.

Completing and Troubleshooting Your Template

As your final action, you will turn off the borders (if you have been working with them) and remove the space between the tables. You will also reduce the size of the placeholder graphic from 50 to 10 pixels. To finish:

1. Select each table (there are three) and change the Border value to 0.

2. Select the lower table. Use your left arrow key to move the cursor to the left of the table. Turn on code view, and remove the <br> tag. Your code should look like the following:

   ```
   </table>
   <table width="100%" border="0" cellspacing="0" cellpadding="0">
   ```

3. The placeholder graphic is between the two graphics in the first row of the first table set to 50. This size should make it easy for you to see the cells. You must reduce it to keep the page from scrolling. Select the graphic and set a new width of 10.

Tip

Invisible graphics are not easy to select. If you know exactly where you have placed the graphic, you can click in that area in design view. Most times, you will find it. However, there are times it is hard, and you should turn to the code view. Place your cursor near where you know there is a spacer graphic and turn on code view. Look for the cursor in code view to find your place. The spacer graphic code for this exercise will look like this: `<img src="art/spacer.gif" width="50" height="1">`. **You can highlight this code and delete from the code view.**

The basics of the test page are now prepared. Your page should look like Figure 19-6. If it does, and you have worked cleanly, you can create your template from this page. However, if you have had to make many adjustments, it is advisable to re-create the page under a different name.

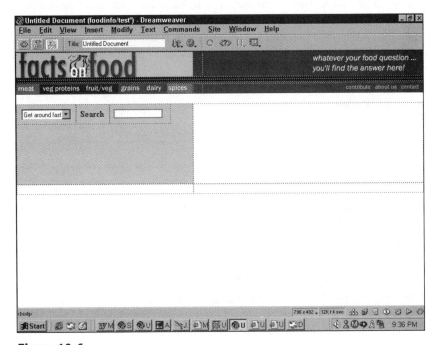

Figure 19-6
The final page ready to be used as a template

If you have any unexplained spaces in your tables, check your code. Look for `</td>` tags that are not on the same line as the content that falls immediately before the tag. For example,

```
<td width="344"><img src="art/logo.gif" width="344"
height="47"></td>
    <td><img src="art/spacer.gif" width="50" height="1"></td>
    <td align="right"><img src="art/answer.gif" width="223"
height="47">
    </td>
```

The first two </td> tags in the preceding code are fine. The last </td> tag is on the row below the table cell it closes, which usually causes a space below the row when the document is previewed in a browser. Although white space should make no difference in code, an extra line space before the </td> is one that consistently causes problems.

This is a perfect time for you to study the code that Dreamweaver produced. See if you can follow along and understand what effect each line of code is creating on the page. If you have studied the basics of HTML and JavaScript, you should understand most of what is going on in the code view. Code that is just ready to be turned into a template is perfect to study. There is usually only a fraction of the code that will be present when the page is complete, yet the code that forms the essential elements for the page is in place.

Done!

In the next session, you will create the template and the library items that are needed for this site.

REVIEW

In this session, you did some fancy table work, and prepared a page to use for the Food Info site template. You covered a lot of ground, although the basic operations were a repeat exercise for you. Here are a few things to remember:

- It is a good idea to create the initial construction of your page, especially when you are creating a template, on a test page. If you have made many changes, you should recreate the page with perfectly clean code.

- You must identify which areas will remain the same on every page and which areas you must be able to edit before you can construct the page that will be your template.

- It is much easier to work with your table borders set to 1, even when the final table will have no borders.

- You cannot trust that a browser will take your cell width values and respect them. You use 100% cells and placeholder graphics to ensure that your pages are rendered as you wish.

- Set the width of an invisible graphic before you deselect.

- Placing just the images from your rollovers and navigation bars is a good idea when you are initially planning your page.

- Using a control row at the bottom of a table is a good way to keep regular content away from the important codes to make you troubleshooting easier.

Quiz Yourself

1. Why is it a good idea to create test tables when designing the layout for your site? (See the "Build Tables for Your Template " section.)

2. What is the only way to guarantee that a cell will display at least as wide as you desire? (See the "Adding content to your tables" section.)

3. Why would you place graphics before setting up rollovers? (See the "Adding content to your tables" section.)

4. Why should you set an invisible graphic width to as large as possible, even when you only need it to establish height? (See the "Adding content to your tables" section.)

5. How do you tell a cell to cover any remaining space on the page? (See the "Adding content to your tables" section.)

6. What is a nested table? (See the "Adding a nested table" section.)

7. What is a common reason for spaces between the graphics in your tables? (See the "Completing and Troubleshooting Your Template" section.)

Preparing Library Items for the New Site

Session Checklist

✔ Organizing with Library items

✔ Using Library items and templates together

✔ Creating Library items to use on sites and templates

✔ Placing your jump menu into your template

✔ Creating the main site template

✔ Creating documents from the site template

**30 Min.
To Go**

I n the previous session, you prepared a test page almost to the point of creating a template. In this session, you will build Library Items to include in that template, and you'll also complete both the main template and a subpage version of the same page.

It might seem as though you are spending a great deal of time and getting nowhere, but you really are making excellent progress. Once your templates are completed, you'll have the power to almost instantly create a page. This is not an exaggeration. The layout is fixed and cannot be edited. What this means is that once you have a solid working template, you cannot inadvertently damage your code; Dreamweaver will not let you. It may be hard to understand how much time this feature alone saves until you have spent hours at a time designing and working with code. No matter how much experience you gain, you can still err and delete a tag or an attribute that changes everything. In fact, you are more likely to do that even when you do have experience.

You are building the Food Info site to be bulletproof. As long as your template is solid and your Library items are well-constructed, you are safe. If you discover a problem on one browser version for a single platform, you will make the changes in the template or the Library item, and Dreamweaver will update the entire site.

Let's take a look at what you will be doing in this Session, and then you'll move on to creating your Library items and the template.

Deciding Between Library Items and Templates

You worked with Library items in Session 15, so you should be fairly comfortable with the concept. Deciding what you want as a Library Item can be a little daunting at first. I must confess that while I was always excited about the idea of Library Items, I worked with Dreamweaver for quite a while before I finally started using them. The same was true for templates. I am now a raging fan, and the difference is not in learning how to create one or the other. The difference is that I spent the time to question whether the item would work as a Library Item. Could this be worked into a template? Once my mind was going in the right direction, it was only a matter of time until I was consistently using both. It took me a while to untangle Library Items and templates; they certainly perform many of the same tasks. Unfortunately, the answer is rarely simple. Fortunately, that also means that you have two great ways in which to solve many of your tedious construction problems.

To template or to Library? That is the question. The answer is: sort of . . . well, it is almost . . . for sure . . . both. It will be easier to look at which areas are definitely one or the other's turf before you choose.

If you want to create a page with many repeated elements, a template is the only answer. If you are creating 75 absolutely identical pages, you can create an entire page with a Library item. But who needs 75 identical pages? Library Items have no options; they are an all-or-nothing concept. Templates, on the other hand, can have both editable and noneditable areas.

Conversely, templates cannot be a portion of a page; they run the show or they do nothing. If you have a small scrap of code that will be added to all second-level pages in your site, templates are of no use. You must use Library Items.

The size of the area you want to automate is actually a good indicator of which function you should choose. If the area is a complete page, choose templates. If the area is merely a portion of a page, choose Library Items.

You can build a page with many Library items and skip the templates. For instance, you could create a header, a footer, and two menus as Library Items. Pop them onto a page and you have an automated, editable page. You have four times the work, however, just in placing the items, not to mention the time you will need to do some of the layout work. Full pages should be created using templates.

The best option, in most all cases, is to use both. Build your pages with templates, and then add the extras and often varying features with Library items. A well-planned site contains very little that cannot be globally edited.

Finally, I want to mention that you can use Library items to keep your code intact. That is why you will create a Library item for your jump menu. Although that particular item is going to appear on your template, and it is the same on every page, Dreamweaver will not select all the code unless you select it by hand in the code view. That is a very good reason for placing an object into a Library item.

Let's move on to creating Library items for your interior menus, and for a button labeled "print this page" that will be placed in different locations throughout your site. You are also going to discover clever workarounds to Dreamweaver's automated file updating as you create one of your Library items.

Creating the Library Items for Your Site

For your first Library Item, you will create a very simple "print this page" button. This script is available from The JavaScript Source at `http://javascript.internet.com/ messages/print-page.html`. I have modified the version that is located on the CD-ROM so that it will be a simple print button. There are more attractive print options available, but this one button has very simple code you can use to create your Library item.

Creating a Library item with a script

Take the following steps to create this button for use at any time in the site:

1. Select File ⇨ Open and select the file `printpage.js` from the Session 20 folder on the CD-ROM.

2. Highlight and copy all of the text that appears in the Dreamweaver window. This is your script.

3. Open the Assets window and activate the Library section. Click the side menu icon and select New Library Item from the menu that appears.

4. Type **printbutton** to name the Library Item.

5. Click the Edit button to open the Library Item edit screen (it will be blank).

6. Select Edit ⇨ Paste HTML. An invisible element marker will appear to represent your script, as shown in Figure 20-1.

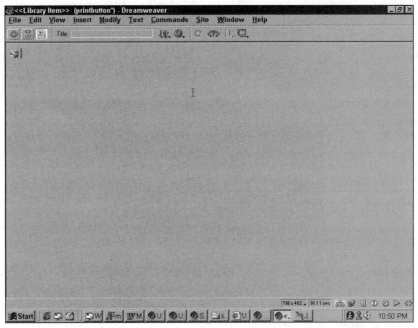

Figure 20-1
The Library edit screen with an invisible element icon representing the script

7. Preview the Library file in all of the browsers that you have listed. You will place this Library item into many locations throughout your site. Although you can easily edit the file, you do want it to be working before you place it. You should see one button that says "Print." When you click the button, your print window should appear. Cancel the print window; this is just a test.

8. Save your Library item and close the window. You can also close the script file that you opened from the CD-ROM.

You will not do any more with this file in this Session, although you will place it independently later in Session 21. You do not want this button on every page, so you will not include it with the template.

Creating a Library item from a menu

**20 Min.
To Go**

Next, you are going to create a Library item that you will deliberately leave unfinished (it will still require some editing). In Session 22, you will come back to this item and create a complex rollover menu. I have included a copy of the completed file in the Session 20 folder of the CD-ROM if you want to peek at what it will be (rollovertest.html). For now, you are simply going to place your graphics in the proper place to create your Library item for editing later.

Copy the Inmen folder from the Session 20 folder of the CD-ROM to the Art folder of your Food Info site. This folder contains the images for your interior menu.

Take the following steps to build your interior menu:

1. Create a new document with the background color #FFCC66. Save the file as rollover.html.
2. Create a table that is five rows by two columns. Set the cell padding and spacing values to 0. Specify the width as 250 pixels and the border as 0. You may want to set your borders to 1 until you complete the menu.
3. Select and merge all of the cells in the second column to create a single cell.
4. Insert the following graphics, one in each row of the first column: `inmen1.gif`, `inmen2.gif`, `inmen3.gif`, `inmen4.gif`, and `inmen5.gif`.
5. You are going to name your images to get ready for your rollovers. Click the first image in the row, the "history" menu item. In the Properties Inspector, type **history** in the Image field to the far left. Click the next image and type **cultural** for the name. Repeat this step for the final three images, using the following names: **methods**, **recipes**, **resources**.
6. In the second column, place the image `inmenblank.gif`. This is an image containing nothing but the background color, so it should be invisible.
7. Name the new image **blank**.

Your page should now look similar to the page shown in Figure 20-2. I have selected the background-colored graphic so that you can see it easily. Note that the Properties Inspector is displaying the image name.

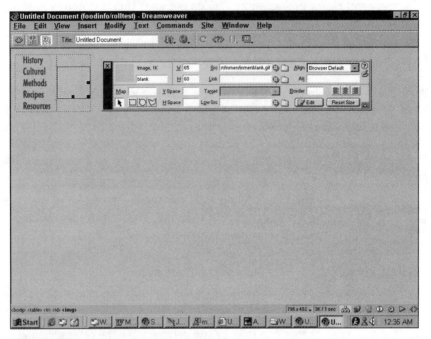

Figure 20-2
The completed menu with the background colored image selected

That is as far as you will go with this menu right now. In Session 22, when you complete the menu, each of the menu items will have a rollover, plus the blank image will swap with an image representing the menu item. Let's turn the menu into a Library item by taking the following steps:

1. Select the table containing the menu items.

2. Open the Assets panel if it is not already open. Click the icon for the side menu and choose New Library Item, or click the New Library Item icon in the lower portion of the Assets panel. Because the table was selected as you created the Library item, the table content is added to the item.

3. Type **interior1** to name the Library Item.

   Even though you have not created the rollovers on this item, you can still place it on your pages if you want to use it for design purposes. When you edit the file, an update will add your rollover information to all instances of the item.

4. Drag the Library item into place beneath the jump menu and search table.

Skirting Dreamweaver's automated file updating

You must now copy the jump menu that you prepared in Session 17. You are going to go around Dreamweaver's automated link correction with this next operation. If you use Dreamweaver's Site window to move your jump menu document to the new site, Dreamweaver would change your links. However, you created the menu with relative links and no directories stated. If you move the file without allowing Dreamweaver to "correct" the links for you, all links will work perfectly from the new location.

See Session 12 for a discussion about relative and absolute links.

To copy without correction, you will use your regular computer file copying method to copy the file containing your jump menu.

Copy the jump menu document, and then create a Library item by taking the following steps:

1. Copy the file `jump.html` from your Weekend site's Resources directory using your normal method to copy files. The Resources folder will be located in the Weekend site root directory that you created in Session 3. Paste the file into the root directory of your Food Info site using your normal method to paste a new file in a folder.

2. Open the file `jump.html` from the Food Info site. You can now create a Library item with this menu.

3. It is best to select an item such as the jump menu from the code window. Start by clicking the menu in Design View. Open the Code View. Make sure your selection covers all of the code from the `<form name="form1">` tag to the `</form>` tag.

4. In the Assets window with the Library section active, create a new Library item. Type **jump menu** as the name. If asked by Dreamweaver, allow any updates.

You now have your jump menu as part of the Food Info site, with the correct links in place. This is a good method to remember when you are sharing assets between sites. Rarely, Dreamweaver's helping nature can cause us problems, and this is a handy trick to remember.

Placing the jump menu in the template page

You can now delete the placeholder jump menu graphic, and then place the Library item, by taking the following steps:

1. Open the file you are using to build your template (it started as `test.html`, but you may have created another).

2. Delete the jump menu graphic placeholder.

3. Drag the jump menu Library Item to the position where you just deleted the graphic.

4. Make sure that all three cells of that table have the cell alignment set to Top.

5. Preview in your browsers to make sure that all is working well.

Your page is in nearly final form to create the template.

Finalizing the Template

You've done your preparation work, and you can now build your final template. You know which areas are going to change and which will stay the same — almost. The one thing you have not yet covered is a color-coding plan for this site.

One of the signs of a good site is that a visitor always knows what page they are on. You are working hard on your menus to give visual clues, but it is preferable to have as many indicators as possible for your visitors. In this case, you have a main menu with many colors. You are going to use the colors from those menu items to give each major section its own color. The upper-right corner of the page will change color and provide the category for the current page — a highly visible indicator for visitors. Figure 20-3 displays how the new title area might look. This adds a great deal of usability to the site, but it must be factored in as you make your final preparations. You will allow for this adjustment when you create editable areas for your template later in this session.

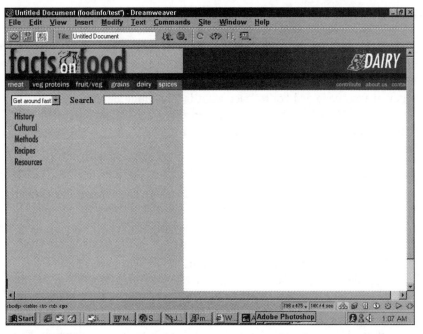

Figure 20-3
The Dairy title is featured in this sample. The red color in the upper portion of the page has been replaced with the blue color matching the Dairy menu item.

Final preparation

Changing your title area means that you will want to leave that area editable in your template. Not only must the image change, but also, you must change the background areas. In this case, you will leave the second and third columns of the first row as editable regions. You will just change the background color for each area in the second column. The third column will have the background color and the image replaced.

Both of your menu areas also must remain editable. You have placed your Library menu as part of your template, but it will remain as an editable region. In Session 21, you will be creating Library Item menus for different pages, and you will replace the original Library Item with one of the newer versions. However, the space will be consistent, so it makes sense to include it as a template item.

Finally, the main content areas will obviously remain editable. You would be unable to place any content if you did not set these areas as editable.

Clean up

As your final act, you should take a look at your code and clean up any areas that might be problem areas. Of course, I am assuming that you have a relatively solid understanding of HTML and/or JavaScript to do this. Even if you do not, it is wise to look at your code and try to trace what is happening on your page.

In addition to reviewing your code, take advantage of Dreamweaver's built-in HTML cleanup feature before you create your template. Follow these steps to use this feature:

1. Select Commands ➪ Clean Up HTML. The Clean Up HTML window will open.

   You will run just the default cleanup, but note the other items that are available. You can strip out comment tags — those tags that provide information only, rather than those that direct the page display. There is also a function to search for specific tags you might want to remove.

2. Make sure that the following functions have checkmarks: Empty Tags, Redundant Nested Tags, and Combine Nested <font> Tags When Possible. If you want to see a report on the changes that have been made, make sure that Show Log on Completion is checked.

   You might get an alert that tells you there is nothing to clean up. You prefer to get those reports — your work is clean. If Dreamweaver has made any changes, a report will be presented.

Never attempt to clean up the Dreamweaver comments if you have any specialized features such as templates or Library Items, as they will be destroyed.

10 Min. To Go

That's the final task, although I have deliberately omitted some areas from this template. You will come back and add a bottom text menu to the bottom of the page and add a few housekeeping details. I wanted you to have the opportunity to edit your pages with content in place to show you that that you really can safely edit templates when the page is finished. It is always disconcerting to set an automatic feature into action. Seeing it work is the best way to build your confidence.

Creating the Template

You have arrived at the big moment. Time to stop the planning, the designing, and the fussing with details, and to get your site rolling. Follow these steps to create the template:

1. If it is not already open, open your template preparation page. Make sure it has been saved.

2. Make sure that the Food Info site is active.

3. Open your Assets panel, if necessary. Activate the Templates area.

4. Select File ⇨ Save As Template. The Save as Template window will open.

5. Select Food Info from the drop-down list of sites.

6. Type **main** in the Save As field. Your window should resemble the window shown in Figure 20-4.

7. Click Save to finish creating your template. The new template will appear in your Assets window, and the title bar of your document window will change to indicate that it is a template.

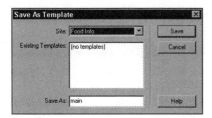

Figure 20-4
The proper settings for creating your template

Setting editable areas

You now have a template. Add your editable regions and you will be ready to start building pages. Take the following steps:

1. With your template open, place your cursor in the second cell of the top row. You want to be able to change the color of this cell. Right-click (PC) or Command-click (Mac) and choose New Editable Region from the menu that is presented (select Modify ⇨ Templates ⇨ New Editable Region).

2. Type **cell space** for the name in the New Editable Region window.

3. Repeat Steps 1 and 2 for the next cell, naming the editable region **title**.

You must stop here and make a small adjustment to your code by hand. Dreamweaver, does not include the <td> tag when a table cell is made into an editable area. I can understand why this is: a template is intended to keep much of your page static, and the <td> tags would not be needed to replace most content.

However, you need to have the <td> tags editable so you can change the title area background. You can get around the default value by hand selecting the code in Code View. Although I could find no way to automatically move the tags, it works like a charm when you move a little code. It is exactly for this type of flexibility that I recommend you become comfortable with your code.

Never change the code for an automatic function without first testing, testing, and then testing again. I tested the method presented here well; I would not have included it if it failed to function properly. Testing is essential. In this case, you are going around a default in Dreamweaver that simply serves to make a template layout safer. Some of the defaults that you will encounter are safety features because an alternate way would not function properly with some browsers.

The problem code for the table is displayed here

```
<td bgcolor="#333399"><!-- #BeginEditable "title%20space" --><img
src="../art/spacer.gif" width="11" height="1"><!-- #EndEditable --
></td>
<td bgcolor="#333399" width="70%" align="right"><!--
#BeginEditable "title" --><img src="../art/titles/dairy.gif"
width="223" height="47"><!-- #EndEditable --></td>
```

Notice how the editable area starts after the <td> tag. Nothing I did while trying to select this code would create a different result, including selecting the entire <td> tag in Code View. However, Dreamweaver will accept the change if you manually move the editable area comment tags.

To change your code so that it includes the <td> tag, follow these steps:

1. In Code View, select the tag <!-- #BeginEditable "title%20space" -->. Select Edit ⇨ Cut, or press Ctrl+X (PC) or Command+X (Mac), to cut the selection.

2. Place your cursor **in front of** the tag <td bgcolor="#333399"> . Select Edit ⇨ Paste, or press Ctrl+V (PC) or Command+V (Mac), to paste the code.

3. Repeat Steps 1 and 2 for the next <td> tag. Your code should resemble the following:

   ```
   <!-- #BeginEditable "title%20space" --><td
   bgcolor="#333399"><img src="../art/spacer.gif" width="11"
   height="1"></td><!-- #EndEditable -->
   ```

```
<!-- #BeginEditable "title" --><td bgcolor="#333399"
width="70%" align="right"><img src="../art/titles/dairy.gif"
width="223" height="47"></td><!-- #EndEditable -->
```

The code seems a little complicated, but I urge you to try it. It is much easier than it looks in print, and it is excellent practice for working with code. If you really do not want to go this far with your template, you can either accept the default background color, or you can change it to another color that will match all of the menu item colors. Simply make the change in your template and change the title image on each page.

Now you're ready to finish setting the editable region by taking the following steps:

1. Select all of the main menu items and create an editable region named **main menu**.

2. Select all of the items in the right menu and name the editable area **menu**.

3. Select the table containing the interior menu and name this editable area **interior menu**.

4. Click in the main content area to the right and create an editable area named **content**.

5. Repeat Step 4 for the left content area and name that area **main content**.

Save your template file. You have a template that you can use to create many similar pages, not worrying about most of the layout. Let's create a few pages.

Copy the Titles folder from the Session20 folder on the CD-ROM to the Art folder in your Food Info site.

Creating pages from your templates

This template will be used to form the entire Food Info site. There are times when you will create two or three versions of a template to use on different types of pages. With this design, however, the design will work for all of your pages.

You will not be completing every page on this site. This menu set up and the site map call for well over 30 pages. I have included this many pages so that you can continue to work on this example and use this site as a test site once you complete the exercises. When you have completed all the sessions, you will be very comfortable with the way this site works — it makes a perfect testing ground for you. You can also benefit from repeating any exercises that you do not fully understand. Simply create or choose a new page and work through the exercise again.

Creating the meat section documents

Take the following steps to create every page for the Meat section:

1. Make sure the Food Info site is active and that the Assets Panel open. Click the side menu icon in the Assets panel and choose New From Template from the menu. A new document will be created with the title Untitled.

2. Choose File ⇨ Save and save the new document as **meathis.html**.

That is really all there is to creating a new page from a template. To change the background color of the title area and replace the existing graphic with the Meat title graphic, take the following steps:

1. Place your cursor in the second cell of the first row and change the background color to #996633 (tan), the same color as the Meat item in the main menu.

When the color palette is open, you can use the eyedropper to select any color on the page. Simply move your cursor off the color palette and click the color you desire. In this case, move your cursor over the background color of the Meat item in the menu. Click anywhere on the background color and that color will be selected.

2. Place your cursor in the third cell — the one containing the graphic — and repeat Step 1.

3. Double-click the title graphic and change it to meat.gif from the Art/titles folder. Your document should look similar to the one shown in Figure 20-5.

4. Save your document.

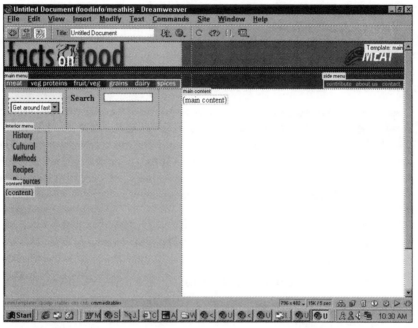

Figure 20-5
The adjusted title area for the meat section is now in place.

Completing the remaining pages

You have now a completed meat section page. You have two choices to complete
the pages for the rest of this section. You can repeat the previous section for each
page, changing the titles as shown in the next exercise. You can also use the
meat.gif file to save the remaining pages. Simply choose File ➪ Save As and specify the new filename as listed in the next paragraph. The new pages will be saved
as exactly the same file with all of the template areas intact. This method should
only be used when you have made few changes to the template, though. When you
have been working on your site for a while, new pages should always be created
directly from your template.

No matter which method you choose, the following are the filenames for the
Meat section documents: meathis.gif (the document you created above),
meatcult.gif, meatmeth.gif, meatrec.gif, and meatres.gif.

Creating the Veg Protein section documents

You do want one more section to be ready for your work. Each section follows this exact format, so as quickly as you can save 30 files, this entire site could be active. You will have no content on your pages, of course, but this is a handy way to have the structure of a site in place in the early stages.

 You are creating these files now, but in a real working situation, you should complete a few pages to make sure you have the right layout and direction. You should not move to creating dozens of pages from a template unless it has been thoroughly tested with content in place. You can make changes to your template, but it is best if they are minor changes.

Take the following steps to create the files for the Veg Protein section:

1. Create a new document from the Main template. Save it as `vegprothis.html`.

2. Change the background color of the cells in the title area to #660000.

3. Change the title graphic to `vegprot.gif` from the Art/titles folder.

4. Save the document.

5. Create the following documents from `vegprothis.html` by repeating Steps 1-4, but using the following filenames: `vegprotcult.html`, `vegprotmeth.html`, `vegprotrec.html`, and `vegprotres.html`.

Done!

You are well on your way to completing a site. Of course, you have not entered any content yet. You will see in Sessions 24 and 25 that when you are working with templates, content addition is not a difficult part of this process.

REVIEW

It has been a long route, but you have finally arrived at the reward stage for your efforts in building components that will help you later. Before you move on, you should review these points:

* It can be confusing to determine whether you should place items in a template or create Library items. As a general rule, Library items are best for self-contained pieces, and templates excel at controlling larger areas.

* It is important to make sure that you have selected the entire area you want to create as a Library item. Check your Code View to make sure.

- There are times when you do not want to use Dreamweaver's automated file updating when you transfer a file. Use normal file copying and moving system to defeat the automated link updating.

- It is important to plan every area of your template for editable areas, and that you design before you commit the file to a template.

- Do not allow Dreamweaver to "clean up" Dreamweaver comment tags in the Clean Up HTML window if you have any automated features, such as templates, in use.

- Occasionally, you must edit your code by hand when you are creating a template so that you can achieve the editable area you require. Test, test, and test again before you proceed with manual changes. Often, Dreamweaver prevents actions for very good reasons.

- It is a good idea to add content to a few pages that are based on a new template, before you create many pages from that template. It is much easier to make major changes to a template before content is added than to edit many dependent pages.

Quiz Yourself

1. What is the main difference between Library items and templates? (See the "Deciding Between Library Items and Templates" section.)

2. What is the main benefit for using Library items for scripts and menus? (See the "Creating the Library Items for Your Site.")

3. Why would you bypass the automated file moving feature in Dreamweaver? (See the "Skirting Dreamweaver's automated file updating" section.)

4. Why must you not use the Dreamweaver automated command to clean up Dreamweaver comments when you are using Library items or templates on your site? (See the "Clean up" section.)

5. How can you include <td> tags as an editable area in a template? (See the "Setting editable areas" section.)

6. When you create a page from a template, what name is assigned to the new page? (See the "Creating pages from your templates" section.)

7. How can you save a new file from a file created from a template, and keep the original template information intact? (See the "Creating the Veg Protein section documents" section.)

PART

IV

Saturday Evening

1. When you are planning a site, what is the most important thing to know about your potential visitors?

2. Why is it important to create a site map before designing a site?

3. What is a jump menu?

4. What is the benefit of a Navigation Bar?

5. What characteristic of a Navigation Bar prevents you from using this feature to create every menu?

6. When you check out a file, does that mean nobody else can get the file or make edits?

7. When you check a file back into the remote site, what is the status of the file on your local site?

8. You can attach design notes in two places. Where are the places?

9. Where can you see a symbol that notifies you that a document has a design note attached?

10. How do you view the contents of a document design note.

11. What is essential to determine before you begin to build a template page?

12. How can you create color stripes that expand and contract with the page width?

13. If you have three columns, with the first two columns set to 200 pixel width, what happens when you set the third column to a width of 100%.

14. Why does it make sense to place graphics in a menu position before you create the rollovers using the same graphics?

15. It can be very hard to select a tiny, invisible graphic, especially if it is in a small column or row. What is often the fastest way to edit or select the graphic?

16. What is a Library Item especially good at handling?

17. What are templates designed to do?

18. Is it reasonable to create a Library Item meant to be detached from the original as soon as it is placed on a page.

19. You want to move files in a Dreamweaver site to another location without the links being updated. What are two ways to accomplish this task?

20. What does it mean when you set an editable area in a template?

☑ Friday

☑ Saturday

☑ **Sunday**

P A R T

V

Sunday Morning

Exploring Dreamweaver's Production Tools

Session Checklist

✔ Going deeper into the Properties Inspector

✔ Using the Objects panel

✔ Using the Assets panel

✔ Setting up and using the Assets Favorites

✔ Speeding up your work

**30 Min.
To Go**

Near the beginning of this book, I stated several times that it was better to learn the program with menus, than with any shortcut. I am not against shortcuts, just against *learning* with shortcuts. I am about to take the restrictions off.

You have constructed one site and prepared the layout for another. You should have a good idea of how the menus work, and how the functions in Dreamweaver are distributed. No doubt, you have explored some of the features I have not covered as you were in the menu system. That's why I believe in using the menus to learn.

However, that was then and this is now. Dreamweaver does offer wonderful shortcuts and visual palettes that can help you produce your pages much more efficiently. I am fully in favor of using every shortcut that saves you time or that makes your work less confusing. No one will use every shortcut or palette. Most of us use one or two windows regularly, and call on many others for specific tasks. Anything that is presented in this session is only to show you what is available, not to suggest that you use any particular aid.

So . . . let's take a look at what Dreamweaver offers. I'll start with the Properties Inspector, because you have already used a tiny fraction of the editing offered in this little wonder panel.

Learning More about the Properties Inspector

In Session 2, you took a quick look at the range of controls that the Properties Inspector offers. At that time, though, you had not covered enough techniques to really look at the full capability contained in this one little window.

You should try at least a few of the following methods on a scrap file. Working through these short exercises will help to train you to use Dreamweaver more efficiently. You will use your template to create a page with objects in place for testing.

1. From the Food Info site, open the Assets window and activate the templates area.

2. Create a new file from the Main template (see Session 20).

3. Select Modify ⇨ Templates ⇨ Detach From Template.

4. Save the file as a name you will know to delete later, such as **trash.html**.

Keep watching your Properties Inspector as you work. When items are selected and you are about to perform an action, check whether the action can be accomplished through the Properties Inspector. There are an amazing number of functions that can be accomplished without ever leaving your document.

Editing code with one click

Most of the options that take up the space on the Properties Inspector do not really give an indication of what is available. Many of the operations that can be accomplished with the Properties Inspector are not evident until you know to look for them. Here are a few of my favorites.

Quick Tag editor

The tiny icon, located at the right of your Properties Inspector and identified in Figure 21-1, has a lot of power. One click of the mouse will bring you to an instant way to edit your code. Not only is it quick to access, but only the selected tag is displayed — your eyes are not distracted by the rest of the code as you work. Change any parameter in the tag. I find that this can be faster than entering the same information in the central portion of the Properties Inspector.

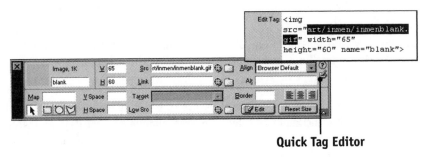

Quick Tag Editor

Figure 21-1
The Quick Tag editor identified and in use

This is also a terrific way to learn HTML because only the selected tag is shown.

Try editing your code with the Quick Tag Editor.

1. Select the table cell containing the search box graphic.

2. Click on the Quick Tag Editor icon and the code for that cell will appear: `<td valign="top">`.

3. Using the Quick Tag Editor, change the background color to black. The code is included here if you do not know the correct syntax: `<td valign="top" bgcolor="#000000">`.

Edit a jump menu or other script

You can use the document menu or a separate Dreamweaver window to edit a script, but you also have one-click access to script editing from the Properties Inspector. When you add a script, an invisible marker is placed. Click on the marker, and your Properties Inspector now has an Edit button.

Edit a script through the Properties Inspector by following these steps.

1. On your test document, drag the Printpage Library item onto your page. You should see an icon to represent the Library item. If not, select View ➪ Visual Aids ➪ Invisible Elements.

2. Make sure your new icon is selected, and Click Detach from Original in the Properties Inspector. This will break the link to the Library item.

3. Click the Edit button on the Properties Inspector and the Script Properties window will open.

4. Change the code `value="Print"` to `value="Print this page"`. Click OK to accept the change.

5. Preview your button in one of your browsers. You have changed the button title from "Print" to "Print this screen" without leaving the main document.

To see another powerful quick-edit feature in the Properties Inspector, click the jump menu in this document to select. You can change any list item and which value displays as the first item right from this screen. There is no need to go to the Behaviors panel for simple jump menu edits. Try this instead:

1. Click on any value in the Initially Selected drop-down menu and watch the value change in the jump menu on your screen.

2. To edit the values in your jump menu, click on List Values in the Properties Inspector. You will be presented with the values that are entered in the jump menu.

3. Click any entry to highlight it. Type new text in the List Values window to replace the highlighted text, as I have done in Figure 21-2. Your jump menu has been edited.

**20 Min.
To Go**

Using context help

Finally, make use of the context help that is available. The ? icon in the upper-right corner of the Properties Inspector will deliver help for the currently selected item. The help screen in Figure 21-3 was called from the Properties Inspector with a table selected. In addition to finding help on exactly the object you are working with, you also gain a better understanding of how the help system is structured.

It is hard for me to leave talking about the Properties Inspector. I have not tried, but I believe you could easily fill an entire chapter describing only the most useful features of this one little window.

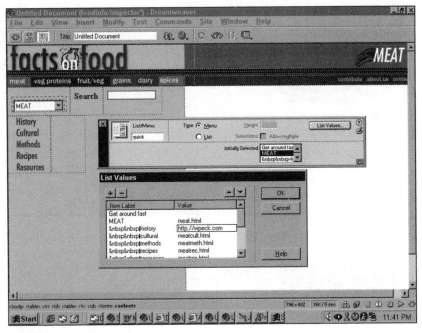

Figure 21-2
Jump menu items displayed for editing through the Properties Inspector

Using the Objects Panel

The Properties Inspector is a wonder once you have objects in your document, but the Objects panel gives you one-click access to adding almost any objects that you need. The panel consists of seven different categories of what amount to shortcut keys: Characters, Common, Forms, Frames, Head, Invisibles, and Special. During the early stages of a site or a new page, I find that the Objects panel is indispensable. As my page nears completion, I rarely open the panel. I also know designers who never close the Objects panel.

Before I explain some of the features of the Objects panel and how to use them, though, I want to show you how to change your preferences for this panel.

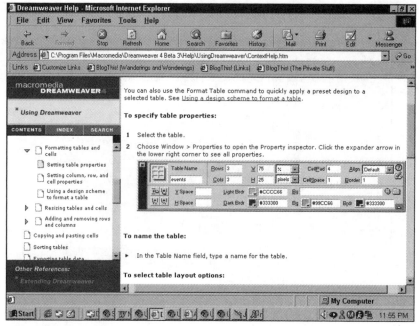

Figure 21-3
Help screen called from the Properties Inspector with a table selected

Changing display preferences

The Objects panel default is to display only icons. If you hold your mouse over the icons, a flag does come up to tell you which object the icon controls, but you may prefer to have the text for that option displayed. You have two other options: text and icons and text only.

I recommend setting your preferences to text and icons. Doing so gives you the benefit of the text plus you learn the icons for the objects that you use most often. The day will come when you can turn your text off, and have a smaller panel on your screen. Figure 21-4 shows all three versions of this panel.

To change the Objects panel preferences:

1. Select Edit ⇨ Preferences. The Edit Preferences window will open. Make sure that General is highlighted in the Category list.

2. Locate the Objects Panel drop-down menu near the bottom right of the window. Choose Icons and Text. Click OK to accept the changes.

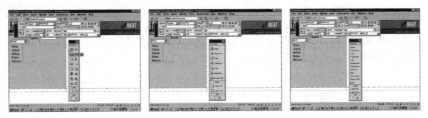

Figure 21-4
The three options for the Objects panel display: icons only (default), icons plus text, and text only

Adding objects with the Objects panel

What makes the Objects panel so efficient is that there are several different displays that you can use for this tiny panel. Click the menu flyout at the top of the panel for a choice of the seven categories. Click any category to change which objects are presented in the panel.

It is also easy to use. In fact, I can't stretch the instructions to more than a paragraph. If you want to add an image, make sure that the panel has Common selected, click Image, and the Insert Image window opens. Click Table and the Insert Table menu opens. Many of the icons lead to a creation window. Others insert an object without a menu.

The Character selection for the Objects panel is an example of direct entry. For example, to enter a (c) symbol, activate the Character listing in the Objects panel. Click the (c) button (or Copyright) and the symbol is entered at the cursor location.

Take a trip through the full selection in the Objects panel. We do not need to step through the functions, because any Objects icon is simply a shortcut to a menu item. You now just have a shorter route to the methods, one that can make a big difference in efficiency over the course of developing an entire site.

Customizing the Objects panel

Most of us use only a few commands repeatedly. You can customize your Objects panel so that all the commands that you use repeatedly are organized in a logical way for your work pattern. You can fully customize which commands display and where they can be found. The panel is controlled by files and folders that can be edited.

Never attempt to customize a program when the change requires editing program files unless you are experienced with file management on a computer. Customizing a program is not the place to learn how to copy, rename, or move a file. Even if you do have experience, make sure that you create a backup of the default settings for easy restoration in case of an error.

To reorganize your default Objects panel display, locate the program files for Dreamweaver 4 on your computer. Within the Dreamweaver folder, locate the Configuration\Objects folder. Each menu item — that is, the flyout menu — has a folder. The individual commands each have an image (GIF) and an HTML file that corresponds to that item. Many also have a JavaScript file.

To move a function to another menu item, simply move all associated files (one HTML, one GIF, and possibly one JS file) to the new folder.

To activate the new settings, press Ctrl or Option as you click the top flyout in the Objects panel. Select Reload Extensions from the menu.

10 Min. To Go

I am not going to cover the Layout View and Table Layout, which are new to Dreamweaver 4. The idea behind Layout view is to make working with tables easier. However, unless you understand *exactly* how a browser works with tables, and how nested tables and table cells react to each other, I do not believe that you should create tables using this feature. Because this book is geared to beginning and intermediate Web developers, my opinion is that this is a dangerous method for creating layout, unless you are an expert. If you would like to know more about it, however, Dreamweaver's Help carries a good section on working in layout view under the main heading Designing Page Layout.

The Assets Panel

I think Dreamweaver fans will soon be referring to time as BA and AA — Before Assets and After Assets. This is the most exciting addition for my work pattern in Dreamweaver 4. The Assets panel lists all the assets that you use in a site, including images, links, colors, and, of course, Library items and templates. This provides click and drag ease for adding elements to your page, but even more important is the consistency that is now so easy.

Using the Assets panel is easy and quite intuitive. I will step through a few procedures and then look at a few of the less obvious tools that are included with this panel.

Using assets

The most powerful feature of the Assets panel is that it is automatic. The first time you open the Assets panel when a site is active, Dreamweaver gathers all the relevant information and presents it to you in the Assets panel. Although that can be a large list, the Favorites function, which I discuss shortly, helps you to organize the assets you use often.

The icons along the left side of the Assets window control which list of assets is active. Holding your mouse over the icon presents the title for that category. Clicking on the icon activates that category. Clicking on an asset in the list presents a preview in the top window of the Assets panel.

To use the assets, you highlight a listing and drag the asset to the location you wish to place it. We have already looked at the Library item and template categories. Let's practice with images, text and links. For this exercise, I selected a graphic and added a link to my site, http://wpeck.com.

Place an image quickly using the Assets panel.

1. To place an image in your document, activate the Images icon in the Assets panel.

2. Select any image from the list presented. Click and drag the listing to your document *or* click the Insert button at the bottom of the Assets panel. Your image will be inserted.

3. To change text color, activate the color icon in the Assets panel. Type **Sample text** anywhere in your document.

4. Highlight your text entry. Click and drag any color listed to the text. Your text will change color.

Although the color list only works automatically with text, you can use the Assets list with the Properties Palette. When you are choosing, for example, a cell background color, from the Properties palette, an eyedropper is presented with the color palette. You can simply click on the color sample includes in the Assets panel color listing to ensure that you are using consistent color.

5. To add a link, activate the Link icon in the Assets panel.

6. Highlight the text you typed. Click and drag any link to the text. The selected text will be changed to a link.

That is the basic operation of the Assets panel. It is truly an intuitive feature that has become so much a part of my Dreamweaver work that it is already hard to remember life BA (Before Assets).

Creating Favorites in the Assets panel

The one drawback to the Assets panel is the number of assets that you gather with even a medium-sized site. For a large site, the number of graphics alone could make the Assets panel nearly unusable. However, the Dreamweaver developers were on their toes, because they also included a feature known as Favorites.

Favorites gather the assets into one easily organized area. You can easily list your most used assets in the Favorites section, and group them into areas that match your workflow. The assets that are featured in the Favorites section remain in the main list. However, as a Favorites listing, you can use your own nickname for the asset without affecting the functional properties — perfect for assigning English names to cryptic or numeric filenames. After you have your Favorites setup, you can view only the Favorites screen if you wish.

Creating and renaming Favorites

To create a Favorite listing:

1. Click the Favorites radio button at the top of the Assets panel. This will display the favorites that you have created; it is currently blank (unless you have been experimenting on your own).

2. Click the Site radio button to return to the main assets listing. Activate the Images section and select an image.

3. Click the Add to Favorites icon, which is the far right icon at the bottom of the Assets panel. You will be prompted with an alert telling you how to get to the Favorites view. I recommend that you disable this alert by clicking the checkbox beside the Don't Show Me This Message Again. Your image is now in Favorites.

4. Return to Favorites view. Your image should be listed there.

   If you would like to change the name in the Favorite view only, you can assign a nickname. This name does not affect the filename at all — it is simply a nickname that you can use in your Favorites listing.

5. To change the nickname for this file, select the image you just copied into the Favorites window. Click again (two distinctive clicks, not a double-click) and rename the nickname. Even though I am sure you have it, let me repeat one more time that this does not affect your filename. You can also click the icon at the top right of the Assets window to present a menu. Choose Edit Nickname from the menu and type in a new nickname.

6. Repeat Steps 2 to 5 to add and create a nickname for another image.

To get the most from your favorites, you should also set up folders or groups of files. You can organize these groups by pages, or perhaps by function, as in menu images. Perhaps you have graphic bullets or other decorative elements that are used throughout your site. You may wish to create a folder that will contain these elements in one place.

Creating and deleting Favorite folders

You must first create a folder and then move your Favorites listings into the folder. To do so, follow these steps:

1. With the Favorites view of your Assets panel active, click the New Favorites Folder icon at the far left of the bottom icons in the Assets panel. A new folder will appear.

2. Type **titles** as the new name for the folder.

3. Repeat Steps 1 and 2 to create another folder. Type **utilities** for the folder name.

4. To move a file into a folder, click and drag the file to the folder. Place one graphic in each folder. Notice that the folders now have + symbols next to the folder icon. Click on the + to expand the folder and see the contents. Figure 21-5 displays a sample of how your Assets should look. Your filenames will be different.

5. To delete a folder or file, simply select the folder or file and click the Remove From Favorites icon at the bottom of your screen. This does not delete the file, just the listing in the Favorites section of the Assets panel.

If you would prefer to have the items in the Site view of your Assets panel sorted by a different parameter, simply click on the title bar for the way you would like the sort to be done. For example, images are listed by filename. If you would prefer to have the images listed by type, click on Type in the title bar of the Assets display.

Locating assets in a site

This is not a major Dreamweaver feature, but on large sites, you can easily lose track of where your assets are stored. To have Dreamweaver take you directly to the location of any file, simply highlight the file and click the icon at the right side of the window to open the flyout menu. Select Locate in site, and you will be taken to the location for that file. Sometimes it is the little things that make all the difference.

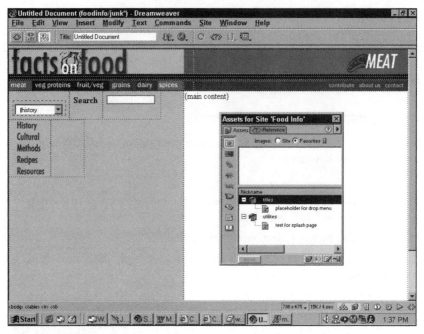

Figure 21-5
Images stored in Favorites in the Assets panel

O'Reilly HTML Reference

Oh, where was this feature when I was learning HTML and wondering about a tag, about what attributes will work with it, or about the tag's defaults? This tab in the Assets panel delivers all the basic information about HTML that you need. You first specify the tag you would like to find from a drop-down list, and a second drop-down menu provides a list of the attributes that can be used with that tag. Either selection then gives a written description as well as examples of correct use.

Anytime you have the Assets panel open, you can simply click on the Reference tab at the top of the Assets panel to open this most valuable resource. (You can also right-click on any tag in any code view to open the HTML Reference.) Figure 21-6 shows the Reference tab active with the IMG tag and Border attribute selected.

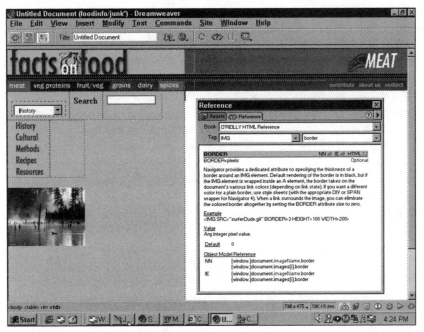

Figure 21-6
O'Reilly's HTML Reference is a complete HTML guide and an integrated part of the Assets panel.

You probably already know this — the F1 key will open the help menu in Dreamweaver (and most other programs). However, you may not know that Ctrl+F1 will take you directly to the Dreamweaver support pages on Macromedia.com. Shift+F1 will open your Assets panel to the O'Reilly HTML Reference window.

Now you understand why I am so excited about the Assets panel addition to this version. Use it for a few weeks, and I will just about guarantee that you will feel the same as I do. You can accomplish almost any task in Dreamweaver by using the Properties Inspector and the Assets panel.

Speeding up your work

We have gone through a tour of some strong production shortcuts. The secret to being highly efficient when using a program is to learn all the features and time-savers so that you can decide which tools to use for a specific task from a position of knowledge. Although it takes a little longer to reach a comfort level with a program if you make a commitment to learn as many ways to accomplish a task as you can, you will be repaid many times over when you find the exact combination that is right for the work you do and how you do your work.

Keep at least two palettes active while you learn. The Properties Inspector is essential, but keep at least one other palette active. Rotate the "palette of the day" until you are comfortable with all of them. Within a few weeks you will know which palettes save you time when you are working on which aspects of your site.

It is also helpful to keep an eye on the shortcuts as you use menu items. They are always listed on the right side of the menu list. By using menus to learn shortcuts, you only learn the keystrokes for the features you use frequently.

I will revisit the subject of increasing productivity in Session 30, when I focus on customizing Dreamweaver. In the meantime, let your mind absorb the production methods that I cover and always watch for methods that seem to save you time.

Done!

REVIEW

You didn't add anything to your site in this session, but you have advanced your Dreamweaver knowledge and production capability by leaps and bounds. Keep using what you have learned, and remember these points:

- The Properties Inspector is the first place you should look when you wish to accomplish a task.

- The Quick Tag Editor provides bite-sized pieces of HTML for quick editing and is a great tool for learning HTML.

- You can edit scripts directly from the Properties Inspector.

- Using Text and Icon display in the Objects panel will help you to learn what each icon represents. When you have them memorized, you can use Icon Only display to save space.

- The Assets panel provides click and drag access to the objects you have used in your site.

- You can create your own listing system for your assets without affecting the original listing through the Assets Panel Favorites window.

- HTML help is right at your fingertips when the Assets window is open, with the O'Reilly's HTML Reference window. You can also reach it by using Shift+F1.

QUIZ YOURSELF

1. What does the Quick Tag Editor in the Properties Inspector allow you to edit? (See the "Editing code with one click" section.)

2. How does the Properties Inspector tell you which object you have selected? (See the "Learning More about the Properties Inspector " section.)

3. What are the three different display settings for the Objects panel? (See the "Changing display preferences" section.)

4. How do you insert an image using the Assets Panel? (See the "Using assets" section.)

5. What are Favorites in the Assets panel? (See the "Creating Favorites in the Assets panel" section.)

6. Where can you find the shortcut for any menu item? (See the "Locating assets in a site" section.)

Placing Graphics and Rollovers in Your Site

Session Checklist

✔ Understanding graphics formats and optimization

✔ Optimizing images for the Web

✔ Adding rollovers to menus

✔ Creating a Navigation Bar for your site

✔ Adding a complex rollover

**30 Min.
To Go**

We have been working with graphics but not talking about them. Although this is not a book about graphics, we cannot have an intelligent discussion about any type of Web development without talking about graphic file types and optimization. Before you return to working with your menu graphics, I will pause and look at JPG and GIF files, and the issue of optimizing graphics. I hope that I can dispel a few myths along the way.

Computer Graphics File Types

Web graphics is a part of the computer graphics family, but computer graphics encompasses a much wider field than just Web graphics. You may think that is a silly or patronizing statement, but it is actually critical to understanding Web graphics. If you have come to computer graphics through the Web world, you will find that much of the information available about computer art is confusing. Many of the same programs are used for both Web and print production, yet they are used in many different ways. I begin by defining graphic file types so that you can better discern what concerns Web production and what does not.

Bitmap and vector

All static images on the Web are *raster* (otherwise known as *bitmap*) images. Raster and bitmap refer to a method of constructing an image. Graphic Interchange Format (GIF), Joint Photographic Experts Group (JPG), and Portable Network Graphics (PNG) images, the only Web-acceptable static images to date, are raster images.

However, in the computer graphics world, there are two basic types of files: raster (bitmap) and vector. Why do we care about vector images if we cannot use them on the Web? There are two reasons. The first is that vector programs are often an excellent choice for preparing Web graphics. Vector images can be easily converted to raster format. The second reason is that vector images are used to prepare animated movies such as those produced by Macromedia Flash or Shockwave and Adobe LiveMotion.

Raster images are produced in programs such as Adobe Photoshop, Jasc Paint Shop Pro, and Corel PhotoPaint. Vector programs include Macromedia Freehand, CorelDraw, and Adobe Illustrator. Macromedia Fireworks and Deneba Canvas are examples of programs that work in both file types.

Raster images are constructed pixel by pixel, similar to filling in a grid, as shown in Figure 22-1. Each pixel, or cell in the grid, contains color information to form an image. Image size and resolution is important to a raster image. File size is directly related to the number of pixels in an image. If you enlarge a raster image, the result is usually poor, because you are simply making the little color areas bigger. Quality degrades rapidly. On the other hand, if you make an image smaller without removing some of the pixels, you have a much larger file size than is necessary. Raster images are usually larger than the equivalent image in a vector program, unless it is a photo-type image.

Vector images are created in an entirely different way, as Figure 22-2 illustrates. The view to the eye is exactly the same as for Figure 22-1, but the construction is completely different. Shapes are mathematically created. Instead of a series of pixels to hold color information, vector images use lines and coordinates to create an object. A blue rectangle would be described as "draw a rectangle from coordinates A to B to C to D and fill with blue." If you enlarge or reduce the image, only the coordinates change, so quality remains the same at any size. Unlike with raster images, increasing the size of a vector image retains smooth edges and detail clarity. A full-page graphic will create a file size that is approximately the same size as one that is 1" × 1".

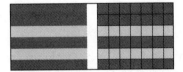

Figure 22-1
Raster images look like the sample at the left, but are created by individual pixels as shown on the right.

Figure 22-2
Vector images are created as objects, mathematically plotted on the page. Compare this sample to the raster version of the same effect.

Ironically, vector images would be wonderful for the Web because many of the graphics that we use in our designs would be miniscule files in a vector format. Unfortunately, using vector images is not an option. Many designers still use vector programs to create Web graphics, or at least design proofs, because the vector work pattern is easier than a raster program for the initial design phase. The graphics must be converted to GIF JPG, or PNG before they can appear on the Web.

The exception to this rule is for movies created with Flash or GoLive. These programs are vector based, but they do require that a special plug-in be installed on the computer. There is also an Scalable Vector Graphics (SVG) viewer that will enable visitors to see vector images, but it is not yet widely enough accepted to use vector images in Web development.

PNG format images

PNG is the Macromedia Fireworks native format. Technically, it is a Web format. Although produced by a hybrid raster/vector program, the resulting files are raster (only Fireworks can access the vector information in a PNG file). Not all browsers recognize this format yet, although it is increasingly being accepted. Although

PNG is a raster format, it has excellent compression and can produce transparent backgrounds on photo-type images. I do not advise using PNG images for Web use yet, although they can be used safely on intranet sites when you know exactly which browser your users have.

Understanding GIF format images

GIF format is one of the Web's "big two" formats. In fact, it is likely that there are significantly more GIF-formatted images on the Web than any other type of image format. GIF format excels for solid color images, such as most menu items and decorative elements (see Figure 22-3). GIF images can also have a transparent background, allowing much more design freedom.

Figure 22-3
The GIF image at the left has clearly defined solid color areas. The JPG image at the right has many more colors and no clearly defined solid color areas.

The drawback to a GIF image is that it can contain a maximum of 256 colors. Although that may sound like a plenty, a photographic image can contain millions of colors. GIF format is best when the image has solid color areas. Images are compressed by reducing the number of colors in the image, an image with only a few solid color areas can have a small file size using GIF format.

Understanding JPG format

The other main Web format, JPG is most at home with photographic-type images (see Figure 22-3), since there are no limits to colors. However, you cannot set transparent areas with this format.

JPG images are compressed to a size acceptable for the Web by removing information. This makes the format excellent for photo-type images, because the eye does not notice the missing information, as long as the image is not overcompressed.

However, solid colors do not fare as well with JPG compression, and quality is often poor for large areas of solid color.

Optimizing Images for the Web

20 Min. To Go

Every image that displays on the Web must be downloaded by the visitor, which places a large responsibility in the hands of every Web designer. Every pixel counts. Although you may have a fast connection, do not assume that most people have the same options. Because I earn much of my living on the Web, I have the best service that is available in my area. Where I live, that "best" is 24,000 bps (on a good day).

Web developers often have Digital Subscriber Line (DSL) or cable connection, and forget that display is not instant for everyone. Do not make that mistake. You are not harming your visitor as much as yourself if your site takes too long to download. Web surfers are impatient people, and with what is available to them, they just move on rather than wait for a bloated page to load.

Images increase your page size much more quickly than text content or code ever will, not that creating clean code is not important — it is. In fact, Dreamweaver keeps track for you. Look at the bottom of the screen for any Dreamweaver document and you will see the total "weight" for your page. This figure, which should be around 20K for our template, includes code, text content, and images. Except in rare circumstances, it should not exceed 45K. Some will likely scream that I am outdated with that number. It has been a standard for years, but many of us are still on the same connections that we were years ago.

We are also moving backward, not forward with connection speed. We have an entire crop of new technology coming into common use — portables, palms, and the like — that are rolling back the average download speed. In North America, local phone access is free, and most of us can connect locally; not so in much of the world. Would you feel differently about file size if you had to pay for every minute on the Web? I sure would and I am already a fanatic on the subject. In fact, many countries with only basic telephone systems are flocking to the Web and will be an important market.

I could go on for pages, giving the reasons why people cannot connect at the high speeds that you, and probably all your contacts, now have. You will have to make your own decision however. You can have great pages with a low file size. It does not take more work, just more knowledge, to create a page that will keep us slowpokes happy.

One of the most comprehensive sources for information about optimizing Web graphics and documents can be found at www.webreference.com/dev/graphics/. **Andy King's series of articles concentrates years of experience into a few pages. These articles are recommended reading for anyone who cares about download time for their work.**

Optimizing GIF images

GIF format files are reduced in size by removing colors. Most graphics programs provide the option to specify how many colors you would like to remain in your image. If your image is a simple button that contains only a few colors, you may get exactly the same result by reducing the number of colors to 8, rather than by using the default of 256. The program discards the information on the other 248 colors and the file size goes down. That is the simple part of GIF optimization. Figure 22-4 shows two similar images that were saved with 256 and 32 colors, respectively, and are of different file sizes. Note that the two images shown here look the same.

Figure 22-4
The image on the left was saved with 256 colors (copy for the Web was in color). The file size is 3.18K. The image at the right was saved with 32 colors (extra colors were necessary for a smooth shadow) and a file size of only 1.52K, which is less than 50 percent of the original file size, with no apparent difference in quality.

There is another way to make your images even smaller though. GIF information is saved in a logical progression horizontally. It reads like we do — across one line, down to the next, across, and so on. If it finds a whole row of one color, it can collect and present that information as a group, rather than reporting on each pixel. That could mean that instead of saving 100 individual pieces of information, it saves 1 piece of information that states that the next 100 pixels are all this color.

Remember this as you design your graphics and ask yourself: Are there places where you can remove tiny areas that interrupt the color gathering information without affecting the look? Can you add horizontal elements to drop the file size? TV scan lines on images have been popular, and wonderful for file size. (Even JPG compresses better with similar horizontal colors.) If you are thinking of adding a vertical texture to a series of buttons, would a horizontal texture work just as well? You will probably save one-half to two-thirds of your file size if you can make the switch.

Optimizing JPG files

JPG format compresses by discarding information, which, of course, affects quality. You are always making choices with JPG images to determine the best combination of small files size with acceptable quality. There certainly are no rules — every image is unique. Occasionally you will run across what I call a "brat" image that will not reduce to a small file size no matter what you do. Fortunately, these are relatively rare.

For most images, you can increase the compression of a JPG image until a fraction of the original information remains. All graphics programs now provide previews that let you see quality as you reduce file size. You make the decision that an image looks good enough, that you can live with the slight quality loss, to gain that smaller file size. See Figure 22-5 for an example.

Figure 22-5
The image on the left is compressed slightly and has a large file size. The image on right is compressed to 20 percent and was a fraction of the size of the first image. If you look closely, you can see that the left image is a little more crisp and detailed, but the second image is one-quarter the file size.

Never resize an image in Dreamweaver. Dreamweaver does not have the right tools to shuffle the information into a smaller size. Graphic programs have complicated capabilities built-in to reduce raster file sizes. But even more important is the "weight" you add to the page. You are forcing your visitor to download an image that is much larger than what they can see. Reducing an image in Dreamweaver does not reduce file size by even 1 byte. Reducing it in a raster program cuts the file size substantially.

Web-safe color

I will not discuss Web-safe color, except to tell you that Dreamweaver offers only Web-safe colors in the color palettes. Use these colors if you are designing for the Web. If you decide to wander from the "safe" colors, be aware that you are more likely to have color shifting (your color will change, sometimes with disastrous results). Colors that are not Web safe can also dither, or have a pattern applied, when Web-safe color is not used.

Although I do not recommend that you use this feature if you are designing for the Web (Intranet design is much more predictable) you can access non-Web safe colors from the Dreamweaver palette. Simply click on the color wheel icon at the top right of the color palette and the Color window will open, presenting the Color window. From here you can select any color.

There are many resources on the Web that cover this extensive subject. The finest, by far, is http://lynda.com. Lynda Weinman has written extensively about Web-safe color. This site is a necessary visit for any serious Web developer.

Graphic optimization is so important to a successful site. As you work through the menus discussed in the rest of this session, count the images we are using. They add up, especially when you are loading two or three sets of images for rollovers. Every byte you save at the graphic production stage is repeated throughout your site.

Adding Rollovers to Menus

**20 Min.
To Go**

Although we have already completed the menu types in this section on our Food Info site, I wanted to go through the menu-building process again now that you understand more about the Dreamweaver interface and placing elements in general. It also helps to have the different construction methods and options presented in one place. Menus and rollovers are important for every site you are likely to create, so this emphasis is important.

You will be working in the main menu and will create simple rollovers for the smaller menu, containing the contribute, about us, and contact menu items, at the right side of the template. You will create a Navigation Bar for the main menu and an interior menu using complex rollovers.

Creating a site menu with a simple rollover

You will create a simple rollover for your smaller top menu. This menu only contains three items. You created this menu with a Navigation Bar when you created the sample menu in Session 17. However, Dreamweaver allows only one Navigation Bar on each page and the extra features offered by the Navigation Bar will save you more time if used for the larger, main menu. You will have to set the down states manually, but because there will be only three pages in the entire site that will be affected by this, it is a reasonable task.

Start by creating a menu with simple rollovers.

1. Open the Main template from the Assets panel or the site window.

2. Select and delete the graphic smmen1.gif. You will replace this graphic with a rollover image. Do not move the cursor.

3. Select Insert ➪ Interactive Images ➪ Rollover Image from the main menu, *or* select Rollover Image from the Objects panel to open the Insert Rollover Image window.

4. Name the image **contribute**.

5. Using the Browse button for the Original Image field, select smmen1.gif from the Art/smmen folder of the Food Info site.

6. Using the Browse button for the Rollover Image field, select smmen1-over.gif.

7. Type **contribute.html** to set the URL. Click OK to complete the rollover.

8. Repeat for the two remaining images using the following files. About Us: name **about**, smmen2.gif, smmen2-over.gif, and URL about.html. Contact: name **contact**, smmen3.gif, smmen3-over.gif, and URL contact.html.

9. Preview the effect in your browser.

10. Save your template. You will set the down state a little later, after you have completed the menus for the template.

Creating your main menu Navigation Bar

**10 Min.
To Go**

Again, this is a repeat performance, because you created a Navigation Bar in Session 17. This time you are working in a template, and have a much larger menu. By the time you finish this menu, you should be comfortable with the method.

To create your new Navigation Bar:

1. Open the Main template from the Assets panel or the site window.

2. Select the images in the main menu and delete. You will replace these graphics with the Navigation Bar.

3. Select Insert ⇨ Interactive Images ⇨ Navigation Bar *or* click on Navigation Bar in the Objects panel to open the Insert Navigation Bar window.

4. Click the Browse button for the Up Image field and select mainmen1.gif from the Art/mainmen folder.

5. Click on the Browse button for the Over Image field and select mainmen1-over.gif.

6. Click the Browse button for the Down Image field and select mainmen1-down.gif.

7. Type **meat.html** for the URL. Do not click OK.

8. To create your next menu item, click on the + at the top of the Insert Navigation Bar. To finish the menu, repeat Steps 4 to 7 using the following files and values:

   mainmen2.gif, mainmen2-over.gif, mainmen2-down.gif, **vegprot.html**

   mainmen3.gif, mainmen3-over.gif, mainmen3-down.gif, **fruitveg.html**

   mainmen4.gif, mainmen4-over.gif, mainmen4-down.gif, **grains.html**

   mainmen5.gif, mainmen5-over.gif, mainmen5-down.gif, **dairy.html**

   mainmen6.gif, mainmen6-over.gif, mainmen6-down.gif, **spices.html**

If your Navigation Bar items are not in proper order, you can adjust menu item position in either the Insert Navigation Bar or Modify Navigation Bar window. Select the menu item you wish to move in the Nav Bar elements list and click on the up or down arrow icons at the top right of the window.

The two preceding exercises were a lot easier the second time around, weren't they? In fact, there are a lot of similarities between all the menu-creation features in Dreamweaver. Now, however, you will move into a new area. Although you made a small sample of a complex rollover earlier, this time you will creat a full menu.

Adding a complex rollover menu

Complex rollovers catch you first as a cool-looking function. But they can also be useful. You can show many images in the space of one image. You can include text (as graphic) descriptions of your menu items. They are still pretty cool, but you can also add a lot of functionality to your site with complex rollovers.

To create the complex rollover using the following steps, you will work in the Behaviors window:

1. Open the Main template from the Assets panel or the site window. You should have a table with the menu featuring History, Cultural, and so on.

   You will take each image, apply a rollover for the menu listing, and have an image appear where there is a blank image now (in the second column). The images should all be named from when you created the template. Check the Properties Inspector to be sure.

2. Select the first image, which is the menu item History. Select Window ➪ Behaviors to open the Behaviors window.

3. Click on the + in the Behaviors window to add a Behavior. Select Swap Image from the menu that pops up.

4. The image History should be selected in the Images list in the Swap Image window. Because you selected this image, you add the next action to it.

5. Click the Browse button next to the Set Source To field. Select inmen1-over.gif from the Art/inmen folder. *Do not click OK.* We still want to replace the blank image with an image to match this menu item.

6. Select blank from the Images list. Click the Browse button next to the Set Source To field. Select inmenim1.gif from the Art/inmen folder. Now you can click OK because we have set both the History image and the Blank image to display different images on mouseover.

7. Repeat Steps 4 and 5 for each of the menu items using the following files:

   inmen2-over.gif and inmenim2.gif

   inmen3-over.gif and inmenim3.gif

   inmen4-over.gif and inmenim4.gif

   inmen5-over.gif and inmenim5.gif

   inmen6-over.gif and inmenim6.gif

8. Preview the results in your browser. They should look like Figure 22-6.

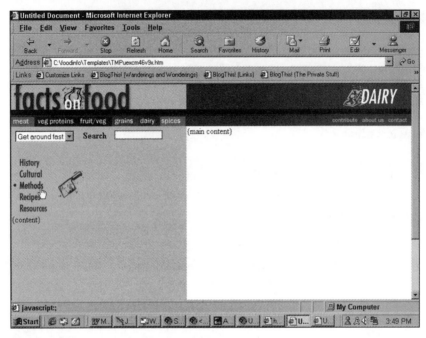

Figure 22-6
Mouse held over the middle menu item on your template preview. Note that the mouseover image is showing as well as the extra image to the right.

You will add the links to this menu as we build our pages over the next few sessions, because this menu will be used on different pages and the links will change on each category of pages.

You now have your menus prepared and will finish them as you put your site together in Session 24.

Done!

You have put a lot of work into your Main template. It is a good idea to make a copy of this file, either under a different name, such as mainbackup, or in a different location.

REVIEW

This is the first time that we have discussed graphics, and it is a bare, introductory primer. However, you will be well on your way to working well with graphics if you remember these points:

- Vector images and raster/bitmap images are constructed in a completely different way. All current formats for static images on the Web are raster formats. Movies, such as those created in Flash and LiveMotion, can display vector-based movies, but a special plug-in is required.

- PNG is best for intranet applications when you know the browser types that are being used, because not all Web browsers recognize the PNG format.

- GIF format images are best for solid-color designs and can have transparent areas.

- Reducing the number of colors used optimizes GIF images.

- JPG format excels for photo-type images but cannot have transparent backgrounds.

- Discarding file information reduces JPG images.

- Only Web safe colors are offered in the default color palette that opens in Dreamweaver. You must use the System Color Picker to choose non-Web safe colors.

- Menus with rollover features can be prepared in many different ways in Dreamweaver, including simple rollovers, complex rollovers, and Navigation Bars.

QUIZ YOURSELF

1. What is a vector image? (See "Bitmap and vector.")
2. What is a raster image? (See "Bitmap and vector.")
3. Why is it important to optimize images even though so many people now have faster connections? (See "Optimizing Images for the Web.")
4. How are GIF images compressed? (See "Optimizing GIF images.")
5. How are JPG images compressed? (See "Optimizing JPG images.")
6. Why should you never reduce an image size in Dreamweaver? (See "Optimizing JPG images.")
7. What color palette does Dreamweaver use as a default? (See "Web-safe color.")

Controlling Text with CSS

Session Checklist

✔ Understanding the differences between Cascading Style Sheets
   and HTML styles

✔ Using and editing HTML styles

✔ Using and editing Cascading Style Sheets

✔ Controlling text with Cascading Style Sheets

✔ Creating linked and class style sheets

✔ Preparing a style sheet for your site

**30 Min.
To Go**

I have not spent much time talking about text. That has been a deliberate
omission, because HTML text is best controlled by Cascading Style Sheets
(CSS). CSS offers many benefits, including significantly less code and a great
deal more flexibility for presenting text. When you take CSS to a linked file, you
can control all the text on your site from one file, which, like a template, can be
edited at any time, with the changes reflected on every page.

CSS is not just related to text control. You can also control positioning, defining
your entire page with dynamic HTML (DHTML) and CSS. However, I do not cover all
of that here. It takes a bigger book to cover all the aspects of CSS, especially when

you are concerned with pages that display properly on all browsers, as you are with this course. Instead, I concentrate on the text capabilities within CSS.

CSS is not to be confused with HTML styles. HTML styles are simply collections of HTML tags that can be applied in one action. I discuss HTML styles first and then move on to CSS.

Understanding HTML and CSS Text Styles

People from the print world have a leg up with the idea of using styles. So do you if you have been using styles with a word processing program. The idea of a style is simple. Instead of applying attributes, such as font or bold, to each section of text, you instead assign a style. You then create a way for your document to tell what each style means.

For example, suppose you wish to have all of your captions in an italic version of the main font. Instead of applying italics to each caption, you instead apply a style called Caption. Within your document, you place a bit of information that tells the document what to do when it hits the Caption style. When the document is displayed, it will first load the information for the styles that you have defined. Then each time the document comes to a Caption style, it will apply the parameters of that style to that paragraph (most styles work on full paragraphs), making all your caption text italic.

Suppose you later decide that you really want your captions to be in a different font and that you would like them to be blue. If you are using styles, you simply change the information in the style definition to the new font and blue color, and remove the italic command. Instantly, all the captions in your document reflect the change, no matter how many pages you have.

That is the true power of styles of any type. In Web design, styles become even more valuable, because you may have hundreds of separate pages. Just remembering what font settings you used, so that you can be consistent, is hard enough. Making changes on every page is a nightmare idea.

Using HTML Styles

HTML styles do not offer the site-wide benefits that CSS does because they only affect the page where they are used. You can use the same styles on many pages, which provides a simple way and is a time-saver, but changing an HTML style does not transfer changes to the pages that you have already created.

HTML formatting, such as the type created when using HTML styles, is not encouraged. With the release of the HTML 4.0 specifications, the W3C (World Wide Web Consortium) discourages the use of HTML formatting in favor of CSS.

However, while CSS is a much more efficient way to control text, HTML formatting is more compatible across browsers. Because it will take precedent over a CSS command, perhaps overcoming a CSS non-compatibility issue, HTML formatting is still commonly used.

Let's apply a style and take a look at the code produced.

Applying an HTML style

To apply an HTML style, follow these steps:

1. Open a new window in Dreamweaver. You will use this just for a text page, so name it **trash.html** or something similar so that you will know to discard it.

2. Type **I will be using an HTML style to change this text. I will then view the code that results.** Check your code after you have this typed, or open the Code/Design View so that you can track changes.

3. Highlight the first sentence. Open the HTML style window by Selecting Window ➪ HTML styles *or* click on the HTML styles icon in the Launcher Bar at the bottom right of the screen. You can also apply styles through the menu by selecting Text ➪ HTML Styles and selecting the correct name, but for this example, we want the HTML Styles window to be open.

4. Click on the Bold listing in the HTML styles listing. The selected text will change to bold.

However, look at your code. Nothing magic has been entered in the code. Our HTML style simply added the <b> and </b> tag to our selected text. Once the style has been applied, the document has no way to determine whether the new code was placed as individual code, or from an HTML style.

Creating a custom HTML style

**20 Min.
To Go**

You can create your own style easily from text that has the parameters you wish to repeat. To create your own HTML style from text, follow these steps:

1. Using the text you typed for the sample above, highlight the word **code**. Apply bold and italic to the text, and change the text color to blue. You will use this text to create a new style.

2. With the formatted word still selected, and your HTML Style window open, click on the + icon at the bottom of the HTML Styles window *or* open the flyout menu at the right top of the HTML Styles window and select New.

3. Type **Important** as the name. Make sure that Selection is highlighted for the Apply To section. Choosing Paragraph here means that when you apply this style in the future, it will be applied to the entire paragraph, not just the selected text.

4. Make sure that the Clear Existing Style option is selected. If you do not use this selection, the attributes included in the style will be added to whatever formatting is already in place.

5. Check that the remaining attributes are correct and click OK.

6. Highlight the word **results**. Click the listing for Important in the HTML Styles window. The style that you just created will be applied, as shown in Figure 23-1.

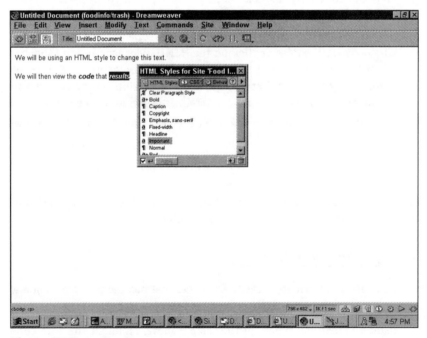

Figure 23-1
A custom HTML style is applied to selected text.

You can create a style from scratch or from another style as well. To create an HTML style without text selected, follow these steps:

1. To start from scratch, make sure no text is selected and select New from the Menu or the New icon. Specify the attributes that you require.

2. To create a style based on another style, select the style you wish to base the new style on and select Duplicate from the flyout menu. Specify the desired attributes as in Step 1.

Editing an HTML style

Finally, to edit an existing style, select the style that you wish to edit and select Edit from the flyout menu. Change or add attributes as you require. Note that editing the style has no effect on the text that has already had the style applied.

HTML styles can save you time, but CSS is a much better choice for text control because you have editing power over your whole site from one file. HTML styles should be used only where you would be using HTML formatting anyway.

Using CSS Styles

By now, you have an idea of how styles are used from working with the HTML styles. However, that is just the beginning of the discussion about CSS style sheets. I focus only on style sheets that are contained in a separate file, but you can also add CSS styles to each page individually.

CSS styles are stored in the head of the document. In the samples you will be doing, only a link to the CSS file is stored in the head. When the document loads, it goes to the CSS file to find out how to display the text. This is a powerful technique because you can change that file, and the next time the document is called by a visitor, it finds the new information when it looks for the CSS file.

Using CSS is a two-step process. First you create a style sheet and then, when preparing the text, you make sure that you are assigning the styles that correspond with the style sheet. Like any feature that can control many pages, solid planning in the initial stages is always an investment. A well-planned style sheet will enable you to work on your design without paying much attention to the text formatting. However, style sheets often grow or change as your project advances.

Although HTML formatting can be applied to text that is controlled by style sheets, and the HTML will override the CSS, you do not want to do that any more often than necessary. Occasionally, you may want one piece of text to be a different color. In that case, HTML formatting makes sense. However, if you use that variation a few times, it would be better to set up a new style. As with any "template"-type document, for consistency and editing speed, it is better to use the master settings to set up everything in your site.

Creating a new CSS style sheet

The best way to understand CSS is to actually use it. You will create a simple, linked style sheet to start, and then will create a page using the styles. Again, you will work on a test page so that you can get your errors out of the way before you create the style sheet for your site. My natural way of working is to create a bare-bones style sheet, containing little more than the font specifications for the <p> tag and the link colors. As I proceed to build the first few pages, my style sheet grows. Usually around mid-construction I reach the end of the changes and pay little attention to the style sheet from that time forward.

Now you will create a new document to test the CSS methods by following these steps:

1. Create a new document. Save the file as testcss.html.

2. Type **This is the text that I will use to test CSS in a linked file.** Click anywhere in the text and check the Properties Inspector. If the format is not Paragraph, select Paragraph from the drop-down list.

3. Select Text ➪ CSS Styles ➪ New Style.

4. The first style you will set is for the <p> tag. The Redefine HTML Tag radio button should be selected in the Type area. Make sure that the Tag field is displaying *p*.

5. You want to create a new style sheet, so you want the Define In selection to be [New Style Sheet File]. Click OK. The Save Style Sheet File As window will appear.

6. Make sure that the active folder is Foodinfo. Type **testcss** in the File Name field. This is the name of our new CSS file. Click Save, and the style sheet will be saved in the root folder as testcsss.css. The Style Definition window you see in Figure 23-2 will open.

   You construct all of your styles in this window. You can attach many styles at one time, although to keep this step simple, you will set the paragraph style. Most of the styles you will apply will be through Type in the Category list. Let's carry on to set the <p> style.

7. With Type selected in the Category list, select Arial, Helvetica, and sans serif from the Font drop-down. When this style is activated on a site, your visitor's browser will check their computer for fonts in the order that they appear. In this case, it would check for Arial, and if Arial is not found, it would look for Helvetica. If neither font was found, the browser would finally accept the computer default sans serif font to display any text in a <p> tag.

Sans serif fonts do not have horizontal design elements, often referred to as *feet.* **Serif fonts do have feet, or the little marks on each character.** Times New Roman **is a serif font and** Arial **is a sans serif font.**

8. Type **10** in the Size field and choose points from the drop-down box next to the size field. This sets the font size to a fixed size of 10 points.

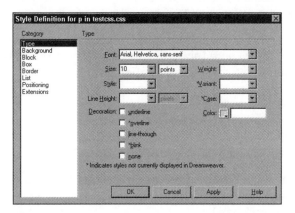

Figure 23-2
The Style Definition window is where all CSS styles are created. The <p> tag is active in this sample, as you can see in the window title bar.

9. Click OK, then Save, and then Done to see the changes. Check your text. It should now be in a sans serif font.

10. Check your code and in the Head area; you will see <link rel="stylesheet" href="testcss.css">. This is the link to our style sheet.

I would like you to see the actual CSS style sheet, although it is not necessary that you understand the syntax for the file. If you try to view the file in Dreamweaver, the window used for editing your style sheet appears, which does show the connection between the document and the files.

To view the CSS file, follow these steps:

1. Open a plain text editor, such as Notepad in Windows. Select File ⇨ Open and navigate your way to the Foodinfo root folder. On a PC, you will have to specify All Files in the Files of Type drop-down selection.

2. Select the file testcss.css and open it.

   The file will contain only the following code:

   ```
   p {  font-family: Arial, Helvetica, sans-serif}
   p {  font-size: 10pt}
   ```

   This is the information that a visitor's browser will use to display the <p> tag in your page. I just wanted you to actually open the separate file to fully understand the connection. We could change this file from the text program, and the changes would be reflected both in the Dreamweaver CSS editor, and in any pages that were displayed with testcss.css.

3. Close the file without saving it.

4. Activate the Food Info site window. Locate the testcss.css file in the root folder. I just wanted you to see the physical location for this file.

Linking to a CSS file

**10 Min.
To Go**

You can now link your CSS file to any other page by following these steps:

1. Create a new document. Type **This is the second document that will be linked to testcss.html.** Make sure that the text is set to Paragraph format. Save the file as **testcss2.html**.

2. You will link the style sheet you created in the last exercise to this document. Select Text ⇨ CSS Styles > Attach Style Sheet. The Select Style Sheet File window will open.

3. Select testcss.css from the root folder of the Food Info site. Click Select to return to your document. Check your code and you will see the same link code as the first document contained after you added the CSS link.

You will edit the CSS next, and you can watch the changes take place in both documents.

Editing a CSS file

After you have your CSS file linked, you can make changes from within Dreamweaver at any time, as shown in these steps:

1. From either document, select Text ⇨ CSS Styles ⇨ Edit Style Sheet. The Edit Style Sheet window will open.

2. Select testcss.css and click the Edit button. The testcss.css window will open.

3. You will now add a style for our links. Click the New button.

4. Make sure the Redefine HTML Tag selection is chosen and select *a*. The Style Definition window will open.

    The *a* or link tag will take on the properties of the <p> style unless you change any attributes. For this example, you will change the link style to be a different font and a light blue color. You will then return to the link tag and change the color again.

5. Select Times New Roman, Times, Serif from the Font drop-down list.

6. Select color #99CCFF from the Color area.

7. Click OK, then Save, and then Done to return to your document.

8. You will see no changes yet, because you do not yet have a link in your text. To create links for testing, highlight the word document in testcss2.hmtl. Type # in the Link field of the Properties Inspector. This sets up a link for testing. Repeat this process in testcss.html, highlighting the word link.

9. Check the code on both documents and you will see that even though we applied a different font, and a new color, there is no formatting code around the link. The color and font is coming directly from the CSS file.

    ```
    <p>This is the second <a href="#">document</a> that will be
    linked to testcss.html.</p>
    ```

10. Repeat the edit process to change the link color to a darker blue.

You now have the basics of creating a CSS linked file. Now, add a few more tags to your style sheet before you move on to a slightly different CSS style type.

1. On a new line, in both documents, type **Headline H1.** Assign Heading 1 formatting to this line. Use your Enter key to create a new line and type **Smaller Headline H2.** Assign Heading 2 formatting to this line.

2. Repeat Steps 1 to 4 in the preceding instructions, but select H1 as the tag to edit. Select Arial, Helvetica, sans serif as the Font, and red as the Color. Accept all screens as you return to your document. Check both documents and you will see that both H1 lines have changed.

3. Repeat for the H2 style, assigning the same font and a green color.

By now, you should be seeing the connection between the file and the documents that you are creating. Don't try to make it harder than it is. When you are editing a CSS style, the changes are written to the separate file testcss.css.

The styles that you have made so far, have all applied to a full paragraph. You can also create a special type of style that can be applied to selected text only.

Creating a custom CSS style

You have been using the predefined HTML tags as a base for your styles. However, you can also create custom CSS styles. Custom styles can be added to a paragraph, but they can also be added to a selection of text. For this example, you will create a style to use for captions. Custom styles can be included on any style sheet.

To create a style for your captions, follow these steps:

1. Type **When I want a caption style, I have the perfect method**. In your Properties Inspector, choose Paragraph from the Format drop-down menu to apply the <p> tag, or Paragraph style, to your text (it may already be Paragraph).

2. Select Text ⇨ CSS Styles ⇨ Edit Style sheet.

3. Select testcss.css and click the Edit button.

4. Click the New button and the New Style window opens.

5. Select Make Custom Style [class] in the Type section.

   Custom styles can be named anything, but it is best to choose a descriptive name. However, the name must be preceded with a period, as in .stylename.

6. Type **.caption** in the Name field. Your New style window should look like Figure 23-3. Click OK.

7. The font will be assigned from the <p> tag if nothing is entered in the Font field. Leave it at default. Select Italic from the drop-down list for Style. Choose a dark color that you have not used yet. Return to your document, accepting changes as you go.

Figure 23-3
Creating a custom style named .caption. Note that the Make Custom Style [class] option is active.

8. Highlight the text that you just typed. Select Text ⇨ CSS Styles ⇨ caption. Each custom style that you create will be listed here.

9. Check your code and you will see that this style application does have an entry in the code.

```
<p class="caption">When I want a caption style, I have the
perfect method.</p>
```

Your custom style is complete. However, this caption is not attractive, so you should edit it.

Editing a custom CSS style

You could probably figure this one out on your own, but I do like to make sure that I have all the bases covered. To make changes in a CSS style sheet after it has been created, follow these steps:

1. Select Text ⇨ CSS Styles ⇨ Edit Style Sheet.

2. Select test.css and click the Edit button.

3. You will see your .caption file at the top of the list. Highlight it and click Edit.

4. Change the font to Times New Roman, Times, serif. Don't click OK yet.
   Dreamweaver offers a preview for your CSS styles, so that you can peek at the results before you accept the changes.

5. Click Apply. The Style Definition window will remain open, but the changes you made are applied to the document. When you are satisfied with the results, click OK and accept changes as you return to your document.

You can also add custom styles to your text through the CSS Styles panel. Select Window ⇨ CSS Styles *or* click the Show CSS Styles icon in the Launcher Bar at the bottom right of your screen. Insert your cursor in a paragraph (to affect the entire paragraph) or select the text you wish to change, and click the defined style in the CSS Styles window.

Preparing CSS for Your Site

Now that you have the basics of CSS, you are ready to create a style sheet for your site. Follow these steps to add a link to the style sheet in your template:

1. From within the Food Info site, open the Assets panel and activate the templates area. Highlight Main template and click the Edit icon at the bottom of the Assets panel.

2. Select Text ⇨ CSS Styles ⇨ New Style. The New Style window will open.

3. Select Redefine HTML Tag and select *p* from the drop-down list for Tag. Make sure that the Define value is [New Style Sheet File]. Click OK.

4. Type **foodinfo** as the filename and click Save.

5. Set the following values for our paragraph style: Font: Verdana, Arial, Helvetica, sans serif; size 10 pt.

6. Continue, using what you learned to create the following styles:

   H1: Font: Arial, Helvetica, sans serif; size: 20 points; color: #663300.

   H2: Font: Arial, Helvetica, sans serif; size: 18 points; color: #990000

7. Now, you will make more exciting links using the CSS selector option. From within the foodinfo.css window, click on the New button.

8. Choose Use CSS Selector for the Type. From the Selector drop-down list, choose a:link. Click OK. This will take you to the Style Definition window in which you can specify how your link will appear. Choose a blue color.

Links should be in blue and underlined for visitor convenience. Many designers scoff at this idea, but observe your own surfing behavior. When you see an underlined, blue section of text, without thinking, you know it is a link. A well-designed page leads the visitor easily to where the visitor wants to go. Standard links help reach this goal.

9. Create a New style, again choosing CSS Selector as the type, but this time select a:hover from Selector drop-down list. Specify #663300 (brown) as the color for this style (see Figure 23-4). When your visitor holds their mouse over a link, this color will appear.

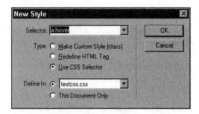

Figure 23-4
CSS selector style is chosen in the New Style window. The a:hover style controls link color when the mouse is passed over.

10. Create a New style, again choosing CSS Selector as the type, but this time select a:visited from the Selector drop-down list. Specify #990000 (dark red) as the color for this style. This is the color that the link will become when the page for that link has been visited.

Done!

11. Accept the changes to your style sheet and return to your template. Save, and allow any pages to be updated when prompted.

REVIEW

I hope you are excited about what you learned in this session. CSS for text is one of the best features for designers, and one that you should use from the start. HTML styles can come in handy as well. Just remember that:

- HTML styles can be used for consistency, but changing a style does not affect text that has already been formatted with an HTML style.
- HTML styles can be created to apply to a full paragraph or a text selection.
- CSS style definitions or links to style sheets are always stored in the head area of the document.
- When you use a CSS linked file, you can change the text style on thousands of pages by adjusting one file.
- When text is formatted with CSS, no formatting appears in the body of the document, significantly reducing the amount of code required for each page.

- You can create a new CSS file or link to an existing file in Dreamweaver.
- Most CSS formatting styles can be applied only to a full paragraph.
- Custom or Class CSS styles can be applied to a text selection or to a full paragraph.

QUIZ YOURSELF

1. What is a CSS text style? (See the "Understanding HTML and CSS Text Styles" section.)

2. What is an HTML style? (See the "Using HTML Styles" section.)

3. What is the benefit of using a linked CSS style sheet? (See the "Using CSS Styles" section.)

4. How do you create a linked style sheet in Dreamweaver? (See the "Creating a new CSS style sheet" section.)

5. How can you link to a style sheet from a new page? (See the "Linking to a CSS file" section.)

6. What is a custom CSS style and how is it applied to text? (See the "Creating a custom CSS style" section.)

7. Why is it important to keep default link colors on your site? (See the "Preparing CSS for Your Site" section.)

Pulling Your Site Together

Session Checklist

✔ Going over the site components

✔ Putting the final touches on the template

✔ Working with section pages

✔ Creating utility pages

**30 Min.
To Go**

I
n this session, you will pull all the loose ends together for your site. You have done a lot of background work up to this point, with many pieces just waiting in the wings to fall magically together and become a site. Well, here is where it happens.

I do not mean to imply that creating a site will always be this organized. I had the site finished before you started working on it, so I was able to use hindsight to plot a wonderfully straight course through to the end. However, the more experience you do get, the more you will find that you try to build a site with components. Even today, the amount of work it takes to pull a site together from start to finish always amazes me. The more you can use well-planned repetitive elements, the better your final site will be.

Let's first review what you have, and then start gluing the whole project together.

Reviewing the Site Components

You have reached the opposite end of the planning that you started with your site map in Session 17. Now you must gather up what you have and make some last minute adjustments to complete all the pieces that you need. You will probably be surprised when you realize how many of the site components you have completed.

- Navigation planned and mapped
- Template prepared and ready to create first section
- Jump menu prepared and inserted into template
- Subpages created
- Rollover menu prepared for subpages
- Utility pages (such as contact) saved and ready for content

Although you have yet to complete one page, you can see that many of the final components for this site are already in place. This is the best way — in my opinion, the only way — to assemble a site, especially one as large as the Food Info site. You can move forward with confidence, knowing that you are building your site with tested pages and that the look will be consistent throughout the site. I promised that your preparation time would be repaid many times over once you reached this stage. You must make a few more template changes, and then I will deliver on that promise.

Finalizing the Template

The major portion of your work went into creating your template. It needs just a few rollover images (the side menu) and the template is ready to be used for your pages. You will be making some adjustments to the new pages that you create, which has been planned all along. You will remove the active link from the main menu, replace the top graphic for each section, and then prepare the three pages you will need to create a "down" state on your small side menu.

There is one more job to complete with your complex rollover menu. You need six different versions of the links in the menu to indicate when a page that is featured in the menu is active. You will create a new Library Item for each menu variation.

Adding rollovers to the side menu

The side menu still has only your placeholder graphics. You must replace the images with a rollover menu to show visitors that it is an active menu. You have had some experience with creating simple rollovers, so I will give you only very general directions. If you have trouble placing the rollovers, refer to Session 13.

1. Select the Contribute menu item image and delete it.
2. Add a rollover image using `smallmen1.gif` as the original image and `smallmen1-over.gif` as the rollover image. All of the images can be found in the Art/smmen folder.
3. Repeat Steps 1 and 2 for the second and third menu item, selecting and deleting the next image in the row. The filenames follow a logical, numerical order.
4. Save the template and, if prompted, allow updates.

Creating Library Items from your rollover menu

To prepare for creating Library Items, you must first build the variations for the rollover menu. Each of the main menu categories requires one of these menus, but the URLs for each of the links is different for each category. Because there are six pages in each main category, it is well worth the few extra steps to have the menus as Library Items.

You created a rollover menu in Session 22, but you did not enter the links for the menu. You will do that now. You will create a Library Item from the menu without links, and then use that menu to create the variations you require.

There are many different ways in which to handle these changing menus. One method has been to include them as you save your section pages (which you will do next). I like to have a Library Item when I can, however, because one of these menus might be the makings of a special page at a later date. It is much easier to drop a Library Item in place than it is to open a file and then cut and paste the menu into another document.

You are going to work in a rather unusual way through this next section, so pay close attention. You will open the template, and you will then create a new page from that template to build the Library Items from your menu. Why not just build them in your template, you ask? Template files are stored in a separate folder, and your links would come from that folder if you created Library Items in the template. You must always be aware of where the file you are using is located in relation to the rest of the site. The new page created from the template will be saved in exactly the same location as the pages where you will be using the Library Items.

Editing the first menu and creating a Library Item

Take the following steps o create your Library menus:

1. Create a new page from the Main template. Save the new page as **interiormenus.html**.

2. You will now edit the rollover menu and save a new Library Item for the Meat main menu pages. Select the graphic menu item labeled "History". In the Properties Inspector, type **meathis.html** in the Link field.

3. Select the "Culture" menu item. Type **meatcul.html** in the Link field. Repeat this step for the remaining menu items, typing the following text, respectively, for the links: **meatmeth.html**, **meatrec.html** and **meatres.html**.

4. When you have specified all of the links, select the table that holds the menu (check your code to make sure you have the entire table selected).

5. Open the Assets window and activate the Library section. Click the + (plus) icon in the lower portion of the Assets window to create a new Library Item. Type **menu meat** for the Library Item title.

When you are creating multiple files with similar names that are used together, as your menus will be, name the item (or file) with the common word as the first entry. In this case, your six menus will all begin with the word "menu," and they will appear together in an alphabetical listing.

You have, in effect, saved this menu by creating a Library Item. To create your next Library menu item, you can simply edit the one you just created, because it is safely saved as a Library Item.

Creating the second menu and Library Item

Your next step is to create a menu with the correct links for the Veg/Protein section. You are starting a little differently with this one, because you have the Library Item that you just created in place. You must first break the Library link, and you must then edit the menu and create a new Library Item. Take the following steps:

1. In your document, select the Library Item rollover menu. In the Properties Inspector, click Detach from Original.

2. Now you are where you started with the previous sample. Type the following link names, as you did in the previous exercise: **vegprothist. html**, **vegprotcult.html**, **vegprotmeth.html**, **vegprotrec.html** and **vegprotres.html**.

3. Repeat Steps 4 and 5 in the previous exercise to create a new Library Item named **menu vegprot**.

You should be able to see the pattern now. Repeat the last exercise to complete a Library Item for the remaining four main menu items: fruitveg, grains, dairy, and spices. Use the same naming pattern for the link names as well as the Library Item name. Figure 24-1 shows the completed list of Library Items.

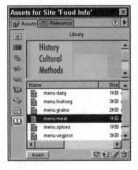

Figure 24-1
Menu variations stored as Library Items. The menus are all listed together because the common word is placed first in the item name.

Creating the First Section of New Pages

**20 Min.
To Go**

I decided early on in this project that this site could be built from a single template. That is always my choice if I can do it, and I often will do a little more work during the construction of the site to ensure that when it is complete, that it is running from one common source.

That does not mean, however, that you cannot use other ways to duplicate and speed your production. You have six main sections to this site — the main menu items. You will create the entry page for each section (such as meat.html), and then save the same page to each of the section titles (such as meathist.html). In this way, all of the changes you make to create the main section page will be passed on to the other section pages, but the original template will remain as the master for every page.

Editing the template for a section main page

Take the following steps to create the meat.html page first, and to then duplicate the page for the rest of the section pages.

1. Select File ⇨ New From Template. Choose Main in the New From Template window list. Save the new file as meat.html.

2. You must change the top menu area for the Meat section. Select the upper-right graphic and replace it with the file meat.gif from the Art folder. Place your cursor in the table cell holding the graphic and change the background color to match the image background (click the image background with the eyedropper). Place your cursor in the cell to the left of the image cell and repeat this step to change the background.

3. The main menu item for Meat must be removed, as well. Click the graphic "Meat" and delete it.

   This sets up the basics for the Meat page. You are ready to add the correct rollover menu. This gets a little tricky because you must delete the current menu and then add the new one. However, if you work with your Code/Design view active, you will have no trouble.

4. Click the Show Code and Design View button in the toolbar to allow you to work in Design View but confirm placement in the Code view.

5. Select the table containing the rollover menu. Your code and document should resemble the document shown in Figure 24-2. Delete the selection by pressing your Enter key. This will expand the menu section and make it easier to place the Library Item.

6. Drag the Menu meat Library Item to the rollover location. You will have to remove the extra <p> tags around the menu. Use your Code view to ensure that the code starts as follows:

```
<!-- #BeginEditable "interior%20menu" --> <!--
#BeginLibraryItem "/Library/menu meat.lbi" --><table
width="150" border="0" cellspacing="0" cellpadding="0">
   <tr>
```

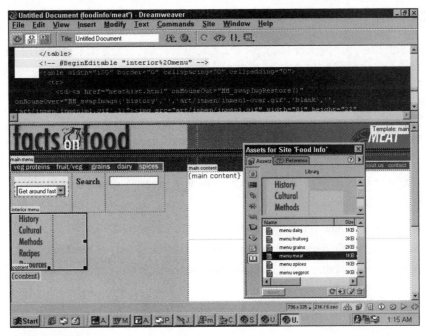

Figure 24-2
Rollover menu selected and ready to be deleted. Code/Design View shown.

Ensure that your code ends as follows:

```
<img src="art/inmen/inmen5.gif" width="81" height="22"
name="resources" border="0"></a></td></tr>
   </table><!-- #EndLibraryItem -->
```

One final little touch is needed. When a visitor is on one of the subpages, they need a way to get back to the main page for that section. With the structure of this site, that will not be a natural pattern. However, you can provide a logical — if not visible — path back to the main page by adding a link to the title image at the top.

7. Select the Meat title graphic. Type **meat.html** in Link field in the Properties inspector. You should remove the link from the actual `meat.html` page once you have made the copies.

The correct menu for the Meat section is now in place, and you are ready to create the rest of the pages in your section.

Creating a subsection page

You will use your perfect Meat page to create the rest of the pages in this section. Check your code to the best of your abilities, because there is nothing more annoying than creating multiple copies of the same error or sloppy code.

Never save multiple copies of a file without first saving the original. It is a common error to start saving the duplicated files before you have saved the final changes to the "master" file.

Once your code is perfect, take the following steps to create new pages:

1. Save meat.html.
2. Save the same file as meathist.html.
3. Immediately save the file (now called meathist.html) as meatcult.html.
4. Continue saving in this manner for meatmeth.html, meatrec.html, and meatres.html.
5. Close all of the files.

When you are working with several identical files, it is a good idea to only work with one open file at a time. Until you can add some distinctive features that identify each page, working with several identical files can easily lead to confusion and errors.

Wow! You have one entire section completed — almost. You are going to make individual changes to the subpage menus.

Finalizing the subpages

Just one more step and you will have an entire section ready to receive content. It is always easier to navigate a site that easily identifies the current page, so you will adjust the rollover menu on the interior pages as a marker for location.

1. Open meathist.html.
2. Select the rollover menu Library Item and click Detach from Original in the Properties Inspector.
3. Select the image for the History menu item and delete it. This removes the image and the rollover behavior for that item.
4. Place your cursor in the empty table cell and insert the file inmen1-over.gif from the Art/inmen folder. Your page should resemble Figure 24-3.

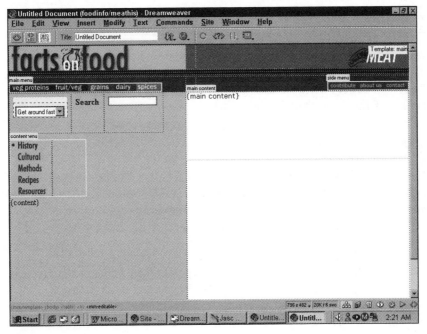

Figure 24-3
The Meat History page with the changed menu

5. Save and close the file.

Your Meat History page is now marked by a different graphic in the menu. Repeat this process for each page in the meat subsection, deleting the menu item that matches the page title and replacing with the "over" image for each item.

Do not **edit the menu on the** meat.html **page. This is your entry page to this section, and there should be no entries shown as active from the submenu.**

Now you *are* finished with this section. You will not go any further with step-by-step instructions, because each section will be created exactly as this one was created — with the filenames changed and a different Library Item menu specified. I would advise that you complete at least one more section while the method is fresh in your mind.

Completing Pages Outside the Main Sections

You have a few pages that do not fit within your main content pages which must be built. These include your entry page (index.html) and the side menu pages. These will be very quick. In fact, your INDEX page is very close to the template. Let's start there.

**10 Min.
To Go**

Creating the Index page

The Index page will be the page that visitors see first. You do not need the rollover menu, because that is accessed through the main section pages. You also must make sure that the graphics and head background color are correct.

Follow these steps to create the Index page:

1. Create a new file from the Main template and name it index.html.

2. The title image may not be correct, depending on where in the process you might have saved your template. The correct image to use is answer.gif from the Art directory. The background color for the center and right cell in the first row should match the image background.

3. Select the table containing the rollover menu. Delete the selection.

   You must remove the rollover menu. You have a few choices here. You cannot remove the editable region, even when you delete the menu. The empty editable region has no effect on the page, and will only be on four pages in the site. You could create a new template, but that would defeat my goal of having a single template. You could break the link to the template and have the editable regions disappear naturally, but you have still lost your one template editing capability. You can try the other methods, but even though I am obsessive about removing extra code, I lean toward keeping the nonintrusive editable regions in the pages that do not have the interior menu in this case.

4. Save the file.

Your index entry page is now ready for content. You will use this page to save the `contribute.html` page, because the side menu pages do not require the interior menus.

Creating the side menu pages

Take the following steps to create side menu pages:

1. With index.html open and saved, save the file as contribute.html.
2. Change the page title image to contribute.gif from the Art/Titles folder. Change the background color for the center and right cells of the heading row to the same color as the image background.
3. Save the file.

   Because the background color for your three side menu pages is the same, you will use contrubute.html to save the other two files.
4. With contribute.html open and saved, save the file as about.html.
5. Immediately save the file again, but this time, save it as contact.html.
6. Return to the last two files and replace the title images with about.gif and contact.gif from the Art/titles folder.

You want to take one more step for the side menu pages. You must let the visitors know where they are, so you will change the image for the menu items on the active page. You also must remove the link to the page when it is active.

Use the following method to create an active state for each of your pages:

1. Open contribute.html.
2. Select the image for the Contribute menu item. In the Properties Inspector, delete the link. This will break the behavior that is applied to the image, as well as remove an active link. You will receive an alert that the behaviors will no longer work. Click OK.
3. Replace the image with smmen1-down.gif from the Art/smmen folder. Your page should resemble Figure 24-4.
4. Repeat Steps 1 through 3 with about.html and contact.html, but use the "down" version of the image you are replacing.

You are ready for content. In the next session, you will place your content and run through some testing and cleanup. You have a few changes to make to your template, and then you will place it on the Web. Then, in Session 26, because you have worked so hard and have the basics down, you will move on to some interesting techniques to add motion and sound to your pages.

Done!

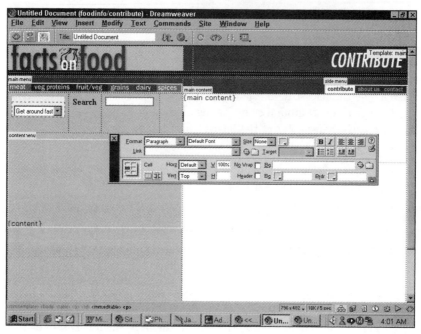

Figure 24-4
The Contribute page with the "down" state image in place

REVIEW

Although much of what you did in this session may have felt like familiar territory, you stretched into some new areas, and you certainly moved into production mode. Make sure you remember the following details:

- When you have finished building the components for your site, it is a good idea to assess what is yet to be completed. Once you move from building to production mode, any omissions or errors are often compounded.

- Create Library Items whenever there is a possibility that you will need to repeat that item. It is much easier to call a Library Item from the Assets panel than it is to copy from one document to another.

- Name files or items that you want to display in sequence, with the first word as the one word that will be common to every object in the series.

- Saving one file from another can help to keep the entire site run by one template.

- Check your code when removing Items from editable regions in a template. There may be some code left behind.
- Always give visitors a visual clue to their location, such as color changes or different graphics for the active listing.
- Removing a rollover image breaks the behavior for that image.

Quiz Yourself

1. Why must you pay close attention to file locations when you are working with templates? (See the "Creating Library Items from your rollover menu" section.)

2. How can you keep files in a series listed together? (See the "Editing the first menu and creating a Library Item" section.)

3. Why is it better to have fewer templates for a site? (See the "Creating the First Section of New Pages" section.)

4. What are two good practices when saving files from other files? (See the "Creating a subsection page" section.)

Creating a Finished Page

Session Checklist

✔ Focusing on accessibility concerns

✔ Placing content text

✔ Cleaning up your page

✔ Checking the target browser

✔ Testing your site

**30 Min.
To Go**

You now have your template finished. I have left one job, adding Alt tags to your images, because that gives you one more chance to edit your template as well as enter the information on the images that are not included in the template. As you move on to adding text, your pages start to take on their own personalities, which, of course, means unique problems. However, because you are working in templates, you can shift content at will without risking your page layout.

In this session, you will also look at important utility tools, such as spell check, search and replace, and Dreamweaver's HTML checker. You'll take a look at how your site will do with a variety of browsers and talk about how you can run your site through its browser paces before you release it to the public.

Your careful work in the earlier sessions should pay off now. Over years of professional work in the computer graphics industry, I have established beyond all doubt that it is much faster to create your pages right the first time, rather than repairing them.

I'd like to start by talking a little about accessibility and adding a key component for accessible pages, Alt tags.

Addressing Accessibility Concerns

Accessibility is geared toward those people who are unable to use the Web in the way that most people do. For example, blind users obviously cannot use any visual clues on a site, but they can still have the benefit of the information when a designer keeps accessibility issues in mind.

Accessibility is a growing issue as more and more businesses and government services move some or all of their services to the Web. If you are working for a government agency, or hoping to work with government agencies, you must be able to create fully accessible sites. For more information, check Bobby, an accessibility information center and page tester at www.cast.org/bobby/. You should also visit www.w3.org/, a site that has information on current Web standards, as well as a section on accessibility.

In the space I have available here, I can do no more than to make you aware of the issue and to guide you through placing an *Alt tag,* which is an extra tag on an image. This tag contains text describing the image, and enables people with limited or no vision to understand the page. As a bonus, sighted people who surf with their graphics disabled can still read about your image, and you can use the Alt tag to provide more direction even when people see your graphics. The Alt tag shows in the browser as a small pop-up flag when the mouse passes over your image.

Adding the Alt tag is a simple process in Dreamweaver. You will add the tags first to the template, as follows:

1. With the Food Info site open, open your Assets panel and activate the templates section. Select the Main template and click on Edit at the bottom of your Assets panel to open the template.

2. Select the logo image in the upper-left corner. At the right side of the Properties Inspector, locate the Alt field (see Figure 25-1) and type **Facts on Food Logo: Click for Home**. Anything you type in this space will show as a mouseover flag in a browser.

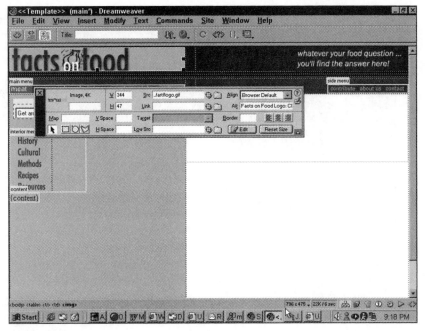

Figure 25-1
Entering an Alt tag for the selected image

3. Click in the center cell of the first row to select our invisible graphic. Here you want to tell a text reader that there is nothing to read. With the invisible image selected, enter the following in the Alt field: **""**. This indicates that there is nothing to read, but still identifies the field. If left blank, the text reader will say unnamed image.

4. Select the Meat menu image and type **Link to Meat section** in the Alt Field.

5. Continue selecting and assigning Alt tags to all the graphics in template. You will still have the new graphics on each page to name, but adding the Alt tags to our template looks after most of the images you have.

6. Save your template and allow updates. Figure 25-2 is an example of this tag in a browser preview.

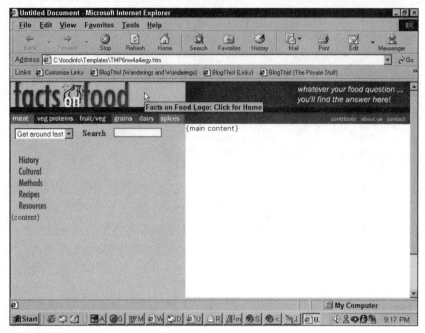

Figure 25-2
Browser preview with Alt tag displayed

Placing Content Text

You have your template in good shape and can enter the text I have been promising. Be warned though, I have left a few things undone in the template, like adjusting margins. You will do your first postcontent template addition in the the "Entering text from a text document" section.

You have two ways to add text to a Dreamweaver document. The first, typing directly into the document, you have already done. The second involves copying and pasting text from a text document, which will be your first content addition. You can copy the text files to your hard drive, but it really is not necessary. I have prepared all the text files as plain text so that you have no word processing compatibility problems. Because no formatting is carried from a word processor to Dreamweaver when pasting text, you can use text from any source as long as you can copy it.

Entering text from a text document

Pasting is probably the most common method for bringing text into Dreamweaver, although there is no reason that you cannot enter your text directly. I write a graphics column for Webreference.com, and the text for my tutorials is entered directly into Dreamweaver. If you are writing your own content, it makes no difference whether you type directly or paste text into your document.

To paste text from another document, follow these steps:

1. Locate and open meathis_intro.txt from the Session 25 folder on the CD-ROM. Select all the text and copy.

2. You will paste the text into the left column of your meathist.html document. This will go into an editable area, the second in this column (the first is your menu table. To make it easier to see the editable area, add a few lines with your Enter key. This opens the area for easier text placement. You will take out any unnecessary paragraph tags when you are finished with the page.

3. Place your cursor at the top-left corner of the left column Content area. Select Edit ⇨ Paste or use Ctrl+V (PC) or Command+V (Mac). Your text has arrived and you can now format.

4. Place your cursor anywhere in the first line of text. This will be your headline. Select Headline 1 from the Format drop-down in the Properties Inspector.

5. Your text may or may not have been imported with the Paragraph style in place. Place your cursor anywhere in a paragraph and check the Properties Inspector Format field. If it says Paragraph, that paragraph has already had the style added. If it says None, or anything else, select Paragraph from the Properties inspector.

Notice how the text is in a sans serif font? Your style sheet is controlling your text, even though you cannot see it. To confirm, select Text ⇨ CSS Styles ⇨ Edit Style Sheet and click on foodinfo.css. The styles that are currently defined will be displayed near the bottom of the window.

Adding margins

Have you noticed that the text is much too close to the margin? Although Web designers tend to use smaller margins than those used for print, text is exceptionally

**20 Min.
To Go**

hard to read if it is jammed right against the side of the screen. Luckily, you have built this site with a template, and can adjust the margins for all of your pages with one change.

Add a margin to your template with the Cell Pad command.

1. Open the Assets panel and activate the template section. Click the Edit button to open the template.

2. Select the table that contains the lower information. Add a Cell Pad value of 10 in the Properties Inspector. Margins appear all around.

3. Save the template and allow updates.

Bonus back pats to anyone who wondered why I had you use two separate tables when you were building the template. Double bonus back pats if you figured out why. I did not want to discuss it at the time, but margins were the main reason. Two tables were needed to make your logo and other graphics go right to the edge of the screen. You could not do that and have cell padding for your text areas, if you were working with only one table.

Now that you have some breathing room for your text, the page is starting to look a little more promising. Your page should look like Figure 25-3. You will fill the space beside the menu in the next session.

But take another look. Your color section no longer lines up with the head area. Why? Well, you just added cell padding to your table. Remember when you made the template, you placed an invisible graphic in the second row of the content table to hold the left column to 344 pixels wide? That image is doing exactly what you asked it to do — it is holding open 344 pixels. However, you have added a 10-pixel margin on either side of your column. Dreamweaver does not know this is an invisible image, so it will not allow it to start until 10 pixels are free. Nor will it end the column until it has added 10 pixels to the other side.

You must adjust your invisible image to be only 324 pixels wide to hold your column at 344 pixels total width. That's 344 − 10 − 10 = 324. To do so, follow these steps:

1. Open the Main template.

2. Select the invisible graphic in the left column of the last table row. Change the width to 324.

3. Save the template and allow updates.

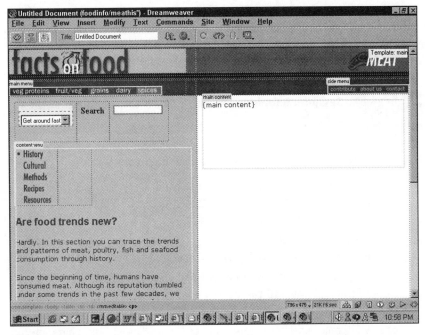

Figure 25-3
Formatting and margins are in place with the editable region labels show-
ing. You can make the labels disappear by selecting View ⇨ Visual Aids ⇨
Invisible Elements. Repeat to turn labels and areas back on.

Your Meat History page should now have perfectly aligned gold areas, and you have just had a valuable lesson in table spacing. You must consider all attributes when you are planning. It is confusing at the start, but, as you have just seen, templates can really help. One little error, such as forgetting your margins or neglecting to factor in spacing, could lead to thousands of keystrokes to fix multiple pages.

Adding decorative touches with images

Plain text is great for information, but it has been long known that images can help to direct the reader through the text. The Web is no exception. In fact, Web readers are probably the least patient readers on the globe. You have to grab attention quickly, get what you have to say said, and catch attention again. Do you doubt that statement? Try to pay attention to the way you look at a new site. Your finger is on that mouse button from the start.

However, images increase the file size. They do, but there are some really good download bargains. Images that are mainly solid colors often have a small file size, and tiny bullets and direction text adds up to only a few bytes. Go ahead and place some text, and then you decide whether the graphics are worth the weight.

 Copy the files bird.gif, animal.gif, and morered.gif from the Session 25 folder on the CD-ROM to the Art folder of the Food Info site.

Follow these directions to place graphic bullets in your text.

1. If it is not already open, open meathist.html. Copy the text from meathis_rock.txt in the Session 25 folder of the CD-ROM. There is no need to copy this file to your computer.

2. Position your cursor at the top of the editable section in the right column. Select Edit ⇨ Paste or Ctrl+V (PC) or Command+V (Mac) to paste the text.

3. Apply Heading 1 to the two one-line paragraphs. These are your titles. Apply Paragraph style to the other two paragraphs.

   You will have to trust me on the next couple of steps. I promise your page will come together before you are finished. And, yes, there are spelling errors in this text. _Do not_ fix them.

4. Place your cursor at the beginning of the line The Flinstones. Insert the image bird.gif from the Art directory. Yes, your text goes down and it looks lousy. This is the trust part.

5. Insert your cursor at the beginning of the next title. Insert the image animal.gif from the Art directory.

   OK, so now you have quite a mess. See Figure 25-4 as confirmation that you have the correct mess. An image will push its way onto a line of text and insist that all other page elements go somewhere else. However, if you add a paragraph justification command to your image, the image will let the text wrap around it.

6. Select the bird image, and select Left from the Align drop-down. If you do not have your invisible elements showing, select View ⇨ Visual Aids ⇨ Invisible Aids to turn them on. You should see a yellow icon next to the first headline. This is your alignment indicator. To move the image, click and drag on the icon, placing it where you would like the image to start. Try moving it down to the first line of the text in the first paragraph to see if you like that look better.

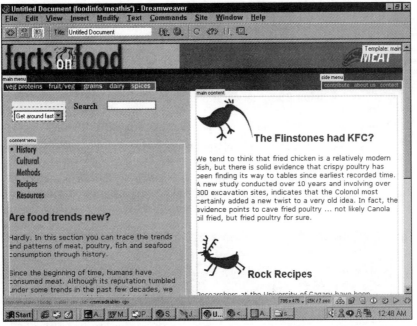

Figure 25-4
Text will not wrap around an image unless you add a paragraph justification command to the image.

7. The image is a little too close to the text. You can add horizontal or vertical spacing on an image in the Properties Inspector. Select the image and type **10** in the H Space field. This will add 10 pixels on each side of the image.

8. Select the animal graphic. You will place this one at the right by specifying Right in the Align drop-down. Add a horizontal spacing of 10 for this image as well.

Now that you have those images under control, you can add some little graphic indicators that there is more information available. These little images, which are used instead of a text link, add almost no weight, but can really spice up a page and give a strong visual cue to your visitor.

1. Place your cursor at the end of the first story paragraph. Insert the image morered.gif from the Art folder. Because this image is small, it will fit within the line of text and does not need to have an align command added.

2. Repeat Step 1 at the end of the second story.

You do not have a link for this image because you are not going to build the text pages. You can type a pound sign (#) in the link field as a placeholder, or create a page and add a link to that page.

3. Type Meat History in the Title field near the top of the screen.

This page is close to complete, and it is starting to look quite good. In Figure 25-5, I turned off the invisible elements and table border views for a fairly accurate view of the finished page. You should preview your page in your browser to make sure that it all looks good in a test.

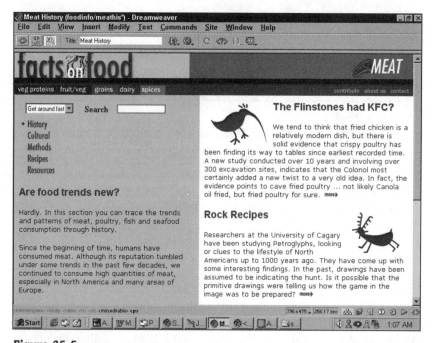

Figure 25-5
Images are now tucked into the text. Invisible elements and table border views have been turned off.

Cleaning Up Your Page

**10 Min.
To Go**

You now have a page nearing completion (you will add a few pieces such as a Flash movie and button, as well as an image map in the next session). You want to make sure that you have as clean a page as possible before you release it to trusted people for testing. Naturally, you will check spelling. Nothing ruins a page more quickly than a spelling error. You will also check your HTML for errors and replace a word using Dreamweaver's search and replace command.

Check spelling

Dreamweaver has a powerful spell checker. You have the option to add words to the list, so there is really no excuse that it is too hard to check spelling (I have heard this from technical people who use industry terms and acronyms that are not in the spell check list).

To check your spelling:

1. Select Text ⇨ Check Spelling or use the shortcut Shift+F7. The first word that come up as misspelled is Flinstones, and the suggestion is Flintiness. Obviously, you cannot accept that choice, so type **Flintstones** in the Change To field. Click Change, or Change All if you have more misspelled Flinstones on the page.

2. KFC will come up next. This you can Ignore, or Ignore All for several on a page. If this is a term you will be using often, select Add to Personal, and it will become listed as a correct spelling.

Never add a word to your personal dictionary without making sure it is spelled correctly. Also, make sure that the word that forms an acronym that works in this document is not a common misspelling of another word.

3. Colonol comes up next. The list of suggestions yields the correct spelling for Colonel. Click the correct word and click Change.

4. Ignore Canola and Change Cagary to Calgary. When the spell check is complete, an alert appears. Click OK.

Run find and replace

When you are working with a template, the search and replace feature is not quite as much a lifesaver as it is at other times. Dreamweaver's replace capability is powerful, and there are times when you need it.

I recently completed a job that took several months to complete. My colleagues and I did the graphics completely, and then we worked with the programmers to add the database functions. We had to replace approximately 30 plain-page links to Active Server Page (ASP) links for nearly 100 pages. A little math will tell you that is a heck of a pile of cut and paste, not to mention the danger of missing some links. It took one person about an hour to complete the job using Dreamweaver's replace command.

You covered the replace feature in Session 10, but I would like to step through it again in more detail. You have a much better understanding now of how Dreamweaver works, and more understanding of what is involved with creating a site. You are going to do a simple replace in the following steps:

1. If it is not already open, open meathist.html. Select Edit ⇨ Find and Replace. The Find and Replace window will open.

2. Open the Find In drop-down list to see your options. You are only doing a document search, but you can also search the full site, a folder, or selected folders in a site. If you chose any folder option, that choice will take you to a browse screen where you can choose your folder. The Find In selection remains until you close the program or change the settings, which is great for multiple replace terms. Choose Current Document.

The Search For option holds the major power of Dreamweaver's search function. You can search for Text, which works much like a word processor's search function, except that it ignores all HTML commands. However, you also have an Advanced Text choice, which lets you search text with qualifiers, such as this word but not when it falls within a certain tag. Source Code allows to you to search for items within an HTML tag, and Specific tag gives you the power to search by tags rather than by what the tag contains. My colleagues and I used a Source Code search across the entire site to replace the codes in the situation I described above, when we replaced all the links in the site with ASP links.

3. To change the University of Calgary to Lakehead University, select Text from the Search For drop down menu.

4. Type **the University of Calgary** in the Search For field.

5. Type **Lakehead University** in the Replace With field.

Watch that your spacing at the end of both the Search For and Replace With fields is the same. If you put a space at the end of the Search For but not at the end of the Replace With content, you will have a royal mess. Also, if you are doing a replace across a folder or site, please make sure that you test the replace thoroughly on one page before you do the full search. Changes cannot be undone if your document is not open when the replace occurs.

6. Click on Find Next. Behind the Search and Replace window, you will see that the University of Calgary is selected.

7. Click on Replace. The new entry is placed and you receive a message that one item has been found and replaced.

If you were doing a site-wide or folder replace, this is your start. After you confirm that the replace is what you require, simply click on Replace All. You will be warned that it cannot be undone. Click OK and all the changes will be made.

Clean up HTML

I have mentioned the value of clean code many times throughout this book. But when you work a page repeatedly, it is common to end up with some extra tags. It can happen even when you are hand coding, so when so much of your work is done with the code hidden, you have to expect that you will leave some extra code. Dreamweaver can go through and check for extra tags and see where tags can be combined.

Follow these steps to clean up your HTML:

1. If it is not already open, open meathist.html.

2. Select Commands ➪ Clean Up HTML. The Clean Up HTML window will open.

3. Select Empty Tags, Redundant Tags, and Combine Nested <font> Tags when Possible. This will clean up most extra code.

Never select Dreamweaver HTML Comments if you are using Library items or Templates. You will break the links.

Most times, you will have few, or even no tags to clean up if you have worked in the way I have described for this site. It is always nice to get the message "Nothing to Clean Up."

Checking the Target Browser

Dreamweaver can give you a list of the attributes in your document that will cause a problem for different browsers. This feature can help you to make decisions on what you will include.

To check for browser problem areas in your document, follow these steps:

1. If it is not already open, open meathist.html.

2. Select File ⇨ Check Target Browsers.

3. Select Netscape Navigator 3 and Netscape Navigator 4 (use Shift or Ctrl to select more than one browser) from the Check Target Browser window list. Click Check.

4. The resulting report (see Figure 25-6) will be placed in a browser window. There are five tags not supported in Netscape Navigator 3 and 4 in Netscape Navigator 4. Of course, both versions of Netscape have listed the same four attributes that are not supported (the zero page margins we are using). The fifth is your link to the style sheet, which means that you will have no control of the text in Netscape Navigator 3. Although your design will not look as good as it does when controlled by the CSS style sheet, it will still be legible. Most designers are only willing to go that far for version 3 browsers.

Testing Your Site

The previous section provided a basic test to see how your site will behave in particular browsers. The best test is to have people troubleshoot your design on every combination possible of platform, resolution, and browser. Although it is hard to hit every combination, it is important to test at least the Netscape Navigator and Microsoft Internet Explorer browsers on both the PC and the Mac, and several monitor resolutions. You can do this by submitting your page to a critique group. One of the most active is the HWG (HTML Writer's Guild) Critique list. You can sign up for this list and many other very active lists at http://hwg.org.

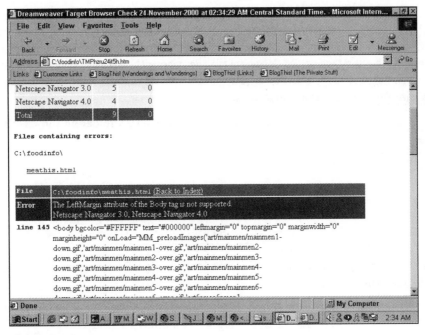

Figure 25-6
The report generated by the Check Target Browsers command

I strongly advise that you sign up for several newsgroups. You cannot measure the value of having expert advice so easily available. I have been "newsgrouping" since 1993, and it never ceases to amaze me how much time people spend helping each other.

See newsgroups.html in the Resources folder on the CD-ROM for a list of newsgroups related to Dreamweaver and Web design.

If you cannot, or do not want to join a newsgroup, you should find people who will take a look at your site before it is released. I use the newsgroups, but I also have people to check for specifics. If you are doing liquid design, testing is even more important.

Well, you are close to being finished with the one page you will do step-by-step. A few fun additions remain, but you have mined what you must learn from the template pages. I urge you to carry on though, with *greeked text,* that is, text that is text that looks real but is actually gibberish. Professional designers use text that does not form words for proofing. You cannot tell what a page will look like until you have content on the page, but using text that is not related to the subject can be distracting. So designers fill the page with text that looks real, but means nothing. Copy this file to your hard drive and store it where you can find it again. Greeked text is a wonderful tool.

You will find greek.txt in the Session 25 folder on the CD-ROM.

Done!

REVIEW

You have stepped through the end tasks for creating a Dreamweaver page. Keep the following details in mind:

- Accessibility must be considered for many large business and government sites. Completing Alt tags is a big step towards this goal.

- Text can be entered either directly or it can be pasted into Dreamweaver from another source.

- Images that are created with solid color areas are usually small files. They can be used to help direct your visitor through your site.

- Adding an Align command to an image will enable the text to wrap around the image.

- You can add horizontal or vertical space to an image with the H Space and V Space fields in the Properties Manager.

- A pound sign (#) can be used to create a placeholder link. It will react like a link, even though it leads nowhere.

- You can add unusual words or acronyms to the spell checker in Dreamweaver.

- Always test one replace before you run a replace function across a site or folder.

- Always test your site on as many different combinations of monitor resolution, platform, and browser as is possible.

QUIZ YOURSELF

1. What are two uses of Alt tags? (See the "Addressing Accessibility Concerns" section.)

2. What are the two ways to enter text into a document? (See the "Entering text from a text document" section.)

3. Margins for text in tables is best added by using which table tag? (See the "Adding margins" section.)

4. How can you add text wrapping to an image in Dreamweaver? See the "Adding decorative touches with images" section.)

5. How can you add words to Dreamweaver's spell checker? (See the "Check spelling" section.)

6. When you are replacing code or phrases in Dreamweaver, what must you watch carefully? (See the "Run find and replace" section.)

7. What information will you receive by using the Check Target Browser command? (See the "Checking the Target Browser" section.)

Placing and Creating the Extras

Session Checklist

✔ Understanding external media

✔ Adding motion and sound

✔ Working with sound and motion files

✔ Creating an image map

✔ Detecting plug-ins

**30 Min.
To Go**

You've worked hard. If you have moved beyond the lessons and created many pages, you have probably been introduced to some of the tedious work of Web design (without Dreamweaver to help, multiply any tedium many times). Now it is time to have some fun.

Many of us are attracted to Web design by its limitless possibilities. In this session, you will learn to place many different types of media into your Web pages, including Dreamweaver's new Flash buttons. This lesson is only about placing movies and other media — not even a scrap about creating it. That is a subject that easily fills several books just for Macromedia Flash or Adobe GoLive, not to mention Director/Shockwave, or even going near editing sound files. Multimedia is a huge and growing field that I will not even brush on here.

Dreamweaver quietly overcomes many of the problems that placing media can present. Placing a Flash movie is much like placing an image. I will take placing an image a little further as well. Finally, you will place an animated GIF and create an image map to round out your visual tools.

This is where you sit back and relax. The work is easy, the results fun.

Using External Media

As much fun as they can be, motion and sound must be treated with respect. All of us have found sites that have so much going on that our eye cannot find a place to rest. Most of us have been quietly surfing when all of a sudden low-quality music comes blaring through the speakers. Having your visitor jump out of their skin will not bring a positive reaction to your site. Most of us leave . . . fast.

Movies can be just as bad. I only have a slow connection to the Internet available to me, and I find it annoying to be forced to watch a full screen, three-minute-download movie that does nothing more that spin a company logo. In fact, I rarely get to see what is on such a site because I leave such sites quickly. Escape routes are important.

The other warning is that you, because you have bought this book, are probably not the average computer user. So many professional developers or interested amateurs assume that the rest of the surfing world has similar equipment and capability. That is so far from true. For many people who surf the Web, computers are not a high priority — computers are more like a simple diversion or entertainment. They are not spending their dollars on the latest and greatest, and often have what seems archaic equipment to us in the industry. Do not forget that you are probably not average.

If you are truly interested in the field of multimedia, I urge you to set up a personal site dedicated to experimentation and the "cool" factor. Do your learning and developing away from commercial or information sites, and you will have the best of both worlds. Many free hosts are available (see the Resource directory on the CD-ROM) for sites of this type. If you have a place to develop your skills and experiment, you are much more likely to use media for good on other sites.

Understanding external media and Dreamweaver

The first thing to understand about media files such as sound and movies is that Dreamweaver is not playing them. You must have a plug-in installed on your computer to play any sound or movie. All modern browsers come with plug-ins to play sounds and most movie types, including Flash. Because you likely have the plug-ins installed, it can seem as if Dreamweaver is working the magic. Not so. Dreamweaver is simply placing the file, and the auto-start settings on your computer will play the file when it is called.

Learn one and you learn them all does not apply to placing media files. Dreamweaver does whittle the differences down for you, because it will place special codes to ensure that your media will play accurately. This does not mean that you should accept the tiny bit of this field that you will learn here, however. If you find that you are placing many media files, you should do your best to research the type of files you are placing. The best information is often found on the software manufacturers' sites, such as Macromedia for Flash/Shockwave information (http://macromedia.com) or RealAudio (www.realnetworks.com/devzone/).

However, the basics of media files are similar from a Dreamweaver perspective. You insert the file, set a few parameters in the Properties inspector and your file will play. Always be aware, however, that no matter how well you place the file, your visitor will require the plug-in to be able to see or hear your content. It is usually a good idea to include a link to download the software (which is free) for the few visitors who do not already have the plug-in.

I have included animated GIF files in this section because they move and can often be interchanged with small Flash movies. Most banners are animated GIF files, although Flash is showing up in that arena as well. However, animated GIF files are simply images, as you will see. All movement is controlled within the file, and as far as Dreamweaver is concerned, an animated GIF is simply an image.

Just before we move on to placing files, I want to talk a little about how to use files with movement and sound.

Making external media count

Adding motion and sound to your pages can help your site to be easy to navigate, pleasant to use, and look more professional. Adding motion and sound to your site can make it hard to navigate, a real trial to use, and have a completely amateur look. The difference is simply in the execution.

Adding motion or sound just because you can is about as bad an idea as exists in the Web-development world. However, if you have a definite reason for adding motion or sound, you can draw attention to features that are important to visitors. Motion and sound can help guide visitors through a page. Recall that graphics can help to guide a visitor to the information they seek. Motion can do the same; it can also set a mood for your site. Although we often talk about using the Web to find information, there is also an entertainment component to the Web. Just as TV commercials are not all white text on a black screen, you do not always have to be all business, even for commercial sites. Building an atmosphere can be important.

However, there is a difference between creating a mood and satisfying your own desires to play with media. As long as you can specifically point to why you have included media, from a visitor's perspective, you are well on the way to responsible media use. Perhaps you have added a new feature to your site. Motion can help draw the visitor's attention to the new area, which is a plus. Or perhaps you have a product that is difficult to explain. Ikea (www.ikea.com) has an excellent example of a Flash movie used to demystify a process. At the site, visit the assembly area to see a Flash movie that is definitely customer oriented.

Always ask the question: What does this do to enhance my visitor's experience?

Most of my warnings are out of the way now. Let's move on and add some media to your pages.

Adding Motion and Sound in Dreamweaver

I begin this section with animated GIF files, which do not officially belong in this section, because they are really graphics. However, animated GIF files not only provide motion, but they are also often used as alternative images for Flash presentations. Animated GIF files can be created from a Flash movie, and used in the same way.

The following files should be copied from the Session 26 folder of the CD-ROM to the Art folder of the Food Info site: banner. gif, separation2m[2].wav, newcontest.swf, newcontest.gif, **and** histbits.gif.

Adding an animated GIF

Animated GIF files provided the first motion on the Web, and have been responsible for many of the warnings I included above, such as distracting from a message, or increasing load time. They can be used well, though, and are indispensable for banner ads and small notices. Animated GIF files are easy to create in most current graphics software, and will display on any browser that will display an image.

You will create a new document to place our animated GIF. I have included a banner ad that will not fit on your site pages. To start, you will create a directory to place your learning files so that they are not mixed with the main documents for your site. To do so, follow these steps:

1. Create a new folder in the Food Info site and name it **resources**.

2. Create a new document in the Resources folder. Name it **mediatest.html**.

3. Place your cursor where you would like the image to appear. Select Insert ⇨ Image and select banner.gif from the Art folder.

4. In the Properties Inspector, type **http://productiongraphics.com/** in the Link field.

5. Preview the file in a browser window to see the animation.

And that is that! Placing an animated GIF in Dreamweaver is the same as placing any image.

Placing a sound file

You have two options when you are placing a sound file. You can simply set up a link to the file, which will play automatically, or, if you want to provide controls for your visitors within your page, you can embed your sound.

Follow these steps to create a link to a sound file:

1. If it is not already open, open mediatest.html.

2. Type **Listen to a clip from Kevin Van Sant's** *Bossa for NG.* Hear the entire clip at http://www.onestopjazz.com/kvansant.

3. Highlight the phrase **Bossa for NG** in the Link field, *or* browse for the file jazure.wav in the Art folder.

4. Preview the file in your browser. Click on the link to make the music play. This gives your visitor control over the file in their own media player.

Some developers prefer to keep controls within their own page. This method, which is outlined in the following steps, is slightly different:

1. In the same document, insert your cursor where you would like to place the sound control. Select Insert ⇨ Media ⇨ Plugin. The Select File window will open.

2. Select the file separation2m[2].wav in the Art folder. A plug-in icon will be placed with Dreamweaver's default value of 32 pixels × 32 pixels.

3. Delete the W and H values to allow the default player size to be displayed.

Preview the results in your browser (see Figure 26-1 for the view in Internet Explorer).

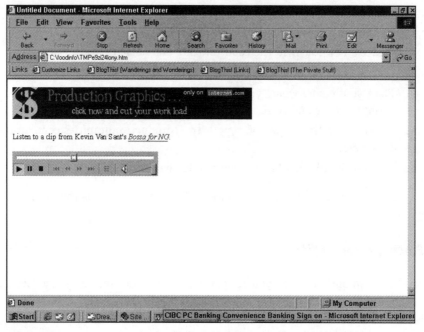

Figure 26-1
The Windows Media Player controls shown in an Internet Explorer preview

You may want to control some of the parameters of your sound clip. The default value is to automatically play the clip. I recommend giving your visitors the opportunity to start any sound. You also may wish the clip to play continuously until it is stopped. You can control both of these parameters through the Parameters button on the Properties Inspector. To do so, follow these steps:

1. Select the sound icon. Click on the Parameters button in the Properties Inspector. The Parameters window will open.

2. Click on the + to add a parameter. Type **LOOP** in the Parameter field and **true** in the Value field. This will loop your sound continuously once it is started.

3. Click on the + to add another parameter as shown in Figure 26-2. Type **autoplay** in the Parameter field and **false** for the value. This will leave the sound off until your visitor starts it.

4. Preview the results in your browser.

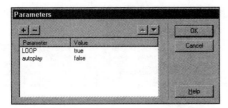

Figure 26-2
Entering the parameters for sound plug-ins in Dreamweaver

You now have two methods to add responsible sound to your site. Visitors should always have a choice.

Inserting a Flash movie

20 Min. To Go

I have prepared a simple little Flash movie to include in our Food Info site. There is no reason that a Flash movie cannot be placed within a template, but for this exercise, you will just place it on the meathist.html page. If you would like this movie on the template page, simply follow the same instructions in a location of your choice in the template document.

1. If it is not already open, open meathist.html.

2. You will add the movie to the table containing your interior menu, but you must first add a column. Place your cursor in the right column of the interior menu table. Select Modify ⇨ Table ⇨ Insert Rows or Columns. Enter 1 column After Current Column for values.

3. Insert cursor in the new column. Select Insert ⇨ Media ⇨ Flash. The Select File window will open.

4. Browse to the Art directory and select the file newcontest.swf. A flash icon will be loaded into the browser at the correct size because Dreamweaver automatically checks and records the size of the .SWF file.

5. You can test the Flash file from within Dreamweaver, and leave it playing while you work on the document, as shown in Figure 26-3. In the Properties Inspector, click the Play button.

6. The details and entry text at the bottom of this movie is set as a link to a page called contest.html. If you would like to try designing a page on your own, create contest.html from the template.

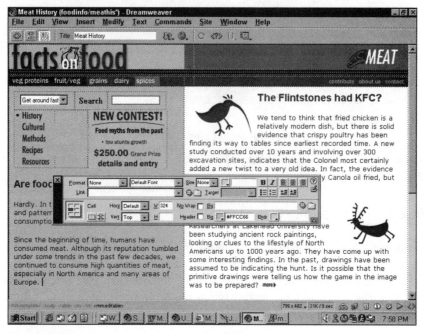

Figure 26-3
Flash movie inserted and playing within Dreamweaver (New Contest section)

I often leave the Flash insert playing while I work. It is a good distraction test. If you wish to have the appearance of the Flash without the movie playing, you can set it to stop looping as you work on the document. Click on the Loop option to deselect looping and click Play again. The movie will play through once and then stop. Remember to click Loop before you save the file again if that is what you intend for the movie.

You can control Flash parameters from the Properties palette. See the preceding Tip to set the movie to play once or to loop continuously. You can also set the size for your movie. Flash is a vector format program, and if you have not included any bitmap images in your movie, you can scale it to any size with no loss of quality. You can also align the movie and provide vertical or horizontal space as for any image.

I will not pretend that creating a full-featured Flash movie is an easy feat. But placing a movie is easy — similar to inserting an image. If you would like to learn more about Flash, visit Macromedia at http://macromedia.com.

A 30-day, full-featured demo version of Flash 5 is included on your CD. See the Software folder. If you cannot see the movie from the exercise above, install the Flash Player, which is also on the CD.

Creating a Flash button

Dreamweaver 4 enables you to create Flash-powered buttons. Choose from several preset styles and customize them with your own text. The buttons come complete with rollover states built in. Building a Flash button is a fill-in-the-blanks exercise, which is outlined in the following steps:

1. If it is not already open, open meathist.html.

2. Insert your cursor at the bottom of the text in the left content columns (below the word *Europe*). Select Insert ➪ Interactive Images ➪ Flash Button. The Insert Flash Button window will open.

3. Scroll through the Style list and select Standard. A sample of the button will appear in the Sample field at the top of the window.

4. Type **NEWSLETTER** in the Button Text field. Select a plain font from the Font list. Select 12 for the font size.

5. Type **newsletter.html** in the Link field. (We will create a page with this name in Session 27.)

Until now we have let all of our links open in the same window as the linking page. This is Dreamweaver's default, and the setting that is recommended in most situations. However, occasionally, you would like to have a new window open when a link is clicked. You can set the link to open in a blank window in the Properties Inspector for any link. Follow these instructions to set this button's link to open in a blank window from the Flash button window:

1. Select _blank from the Target drop-down list. The link will open in a new window when it is clicked.

2. Select the background color for the button. The number is #FFCC66 or simply click the eyedropper on the background color behind the Flash Button window.

3. Type **newsletter.swf** in the Save As file. Flash buttons must be saved in the same directory as the document.

4. Click Apply to see your finished button (move the Flash Button window if you cannot see your button in place) and make any changes to font or

font size, or feel free to find a button you like better. When you are satisfied with the button, click OK.

5. Preview your button in your browser. Hold your mouse over the button to see the mouseover state.

6. As a text exercise, try to format the button with the text **Get all the news:** as I have in Figure 26-4. *Hint:* I used a table.

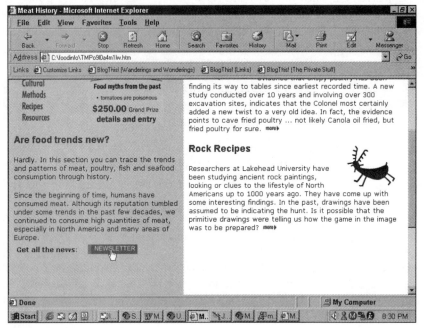

Figure 26-4
Flash button in place with mouseover state shown in browser preview

Creating an image map

10 Min. To Go

You have survived all the tough ways to create a link from an image. I will end this section with an easy way to create a series of links: image maps created with HTML code that are added to an image link. This code sets different areas of the image to link to different places. No JavaScript is involved, which makes this method of creating links compatible for almost every browser in use.

However, you do give up the visual cues that a rollover produces. The browser will display the hand icon, indicating a link, when the mouse is held over a link. It is especially important to use Alt tags when creating image maps, because the flag that carries the Alt tag information can help guide your visitor to identify the link areas.

To create an image map, you insert an image and then define the link areas, as follows:

1. If it is not already open, open the mediatest.html file.

2. Insert your cursor below the other content on the page. Insert the image histbits.gif from the Art directory.

3. We must now define three areas that will have separate links. Make sure that the image is selected. Type **historybits** in the field beside the word Map in the Properties Inspector. This is your image map name.

4. Select the blue rectangle in the lower-left corner of the Properties Inspector. This will draw a rectangular area as a link. This area is known as a *hotspot*. The Oval Hot Spot tool will draw an oval area, and the Polygon Hotspot tool allows for freehand hotspots. With the Rectangular Hot Spot tool selected, draw a rectangle that encloses the entire area over the bread illustration and the word *bread*. The Properties Inspector will change to receive information for that hotspot. Figure 26-5 displays a hotspot in progress.

5. Type **histbit.html#bread** in the Link field of the Properties Inspector. This will link to a document called histbit.html and jump to a named anchor called bread.

 If you want the practice, try creating the histbit.html document, fill it with greeked text, and place the anchors for this image map. I have covered all the techniques that you need to create this page.

6. Type **Link to Bread history** in the Alt field. Note that the map name is displayed in the lower-left corner of the Properties Inspector. This will be consistent for the three hotspot areas that you will create.

7. Repeat Steps 4 to 6 for the next two areas, using the named anchors of #wine and #sugar, and adjusting the Alt tag to match.

8. Preview the document in your browser to see the image map in action. The links will not work unless you have created the histbits.html page, but you will be able to see the Alt tag flag. Check the status bar at the bottom of the window to see the link information.

9. To edit any hotspot on your image map, select the large arrow in the hotspot area in the bottom left of the Properties Inspector. Click on the hotspot in your document and make your changes. Figure 26-5 shows the first hotspot selected.

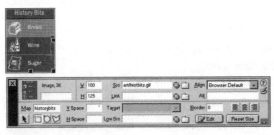

Figure 26-5
Information for a selected hot spot is displayed in the Properties Inspector.

Your image map is now complete. Look at the code that was produced as you created the map. In the partial sample of code I have included here, the map is named and one hot spot is defined.

```
<map name="historybits">
    <area shape="rect" coords="1,20,100,56"
href="histbits.html#bread" alt="Link to Bread history"
title="Link to Bread history ">
```

There are times when an image map is the perfect way to include links. Keep the idea in your growing bag of tricks.

Checking for plug-ins

Although most visitors will have the major plug-ins installed, you may wish to be safe and create a page that works even when they do not have the plug-in you are using. In this example, you will use our Behaviors palette to create a JavaScript check for the Flash player. If the visitor has the player, they will go to the page containing Flash. If they do not have the player installed, they will be directed to an identical page that has an animated GIF file replacing the Flash.

Create a script that will check for the Flash player by doing the following:

1. Open the mediatest.html file. If it is already open, make sure that you have saved all changes.

2. Save the file as **mediatestnoflash.html**. You will replace the Flash movie with an animated GIF file.

3. Select and delete the Flash movie. In the same location, insert the image newcontest.gif. Save and close this document.

4. Open mediatest.html again. You will place the Flash detector on this page. If a visitor has the Flash player, nothing will happen. If they do not have the player, you will send them to the page that you just created.

5. Click the <body> tag in the lower-left corner of the document window.

6. Open the Behaviors panel. Click the + and select Check Plugin. The Check Plugin window will open.

7. Choose Flash from the Plugin: Select drop-down list.

   You do not need to direct your visitors who already have the plug-in to any other page, so you will leave the If Found Go to URL field empty.

8. In the Otherwise, Go To URL field, type **mediatestnoflash.html** or browse to find the file. See Figure 26-6 for the correct settings.

9. Click OK.

Figure 26-6
Create a detector that sends visitors without the Flash player to a page with a GIF image as a substitute for the Flash movie.

If the detector cannot find the plug-in for any reason, and there are reasons other than that the plug-in is not present, this script will automatically send visitors to the alternate page. If you would prefer that the detection assume that the plug-in *is* present when it cannot positively determine the answer, check the option Always go to first URL if detection is not possible. Because your information is in much the same form on both pages, you will not take a chance; instead, you will just send visitors to the "safe" page and leave it unchecked.

Done!

When a visitor arrives at your page now, the detector will quickly check for the Flash player and if it cannot determine that the player is present, it will deliver the alternate page instead. This can be a valuable tool when you want to include some exciting technologies but don't want to leave some visitors behind.

REVIEW

That was fun. Placing the "extras" is not hard (although creating them is a bit more involved). You should pay special attention to the following details, however:

- Always ensure that you are adding to your visitor's experience before you add any motion or sound to your site.
- An animated GIF can be added to your documents in the same way that any image can be added.
- Sound files can be included as links or embedded in the page. Regardless of the method used, you should always make sure that your visitor has the option to start and stop the sound file.
- Flash movies can be previewed in the Dreamweaver document.
- Flash movies are created in a vector format, which enables them to be scaled without quality loss as long as there are no raster images included in the file.
- Leaving a Flash movie playing as you work on the page can be a great test for the aggravation factor of the motion. You can also stop the movie from looping so that you can see the general effect without working with the constant motion.
- Image maps create a simple multiple link image. Make sure you use Alt tags when you are using image maps as they can help your visitor identify the hotspots as links.
- You can create an alternate page for visitors that do not include the plug-in on a page. It is easy to create a plug-in detector in Dreamweaver.

QUIZ YOURSELF

1. Why must you be careful with external media on your pages? (See the "Using External Media" section.)

2. What is a media player and why must it be installed before you can test media in Dreamweaver? (See the "Understanding external media and Dreamweaver" section.)

3. What is an animated GIF? (See the "Understanding external media and Dreamweaver" section.)

4. What is the only valid reason for adding media to your pages? (See the "Making external media count" section.)

5. How can you test an animated GIF in Dreamweaver? (See the "Adding an animated GIF" section.)

6. How is a Flash movie previewed in Dreamweaver? (See the "Inserting a Flash movie" section.)

7. How do you preview a Flash button in Dreamweaver? (See the "Creating a Flash button" section.)

8. What is a hotspot on an image map? (See the "Creating an image map" section.)

9. Why would you add a browser detection script to your site? (See the "Checking for plug-ins" section.)

PART

V

Sunday Morning

1. You can edit jump menu items from the Properties Inspector. How?

2. How can the Properties Inspector help you learn Dreamweaver?

3. You can customize the Objects panel to display icons only, text only, or icons and text. Where do you make this choice?

4. A site's assets are listed in the Assets panel. At times, you may lose track of where an asset is located. How can you use the Assets panel to find the lost asset?

5. JPG files are best for which type of images?

6. GIF files are best for which type of images?

7. What does the term *optimizing images* mean?

8. What is the difference between an HTML style for text and a separate CSS style sheet file for text?

9. When you create a style sheet through the Attach New Style Sheet command from the Text ⇨ CSS styles menu, what actually happens.

10. What is the route for editing a CSS style sheet you have already attached to your document?

11. How can you ensure that files in a series are stored together in a file listing for easy retrieval?

12. When you are using a page as a base to save other pages, what is very important to remember?

13. Why is it important to include an *active* state image when you are preparing your menu items?

14. What is an Alt tag?

15. How can you make text wrap around an image?

16. When you choose Add to Personal in the Check Spelling window, what is the result?

17. When you have been working with a document for quite a while and have made many changes, what is one thing you can do to make sure you have not left redundant code behind?

18. If you are interested in cutting-edge media, how can you learn and experiment without including inappropriate items on a commercial page?

19. Sound can add to a page, but one thing should always be included with sound. What is it?

20. A Flash button or buttons can be used for site navigation. What is necessary for a Flash button to work?

PART

VI

Sunday Afternoon

Using Layers for Layout

Session Checklist

✔ Understand layers

✔ Working with layers

✔ Creating layers in pages

✔ Converting layers to tables

✔ Deciding whether to use tables or layers

**30 Min.
To Go**

ayers are almost irresistible for those who have come from the print world. Layers have been used almost since the beginning of the computer graphics field. Watching a page fall together with layers will seduce even those of us who have never sent a file to print. However, like all Web technologies, anything really fun comes with a long list of cautions. Although learning to use layers is relatively easy — certainly easier than tables — not all browsers interpret layers in the same way. From a Dreamweaver perspective, layers are a click-and-drag operation. Learn a few rules, such as how to enlarge, move and place one layer inside another, and you will have much of the technique mastered. In reality, the Web is never that simple.

Let's start by looking at layers and why they require caution, and then let's move on to building a page using layers.

Understanding Layers

Working with layers is relatively easy. You drag a layer shape onto your page, place some content, and then repeat. There are no columns or rows to create, delete, or merge to achieve your look. In the initial stages, working with layers is similar to working with a page layout program. Create a layer, add some content, and you are set. However, in practical applications, getting your page to display in a browser is an entirely different matter.

Layer position on the screen is set into code by CSS. Remember the warnings you learned about using CSS for text only? It is no better for positioning. Not all browsers support every command. Buggy is the word you often hear associated with layers and CSS. You can create a document using layers and CSS, and it will go together very quickly. In addition, layers offer routes around much of what frustrates us when working with tables. The tricky part is getting it to display on a variety of browsers.

See Session 23 for a discussion of CSS.

How can layers be so popular if they are so buggy? Intranets offer one clue. You see the Web, and you can understand the growth in this world, but Intranets also have become extremely popular tools for large businesses and organizations to share information and resources. Intranets are a controlled environment. The designer often knows which browsers or platform site visitors will use. If I were working in an intranet environment, I would work exclusively with layers.

Others use layers to create a layout, and then convert the layers into tables. You will learn how to complete this operation in this session, as well. I would, however, like to offer an extra caution. Tables will display, even in older browsers. However, as you have seen in earlier sessions, you must construct tables very carefully to avoid surprises in many browsers. Creating your page in layers does not remove that requirement. Once you convert layers to tables, you still must have very clean work and a layout that fits into the table format, which takes away many of the benefits of working with layers.

So why teach — and more important to you — why learn layers. You may be interested in Intranet design. That is reason enough. Some people are just more comfortable with the layers concept for construction. That is reason enough, as long as the work is done with tables in mind while you work. But the biggest reason of all is that the day will come when you can freely use layers. Every month that passes takes us closer to the day when there are few disadvantages and many advantages to working with layers. You may already be designing for a target group that is likely to have only the most modern browsers, and you may be willing to go through the extensive debugging process required even for a specific Web group (you will not have time or space to enter that arena at all). Layers should not be ignored.

Do we have a good DHTML book to recommend here?

Working with Layers

You will create a page for just the first few exercises in this session. Before you build a page for your site, you should be comfortable with how layers are created and manipulated. Much of what you learn in the first portion of the layers work cannot be used for your site because it cannot be converted to layers. But you should look at what layers can do when you are not restricted. You also will need some of these techniques for Session 28.

Creating a layer

Use the following steps to create a new document to be placed in the Resources folder that you created in Session 26:

1. Create a new document in the Food Info site Resources folder. Name the document **layerstest.html**.
2. Select Window ➪ Layers to open the Layers panel. Make sure the Prevent Overlaps option is selected.
3. Select Window ➪ Objects to open the Objects panel. Make sure that you can see your Invisible Elements.
4. To create a layer, click the Draw Layer icon in the Objects panel. Click and drag anywhere on the page to define your layer. A rectangular area with a tab at the top will appear. This is your layer. Check your Layers panel and you will see Layer1 listed.

5. To select the layer, click the tab at the top or on any border. Selection handles will appear around the border of the layer. Note that the Properties Inspector now has Layer options displayed. Type **firstsample** in the Layer ID field in the Properties Inspector.

6. Take a look at the L, W, T, and H values in the Properties Inspector. These are the coordinates and size for your layer. L represents where on the page the left edge of your layer is positioned in relation to the left edge of the page. T represents where the top of your layer is positioned on the page in relation to the top of the page. Click and drag your layer and you can watch this value change. (When you create nested layers later in this session, these values will refer to the position in relation to the parent layer when a child layer is selected.)

7. The W and H values are the width and height for your layer. Click and drag a resizing handle for your layer in your document and watch the values change in the Properties Inspector.

Let's pause for a moment and take a look at the following code that Dreamweaver produced to display your layer:

```
<div id="firstsample" style="position:absolute; left:185px;
top:70px; width:252px; height:208px; z-index:1"></div>
```

Reading through the code, most will make sense if you compare it to the Properties Inspector values. Note the style reference; that is your CSS positioning. The z-index refers to the layer position in relation to other layers. Let's create another layer to see the z-index in action.

1. Activate the Draw Layers icon in the Object panel. Click and drag to create another layer that is close to, but not touching, the first layer. Name the layer **secondsample**. Note that the Layers panel now lists both layer names, and that the z-index value is 1 for Firstsample and 2 for Secondsample.

2. Click the Secondsample listing in the Layers panel and drag below Firstsample. The listing order changes, as does the z-index value. This becomes very important when you start working with DHTML in the next session. Figure 27-1 shows how the page should look. Your layer size and position will be different.

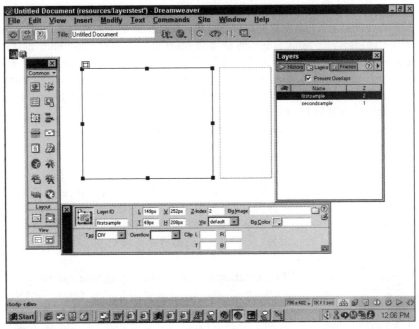

Figure 27-1
Two layers are drawn, with one selected. Note that the Properties Inspector lists the positioning information, and that the selected layer is also highlighted in the Layers panel.

Creating a nested layer

**20 Min.
To Go**

To use the stacking benefits of layers, you will be placing layers inside of layers. This is the equivalent to nesting tables when you are working without layers. However, you cannot convert nested layers to tables. Right now, you are simply going through a tour of layers and how to work with them. You will then move on to create a page for your site that you can convert to layers.

First, let's look at the Prevent Overlaps command in the Layers panel. This option is essential if you are planning to convert your layers to tables when your page is complete. Layers can be placed anywhere — over, under, overlapping, or even in the middle of nowhere. There are no bounds. However, tables are not as easy to get along with. If layers are table-bound, you must keep the design under control. One way to prevent creating a page in layers that cannot be reasonably transferred to tables is to activate the Prevent Overlaps option. Dreamweaver will prevent you from placing layers where a table would be unable to duplicate the position.

The Prevent Overlaps command takes away the click-and-drag ability for nested tables. You still can create a nested table through the menu, but you will have to toggle the Prevent Overlaps option on and off if you want to draw your nested layers directly on the screen. I find it difficult to work with the nested layers when the Prevent Overlaps feature is on because the size and position must be changed numerically. If you are working with nested layers, you cannot convert the result to tables, so there is no reason to keep it turned on.

Take the following steps to create a nested table:

1. Turn off the Prevent Overlaps option.

2. Click the Draw Layer icon in the Object panel. With your Alt (PC) or Option (Mac) key pressed, click and drag within the first layer to define a new layer. If Prevent Overlaps is activated, you still can add a nested layer, but you must use Insert ⇨ Layer to place the layer and numerical control in the Properties Inspector to edit the size or position.

If you will be creating many nested layers, you can set your preferences to automatically allow nested tables. Select Edit ⇨ Preferences and click Layers from the Category list. Activate Nest When Created within a Layer. You will now be able to draw nested layers without holding down the Alt (PC) or Option (PC) key. Using the Alt or Option keys will then allow you to create a layer that is not nested.

3. Name the new layer **firstchild** in the Properties Inspector. Note the values in the Properties Inspector. When the new layer — which is considered to be a child of the layer that contains it — is selected, the L and T values reflect the position of the child layer within the parent layer. These values have no relation on the child's position on the page. Also note that the Firstlayer listing in the Layers panel now has a sublisting to reflect the addition of the child layer.

4. Set the child layer to be in the upper-left corner of the parent layer. You can either type 0 for both the L and T value, or you can drag it into position. When dragging, move it close to the desired location and use your arrow keys to move the layer one pixel at a time.

5. Select the Firstsample layer and select a light gray background from the bg color field in the Properties Inspector. Select Firstchild and assign a white background color. See Figure 27-2 for the final result.

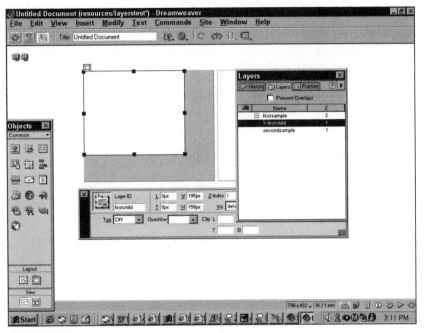

Figure 27-2
Parent layer with gray background and selected child layer with a white background. Note that the child layer position is relative to the parent layer, not the page.

Positioning layers

To move a layer, you simply select the layer and then click and drag it to the new position. To resize a layer, select and then resize with the handles at the sides or corners of the layer.

You might decide that you require a layer in a different stacking order. If this is the case, follow these steps:

1. Select the layer Secondsample and assign a red background color.

2. Draw a large layer over all the layers now on the page.

3. Apply a dark blue background color to the new layer. It should hide all the layers that are on your page.

4. Select the new layer. In the Properties Inspector, change the z-index value to 1.

5. Select Secondsample layer and change the z-index value to 2 (Firstsample already has a value of 2).

6. Deselect all layers and you will see that the two smaller windows now appear on top of the blue window.

Adding content to layers

Content is added to layers in the same way that it is added to the page. Images, media, or text are added to the layer at the cursor position. Insert an image in your layer following these steps:

1. Click inside the white layer to position the cursor. Insert animal.gif from the Art folder.

2. Click inside the red layer. Using white, bold type, type enough words to fill several lines.

3. Select the gray parent layer. In the Properties Inspector, add back8.gif from the Art director as the Bg Image. This creates a background for the gray layer only. See Figure 27-3 for the final result.

Doesn't that feel familiar? Layers are similar to minipages. However, before your imagination takes off with the wonderful designs you could create, it is time for a reality check. This looks great on the Dreamweaver page. It will probably display properly on a PC version of Internet Explorer 5, and perhaps even a Mac version of Internet Explorer. But you know for sure it that will be buggy, at best, in Netscape. This is the problem with layers.

As I stated before you started the exercise, if you are designing for a controlled environment such as an Intranet, layers are wonderful. If you are cautious in their use, you also can create tables from the layers document, which you will do shortly as you create a page for your site.

Let's move on to the real world of layers. You will turn on Prevent Overlaps and abstain from nested layers so that you can create a page which can be converted to layers and will display in all browsers.

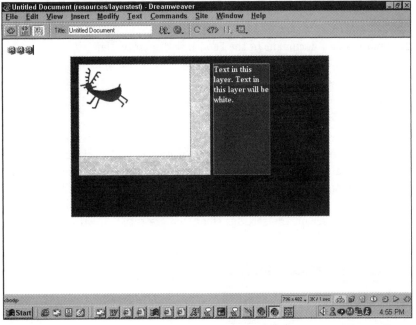

Figure 27-3
*Your layers with content. Note the three "invisible content" markers at the
upper-left of the screen. These are placed with your layers and contain the
layer positioning information.*

Creating a page with layers for tables

**10 Min.
To Go**

Here you are on the other side, ready to use layers that you can put on the Web.
What is different? Well, you are working with layers that cannot be nested or over-
lapped. You also are going to have to keep the structure of a table in mind as you
create your layers document. Because you will be converting the layers to tables at
the end of the exercise, you might as well work within those bounds right from
the start.

**Copy the image logonews.gif from the Session27 folder on the
CD-ROM to the Art folder of the Food Info site.**

Follow these steps to create a window to be used as a sign-up window for your newsletter:

1. Create a new document in the Food Info directory. Name it newsletter.html. You will create this document using layers.

2. First, you will turn on a grid to help line up the layers. Select View ⇨ Grid ⇨ Show Grid. This shows the default grid. You will slight adjust the grid to create a finer grid.

3. Select View ⇨ Grid ⇨ Edit Grid. Make sure the Snap to Grid and Show Grid options are checked. Type **20** in the Spacing field. Select Dots as the Display value. Then click Apply to see the results. The color setting has been changed in the example shown in Figure 27-4 to help it display better in the image. As long as you can see the grid, a light color is better. Click OK to accept the settings when you are satisfied with them.

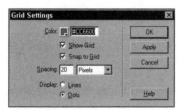

Figure 27-4
Grid Settings window with customized settings

4. Open the Layers panel and the Object panel if they are not already open. Make sure that the Prevent Overlaps option is selected in the Layers panel.

5. Set the background color for the page to FFCC66 (gold).

6. Attach the style sheet foodinfo.css to the document.

7. Click the Draw Layers icon in the Object panel. Draw a layer in the upper-right corner that is 300 pixels wide by 60 pixels high. Name the layer **Logo**.

8. Place your cursor in the Logo layer and insert the image logonews.gif from the Art folder. Center the image in the layer.

9. Create another layer beneath the Logo layer, starting 20 pixels in from the edge and 20 pixels down from the Logo layer bottom. Label the layer Text. Insert your cursor in the Type layer and type the following text, pressing Enter after each line:

Facts on Food Newsletter

Delivered monthly . . . filled with food history, lore, tips, trivia and recipes. Guest articles with every issue. Free!

Apply Paragraph style to both lines. Highlight the headline and apply bold and a font color of 990000.

10. Create a layer 20 pixels down from the Text layer, aligned with the left edge which is 140 pixels by 60 pixels. Label the layer **Form**. Type **Email address**. Make sure that Paragraph style is applied. Insert a <br> tag (Shift Enter). Add a form and a text box form object.

11. Create a layer 100 pixels by 60 pixels that is 20 pixels down from the Text layer, aligned with the right edge of that layer. Label the layer **Explain**. Type **Simply type in your email address.** Make sure that Paragraph style is applied.

12. Create a layer 80 pixels by 20 pixels, aligned with the right edge of the Explain layer and right against the lower edge of that layer. Label the layer **Close**. Type **X Close window**. Make sure Paragraph style is applied. Select the text and set to Size 1 and font color 000066.

13. Type **Newsletter Sign-up** in the Title area near the top of your page.

That's your layout. You are almost ready to create a table from your layer page. Check to make sure that all alignments are as you want them. See Figure 27-5 for an example of how it should look in Dreamweaver.

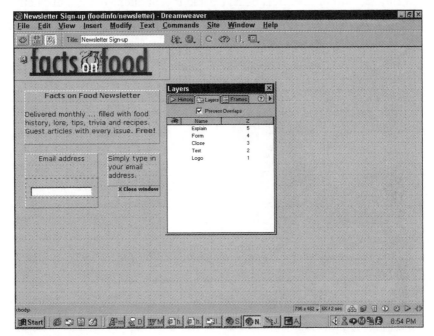

Figure 27-5
The completed layer view of your page. It is ready to be converted to a table.

Converting layers to tables

This is going to be a little anticlimatic. You have worked through this entire session to get here and you are going to accomplish your goal in one operation. I could make it harder, but I don't think you would appreciate that, either. Follow these steps to create a table:

1. Select Modify ⇨ Convert ⇨ Layers to Table. The Convert Layers to Table window will open.

2. Select Most Accurate for the Table Layout. Choosing Smallest will deliver a less complicated table, but it will not be as accurate. Any cells below the size you specify will be included with a neighboring cell to reduce columns and rows. Use this feature if accurate layout is not crucial.

3. Make sure that Use Transparent GIFs is checked. Dreamweaver will place the invisible images you require to prevent collapsing cells.

4. Make sure that the Center on Page option is unchecked.

5. Check Prevent Layer Overlaps. This is a safety feature, because you should have no overlapping layers.

6. Check Snap to Grid if your layout is dependent on a grid. This will prevent tiny columns or rows from being created if your alignment is a little off.

7. Click OK. Your document should look resemble Figure 27-6.

Figure 27-6
Dreamweaver view of your page immediately after converting your layers to a table

You can change your page back to layers if you decide to add or change content, or you can edit it in table form. You may want to see if there is any way to reduce the number of columns or rows. However, if you find you are doing too much editing on the table that is created by Dreamweaver, you might want to consider using tables from the beginning of the process.

Those are the basics of layers. You now know how to produce pages with layers or with tables. The remaining piece is deciding which is best for you.

Using Tables or Layers

The decision to use layers or tables for your work must come next. Try creating your pages with layers and tables to find the way that is the most comfortable for you. The type of content you produce also can determine which method is most appropriate for you.

Creating tables from layers definitely produces more code. This matters to me, and it is one of the main reasons I use tables for most of my page construction. But as I mentioned earlier, layers are terribly seductive. The process is much more intuitive than creating an exciting layout with tables — it can resemble a math process more than art. Having control over every column and row is comforting, especially when I am trying to stretch what tables were meant to do.

Your list of pros and cons for each method will likely be different than mine. You may never make a solid decision. You should, however, make sure that you are comfortable with both methods. That is the best way to make production decisions. When you know both methods with equal comfort, you are more likely to make your decisions based on the best that each can deliver.

Done!

REVIEW

You now have the tools to create your pages with layers rather than tables. The methods are straightforward, as long as you remember the following details:

- Layers depend on CSS for positioning, which is what prevents you from using layer-based documents for general Web use. Even current browsers cannot be trusted to correctly display layers.

- The Properties Inspector provides all control for layer positioning. The Layers panel displays and controls layer stacking order. The Object panel provides the drawing tool for click-and-drag layers.

- Nested layers cannot be used for documents that will be converted to tables.
- The Prevent Overlap option helps create layers that will easily convert into tables.
- Content is added to each layer in the same way as it is added to a page. Each layer is like a minipage.
- Naming your layers helps to keep your work organized.
- Layers can be converted to tables, and the same page converted back to layers — although it is best to convert back and forth as little as possible.
- The best way to decide whether table or layer construction is right for you is to learn both methods very well. Each has strengths and weaknesses, and every person will have a preference.

QUIZ YOURSELF

1. What is the only safe place to use layers for final production of your pages? (See the "Understanding Layers" section.)

2. What does the Prevent Overlaps command do for layers? (See the "Creating a nested layer" section.)

3. How do you move a layer? (See the "Positioning layers" section.)

4. Content will be added to the active layer at what point? (See the "Adding content to layers" section.)

5. What is one benefit and one drawback of creating tables from layers, as opposed to creating tables from the start? (See the "Using Tables or Layers" section.)

Session Checklist

✔ Recognizing the limitations of DHTML

✔ Working with DHTML

✔ Understanding timelines

✔ Seeing DHTML at its best

30 Min.
To Go

I n the last session, you learned how to create layers for layout. As you move into DHTML, you will put layers to a completely different use. Until now, you have used code only for static objects. Images, text, tables are all static. In fact, even the animated GIFs and the Macromedia Flash object you placed on your page were static. The file caused motion on the screen, but the image or movie remains static on the page. DHTML actually moves layers across your screen. Objects are placed in layers which positioned by CSS and moved by JavaScript. As with most things that move from one coordinate to another, you must pay attention to what you are doing and plan your work well, but the concept is surprisingly simple to create in Dreamweaver.

Recognizing the Limitations of DHTML

"Okay," you're asking, "where are the warnings?" Yes, they are coming. You will be using layers, which of course come with compatibility issues that were well covered in the last session. When you used layers for your layout, you could convert to tables so that all browsers could see page. There is no way to make a table cell move, though, so you have no alternative when using layers for DHTML. Again, Intranets — with their controllable environment — offer an ideal place to use DHTML.

DHTML can be used to build features that cannot be accomplished in any other way. Menus that unroll over text and disappear when not in use are highly attractive for sites with masses of information. If you know the majority of your audience will be using more recent browsers and you are prepared to delve deeply into discovering all the quirks with each browser, you can put DHTML to use in documents for the Web.

Never use DHTML for a function that will make your site unusable if the visitor's browser does not recognize your code. I recently asked a developer who makes most of her living working with DHTML and CSS whether it was practical to use DHTML at all. Her reply was very descriptive: "For Intranet — absolutely. For the Web, use it for nothing that is mission critical." If you are building menus with DHTML, please make sure you have an alternative way to navigate your site.

Working with DHTML in Dreamweaver

DMHTL is actually a combination of JavaScript and CSS controlling the position of layers. Objects are placed on layers, and they can be moved from on location to another with timelines or with JavaScript commands. Layers also can be made visible or invisible by position or mouse action, further adding to its capabilities.

Think back to your layers exercise in Session 27. You placed objects on layers for positioning. Remember the code that placed that layer where you wanted it on the page? Now picture that you could add instructions to the placement code that told the browser to change the coordinates after a certain time, or when the visitor performs a mouse action. Then imagine that you can tell that layer to be visible or invisible in the same way.

Creating layers for DHTML

Let's start by creating a document with layers that can be moved. The following exercise will create an extremely simple puzzle just to introduce the idea of moving layer position:

1. Create a new document in the Food Info site and the Resources folder. Name the file **layermove.html**.

   Turn on your grid to make positioning your layers easier. Because you are working with a few large objects, you can set your grid to a high value.

2. Select View ⇨ Grid ⇨ Edit Grid. Set the Spacing value to 50, and select Snapto Grid. Make sure that the Show Grid option is checked.

3. Create a layer with a width of 93 pixels and a height of 111 pixels. Select the layer, and then assign the name **A** to the layer. Position the layer close to the top of the page.

4. Insert the image movea.gif from the Art directory into the A layer.

5. Repeat Steps 3 and 4 twice, naming the new layers B and C, respectively, and inserting moveb.gif and movec.gif in the respective layers. Use the grid to place the layers equally. The result should be similar to Figure 28-1.

6. Select all three layers by holding down your Shift key as you click each layer. Select Modify ⇨ Align ⇨ Top to align the layers.

7. Create a new layer at the left edge of the page, approximately 350 pixels from the top edge, and name it Question 1. Type **A car that can be rented for a very short period of time.** in the layer.

You have just created three layers containing an image (layers A, B and C) which a visitor will be able to drag into position once you have completed the next exercise. The final layer that you created, called Question 1, contains the question that will be answered by dragging letter layers into the correct order. The question layer will remain static.

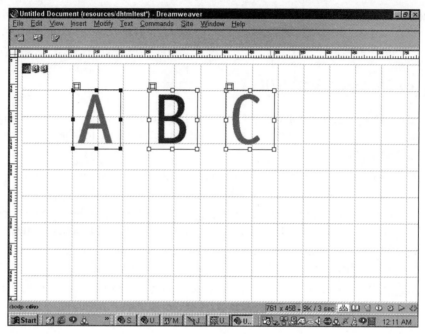

Figure 28-1
*Here are three layers created and aligned. The grid shown here is set to 50
pixels by 50px.*

Adding behaviors for layers

You are now going to create a behavior that will allow you to drag each of the layers to a new position when the page is displayed in a browser. When the layers are
dragged into position, the letters will spell "cab." You add the behavior to the
<body> tag.

Add the JavaScript that will allow visitors to drag layers by following these steps.

**20 Min.
To Go**

1. Open the Behavior window. Click the <body> tag in the lower-left portion
   of your screen.

2. Click + (plus) in the Behavior window to create a new behavior. Choose
   Drag Layer and the Drag Layer window will open.

3. Select layer "C" from the Layer list.

4. Set the Drop Layer values to Left **0** and Top **200**. Set the Snap if Within value to **50**. When the page is displayed in a browser, Layer C (and any contents of layer C, of course) will snap into a position at the left edge, 200 pixels from the top edge of the window. When dragging, the layer will snap into this position as long as the layer is dragged to within 50 pixels of the new location. Click OK to create the behavior.

5. Repeat Steps 2 through 4 for the A and B layers, using Top 200 for both and Left 100 and 200, respectively.

6. Preview the page in a browser. Click the C image and drag it close to the area above the text layer. It will snap into place when your mouse pointer is close enough to the specified position. Repeat this step for the other letters.

This is a very simple example of the way layers can be used to build a puzzle or other interactive features. Experiment with different behaviors and values. Remember that you will have to preview your page to see the results.

As you experiment, you will begin to realize how powerful layers and behaviors can be. However, do not forget that this is not a well-supported feature. If you want to work with DHTML for general Web use, you will have to study the topic in much more depth than you can cover here. DHTML is not supported by version 3 browsers. Even for version 4 and later browsers, perfect operation requires intensive troubleshooting.

Understanding Timelines

Layers and behaviors can produce some powerful capabilities, but when you add the ability to control when an action takes place, you realize the full power of DHTML. You can move layers, turn them on and off at a certain time or when the visitor completes an action, and so on — all can be added with Dreamweaver's timelines.

The timeline control in Dreamweaver will be familiar if you have ever worked on animated production, such as Macromedia's Flash or Shockwave. The action is controlled by frames (these are no relation to the frames in browsers that you will cover in the next session). In the simplest form, each frame tells the browser where to place the contents of the layer.

Note

To avoid any confusion with previous exercises, as well as those to come in this session, this example has no relation to any other exercise. It is simply a sample.

Figure 28-2 shows the Timeline panel. Each frame contains information that tells the contents of a layer where to be on the page. In the example shown here, the layer containing the logo image is moved on a curved path. It will start automatically and continue moving because the Autoplay and Loop options are active. Clicking any frame along the timeline will move the layer containing the image to the correct position as set in the timeline.

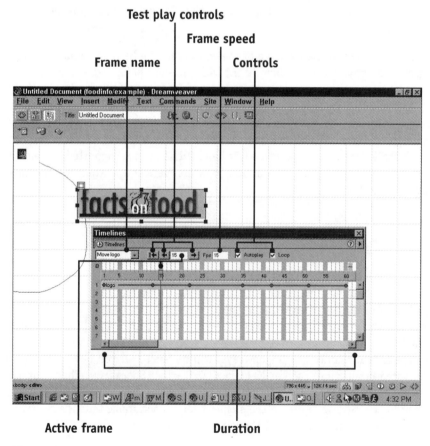

Figure 28-2
The Timeline panel

**10 Min.
To Go**

The sample shown earlier in Figure 28-2 is set to the default value of 15 fps (frames per second). Because this full timeline is 60 frames long, it will take 4 seconds to complete the action (60 ÷ 15 = 4). You can test your timeline actions within Dreamweaver by using the forward and back arrows, by adjusting the speed of the playback, or by editing the number of frames. You can edit each frame individually.

You will automate the action from the last exercise in the previous section, "Adding behaviors for layers." To start, you will remove the behaviors from the layers and add a timeline to automatically move the layers (without the visitor dragging the layer). You also will add a behavior that will require visitors to initiate the layer movement.

Using a Timeline to Control Layers

Now that you have had a peek at the Timeline window, you will add a timeline to the quiz document that you created in the first two exercises in this session. Start by saving the file with a different name and removing the existing behaviors.

Follow these steps to save the file with a different name and delete the original behaviors:

1. Open the file dhtmtest.html if it is not already open. Save the file as **timetest.html**.

2. Open the Behaviors window. The behaviors that you added to the layers should be visible if there is nothing selected in the document.

3. Click the first behavior and click the – (minus) button at the top of the Behaviors window, or press the Delete key to remove the behavior.

4. Repeat Step 3 for the remaining two behaviors.

Adding a timeline

Now you can add a timeline to each of the layers. To prevent confusion and to allow for easier editing, you should use a new timeline for each section of the page, even when different areas will be affected at the same time. For your example, you can use the same timeline to move three layers.

Select Window ⇨ Timelines to open the Timelines panel, which controls all timelines (see Figure 28-3). The drop-down list in the upper-left portion of the window lists the timelines within the document. The numbers across the top of the window represent the frames that create a timeline. The numbers on the left side of the window represent the layers that have been added to the timeline.

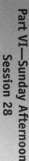

Follow these steps to add the three layers containing images to one timeline, setting a beginning and end position for each of your images. Each layer must be individually added.

1. Select layer "C," making sure that the layer is selected and not just the image.

2. Before you can add any action to the layer, you first must add the layer to the timeline. Select Modify➪Timeline➪Add Object to Timeline. You also can add the layer to the timeline by dragging the layer to the first frame of the timeline, as shown in Figure 28-4. The layer name will be added to the timeline.

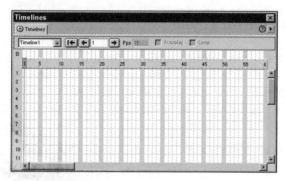

Figure 28-3
The Timelines panel

3. Repeat Step 2 to add layer A and B to the timeline.

4. The layers have been added to the timeline, but there is no action at this point. You must set the end position for the layer to complete the action. Select the last frame of the C layer in the timeline. Drag the layer to the final position. Figure 28-5 shows the result.

5. Repeat Step 4 for the remaining layers, moving them into position to spell the word "cab."

6. Preview the timeline action by holding down the right-arrow next to the frame number in the Timelines panel. The letters should continually move from the original position to the new position.

You now have your action determined, but you need to tell the timeline when to operate. You will add behaviors to the timeline. Then, you will edit the behavior to operate on a click from the visitor rather than the mouseover created by the behavior.

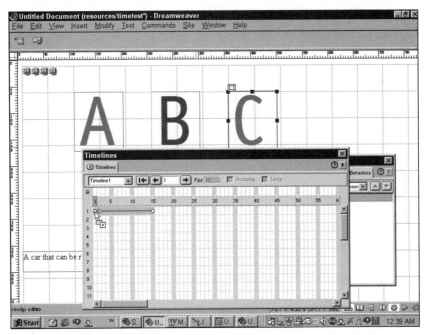

Figure 28-4
Layer "C" is dragged to the timeline.

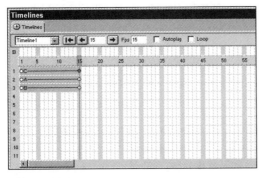

Figure 28-5
*Last frame for layer C is selected and the layer is dragged to the final posi-
tion. The diagonal line represents the path for the layer as the timeline is
played.*

Adding behaviors to a timeline

You mapped out the locations for your images at different times in the previous exercise, but you must now tell the timeline function when to start. Timelines are controlled by JavaScript that you will enter through the Behaviors panel. For this example, you will attach the behavior to a text link.

To add a Behavior to your timeline and then edit the JavaScript to customize it, complete the following steps.

1. Create a new layer beside the text layer and type: **Click here to display answer.**

2. Select the text you just typed. In the Properties Inspector, type **#** (pound) in the Link field. This creates a link that will receive your behavior.

3. Open the Behavior panel window. With the text still selected, click + (plus) and choose Timeline ⇨ Play Timeline. The Play Timeline window will open.

4. Accept Timeline 1 as the timeline to play.

Your timeline is now set to play when the mouse pointer is passed over the link with the attached behavior. Preview the page in Tour Document to see the result when you pass your mouse pointer over the link. However, it will be less confusing for visitors if you set the timeline to play when the link is clicked, rather than just on a mouseover. The following simple edit to the behavior will change this action:

1. With your text still selected, open your preferred Code view. The code for the link will be displayed.

2. Locate the following line of code:

   ```
   <a href="#" onMouseOver="MM_timelinePlay('Timeline1')">Click
   here to display answer.</a>
   ```

3. Change onMouseOver to onClick. The timeline will be played when the visitor clicks the link. Return to your regular view.

4. Preview the page in your browser. Click the link to start the timeline action. If you want to see it again, simply reload the page in your browser and click the link again.

I will again make a case for learning the code behind the Dreamweaver document. When you are familiar with the way code works, you can use the convenience of Dreamweaver's behaviors, yet still be able to edit the code for your particular needs. Having said that, changing the onMouseOver to an onClick option can be completed in the Behaviors window. Place your cursor in the link text (the behavior is attached to this link) and highlight the behavior in the Behavior window. Click the arrow in the center of the behavior listing and choose onClick from the drop-down menu that appears.

Editing a timeline

Once you have your basic timeline created, you may want to make minor adjustments to perfect your actions. Follow these steps to add frames to the timeline and then increase the speed:

1. If it is not already open, open the document timetest.html. Make sure that the Timelines panel is open.

2. You are going to add 10 frames to the movement of the second layer, and 20 frames to the third layer so that the letters fall into place at different times. Click the last frame of the "A" layer. Drag the frame to 25. To make this action start a little behind the movement of the first layer, click and drag the first frame of the "A" layer to 5.

3. Click and drag layer "B" to make 35 the last frame. Click and drag the first frame of this layer to 10. The movement will now be staggered.

4. Change the frames per second (Fps) setting to 20, which will increase the speed of the action. Figure 28-6 shows the correct settings.

Not all browsers will adjust the speed of a timeline.

5. Preview the document in as many browsers as you can. This is the most important part of working with layers and timelines and it should not be skipped.

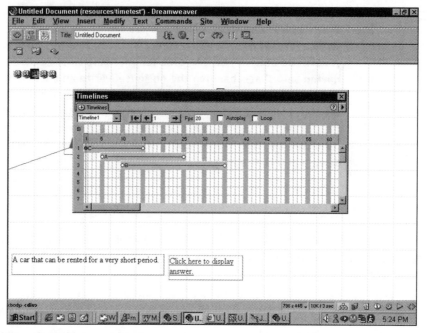

Figure 28-6
The final settings for your timeline. Note how the layer action now starts at different times.

Testing pages with timelines

Creating a page that will work in Dreamweaver — and which will preview correctly with the browsers on your computer — is just the beginning. Your initial testing in Dreamweaver is an efficient way to create the correct motion and speed for your animation. However, you also should upload your page to the server and have as many people as possible test your page to see if the layers and timelines are working as they should.

When you are working with any documents built with layers, testing across platforms and browsers is essential. It is a good idea to develop a network of testers, which can most easily be accomplished by joining Web development newsgroups. See the CD-ROM Resources folder for a list of newsgroups that provide expert advice, as well as the opportunity to have your pages tested on a wide variety of computers.

DHTML at Its Best

Before you assume that DHTML is only about animation, I would like to bring your attention to the best use for DHTML. You probably have seen menus that drop down over the content on the page while you are making a selection. This is usually DHTML at work (there are drop-down Java applet menus, as well, although they are not common). On content-rich sites, it is very tempting to use DHTML menus. If you have a controlled customer base, or you are working on Intranet sites, you have every reason to move into this technology.

 There are several great educational sites that focus on DHTML. The DHTML section of webreference.com features an ongoing series about DHTML menus. See this series at http:// www.webreference.com/dhtml/**. Another source for DHTML/JavaScript/CSS is** http://www.pageresource.com/ dhtml/index.html.

With many technologies that are not well accepted, I recommend that you learn them only for fun and for use on personal sites. However, as buggy as using layers and CSS can be, I still urge anyone who is interested in this method of creating documents to study hard. Many believe that the future of Web design will be layers, and that eventually, browser standards will reach a point that this technology will be safe to use. The time you spend to learn DHTML will not be wasted.

This has been a very brief introduction to the DHTML capabilities within Dreamweaver. The subject is very deep, and I again urge you to learn the code behind the actions you create in Dreamweaver. Troubleshooting and applying fixes so that your actions will play in all browsers is the biggest part of DHTML.

REVIEW

DHTML provides exciting possibilities, and also can be confusing. With Dreamweaver's assistance, it can be done, however, as long as you keep these few things in mind:

- DHTML is a combination of CSS and JavaScript which are applied to layers.
- DHTML is best at this time for Intranets rather than for the general Web. Browsers and computer platforms are usually easy to determine with Intranets, which removes much of the uncertainty that plagues DHTML.

- If you are using DHTML or layers for general Web use, make sure that you are not using the features for critical functions that will render your site unusable if the DHTML does not work properly in the visitor's browser.

- Action is added to timelines with behaviors in Dreamweaver. Behaviors add the JavaScript required for DHTML.

- Timelines control layer movement frame by frame. Each frame can be edited individually, or you can edit them manually by setting the beginning and end positions.

- Objects must be placed in layers to be used with timelines.

- You can preview actions in Dreamweaver by using the controls in the Timeline panel.

- Timelines can be edited after creation.

- Any document created with layers — especially when timelines have been used — must be tested across every combination of browser and platform.

QUIZ YOURSELF

1. Why is DHTML best left to Intranet development and noncritical portions of sites designed for the Web? (See the "Recognizing the Limitations of DHTML" section.)

2. DHTML is a combination of which Web development features and languages? (See the "Working with DHTML in Dreamweaver" section.)

3. DHTML is based on layers. What is used to move the layers in the browser? (See the "Adding behaviors for layers" section.)

4. What is the main purpose for timelines in Dreamweaver? (See the "Understanding Timelines" section.)

5. How can you preview and test a timeline? (See the "Adding a Timeline," and "Testing pages with timelines" section.)

6. What type of menus use DHTML? (See the "Testing pages with timelines" section.)

Working with Frames

Session Checklist

✔ Learning about frames

✔ Working with frames to create documents

✔ Using frames to your advantage

✔ Imitating frames

**30 Min.
To Go**

F rames have controversial in Web design since they were first introduced. The problem — as always — is the different way in which browsers interpret frames, complicated by the loss of screen space for lower-resolution browsers. Most designers do not use frames unless a very good case can be made that frames are the best way in which to handle an information presentation problem. To make this decision for yourself, let's start by looking at exactly what frames are, and where they can be used.

Understanding Frames

The concept of frames is very simple. Each frame is an individual HTML document. The collection of two or more frame documents within a page is controlled by a single document known as a *frameset*. The frameset contains no information other than to tell the browser which documents to display within the page, and where they should be placed. You will start with a very simple frameset page, and you will change the background colors on each frame to trace exactly what is happening on the page. This should help you understand exactly what you are doing when you are using frames.

Creating a framed document

You will start by creating a directory to hold your frame documents. It is not necessary that you create a special folder for your frame documents, but it will help you to keep track of exactly the documents which are making up your framed document.

Create a folder for your frame files, and then start building your framed page, using the following steps:

1. Create a new folder within the Resources folder of your Food Info site. Type **frames** for the name of the new folder.

2. Create a new document. **Do not** save this document yet.

3. Select Insert ⇨ Frames ⇨ Left and Top. Your document will divide into four sections, as shown in Figure 29-1.

Figure 29-1
Page divisions, or frames, are created when you add left and top frames to a page.

Select View ⇨ Visual Aids ⇨ Frame Borders if you cannot see gray lines between the sections.

4. Insert your cursor into the top left section and type **corner.html**. You will be naming this frame with this same name; this text entry is simply to provide easy identification as you move along in the exercise.

5. Insert your cursor in the upper-right section and type **topright.html**. Repeat this step, typing **lowerleft.html** in the second section on the left side, and **maincontent.html** in the large area at the lower-right section. Remember that these are simply text entries.

At this point, you have a framed document that is unnamed. You will go through and name each frame and save the frameset, which will tell the browser how to display your collection of frames.

Naming frame documents

Individual frames must be named because each frame is a separate document. The frameset that you create as your last action will be the one that is displayed in the browser, calling on each of the individual documents you have created to display the page.

Follow these steps to name and save your frames:

1. Insert your cursor into the upper-left section and select File ⇨ Save Frame As. The Save As window will open. Browse to the Frames directory that you created in the previous exercise. Name the document **corner.html**.

2. Insert your cursor into the upper-right section and repeat Step 1, this time naming the document **topright.html**. Repeat Steps 1 and 2 for the remaining two sections, using the text entry names that you typed as the filenames.

   You should now have four files saved. As you will see later in this session, each of these four documents can be opened as you would open any other document — separate from the frames. It is the frameset that creates the framed page. Now, you will save the frameset.

3. Click one of the gray borders and select File ⇨ Save Frameset As. Make sure that the Save As window has the Frames folder active, and then type **testset.html**. Figure 29-2 displays the results. Note how the window's title bar shows the name of the frame that is active; in this case, corner.html.

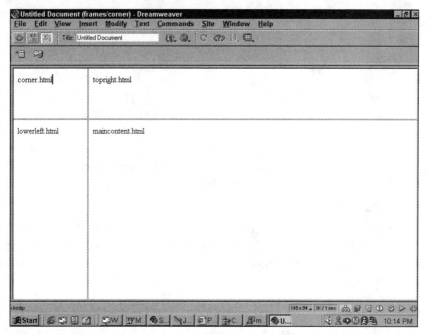

Figure 29-2
Framed page with four frames. Note that the active frame's name is displayed in the window's title bar.

Editing frames

To make it easier to identify each of the frames, you will change the background color of each frame. Please note that this is a page property you will be using to change the color. Normally, the entire page changes to the same color. Because frames are individual documents, you can apply a separate background or background image to each frame.

Change the page properties for each frame page to set the background color as follows:

1. Insert your cursor into the corner.html frame. Select Modify ⇨ Page Properties, and change the background color to a light gray. Only the top corner frame will be affected.

2. Insert your cursor into the topright.html frame and repeat Step 1, choosing a different light color. Repeat Step 2 for each of the remaining frames. Your document should resemble Figure 29-3.

 You are using a light color simply because you have black type. Any color or background image can be used.

3. You have made changes to each frame (document). To save the changes, select File ⇨ Save All Frames. Any changes you have made to any frame will be saved.

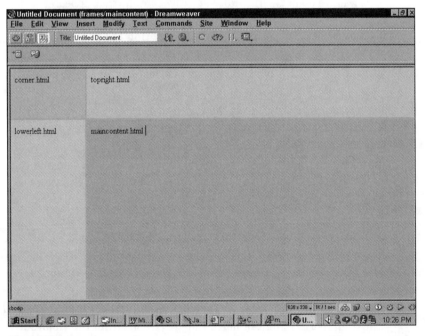

Figure 29-3
The color for each frame has been set using the page background color. This illustrates that each section of the page is an individual document, because changing a background color affects the entire page.

Touring your frames and frameset

Let's take a look at what you have created. By the end of this tour, you will have the concept of frames well established. As you move on to creating more interesting framed documents, you will have a solid base from which you can work.

In this exercise, you will add content to pages in a frameset, both from within the frameset and with the pages that form the frameset independently opened.

1. Activate the Food Info site window. Browse to the Frames folder in the Resources folder. The frames folder should contain five files: corner.html, lowerleft.html, maincontent.html, testset.html, and topright.html. All five files are necessary to create your page.

2. Close all documents, leaving only the site window open. Double-click corner.html to open the file. Note how the content that appeared in the upper-left corner of the framed page is shown on the page, but without the other frames. This is one of the frames within the frameset. When it is opened alone, is a simple HTML document.

3. Highlight the text in the document and change the font color to blue. Save and close the file.

4. Open testset.html. Notice that the text in the upper-left corner frame of the page is now blue. The upper-left frame contains the file corner.html, which you just edited.

5. Close all files again. Open maincontent.html. Create a new line and type you can insert an image in any frame. Insert another line and insert bird.gif from the Art directory of the Food Info site. Save and close the file.

6. Open testset.html. Note that the changes you made to the maincontent.html frame are now included in the framed page.

7. Preview the document in your browser. It should resemble Figure 29-4.

It does not matter where you edit documents that are part of a frameset. You can make changes from within the frameset, or you can open the document individually as you did earlier. The result will be the same in either case.

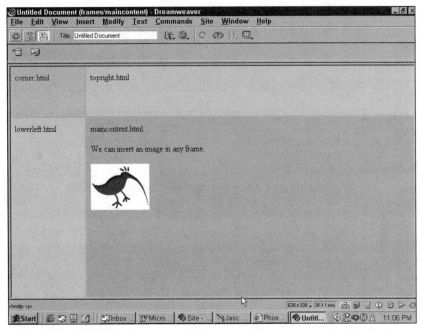

Figure 29-4
Final framed page as previewed in Internet Explorer. Note that the borders around each frame, which displayed in Dreamweaver, have disappeared. Because the default value is that borders are disabled, the Dreamweaver display is showing only construction borders.

Although you have not created an exciting page, you should feel fairly comfortable with the idea of how frames and framesets interact. Let's take a look at the code from the frameset to make sure that you fully understand what is happening. The following code is copied from testset.html, which is your frameset document.

```
<frameset rows="94,338*" cols="145,638*" frameborder="NO"
border="0" framespacing="0">
  <frame name="cornerFrame" scrolling="NO" noresize
src="corner.html" >
  <frame name="topFrame" scrolling="NO" noresize
src="topright.html" bordercolor="#000000" frameborder="NO" >
  <frame name="leftFrame" scrolling="NO" noresize
src="lowerleft.html">
  <frame name="mainFrame" src="maincontent.html">
</frameset>
```

For now, ignore the attributes frameborder, border, framespacing, scrolling, and noresize. The important entries right now are the coordinates for the frameset rows and columns, as well as the source value. Note how the source corresponds to the filenames that you created for each of your frames. You will edit the name of the frame later, but the src value refers to the actual file that will be placed in the specified location.

As you work with frames and learn more advanced techniques, keep checking your code to follow the changes with each edit. Frames can be confusing. If you understand the code behind frames, you will have a much better chance of troubleshooting problems and using frames for creative solutions.

Now that you have the basics, let's create a page using frames.

Creating a Frame-Based Document

20 Min. To Go

As in most Web development, planning your frames well from the start will save many headaches later. You are going to create a page for your Food Info site that will feature an alternative for the history bits section for this site.

For this page, you will create your frames and then add content. Most of the content will be created on the page, but you want to include the menus from your other pages, and you also will create a page separately to be used in your frame.

Creating your framed document

You will create a frame that extends across the top of the document to hold the logo and title, and another frame across the top to hold your menus. You will then create a frame for the left section of the page — below the top frames — to hold a text menu. Clicking the text menu will open that selection in the right frame. You will require four frames.

Create a new framed document with four frames using the following steps:

1. Open a new window from the Food Info site window.

2. Select Insert ⇨ Frames ⇨ Top. This will insert a frame across the top of the page. Don't worry about size right now.

3. Repeat Step 1 to create another frame that spans the top of the frame.

4. With your cursor in the lower frame, select Insert ⇨ Frames ⇨ Left. This will insert a frame to the left of the lower section. Your document should resemble Figure 29-5. The frames for your document are complete, but you still must save the frames and frameset.

5. Save the frames with the following names, starting with the top two frames, and then saving the left and right frames, respectively: framelogo.html, framemenu.html, frameleft.html, and frameright.html.

Naming your frames

Pause here to make sure that you do not trip in this section. In the last exercise, you named your frame documents. In the next exercise, you will actually name your frames to help identify your framed sections and work with your code. Think back to Session 13 when you named your images to use with the JavaScript for your complex rollovers. The name you assigned in the Properties Inspector had no relation to the filename. Naming your frames is exactly the same. You will use a combination of the Frame panel and the Properties Inspector to create names for your frames.

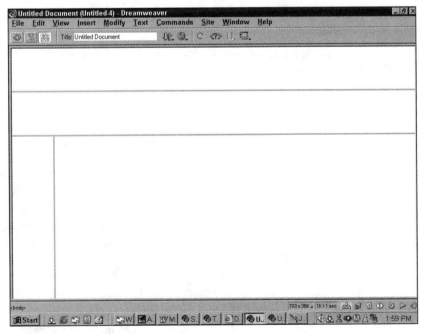

Figure 29-5
Frameset with four frames

The following steps will guide you through naming your frames:

1. Select Window ➪ Frames to open the Frames panel. Open the Properties Inspector.

2. Click the top frame in the Frames panel. This will present the information for that frame in the Properties Inspector. Type **Logoframe** in the name section. Note how the name you changed is reflected in the Frames panel.

3. Click the second frame and type **Menuframe** to name. Repeat this Step for the two lower frames, naming them **Leftframe** and **Maincontent**, respectively.

4. Click the gray border in Dreamweaver to select the frameset. Check your code and you will see that the new frame names are reflected in the frameset code. This will help when you must make minor adjustments to the code, because each frame can now be clearly identified.

5. Select File ➪ Save All Frames to save the changes.

Adding content to your frames

Now follow these steps to add your content and adjust the size of the frames to match that content:

 Copy histbits.gif from the Session 29 folder of the CD-ROM to the Art folder of the Food Info site.

1. With your cursor in the top frame, insert a table with two columns and one row, specify no cell padding or spacing, and set a width of 100%. You want your images to be justified both left and right, so you must separate them. You could create an extra frame for this purpose, but it is best to use the smallest number of frames possible to eliminate confusion, increase stability, and decrease download time.

2. With your cursor in the first cell of the table, insert the image logo.gif from the Art folder. Don't worry about how it looks right now. Apply left justification to this cell. With your cursor in the right cell of the table, insert histbits.gif. Apply right justification for this cell.

3. Set the background color for the first cell to match the background of the logo. Set the background color of the second cell to match the background of the title. Now you must correct the margins and the size of the top frame.

Adjusting page properties and size for frames

Remember that frames are simply HTML documents collected into a single page. You want your top frame to be right against the top and left border where the logo and titles are on other pages. To do this, you must set your page margins for the framelogo.html document of this frameset to 0. You will use a combination of the Frame panel and the Properties Inspector to accomplish this.

You also can set the margins by opening the framelogo.html document and setting page properties as you did in Session 9.

Follow these steps to adjust the page properties and the size of your frames:

1. Select Window ⇨ Frames to open the Frames panel. Open the Properties Inspector.

2. In the Frames panel, click the Logoframe frame to select. In the Properties Inspector, set both the Margin Width and Margin Height to 0.

    Your content should now reflect no margins. Now, you will adjust the size of the frame to match the content. You can click and drag the frame borders to adjust the size, or you can set values in the Properties Inspector. Remember that it is your frameset that controls the frame position and sizing.

3. Click the gray border to select the frameset.

4. Click and drag borders to meet the lower edge of the logo image. Preview the frame in your browser to ensure that you have the exact positioning.

5. You also can set the value to 47, which matches the image height in the Properties Inspector.

Creating a frame from an existing document

You worked hard to create your menu look when you were working in the main site. Rather than repeat that work for this document, you can create an HTML document that contains only the menu. You will then open that document in the appropriate frame of your frameset.

Carefully follow these steps to create a document that you will use for frame content.

1. In the Food Info site, create a new document from the Main template.

2. Break the link to the template. You will be using only the menu portion of this page. Save the document as **framemenu.html**.

3. Delete everything on the page except the table holding the menu and the decorative stripes above the menu. The easiest way to do this is to delete the content row by row. Your document should resemble Figure 29-6 when you have completed this step.

4. Save the document and close.

5. Return to your framed document and add the menu that you just prepared. With your cursor in the Menuframe frame, select File ➪ Open in Frame and choose framemenu.html. The document will open in your frame. With a few adjustments, you now have the menu added to your framed document.

6. Adjust the frame borders so that the upper two frames are exactly positioned to contain the logo and title image, as well as the menu document.

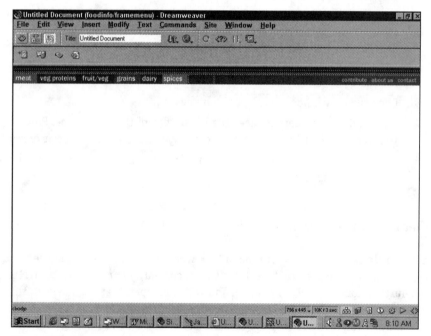

Figure 29-6
All information removed from the page except the menu you require. This document will be added to your frameset.

Any document can be added to a frameset using this method. Again, it is most important to retain the concept that you are placing full HTML documents into a pattern described by the frameset.

Finally, you are going to create a text menu in the left column of the second frameset and direct the links from that menu to open in the main content area. This is one of the best reasons for using frames. When you need content to change in one area of the page, but it is best that the visitor has constant, easy access to the menu items.

Create a text menu to use with your framed page by taking the following steps:

1. Attach the foodinfo.css style sheet to the document.

2. Type the following to create a menu. **Bread**, **Wine**, and **Sugar** will be typed using Paragraph style with Bold, and the remaining entries will be Paragraph style only. Set the font color to # 663300 (brown). The menu items with links will change to blue when the links are added.

Bread
Preparing Grain
Developing Trends
Commercial
   Wine
Trends in Fruit
Preparation
   Sugar
Production
Health Trends
Shortages

This is your menu. Next, you will add links to the menu and specify that the links will open in the right frame by creating targeted links.

Creating targeted links

You will use the Target field in the Properties Inspector so that the links will open where you specify. To make it easier, I have included three HTML files to use as link files.

10 Min.
To Go

Create a new folder in your Food Info site called histbits. Copy the following files from the Session 29 folder on the CD-ROM to the new folder: commerc.html, devtrends.html, and prepgrain.html. The documents should be placed in a separate folder to keep the main folder more manageable.

Create targeted links for your framed page by following these steps.

1. Highlight the text "Preparing Grain" in the Bread section of the menu. Use the browse feature of the link field in the Properties Inspector to locate and select prepgrain.html in the Histbits folder.

2. Select Maincontent from the Target drop-down list. This will place the contents of the linked file into the Maincontent frame in your document.

3. Repeat Steps 1 and 2 for the next menu item, using devtrends.html for the link and Maincontent as the target. Repeat Steps 1 and 2 for the third menu item. using commerc.html for the link and Maincontent as the target.

4. Preview the document in your browser to see the results. When the page is first presented, you will see a blank white page. Click any of the prepared links and the right portion of the screen will fill with the linked document.

If you want, you can create more links for this page using the samples I have included as a base file, and then saving the new files in the Histbits folder. You also can prepare a document that will serve as the initial view for the Maincontent frame. I have left it blank to make it clear how the links are operating. Normally, you would have content presented on this page. You can create a page separately and open it as you did for the menu, or you can create the page within the frameset, saving the frame to replace the blank frame that is presently in place.

You now have the basics of creating a framed document. What remains is deciding when to use them.

Deciding When to Use Frames

Frames can make navigation easy. and they generally are easier for the designer to work with than nonframed pages. However, many visitors do not like viewing pages with frames, and they do create problems. The most important problem for designers is that framed pages are difficult to bookmark. It is quite common for an entire site to be created with one frameset, with information changing within the frame documents. When the site is bookmarked by the visitor, only the main page will be saved, making it difficult for your visitor to mark specific information. The designer must provide a "bookmark this page" script to ensure that visitors can return to the correct page.

Printing pages also is more difficult. A Web savvy visitor can print just the frame they are interested in, but not all visitors will know how to do this. If printing is important to your visitors — and many people still want their information on paper — you might want to add a special "print this article" script to ensure that you are not frustrating your visitors with your frames.

Download time also is affected. It should be clear now that you have created framed documents. You are asking the visitor to download not one page, but several. Also, any technique that calls for exacting positioning must be tested in many browsers across both platforms to ensure that the framesets are read as you intended.

What is the benefit of frames? You saw an example with the page you created. Often, frames are the best answer to displaying many similar files, whether they contain text or images. Photographers often place thumbnail images of their work in a framed page; when the visitor clicks to see the image in a larger size, the image is displayed on the same page with the thumbnail images still in view.

Personally, I avoid frames unless they are the only way to create a function. You should not be using frames simply because it will present a more stable, artistic look. If you can improve the function of a document for your visitor with frames, it is an admirable addition. I will use frames, but I must prove to myself that doing so is the best way to make my visitor's experience rewarding. If that proof is not there, I always bow to simpler methods, even if I must work a little harder to create the same look.

Simulating Frames

One of the main reasons designers use frames is to have a small area of scrolled text within a static page. Here is a very easy workaround for this that does not involve frames:

1. Create a new document in the Food Info site.
2. Insert a table with two columns and one row. You are going to insert a form in the second cell so that you can place text at the right side of the document.
3. With your cursor in the second cell, select Insert ➪ Form Item ➪ Text Field. Click Yes when you are asked if you want to add a form tag.
4. Select the text field and select Multi line for the Type.
5. Set the Char width value to 50 and the Num Lines value to 20.
6. Change Wrap to Virtual.

7. In the Initial Value field, type **This is a sample of a frame-like form included in a document. The rest of this area will be filled with greek text.** Insert greek text to create more text.

8. Preview your results in a browser. Figure 29-7 shows this form in Internet Explorer.

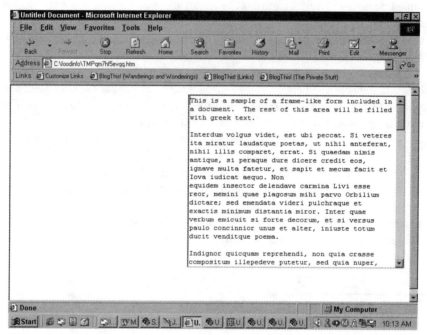

Figure 29-7
Using a text field to present information that will scroll without using frames

Done!

This is a very handy tip that will help you avoid the use frames in many cases. The form has no interactive purpose; it is used to create a scrolling text area. Many creative designers have developed methods to create the same look that might be created with frames, but without the problems that come along with them. Keep your eyes open for innovative design, as well as for exceptional use of frames. I have seen some brilliant frame uses, and would never recommend totally ignoring this technique.

REVIEW

Frames are a simple concept and can be very effective for some pages. Remember these details about frames:

- Each frame is an individual document.
- Frame documents can be edited within a frameset or as an independent document.
- It is a good idea to check the code as you build your first framed documents so that you understand what is happening as you create the document.
- Each document within a frameset has a unique filename. It also is wise to give each of your frames a name to use with the Frames panel and when you are directly editing code.
- Content can be added to individual frames within the frameset document. You must use Save All commands or save each frame individually.
- You can create a frame from an existing document.
- Links can be created that will appear in the frame that you specify.
- You can create a text field that will simulate frames.

QUIZ YOURSELF

1. What is the basic concept of frames? (See the "Understanding Frames" section.)

2. How is each frame saved? (See the "Naming frame documents" section.)

3. What is a frameset? (See the "Touring your frames and frameset" section.)

4. You can edit frame documents in two ways. What are they? (See the "Touring your frames and frameset" section.)

5. What is the difference between naming a frame and naming a frame document? (See the "Naming your frames" section.)

6. What effect do page property settings have on frames? (See the "Adjusting page properties and size for frames" section.)

7. How do you set where links in framed will open? (See the "Creating targeted links" section.)

8. What trick can be used to create a scrolling text portion of a page without using frames? (See the "Simulating Frames" section.)

Increasing Productivity

Session Checklist

✔ Changing defaults and preferences

✔ Taking advantage of the Repeat command and History palette

✔ Downloading and installing Dreamweaver extensions

✔ Working efficiently

**30 Min.
To Go**

Y̲ou have created pages using nearly all of Dreamweaver's capabilities. I hope you have taken the time to do some of the extra assignments, because this is a very powerful program that can only be learned well by working with the features.

I also have kept you to a pretty basic level of operation as you stepped through the techniques. In the early chapters, I warned you that I was going to do this, believing that the correct order to truly learn a program was to learn the basics and then move to the shortcuts. That certainly does not mean that I do not believe in shortcuts. Once you understand the way a program works, it is an excellent idea to look for any shortcut you can find to make your work progress faster. Shortcuts and automated tasks also can help to keep your work consistent, which is vitally important when you are working on large sites. There are times with major sites that I do not touch a page for a month once the site has been designed or created from a template. It is much easier to keep total consistency if I can depend on automated features to accomplish the exact task many days or weeks later.

In this final session, we will look at customizing Dreamweaver's settings and creating automated actions to assist your work. You know how to operate Dreamweaver, so let's turn up the speed.

Changing Defaults and Preferences

Many of Dreamweaver's preferences can be set in one comprehensive window. In fact, there are too many to go through one by one here. The manual and online help are good sources for information on all the preference settings. We will look at the preferences you are most likely to change in this session.

The preferences are all reached through a single menu:

1. Select Edit ⇨ Preferences and the Preferences window will open.

2. Click the Category listing to select one of its options, as shown in Figure 30-1.

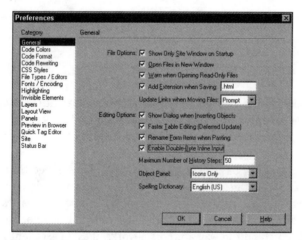

Figure 30-1
The Preferences window with the General category selected

3. Click checkboxes to enable or disable an option. Select options from drop-down lists to activate them.

4. One change I recommend is to change the Add Extension When Saving value to **.html**. This will save any HTML file with the extension of .html instead of .htm.

5. You can change options in many categories in the same Preferences session. Simply click another category when you are finished with the first and make your changes. Continue until you have made all changes in the categories you desire and click OK. Changes will usually take place immediately, although you will occasionally have to restart the program to see the effect.

Table 30-1 lists commonly adjusted preferences, along with an explanation about the adjustment.

Table 30-1
Common Preferences

Category	Feature	Purpose
General	Spelling Dictionary	Change the spell check to another version.
General	Faster Table Editing	Prevents tables from redrawing when you are typing. You can force a redraw by pressing Control+Spacebar (PC) or Command+Spacebar (Mac).
Code Colors	Default colors for properties and code	Change to match team specifications, or to speed up your work if you often change page properties.
Code Colors	Specific tags	Makes it much easier to identify specific tags when you will be working with a Code view.
Code Format	Line Breaks	Extra lines can be added to code when transferring files through FTP. Change the value for the platform you are using.
Code Rewrite	Never Rewrite Code	Set the file types that will never have code rewritten.

Continued

Table 30-1 *Continued*

Category	Feature	Purpose
File Types/Editors	External Code Editor	Set the program that will open when you click Edit in Code view.
Highlighting	Editable Regions, etc.	Change the color that is used to specify special features in Dreamweaver.
Invisible Elements	All	Toggle on an off for the elements that will show when Invisible Elements are enabled.
Layers	All	Set preferences for code and default values for layers.
Panels	Show in Launcher	Set which features can be accessed through the Launcher Pad at the lower edge of the screen.
Preview in Browser	Browsers	Add browsers and set to Primary or Secondary browsers.
Site	Always Show	Change the local file to the left side, if desired (which many people prefer).
Site	FTP Timeout	Increase the value if you have a slow connection and you receive frequent time-outs.
Status Bar	Connection Speed	Sets the speed that determines the download speed shown in the lower portion of the screen for every document.

This is only a partial list of the preference settings that can be adjusted in Dreamweaver. I recommend that you read through the online help section on preferences, because each Web developer has different needs and I may have missed a feature that could be very important to you.

Repeating Steps

Dreamweaver provides two different methods for repeating steps that you have already taken be applied to another area of your document. For simple one-step changes, the Repeat command is quick and easy. For more complex actions, you can use the History palette to replay your steps.

Repeat command

Occasionally, you will find that you are doing repetitive, simple tasks, such as removing the bold command from several words in different locations. For example, simple operations such as this, simply highlight the word and remove the bold. You can then repeat the action any number of times by highlighting the next word and selecting Edit Repeat. It really only pays in time when you use the shortcut Ctrl+Y (PC) or Command+Y (Mac).

Using the History palette

**20 Min.
To Go**

When you want to repeat more than one step, or you want to call the action when you have completed other actions, you can use the History palette to automate repetitive tasks, as shown in the following steps:

1. Select Window ⇨ History to open the History panel. As you work through the next few steps, keep your eye on the History panel to see how it enters every step, including backspaces, that you type.

2. Type a few lines of text. Insert any image. Note how the History panel tracks every addition.

3. Insert a table with any parameters. Type a few more lines of text.

4. Now you will use the History palette to insert a table that is identical to the one you just typed. In the History panel, click the entry for inserting the table. Click Replay at the lower edge of the History panel. The identical table will be inserted at the current cursor location.

You also can select more than one step to replay, and you can even select noncontinuous actions. To select continuous steps for replay, click the first action and press down the Shift key while you select the last action you want to replay. To select noncontinuous actions, select each action with your Ctrl key (PC) or Command key (Mac) pressed down. Click Replay when you have selected the actions you want to replay. Figure 30-2 shows the insert table command selected and replayed.

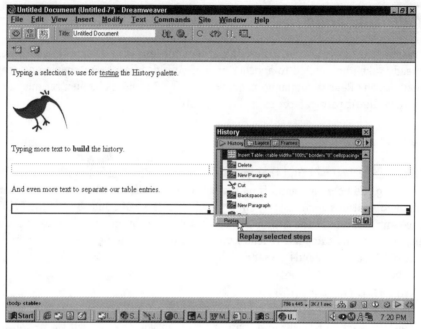

Figure 30-2
*Table insertion listed and selected in the History panel. Clicking the Replay
button in the History panel inserts an identical table.*

Copying History panel steps between documents

Although replaying a step within the same document can save time and create
consistent work, this feature is even more valuable when it is applied across documents. You can copy any series of history steps from one document to another for
total consistency and great time savings, because you would otherwise have to
compare the attributes from one document to another.

Copy a table from one document to another using the following steps.

1. Create a new document.

2. If it is not already open, open the document you created in the last exercise.

3. Select the table creation step (Step 2) from the previous exercise again.

4. Right-click the entry, or click on the side menu of the History panel, and
   then select Copy Steps from the menu that appears.

5. Activate the new document and place the cursor where you would like the
   table to appear.

6. Select Edit ⇨ Paste and the table will be inserted.

Saving History steps as commands

The History panel is cleared when you close your document. But there might be times that you would like to save a series of steps for later use. Dreamweaver offers this option through Commands, as illustrated in the following steps:

1. Return to your first document. There should be an Insert Table and New Paragraph command together in the History panel. Select both.

2. Right-click the entry, or click on the side menu of the History panel, and then select Save As Command from the menu that appears. Type **2 Column Table** in the Save As Command window.

3. Your command is stored in the Command menu. To use it, place your cursor where you want the table to appear and select Command ⇨ 2 Column Table. Figure 30-3 shows the result.

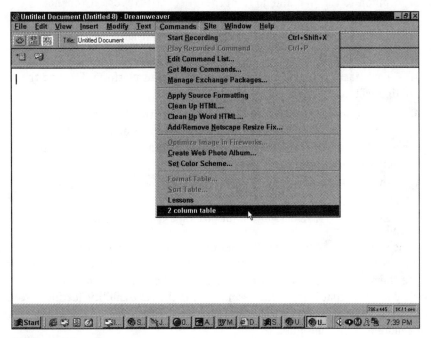

Figure 30-3
The History steps have been saved as a command and now appear in the Command menu.

Adding extensions to Dreamweaver

Macromedia is well known for the support it offers through its Web site. You can reach the Dreamweaver help through `http://macromedia.com/support/dreamweaver/`. Make sure that you visit this site and become familiar with the support system.

One of the most exciting sections of the Macromedia site contains extensions. Extensions are small scripts that are written specifically to enhance Dreamweaver capabilities, and which are free to download from the site.

Until Dreamweaver 4 was released, you had to download a special program to manage extensions. That is now built into Dreamweaver making it easier than every to access the extras that are provided by Dreamweaver and other individuals.

Let's step through the process downloading a file with extra Flash button styles and installing the extension using the following steps:

1. Sign on to the Web and go to `http://macromedia.com/exchange/dreamweaver/`. If you have not registered, you must complete the free registration before you can download any extensions.

2. Click Additional Flash Button Styles to proceed to the download page.

3. Select Macintosh or Windows, according to your platform. Clicking the link will automatically start the download.

4. Locate the file in the folder you specified for the download and double-click it. The file will automatically extract and present you with Macromedia's disclaimer. Read and click Agree if you are comfortable with the terms.

5. If Dreamweaver is running, shut it down and restart. The new Flash buttons will now be available through Insert ➪ Interactive Images ➪ Flash Button. (See Session 26 for placing a Flash button.)

It is worthwhile to visit the Macromedia site often, because new extensions are regularly added. If you would like to create your own extensions — and perhaps share them with other Dreamweaver users — all the information you need is on the same page. One that I especially recommend is the Accessibility Testing extension. This little script will check your page for accessibility issues and will help you to be a more inclusive designer.

Working Smart: Production Tips

**10 Min.
To Go**

This is the final section of the book, and I want to leave you with a few tips that I have developed and gleaned from other designers over the years. If you are expecting a list of keyboard shortcuts, you will be disappointed; those are listed at the back of the Dreamweaver manual. What you will find here are tips to speed production and assure quality that we use every day. I do not remember where most of these ideas originated. Some I developed, while others came from books or other designers. Some techniques are translations from the print world, while still others were prompted by questions from students. The source is unimportant. That they are tried and tested, day-to-day working solutions, is what counts.

Organize your work

One word into this tope and I am about to hop onto a soapbox. I cannot stress enough the importance of solid organization for any computer graphics work. Web work is the most susceptible to going out of control with lack of organization.

Make folders

With Dreamweaver, you easily move can files and keep your links intact. If you err, err with too many folders. You can always combine folders at a later time, but file numbers grow very quickly when you are working on a Web site.

See Session 3 to review site structure and folder creation.

Plan ahead

Before you create your site, create a site map. Before you create your pages, know where you are going. Most time-consuming troubleshooting that I have done has been caused by making many changes on a page. I still design in Dreamweaver, which often means that I am making serious changes such as redesigning tables. Once my design is established, however, I usually will create a file from scratch. This removes any chance that extra code has been left behind.

See Session 17 for a discussion of site maps.

Use templates

Even if you are going to break every template that you use, it is still worthwhile to start with a template. Once the template is broken, there is no difference between that file and any other, yet you gain great time savings and consistency if you start with the same template for every page. Spend the time to make your template perfect, and test it well before you create new pages. Your troubleshooting, as a result, will be held to a bare minimum.

See Session 16 for a discussion of templates.

Do your design layout in a graphics program

As much as I love Dreamweaver, it was never meant to be an art tool. I create all of my draft sites either in an illustration program such as CorelDraw or Adobe Illustrator, or I use a raster art program that will accomplish slicing like Adobe Photoshop or Jasc Paint Shop Pro. Macromedia Fireworks is an unusual combination of the two program types mentioned earlier, and which works seamlessly with Dreamweaver. You can slice your graphics in the graphics program, create draft files of the entire page for client approval, or use the image as a tracing image in Dreamweaver. You start this process by creating a full-page mockup of your design. I have included a copy of a full-page mockup for the food info site on the CD-ROM.

Copy the file tracing.gif from the Session 30 folder on the CD-ROM to the Art folder of your Food Info site.

Take the following steps to use an image for tracing in Dreamweaver:

1. Create a new document in the Food Info site. Save it as **tracetest.html** in your Resources folder.

2. Select Modify ⇨ Page Properties to open the Page Properties window. Use the Browse button for the Tracing Image field near the bottom of the window to locate the file tracing.gif.

3. Set the Image Transparency to 50%.

4. Set the Left Margin, Top Margin, Margin Width, and Margin Height settings to 0. Click OK to return to your document. Figure 30-4 shows the result.

A full-page image is showing in the background. You can use this tracing image to build your page. You might want to use a lower transparency to make the background fade even more and keep it from distracting your view. When you have completed your page, you can remove the tracing image.

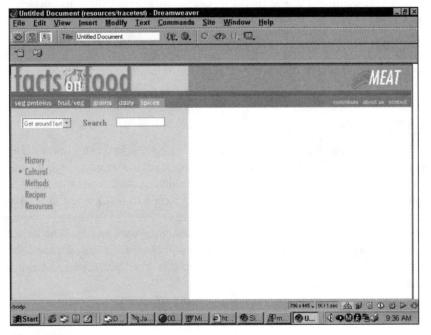

Figure 30-4
Tracing image applied to a blank page. Your page can be built using the tracing image as a pattern.

Working carefully

I participate in a lot of newsgroups, and one of the most common statements I hear is, "Oh, right, I meant to fix that." It is easy to get caught up in the production and leave good code practices behind. I understand this, because it is very much my natural way to work. After all, I am an artist at heart. However, I have learned the hard way that Web work is not forgiving when you are running with the muse. Do it right the first time is a perfect motto for Web work.

Learn to read code

At one time, I could hand code HTML pages. Today, I suppose I could, but it would not be easy. I have been spoiled by Dreamweaver's wonderful features. However, I still "read" code fluently, and this — more than any other skill — has saved me a great deal of time. No, knowing code is not a purist activity. It is purely and simply a time-saver. Learn HTML by taking a course, studying a book (such as Greg Perry's HTML 4.01 Weekend Crash Course), or religiously following your code as Dreamweaver creates it. You will save hundreds of hours for every hour you spend learning code.

Follow your code

I am surprised that I do not wear out my Code view toggle when I am working with Dreamweaver. I do my design almost completely in Design view, but I am constantly toggling back and forth to Code view. I do not do this because I like code; quite the contrary. I keep a constant eye on my code to make sure that I have not accidentally added extra code (which is easy to do when you change your mind), or that extra spaces have been entered. Dreamweaver does an excellent job with code. Most little extras that get into my pages go there from my own hand, but it is much easier to find them step-by-step than it is when you are having trouble with your page in the testing phase.

Work within the limits of HTML

In Web work, the mark of a professional is often that they have learned to work with HTML limitations. This language was never meant to create the beautiful pages we create today in word-processing and page layout programs. You can do almost anything your artistic heart desires, but the cost is often long download time and unstable pages. At this time, we still must depend on tables for general Web layout. Tables are square. If you find yourself nesting three or four tables just to place an artistic element, stop and think: Is there another way to do this? Does this extra table improve my visitor experience or just make me feel good? Great Web pages are simple pages that download quickly and work in every browser. That does not mean they are ugly pages. Start reading the source code on professionally designed pages and you will see that the best use simple layouts and depend on their creativity to make them visually appealing.

Save, save, save

Dreamweaver does not have any type of automatic feature to prevent you from losing your work. Save every time you stop. It is easy to become lost in your work and let an hour go by. I cannot say that Dreamweaver causes me many problems, but I often work with many other active programs and I do occasionally crash my system. My tolerance for losing work is very low, and I am an obsessive saver.

Be a perfectionist

I am usually cautious about tossing the word perfectionist out to an artistic crowd. However, in Web work, perfection is well rewarded. The minute you say, "That's good enough," warning bells should go off. You often are building new features on top of previously created features. The original problem is not always the one that shows. When I first started using CSS, I neglected to check what would work with a linked CSS file — it must be the same as inline CSS, I thought. I spent an entire day trying to figure out why my graphics were flying all over my page in version 3 browsers. The text was fine. I was very lucky to hear from a woman who had had the same problem, which was caused by one command in a linked CSS file. It had NOTHING at all to do with my graphics. I changed that CSS command to an inline style and the problem was fixed, but it was caused when I did not carry my homework to the level of perfection. That incident taught me a lot. Web design is not fun when you spend and entire day chasing "ghosts."

Use Dreamweaver to its fullest

I am going to end on this note. Dreamweaver is a very powerful program. Dreamweaver's designers have done an excellent job in creating a program for both professional and serious amateur Web designers. They have included features that take the tedium and massive organization tasks of a large Web site and made them child's play. But you have to learn these features well and use them from the beginning of each project to reap the full benefit. Use the check-in/check-out system. Build your pages with templates and library items. It seems like too much front-end work at times, but the savings are gigantic at the other end of your project. Trust me on this one.

Done!

And there we have it. If you have followed every session and completed each exercise, you have a solid working knowledge of Dreamweaver. Keep your skills active, even if you only use them for personal sites. This field moves too fast to relax even for a few months. Keep surfing for the latest trends and information about how new browsers handle code. This is an exciting field that will never bore you if you make a commitment to stay with it. That — more than any other feature of this career — makes me feel that this is my "real" career.

REVIEW

In this session, you have done a lot of review, but I would like you to take these special notes with you:

- Defaults and preferences can be changed from the Preferences window. Simply click the category you want to change and make the adjustments.

- You can save time by using your History palette to repeat steps.

- History steps can be saved as commands that are available through the Command menu.

- Macromedia's Web site provides great support, and you can download scripts for specific tasks.

- Organizing your work is the best production enhancement for any Web work.

- Working carefully as you create your pages is the best way to prevent aggravating and time-consuming troubleshooting.

- Dreamweaver has powerful features. Use them.

QUIZ YOURSELF

1. Where can you find the settings for most Dreamweaver settings? (See the "Changing Defaults and Preferences" section.)

2. The Repeat command can be used only in what circumstance? (See the "Repeat command" section.)

3. How can the History palette be used to repeat commands? (See the "Using the History palette" section.)

4. When you wish to use a series of steps from the History palette at a later date, how can you save the information? (See the "Saving history steps as commands" section.)

5. What are Dreamweaver Extensions? (See the "Adding extensions to Dreamweaver" section.)

6. Why is a tracing image different from any other image in Dreamweaver? (See the "Do your design in a graphics program" section.)

7. Why is it important to learn to work with HTML capabilities? (See the "Work within the limits of HTML" section.)

PART

VI

Sunday Afternoon

1. Although layers make creating a page easy, they come with a serious disadvantage. What is it?

2. How is CSS used with layers?

3. Dreamweaver allows you to design with layers but to overcome the problems associated with displaying layer-built pages. How?

4. When working with layers, what is the Prevent Overlaps option designed to do?

5. When you have a nested layer, the nested layer is referred to as the *child* layer. What do the coordinates of this layer refer to?

6. If you are going to use DHTML in pages for the Web, what is an excellent policy to use?

7. What part do Dreamweaver behaviors play in DHTML?

8. How can you add animation with DHTML in Dreamweaver?

9. How can you tell an animation when to start in Dreamweaver?

10. When using DHTML for your pages, no matter what you do, one thing is absolutely essential? What is that critical step?

11. What is a frameset?

12. What is the difference between naming a frame and saving a frame?

13. What is a frame?

14. What are the drawbacks with framed documents?

15. When you are adding content to a frame or editing a frame, what should you keep in mind?

16. How can you use a form item to simulate a framed area?

17. Where do you use the Repeat command?

18. The History panel can be used to repeat a series of steps. How?

19. Why is it important for Web developers to learn to work within the limits of HTML?

20. Perfection is always nice. With Web development, it is essential. Why?

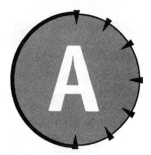
Answers to Part Reviews

Friday Evening Review Answers

1. Although you can produce Web pages in Dreamweaver without knowing HTML code, you can customize your work more easily with knowledge of HTML. Troubleshooting a display problem can be very frustrating if you do not understand enough about HTML code to find where a small code error is producing the problem.

2. No standards are accepted by every browser manufacturer, so each browser interprets some code in a different way. Not only do differences exist among brands of browsers, but often the same browser interprets code in a different way on a Mac or a PC.

3. The text that displays on a Web page uses the fonts installed on the viewer's computer. There is no way to guarantee that the viewer has the required fonts installed. To overcome this variation, we design pages with fonts commonly installed on all computers, plus provide a generic choice.

4. The Assets manager offers tracking of all images, colors, external URLs, scripts, Flash, Shockwave and QuickTime movies, templates and library items in your site.

5. The Site window is used to manage all the files in your site. Dreamweaver keeps track of links and can be set to make sure that the local and remote sites are the same at all times.

6. When you use menus rather than keyboard shortcuts, you are exposed to the structure of the entire menu containing the command you choose.

If you watch for the keyboard shortcut always listed with the menu item, you also learn the shortcuts for the commands you use most often.

7. A context menu is a pop-up menu that contains only commands for a specific task. For PC users, right clicking an object opens a context menu. Mac users use Ctrl-Click to open a context menu.

8. Dreamweaver panels are the windows that can be opened, providing shortcuts to most commands.

9. To preview a Dreamweaver document in a browser, you must specify the location for the application file for the desired browser. You can specify up to 12 browsers to use for previews.

10. No. You can preview your document without saving it, which is a handy feature. You can check the results of a command and easily undo the command if the results are not satisfactory.

11. Getting a file means copying a file from the remote site to the local site. Putting a file means copying a file from the local site to the remote site.

12. Design notes are small text files added to a document. They do not display as part of the page, but anyone with Dreamweaver can read the notes. Usually, you use design notes when you are working in a team setting.

13. The Root Folder is the top folder for all your site files and should contain the entry page for your site.

14. An HTML document cannot be more than one page. There is no limit to the size of the page, but there is no way to specify more than one page. Each HTML page in a site is a separate document.

15. Dreamweaver creates a Site Map, or graphic illustration of the files in your site, showing the relation of one file to another through links.

16. F10 opens and closes the HTML Inspector.

17. When a page is viewed on the Web, the browser uses font information from the viewer's computer. Dreamweaver only lists the fonts included on almost all computers.

18. Adjust font color and attributes in the Properties Inspector.

19. Creating hundreds of graphic images when creating a site is not unusual. If the images are not placed in a separate folder, managing your site becomes a nightmare.

20. The most common graphic file types are GIF and JPG. Any browser displays these formats. Many browsers also display PNG format images. You

can place files in any of these formats in Dreamweaver, although PNG is best saved for Intranet use.

Saturday Morning Review Answers

1. You must use Dreamweaver's FTP function if you wish to use the automated site management features. All file management features are handled through the Site window in Dreamweaver.

2. You must have the host address, the host directory, your login name and password.

3. Dragging the root directory on the local site to the remote site transfers the entire site.

4. Nested tables take longer to load and can cause display problems on some browsers if too many levels of nested tables exist.

5. Editing tables can often lead to errors. If you plan your tables well, you are much more likely to achieve what you desire quickly, while maintaining excellent code.

6. Working with your table borders turned on can help to keep the table structure in clear focus. You can turn the borders off as soon as you have your table areas well defined.

7. When you set a table to a fixed size, such as 500 pixels, the table displays at that size as long as the total width of graphics contained is less than the table width. However, if you specify that a table is to be 100%, the table stretches across the screen regardless of monitor resolution. The table may be 600 pixels, 800 pixels, or 1200 pixels wide depending on what the maximum resolution is for the monitor viewing the page containing the table.

8. If you place an invisible graphic, usually a transparent GIF image, that is 200 pixels wide, the image forces the column to a minimum of 200 pixels.

9. When a table is inserted into another table cell (called nesting) and is set to a percentage width, the size for the nested table is calculated from the size of the cell containing it.

10. Yes. You can specify fixed or percentage widths or a combination for columns within the same table.

11. In Dreamweaver, as long as your cursor is in the cell you wish to add a background color to, you simply select the color from the Bg palette on the Properties Inspector. Dreamweaver automatically adjusts the <td> tag.

12. Select the cell, row, column or table you wish to remove the background from, and delete the entry in the Bg field.

13. When a table has more than one cell, Netscape Navigator starts the pattern over for every cell and leaves any cell-spacing areas blank.

14. Internet Explorer ignores any reference to a background in the <tr> tag. However, it displays a background as part of the <td> tag, so careful planning still allows most effects to be completed.

15. Page backgrounds are added in the Modify ⇨ Page Properties menu item.

16. Internet Explorer and Netscape Navigator demand their own codes to set page margins. Dreamweaver makes it easy by allowing you to specify Left Margin, Top Margin, Margin Width, and Margin Height, which covers all the code needed for both browsers.

17. In Dreamweaver, you add a link to a selected image in the Link field of the Properties Inspector.

18. In Dreamweaver, you have the option to search for code and to replace it with new code. To replace your page margins, enter the current page margin code into the Find field in the Find and Replace window; enter the desired code in the Replace With field, and choose Entire Site from the Find in drop-down box. Click OK, say OK to the alert that appears, and the changes are made.

19. Select the files you wish to move and drag to the location you wish to place the files.

20. When you use site synchronization, you can ensure that both your remote site and local site contain the same files at all times. Synchronizing saves a lot of time for a complex site because it is often hard to remember if you have uploaded all files you have edited.

Saturday Afternoon Review Answers

1. The best way to work with code in Dreamweaver is the way that is most comfortable for you. There is no difference in the results when you enter or edit code with the split design/code window, the Code Inspector, the

full code screen, or even the Quick Tag Editor. Most likely, you will find yourself using several different code view options.

2. There is no difference if you hit your Enter key three times when you are working in code view. Browsers ignore white space in HTML documents.

3. If you find you are often looking for a specific tag, it can save a lot of time to specify a color you can easily spot for that tag.

4. Script code is usually placed in the Head area of the document and is part of the `<body>` tag.

5. A link to another site must be given in absolute terms, or the full address must be included, such as `http://wpeck.com`.

6. A Named Anchor is marked with an Invisible Element marker as long as Dreamweaver has been set to show Invisible Elements.

7. You can update many instances of a link through Dreamweaver's Change Links Sitewide command.

8. Highlight the marker for the JavaScript you wish to edit, and click the Edit button in the Properties Inspector. The script is presented and can be edited.

9. A simple rollover is simply one image replacing another when a mouse is passed over the original image.

10. Rollovers must be tested in a browser preview because the action does not occur in Dreamweaver.

11. The Behaviors panel is used to add JavaScript.

12. You use tables to layout a form for the same reason you use them to layout your pages. You cannot add format commands to a form or form object, so you must place the form objects in table cells to create an easy-to-follow form.

13. In the Properties Inspector, when the form is selected, click the Action button, and direct Dreamweaver to the CGI script you wish to use to collect and return the data from your form.

14. Radio buttons are used when only one choice is allowed. Checkboxes are used for multiple selections.

15. A hidden field is used to tell the script running a form what information to collect and where to send the results.

16. The Assets panel gathers all the colors you have used in a site and presents them when the Color icon is active in the Assets panel.

17. You can create a Library Item from scratch or highlight an existing section of your page and create a Library Item from that content.

18. When you delete a Library Item from the Assets panel, the link to that Library Item is broken for any instances where the item has been placed, but the item is not removed from the pages. To delete the instances of a Library Item, you must remove them from every page.

19. You must return to the template file to make changes to a non-editable area of a template page. You can also break the link to the template, which makes the entire page editable.

20. If you delete a template file outside the Assets panel, the Assets panel will assume it is still there and continue to look for the template, indicating an error every time the Assets panel is opened.

Saturday Evening Review Answers

1. The number one thing to understand before you start designing a site is why your visitor visits your site. Without that information, you have a hard time making decisions on the look of the site, how navigation should work, and what type of information should be placed in which location.

2. A site map helps you see how each page is connected or should be connected. It can help you determine the navigation for the site and often leads directly to the perfect route for placing content.

3. Jump menu is the name of a drop-down menu, offering many choices in a very small space.

4. Even a Navigation Bar containing many items can be easily created from one menu.

5. The one drawback to a Navigation Bar is that you can only have one per page.

6. No. The Check Out command simply places a check mark beside the file to notify others that you are working on the file. However, they can still get the file and make changes because the file is not turned into a read-only file on the server.

7. When you check a file in to the remote site, the file on your local site becomes a read-only file until you check that file out again.

8. You can attach design notes to full documents or to individual images.

9. Files that include design notes appear in the Site window with an icon beside the filename, indicating the presence of a note.

10. Select File ⇨ to view the design notes screen.

11. The most important task when you are building a template is to identify which areas can remain identical on every page created with the template and which areas must be editable.

12. You can create stripes by creating table rows with background colors. Transparent GIF files are used to set the height of the stripe. The table containing the stripe rows must be set to 100% for the color to stretch across the entire page.

13. With two fixed-width columns and a third set to 100%, the third column should always fill whatever space remains. However, in most cases, if only text fills the third column, you still require a transparent GIF file set to a width of at least half of the smallest width the third column will be. If you do not have this graphic in place, the browser may decide to share some of the third column width with the fixed-width columns.

14. It is often best to place plain images for a menu until you have your final position and layout determined. It is a lot easier to move and adjust individual images than images with attached behaviors.

15. It is often faster to turn to your code view to select an invisible image. Place your cursor in the table cell that contains the graphic, and change to a code view. The image should be easy to see in this view because it is the same as any other image when written in code. Make your changes in the code view, or select the image code, and return to the design view. The image remains selected.

16. A Library Item is an excellent way to add small pieces of content to many pages. Because it is stored in the Assets panel, you can easily drag a Library Item into any document.

17. Templates are designed to provide a consistent starting point for many pages.

18. Sure. You can create a Library Item for a menu and then detach it from the Library Item to make an adjustment to the active page menu item. You still save time, and consistency is still there. However, because the link is broken, you do lose the ability to update the Library Item automatically on all the pages containing the item.

19. You can move the files from outside Dreamweaver, and the links do not change. You can also tell Dreamweaver not to update the files when you move them, and the Update Files alert appears.

20. An editable area in template-based documents can be changed in any way. In a template, editable areas are the only areas you can edit unless you detach the document from the template.

Sunday Morning Review Answers

1. Select the jump menu, and click List Values in the Properties Inspector. You can add, remove, or edit menu entries.

2. So many of Dreamweaver's commands can be accomplished through the Properties Inspector. Just by always watching this little window, you can see where operations are completed even when you do not need that feature today.

3. You can change the way the Objects panel displays options in the Preferences window.

4. Select the asset in the Assets panel, and choose Find in Site from the side menu.

5. JPG images are best for images containing graduated color changes, such as photographs.

6. GIF images are best for images with large areas of solid color.

7. Optimizing images means reducing file size as much as possible without compromising quality.

8. Although you can create much the same effect with an HTML style as you can with CSS, HTML styles only work for one page. CSS styles can be assigned to many pages. Plus, with a CSS style sheet, you can change the style, and all text with that style changes. HTML styles do not affect text that has already been created.

9. When you use the Attach New Style Sheet command, Dreamweaver creates a separate document to hold your CSS styles and attaches a note in your document to look for the text styles in that location.

10. Select Text ➪ CSS Styles ➪ Edit Style Sheet to make changes to an existing style sheet.

11. When you are naming a series of graphics, like in a menu, make sure you start the filename for each image with the same word or set of characters, like `menuhome.gif`, `menucontact.gif`. This is much more convenient when locating files than using names such as `homemenu.gif`, `contactmenu.gif`.

12. When you create a page, and want to use that page as the base for a page with a new name, make sure you save any changes to the original page before you save the file with the new name.

13. An "active state" graphic is the way you let your visitor know that he or she is on the page represented by the corresponding menu item. It can have any effect as long as it is not the same as the original graphic.

14. An Alt tag is the text that appears when the mouse is held over a graphic. You enter an Alt tag in the Alt field of the Properties Inspector.

15. Adding an alignment command to an image in the Properties Inspector allows text to wrap around that image.

16. Adding to Personal when checking spelling adds the active word to your personal dictionary. That word is no longer considered a spelling error, so be careful when you are using this command.

17. You can use Clean Up HTML to remove redundant or empty tags.

18. Create a personal page to satisfy your desire to experiment and to learn new techniques.

19. Visitors should always have the option to stop sound or, better yet, be invited to start sound.

20. The visitor must have the Flash player installed before he or she can see or use a Flash button. Although browsers have included the Flash button for some time now, it is still a consideration.

Sunday Afternoon Review Answers

1. Layers are not fully supported by all browsers and can cause some serious problems when viewed on the Web.

2. CSS is used to position layers.

3. Dreamweaver allows you to convert layers to tables, which display properly in almost every browser in use today.

4. The Prevent Overlaps command should be used when you intend to covert layers to tables at any point. This prevents layers from overlapping, which would prevent tables from being created.

5. The coordinates on a child layer are stated in reference to the parent layer.

6. It is a good idea to not use DHTML for features on your site that render it useless if the visitor's browser does not support DHTML.

7. Behaviors provide the JavaScript that allows layers to move in DHTML.

8. The Dreamweaver Timeline function provides the method to animate layers.

9. You use the Dreamweaver Behaviors panel to add the JavaScript to a link that starts an animation.

10. It is absolutely essential that you test, test, and test again when you are creating pages with DHTML. More skill is required to troubleshoot DHTML than to build pages with it.

11. A frameset is a document that collects HTML pages into a specified arrangement on a page.

12. Naming a frame assigns a name to the frame in the same way you assign a name to an image. This is done in the Properties Inspector. Saving a frame creates an HTML document that the frameset calls to create a page.

13. A frame is actually a separate HTML document that can be created separately and just called into a frameset. You can also create a frame from within the frameset page. No matter how you create it, a frame remains a separate document.

14. Framed documents are a designers dream, but they can cause problems. Framed documents are hard to bookmark and print for visitors who are not Web savvy. Search engines have a hard time finding information on framed documents, and people with low-resolution monitors often dislike frames because frames can create a cramped document.

15. Frames are easy to understand if you always remember that each frame is an individual document. If you wish to change the background color, you can use Page Properties to set the color. To change the margins, you also use Page Properties.

16. If you insert a multiline text area in a document, you can enter text and have that text scrollable without using frames.

17. The Repeat command is used to repeat the exact action many times, as in changing background colors in nonconnected cells in a table.

18. When you complete an action in Dreamweaver, the History panel records that action. You can open the History panel and can select the action you want to repeat. With your cursor in the position you wish the action to be repeated, click Replay in the History window. You have an instant repeat of that action. You can also save History steps for later use or for use in other documents.

19. Effort spent to find creative ways to produce interesting, effective work within the limitations of HTML is better than trying to push the limits of HTML to the point where you are creating pages that contain tags that are not well supported. Learning HTML is one of the best things you can do to help you make the most of the language. An excellent understanding of HTML, and accepting what it can and can't do, allows you to spend your time designing rather than troubleshooting and testing.

20. Although HTML is not officially a programming language, it is still fussy. Browsers are not standardized. Monitors are far from standard. People reach Web pages by using everything from very slow modems to screaming fast, cutting-edge, direct connections. Plus, they may be using a Mac or a PC — no way to tell ahead of time. Given the variables in the Web world, it is a wonder that any pages display properly. Every error you make with code, or extra demands you make with things such as several nested tables, can set a chain reaction in motion. In Web development, perfection is not just a nice thing to have; it is the key to creating successful pages.

What's on the CD-ROM?

The CD-ROM included with this book contains all the images, scripts, and sample files you require to complete the exercises, resources for Web development and trial versions of software programs often used with Dreamweaver (see Appendix C to learn more about these programs). You will also find a self-assessment test to help you determine your current level of expertise and to track your progress.

Files required for exercises

To complete most of the exercises in this book, you require image files or text files. Watch for CD-ROM notes that tell you which files you require and where to place these files on your computer. The files on the CD-ROM are in folders that correspond to session numbers. Some sessions do not have folders.

Resource files

In addition to files you require to complete exercises, the CD-ROM also contains several resource files that help you locate important Web sites. Watch for CD-ROM notes throughout the book that refer you to the resource file that corresponds to the session topic. The resource files are HTML pages, and you can view them by using your standard browser; you can click the links when you are connected to the Web for easy access.

Software programs

Dreamweaver does not work alone. You must create the images you require in graphics programs like the ones included on the CD-ROM, and you also require Internet Explorer and Netscape Navigator for testing your pages.

Internet Explorer/Netscape Navigator

When you are designing Web pages, you should have both of these browsers installed on your computer for testing your pages.

Adobe Photoshop

Adobe Photoshop 6 is a tryout version of Photoshop, the most popular graphics editor among professional designers. This powerful program offers image editing and special effects and includes ImageReady3, a program dedicated to producing images for the Web.

Macromedia Fireworks

Macromedia Fireworks is a 30-day, fully functional trial version of Macromedia's specialized Web graphic creation program. This program integrates seamlessly with Dreamweaver and is powerful and easy to learn.

Jasc Paint Shop Pro

Enjoy a 30-day evaluation version of Jasc Paint Shop Pro, a powerful yet easy-to-learn program. Its popular price makes it a choice for many designers, including professional Web developers.

Xat Image Optimizer

A shareware version of Image Optimizer is included on the CD-ROM. This optimization program can help you to create Web graphics with excellent quality and a small file size.

Macromedia Flash

Macromedia Flash is another Macromedia product designed for Web development. Try your hand at creating movies for the Web with this full-featured, 30-day trial.

Macromedia Freehand

Freehand is a vector program, which many designers find valuable for initial Web layout and for creating graphics for the Web. This version of Freehand offers a full-featured, 30-day program, so you can fully test its capabilities.

Working with Other Software

Dreamweaver is a powerful program, but it cannot work alone. In fact, Dreamweaver is nothing more than a gathering tool for Web-bound content. To complete Web sites, you need at least one graphics program. Choosing can be a daunting task. To help clear the initial fog, I have compiled a short description of the most popular graphics programs Web designers use.

See Session 22 for more about raster and vector graphics formats.

Adobe Photoshop 6/ImageReady

Photoshop is probably the most popular graphics program in the world, and it is an excellent tool for Web design. It is primarily a raster program, with limited vector capability. Photoshop comes bundled with ImageReady 3, a full-featured, Web graphics preparation program. Photoshop is often used for creating the initial design, with ImageReady preparing sliced images, HTML for Web pages, and animated GIF images. Photoshop can handle any image-preparation task, and ImageReady is one of the best pre-Web preparation programs. However, this package comes with a high price tag, and because of the power it contains, it does have a long learning curve. Photoshop is available for both Mac and PC platforms, with an abundance of tutorials available on the Web. (A Photoshop demo version is included on this book's CD-ROM.)

Jasc Paint Shop Pro

Paint Shop Pro (PSP) is an amazing graphics-preparation program and is perfect for Web design, although it is only available for the PC platform. It is primarily a raster program, with limited vector capability. Don't dismiss this program because of its low price tag (well under $100 in the United States). Many professional Web designers use PSP exclusively. You can use PSP for initial design, image preparation, slicing images, and creating animated GIF files (Jasc Animation Shop is included with PSP). Many people find that PSP is one of the easiest graphics programs to learn, and it is well supported with Web-based tutorials. (A Paint Shop Pro demo version is included on this book's CD-ROM.)

Macromedia Fireworks

Fireworks is an interesting hybrid program, combining powerful raster editing features with strong vector creation tools. Fireworks has led the industry in image slicing capability and has the advantage of working seamlessly with Dreamweaver, which can be important if you are using your graphics program to create HTML for sliced images. You should try Fireworks if you are working with Dreamweaver. (A Fireworks demo version is included on this book's CD-ROM.) Animations are created in Fireworks and can be exported as animated GIF files or as a Flash SWF file (see Flash later in this appendix).

Vector programs

Vector programs such as CorelDraw, Adobe Illustrator, and Macromedia Freehand can also be used to create Web graphics. Many designers, especially those who have a print background or those who supply print graphics, in addition to Web content, to clients still do much of their design in vector programs. I do. Vector programs are object based, which means there is no need to work in layers to keep objects separate. However, this class of programs is secondary for Web design. Many designers are working without a vector-based graphics program, but few are working without a raster-based graphics program.

Macromedia Flash/Adobe Live Motion/Corel R.A.V.E.

Flash is well known for creating movies for the Web. LiveMotion and R.A.V.E. are Adobe and Corel's competing programs. Flash is still the leader, especially for scripting, the ability to use programming to control how the movie behaves. Some designers are completing entire sites, including the site navigation, in Flash. LiveMotion and R.A.V.E. claim to be easier to use — easier for designers than programmers. Luckily, demo versions are available for all three programs. (A Flash 5 demo version is included on this book's CD-ROM.) Although beginning Web designers do not need to know how to make a movie, it is a good idea to learn to create a basic movie as you build your skills.

Choose your graphics program based on your needs

There is no right or wrong program for creating Web graphics. As long as you can create well-optimized, quality graphics, you are using the right program. Web developers tend to become very attached to their programs and often speak strongly for or against specific programs. Listen to any valid points they may have for choosing or avoiding a software program, but always remember that each designer works in a different way. Use trial versions whenever you can to see whether a place in your workflow exists for a specific program. Trust your own instincts in the end.

Index

Symbols and Numerics

+ (add), 212
&#149 (bullet), 268
<> icon, 176
+ icon, 362
? icon, 332
– (minus sign), 288
 # (pound sign), 396, 446

A

absolute links, 192, 194. See also links
accessibility for people with disabilities, 149,
*   388–390, 476*
Accessibility Testing extension, 476
Activate Preload Images command, 273
Active state image, 383
add (+) symbol, 212
Add Browser window, 129
Add Extension When Saving Value option, 471
Add Object to Timeline option, 443
Add to Favorites icon, 338
Adobe
  GoLive, 347
  Illustrator, 346, 478, 502
  ImageReady, 271, 501
  LiveMotion, 346, 502–503
  Photoshop, 62, 271, 346, 478, 500, 501
Advanced Text search option, 398
aligning
  Align Center icon, 139
  Align option, 439
  cell content, 97–99, 297
  graphics, 394–395
  layers, 432, 433, 439
  table, 88–90
All Info option, 288
Alt tags, 148–149, 388–390, 415
Always Go To First URL option, 417
Amazon.com Web site, 151
Apply Template to Page option, 252
Assets Manager, 14
Assets panel
  Alt tags, adding, 388–389
  assets, locating, 339
  drag-and-drop feature, 229, 237
  Favorites feature, editing, 338–339
  HTML Reference, O'Reilly's, 340, 341
  images, inserting, 337
  Library section, 310
  links, adding, 337

  New Favorites Folder icon, 339
  New From Template option, 320
  New Library Item option, 310, 312
  overview, 228–229, 336–337
  Properties palette option, 337
  sorting items in Site view, 339
  text color, changing, 229–230, 233, 337
  timesaving tips, 342
  title bar, 339
Attach Style Sheet option, 366
attributes. See also Cascading Style Sheets (CSS);
*   HTML (Hypertext Markup Language) styles*
  applying to fonts, 57
  checking target browsers, 400
  code color, 182–184
  compatibility issues, 340, 400
  for links, 195, 367, 370–371

B

<b> tag, 361
background
  Bg color field option, 119, 120
  browser interpretation of, 131–134
  cell padding and spacing, 124
  color, changing, 320
  color, deleting, 123
  color codes, 183, 295
  compatibility issues, 133–134
  frames (HTML), adding to, 454–456
  issues with Netscape, 126
  overview, 118–119
  page color, 140
  page image, 141–142
  properties, 140, 141–142
  table color, 119–125
  table image, 125–128
  template, adding to, 249–250, 320
banner ads, 408–409
behaviors
  checking for plug-ins, 417
  definition, 204
  deleting, 383, 443
  editing, 447
  rollovers, attaching to, 212
  timelines, attaching to, 446–447
Behaviors palette
  behaviors, adding, 212
  Drag Layer option, 440
  jump menus, editing, 270
  rollovers, 209, 212, 355

Hungry Minds, Inc.
End-User License Agreement

READ THIS. You should carefully read these terms and conditions before opening the software packet(s) included with this book ("Book"). This is a license agreement ("Agreement") between you and Hungry Minds, Inc. ("HMI"). By opening the accompanying software packet(s), you acknowledge that you have read and accept the following terms and conditions. If you do not agree and do not want to be bound by such terms and conditions, promptly return the Book and the unopened software packet(s) to the place you obtained them for a full refund.

1. **License Grant.** HMI grants to you (either an individual or entity) a nonexclusive license to use one copy of the enclosed software program(s) (collectively, the "Software") solely for your own personal or business purposes on a single computer (whether a standard computer or a workstation component of a multi-user network). The Software is in use on a computer when it is loaded into temporary memory (RAM) or installed into permanent memory (hard disk, CD-ROM, or other storage device). HMI reserves all rights not expressly granted herein.

2. **Ownership.** HMI is the owner of all right, title, and interest, including copyright, in and to the compilation of the Software recorded on the disk(s) or CD-ROM ("Software Media"). Copyright to the individual programs recorded on the Software Media is owned by the author or other authorized copyright owner of each program. Ownership of the Software and all proprietary rights relating thereto remain with HMI and its licensers.

3. **Restrictions On Use and Transfer.**

   (a) You may only (i) make one copy of the Software for backup or archival purposes, or (ii) transfer the Software to a single hard disk, provided that you keep the original for backup or archival purposes. You may not (i) rent or lease the Software, (ii) copy or reproduce the Software through a LAN or other network system or through any computer subscriber system or bulletin-board system, or (iii) modify, adapt, or create derivative works based on the Software.

   (b) You may not reverse engineer, decompile, or disassemble the Software. You may transfer the Software and user documentation on a permanent basis, provided that the transferee agrees to accept the terms and conditions of this Agreement and you retain no copies. If the Software is an update or has been updated, any transfer must include the most recent update and all prior versions.

4. **Restrictions on Use of Individual Programs.** You must follow the individual requirements and restrictions detailed for each individual program in the "About the CD-ROM" appendix of this Book. These limitations are also contained in the individual license agreements recorded on the Software Media. These limitations may include a requirement that after using the program for a specified period of time, the user must pay a registration fee or discontinue use. By opening the Software packet(s), you will be agreeing to abide by the licenses and restrictions for these individual programs that are detailed in the "About the CD-ROM" appendix and on the Software Media. None of the material on this Software Media or listed in this Book may ever be redistributed, in original or modified form, for commercial purposes.

5. **Limited Warranty.**

    (a) HMI warrants that the Software and Software Media are free from defects in materials and workmanship under normal use for a period of sixty (60) days from the date of purchase of this Book. If HMI receives notification within the warranty period of defects in materials or workmanship, HMI will replace the defective Software Media.

    (b) **HMI AND THE AUTHOR OF THE BOOK DISCLAIM ALL OTHER WARRANTIES, EXPRESS OR IMPLIED, INCLUDING WITHOUT LIMITATION IMPLIED WARRANTIES OF MERCHANTABILITY AND FITNESS FOR A PARTICULAR PURPOSE, WITH RESPECT TO THE SOFTWARE, THE PROGRAMS, THE SOURCE CODE CONTAINED THEREIN, AND/OR THE TECHNIQUES DESCRIBED IN THIS BOOK. HMI DOES NOT WARRANT THAT THE FUNCTIONS CONTAINED IN THE SOFTWARE WILL MEET YOUR REQUIREMENTS OR THAT THE OPERATION OF THE SOFTWARE WILL BE ERROR FREE.**

    (c) This limited warranty gives you specific legal rights, and you may have other rights that vary from jurisdiction to jurisdiction.

6. **Remedies.**

    (a) HMI's entire liability and your exclusive remedy for defects in materials and workmanship shall be limited to replacement of the Software Media, which may be returned to HMI with a copy of your receipt at the following address: Software Media Fulfillment Department, Attn.: *Dreamweaver® 4 Weekend Crash Course™*, Hungry Minds, Inc., 10475 Crosspoint Blvd., Indianapolis, IN 46256, or call 1-800-762-2974. Please allow four to six weeks for delivery. This Limited Warranty is void if failure of the Software Media has resulted from accident, abuse, or misapplication. Any replacement Software Media will be warranted for the remainder of the original warranty period or thirty (30) days, whichever is longer.

(b) In no event shall HMI or the author be liable for any damages whatsoever (including without limitation damages for loss of business profits, business interruption, loss of business information, or any other pecuniary loss) arising from the use of or inability to use the Book or the Software, even if HMI has been advised of the possibility of such damages.

(c) Because some jurisdictions do not allow the exclusion or limitation of liability for consequential or incidental damages, the above limitation or exclusion may not apply to you.

7. **U.S. Government Restricted Rights.** Use, duplication, or disclosure of the Software for or on behalf of the United States of America, its agencies and/or instrumentalities (the "U.S. Government") is subject to restrictions as stated in paragraph (c)(1)(ii) of the Rights in Technical Data and Computer Software clause of DFARS 252.227-7013, or subparagraphs (c) (1) and (2) of the Commercial Computer Software - Restricted Rights clause at FAR 52.227-19, and in similar clauses in the NASA FAR supplement, as applicable.

8. **General.** This Agreement constitutes the entire understanding of the parties and revokes and supersedes all prior agreements, oral or written, between them and may not be modified or amended except in a writing signed by both parties hereto that specifically refers to this Agreement. This Agreement shall take precedence over any other documents that may be in conflict herewith. If any one or more provisions contained in this Agreement are held by any court or tribunal to be invalid, illegal, or otherwise unenforceable, each and every other provision shall remain in full force and effect.

The CD-ROM that accompanies this book contains all the images, scripts, and sample files you require to complete the exercises, resources for Web development, and trial versions of software programs often used with Dreamweaver (see Appendix B to learn more about these programs). You will also find a self-assessment test to help you determine your current level of expertise and to track your progress.